Julian Hawthorne, Thomas Colley Grattan

Holland

The History of the Netherlands

Julian Hawthorne, Thomas Colley Grattan

Holland
The History of the Netherlands

ISBN/EAN: 9783337326562

Printed in Europe, USA, Canada, Australia, Japan

Cover: Foto ©ninafisch / pixelio.de

More available books at **www.hansebooks.com**

THE DUKE OF ALVA DEPOSES MARGARET OF PARMA
Frontispiece, Holland.

HOLLAND

THE HISTORY OF

THE NETHERLANDS

BY

THOMAS COLLEY GRATTAN

WITH A SUPPLEMENTARY CHAPTER OF RECENT EVENTS

By JULIAN HAWTHORNE

CONTENTS

CHAPTER I

FROM THE INVASION OF THE NETHERLANDS BY THE ROMANS TO THE INVASION BY THE SALIAN FRANKS

B.C. 50—A.D. 250

Extent of the Kingdom—Description of the People—Ancient State of the Low Countries—Of the **High** Grounds—Contrasted with the present Aspect of the Country—Expedition of Julius Cæsar —The Belgæ—**The** Menapians—**Batavians**—**Distinguished** among the Auxiliaries of Rome—Decrease of national Feeling in Part **of** the Country—Steady Patriotism **of** the Frisons and Menapians—Commencement of **Civilization—Early Formation** of the Dikes—Degeneracy **of** those who became united to the Romans—Invasion of the Netherlands **by the Salian Franks** . . 17

CHAPTER II

FROM THE SETTLEMENT OF THE FRANKS TO THE SUBJUGATION OF FRIESLAND BY THE FRENCH

A.D. 250—800

Character of the Franks—The Saxon Tribes—Destruction of the Salians by a Saxon Tribe—Julian the Apostate—Victories of Clovis in Gaul—Contrast between the Low Countries and the Provinces of France—State of Friesland—Charles Martell—Friesland converted to Christianity—Finally subdued by France 27

CHAPTER III

FROM THE CONQUEST OF FRIESLAND TO THE FORMATION OF HOLLAND

A.D. 800—1000

Commencement of the Feudal System in the Highlands—Flourishing State of the Low Countries—Counts of the Empire—For-

(3)

mation of the Gilden or Trades—Establishment of popular
Privileges in Friesland—In what they consisted—Growth of
Ecclesiastical Power—Baldwin of Flanders—Created Count—
Appearance of the Normans—They ravage the Netherlands—
Their Destruction, and final Disappearance—Division of the
Empire into Higher and Lower Lorraine—Establishment of the
Counts of Lorraine and Hainault—Increasing Power of the Bishops of Liege and Utrecht—Their Jealousy of the Counts; who
resist their Encroachments 34

CHAPTER IV

FROM THE FORMATION OF HOLLAND TO THE DEATH OF LOUIS DE MALE

A.D. 1018–1384

Origin of Holland—Its first Count—Aggrandizement of Flanders—
Its growing Commerce—Fisheries—Manufactures—Formation
of the County of Guelders, and of Brabant—State of Friesland
—State of the Provinces—The Crusades—Their good Effects on
the State of the Netherlands—Decline of the Feudal Power, and
Growth of the Influence of the Towns—Great Prosperity of the
Country—The Flemings take up Arms against the French—
Drive them out of Bruges, and defeat them in the Battle of
Courtrai—Popular Success in Brabant—Its Confederation with
Flanders—Rebellion of Bruges against the Count, and of Ghent
under James d'Artaveldt—His Alliance with England—His
Power, and Death—Independence of Flanders—Battle of Roosbeke—Philip the Bold, Duke of Burgundy, obtains the Sovereignty of Flanders 44

CHAPTER V

FROM THE SUCCESSION OF PHILIP THE BOLD TO THE COUNTY OF FLANDERS TO THE DEATH OF PHILIP THE FAIR

A.D. 1384–1506

Philip succeeds to the Inheritance of Brabant—Makes War on England as a French Prince, Flanders remaining neuter—Power of
the Houses of Burgundy and Bavaria, and Decline of Public
Liberty—Union of Holland, Hainault, and Brabant—Jacqueline,
Countess of Holland and Hainault—Flies from the Tyranny of
her Husband, John of Brabant, and takes Refuge in England—
Murder of John the Fearless, Duke of Burgundy—Accession of
his Son, Philip the Good—His Policy—Espouses the Cause of

CONTENTS

John of Brabant against Jacqueline—Deprives her of Hainault, Holland, and Zealand—Continues his Persecution, and despoils her of her last Possession and Titles—She marries a Gentleman of Zealand, and Dies—Peace of Arras—Dominions of the House of Burgundy equal to the present Extent of the Kingdom of the Netherlands—Rebellion of Ghent—Affairs of **Holland and Zealand**—Charles the Rash—His Conduct in **Holland—Succeeds his** Father—Effects of Philip's Reign **on the Manners of the People**—Louis XI.—Death of Charles, and Succession of **Mary**—Factions among her Subjects—Marries Maximilian **of** Austria—Battle **of** Guinegate—Death of Mary—Maximilian unpopular—Imprisoned by his Subjects—Released—Invades the Netherlands—Succeeds to the Imperial Throne by the Death of his Father—Philip the Fair proclaimed Duke and Count—His wise Administration—Affairs of Friesland—Of Guelders—Charles of Egmont—Death **of** Philip the **Fair** 60

CHAPTER VI

FROM THE GOVERNMENT OF MARGARET OF AUSTRIA TO THE ABDICATION OF THE **EMPEROR CHARLES V**

A.D. 1506—1555

Margaret of Austria invested with the Sovereignty—Her Character and Government—Charles, Son of Philip the Fair, created Duke of Brabant and Count of Flanders and Holland—The Reformation—Martin Luther—Persecution of **the** Reformers—Battle of Pavia—Cession of Utrecht to Charles **V.—Peace of** Cambray—The Anabaptists' Sedition at Ghent—Expedition against **Tunis** and Algiers—Charles becomes possessed of Friesland and **Guelders**—His **increasing** Severity against the Protestants—His **Abdication** and Death—Review—Progress **of Civilization** 82

CHAPTER VII

FROM THE ACCESSION OF PHILIP II. OF SPAIN TO THE ESTABLISHMENT OF THE INQUISITION IN THE NETHERLANDS

A.D. 1555—1566

Accession of Philip II.—His Character and Government—His Wars with France, and with the Pope—Peace with the Pope—Battle of St. Quentin—Battle of Gravelines—Peace of Câteau-Cambresis—Death of Mary of England—Philip's Despotism—Establishes a Provisional Government—Convenes the States-General at Ghent—His Minister Granvelle—Goes to Zealand—Embarks for Spain—Prosperity revives—Effects of the Provisional Government — Marguerite of Parma — Character of Granvelle—Viglius de Berlaimont—Departure of the Spanish Troops—Clergy — Bishops—National Discontent—Granvelle appointed Cardinal—Edict against Heresy—Popular Indignation—Reformation—State of Brabant—Confederacy against Granvelle—**Prince of Orange—Counts** Egmont and Horn join the Prince **against** Granvelle—Granvelle recalled—Council of Trent—Its **Decrees** received with Reprobation—Decrees against Reformers—**Philip's** Bigotry—Establishment of the Inquisition—Popular **Resistance.** 95

CHAPTER VIII

COMMENCEMENT OF THE REVOLUTION

A.D. 1566

Commencement of the Revolution—Defence of the Prince of Orange—Confederacy of the Nobles—**Louis** of Nassau—De Brederode—Philip de St. Aldegonde—Assembly of the Council of State—Confederates enter Brussels—Take **the Title of** *Gueux*—Quit Brussels, and disperse in **the Provinces—Measures of** Government—Growing Power of the Confederates—**Progress** of the **Reformation—Field** Preaching — Herman Stricker — Boldness of the Protestants—Peter Dathen—Ambrose Ville—Situation of **Antwerp—The** Prince repairs to it, and saves it—Meeting of the **Confederates at** St. Trond—The **Prince of** Orange and Count **Egmont treat** with them—Tyranny of Philip and Moderation **of the Spanish** Council—Image Breakers—Destruction of the **Cathedral of Antwerp—Terror of** Government—Firmness of **Viglius—Arbitration between the** Court and the People—Concessions made by Government—Restoration of Tranquillity . . 120

CHAPTER IX

TO THE ADMINISTRATION OF REQUESENS

A.D. 1566—1573

Philip's Vindictiveness and Hypocrisy—Progress of Protestantism—Gradual Dissolution of the Conspiracy—Artifices of Philip and the Court to disunite the Protestants—Firmness of the Prince of Orange—Conference at Termonde—Egmont abandons the Patriot Cause—Fatal Effects of his Conduct—Commencement of Hostilities—Siege of Valenciennes—Protestant Synod at Antwerp—Haughty Conduct of the Government—Royalists Repulsed at Bois-le-duc—Battle of Osterweel, and Defeat of the Patriots—Antwerp again saved by the Firmness and Prudence of the Prince of Orange—Capitulation of Valenciennes—Success of the Royalists—Death of De Brederode—New Oath of Allegiance; Refused by the Prince of Orange and others—The Prince resolves on voluntary Banishment, and departs for Germany—His Example is followed by the Lords—Extensive Emigration—Arrival of the Duke of Orleans—Egmont's Humiliation—Alva's Powers—Arrest of Egmont and others—Alva's first Acts of Tyranny—Council of Blood—Recall of the Government—Alva's Character—He summons the Prince of Orange, who is tried by Contumacy—Horrors committed by Alva—Desolate State of the Country—Trial and Execution of Egmont and Horn—The Prince of Orange raises an Army in Germany, and opens his first Campaign in the Netherlands—Battle of Heiligerlee—Death of Adolphus of Nassau—Battle of Jemminghem—Success and skilful Conduct of Alva—Dispersion of the Prince of Orange's Army—Growth of the naval Power of the Patriots—Inundation in Holland and Friesland—Alva reproached by Philip—Duke of Medina-Celi appointed Governor—Is attacked, and his fleet destroyed by the Patriots—Demands his Recall—Policy of the English Queen, Elizabeth—The Dutch take Brille—General Revolt in Holland and Zealand—New Expedition of the Prince of Orange—Siege of Mons—Success of the Prince—Siege of Haarlem—Of Alkmaer—Removal of Alva—Don Luis Zanega y Requesens appointed Governor-General 136

CHAPTER X

TO THE PACIFICATION OF GHENT

A.D. 1573—1576

Character of Requesens—His conciliating Conduct—Renews the War against the States—Siege of Middleburg—Generosity of the Prince of Orange—Naval Victory—State of Flanders—Count Louis of Nassau—Battle of Mookerheyde—Counts Louis and Henry slain—Mutiny of the Spanish Troops—Siege of Leyden—Negotiations for Peace at Breda—The Spaniards take Zuriczee—Requesens dies—The Government devolves on the Council of State—Miserable State of the Country, and Despair of the Patriots—Spanish Mutineers—The States-General are convoked, and the Council arrested by the Grand Bailiff of Brabant—The Spanish Mutineers sack and capture Maestricht, and afterward

CONTENTS

Antwerp—The States-General assemble at Ghent and assume the Government—The Pacification of Ghent . . . .

CHAPTER XI

TO THE RENUNCIATION OF THE SOVEREIGNTY OF SPAIN AND THE DECLARATION OF INDEPENDENCE

A.D. 1576—1580

Don John of Austria, Governor-General, arrives in the Netherlands—His Character and Conduct—The States send an Envoy to Elizabeth of England—She advances them a Loan of Money—The Union of Brussels—The Treaty of Marche-en-Famenne, called the Perpetual Edict—The impetuous Conduct of Don John excites the public Suspicion—He seizes on the Citadel of Namur—The Prince of Orange is named Protector of Brabant—The People destroy the Citadels of Antwerp and other Towns—The Duke of Arschot is named Governor of Flanders—He invites the Archduke Mathias to accept the Government of the Netherlands—Wise Conduct of the Prince of Orange—Ryhove and Hembyse possess themselves of supreme Power at Ghent—The Prince of Orange goes there and establishes Order—The Archduke Mathias is installed—The Prince of Parma arrives in the Netherlands, and gains the Battle of Gemblours—Confusion of the States-General—The Duke of Alençon comes to their Assistance—Dissensions among the Patriot Chiefs—Death of Don John of Austria—Suspicions of his having been Poisoned by Order of Philip II.—The Prince of Parma is declared Governor-General—The Union of Utrecht—The Prince of Parma takes the Field—The Congress of Cologne rendered fruitless by the Obstinacy of Philip—The States-General assemble at Antwerp, and issue a Declaration of National Independence—The Sovereignty of the Netherlands granted to the Duke of Alençon . . . .

CHAPTER XII

TO THE MURDER OF THE PRINCE OF ORANGE

A.D. 1580—1584

Proscription of the Prince of Orange—His celebrated Apology—Philip proposes sending back the Duchess of Parma as Stadtholderess—Her Son refuses to act jointly with her, and is left in the Exercise of his Power—The Siege of Cambray undertaken by the Prince of Parma, and gallantly defended by the Princess of

CONTENTS

Epinoi—The Duke of Alencon created Duke of Anjou—Repairs to England, in hopes of marrying Queen Elizabeth—He returns to the Netherlands unsuccessful, and is inaugurated at Antwerp—The Prince of Orange desperately wounded by an Assassin—Details on John Jaureguay and his **Accomplices—The People** suspect the French of the Crime—Rapid **Recovery of the Prince,** who soon resumes his accustomed **Activity—Violent Conduct** of the **Duke of** Anjou, who treacherously **attempts to** seize **on** Antwerp—He **is** defeated **by the** Townspeople—His Disgrace and Death—Ungenerous **Suspicions** of the People **against** the Prince **of** Orange, who **leaves Flanders** in Disgust—Treachery of the Prince of Chimay and others—Treason of Hembyse—He **is** executed at Ghent—The States resolve to confer the Sovereignty on the Prince of Orange—He is murdered at Delft—Parallel between him and the Admiral Coligny—Execution of Balthazar Gerard, his Assassin—Complicity of the Prince of Parma . . . **180**

CHAPTER XIII
TO THE DEATH OF ALEXANDER, PRINCE OF PARMA
A.D. 1584—1592

Effects of William's **Death on the History of his Country—Firm Conduct of the United Provinces—They reject the Overtures** of the Prince of Parma—He **reduces the whole of Flanders—De**plorable Situation of **the Country—Vigorous Measures of the** Northern States—Antwerp **besieged—Operations of the Siege**—Immense Exertions of the **Besiegers—The Infernal Machine—**Battle on the **Dike of Couvestien—Surrender of Antwerp—Ex**travagant **Joy** of Philip II.—The **United Provinces solicit the** Aid of France and England—Elizabeth **sends them a supply of Troops under the** Earl **of Leicester—He returns to** England—Treachery **of some English and Scotch** Officers—Prince Maurice commences **his Career—The Spanish** Armada—Justin of Nassau blocks up the Prince **of Parma** in the Flemish Ports—Ruin of the Armada—Philip's **Mock Piety** on hearing the News—Leicester dies—Exploits and **Death of** Martin Schenck—Breda surprised—The Duke of Parma leads his **Army** into France—His famous Retreat—His Death and Character **196**

CHAPTER XIV
TO THE INDEPENDENCE OF BELGIUM AND THE **DEATH OF PHILIP II.**
A.D. 1592—1599

Count Mansfield named Governor-General—State of Flanders and Brabant—The Archduke Ernest named Governor-General—

Attempts against the Life of Prince Maurice—He takes Groningen—Death of the Archduke Ernest—Count Fuentes named Governor-General—He takes Cambray and other Towns—Is soon replaced by the Archduke Albert of Austria—His high Reputation—He opens his first Campaign in the Netherlands—His Successes—Prince Maurice gains the Battle of Turnhout—Peace of Vervins—Philip yields the Sovereignty of the Netherlands to Albert and Isabella—A new Plot against the Life of Prince Maurice—Albert sets out for Spain, and receives the News of Philip's Death—Albert arrives in Spain, and solemnizes his Marriage with the Infanta Isabella—Review of the State of the Netherlands 211

CHAPTER XV

TO THE CAMPAIGN OF PRINCE MAURICE AND SPINOLA

A D. 1599—1604

Cardinal Andrew of Austria Governor—Francisco Mendoza, Admiral of Aragon, invades the neutral States of Germany—His atrocious Conduct—Prince Maurice takes the Field—His masterly Movements—Sybilla of Cleves raises an Army, which is quickly destroyed—Great Exertions of the States-General—Naval Expedition under Vander Goes—Its complete Failure—Critical Situation of the United Provinces—Arrival of the Archduke in Brussels—Success of Prince Maurice—His Expedition into Flanders—Energy of the Archduke—Heroism of Isabella—Progress of Albert's Army—Its first Success—Firmness of Maurice—The Battle of Nieuport—Total Defeat of the Royalists—Consequences of the Victory—Prince Maurice returns to Holland—Negotiations for Peace—Siege of Ostend—Death of Elizabeth of England—United Provinces send Ambassadors to James I.—Successful Negotiations of Barneveldt and the Duke of Sully in London—Peace between England and Spain—Brilliant Campaign between Spinola and Prince Maurice—Battle of Roeroord—Naval Transactions—Progress of Dutch Influence in India—Establishment of the East India Company 223

CHAPTER XVI

TO THE SYNOD OF DORT AND THE EXECUTION OF BARNEVELDT

A.D. 1606—1619

Spinola proposes to invade the United Provinces—Successfully opposed by Prince Maurice—The Dutch defeated at Sea—Desper-

ate Conduct of Admiral Klagoon—Great naval Victory of the
Dutch, and Death of their Admiral Heemskirk—Overtures of
the Archdukes for Peace—How received in Holland—Prudent
Conduct of Barneveldt—Negotiations opened at The Hague—
John de Neyen, Ambassador for the Archdukes—Armistice for
Eight Months—Neyen attempts to bribe D'Aarsens, the Greffier
of the States-General—His Conduct disclaimed by **Verreiken**,
Counsellor **to** the Archdukes—Great Prejudices **in Holland**
against **King James** I. and the English, and Partiality toward
France—Rupture of the Negotiations—They are renewed—Truce
for Twelve Years signed at Antwerp—Gives great Satisfaction
in the Netherlands—Important Attitude of the United Prov-
inces—Conduct of the Belgian Provinces—Disputes relative to
Cleves and Juliers—Prince Maurice and Spinola remove their
Armies into the contested States—Intestine Troubles **in the
United Provinces—Assass**ination **of Henry** IV. of France—His
Character—Change in Prince Maurice's Character **and** Conduct
—He is strenuously opposed by Barneveldt—Religious Disputes
—King James enters the Lists of Controversy—Barneveldt **and
Maurice take opposite Sides**—The cautionary **Towns released**
from the Possession of England—Consequences of **this Event**—
Calumnies against Barneveldt—Ambitious Designs of Prince
Maurice—He is baffled by Barneveldt—The Republic assists its
Allies with Money and Ships—Its great naval Power—Outrages
of some Dutch Sailors in Ireland—Unresented by **King James**—
His Anger **at** the manufacturing Prosperity of **the** United
Provinces—Excesses of the Gomarists—The Magistrates call out
the National Militia—Violent Conduct of Prince **Maurice**—**Un-
compromising Steadiness** of Barneveldt—Calumnies against
him—Maurice **succeeds** to the Title of Prince of Orange, and
Acts with increasing Violence—Arrest of Barneveldt **and his
Friends—Synod** of Dort—Its Consequences—Trial, Condemnation, and **Execution** of **Barneveldt**—Grotius and **Hoogerbeets**
sentenced **to perpetual Imprisonment — Ledenburg commits**
Suicide 283

CHAPTER XVII

TO THE DEATH OF PRINCE MAURICE

A.D. 1619—1625

The Parties of Arminianism quite subdued—Emigrations—Grotius
resolves to attempt an Escape from Prison—Succeeds in his Attempt—He repairs to Paris, and publishes his "Apology"—
Expiration of the Twelve Years' Truce—Death of Philip III. and

of the Archduke Albert—War in Germany—Campaign between Prince Maurice and Spinola—Conspiracy against the Life of Prince Maurice—Its Failure—Fifteen of the Conspirators executed—Great Unpopularity of Maurice—Death of Maurice . . 261

CHAPTER XVIII
TO THE TREATY OF MUNSTER
A.D. 1625—1648

Frederick Henry succeeds his Brother—Charles I. King of England—War between France and England—Victories of Admiral Hein—Brilliant Success of Frederick Henry—Fruitless Enterprise in Flanders—Death of the Archduchess Isabella—Confederacy in Brabant—Its Failure, and Arrest of the Nobles—Ferdinand, Prince-Cardinal, Governor-General—Treaty between France and Holland—Battle of Avein—Naval Affairs—Battle of the Downs—Van Tromp—Negotiations for the Marriage of Prince William with the Princess Mary of England—Death of the Prince-Cardinal—Don Francisco de Mello Governor-General—Battle of Rocroy—Gallantry of Prince William—Death of Cardinal Richelieu and of Louis XIII.—English Politics—Affairs of Germany—Negotiations for Peace—Financial Embarrassment of the Republic—The Republic negotiates with Spain—Last Exploits of Frederick Henry—His Death, and Character—William II. Stadtholder—Peace of Munster—Resentment of Louis XIII.—Peace of Westphalia—Review of the Progress of Art, Science, and Manners — Literature — Painting — Engraving—Sculpture—Architecture—Finance—Population—Commercial Companies—Manners 271

CHAPTER XIX
FROM THE PEACE OF MUNSTER TO THE PEACE OF NIMEGUEN
A.D. 1648—1678

State of the Republic after the Peace of Munster—State of England—William II. Stadtholder—His ambitious Designs and Violent Conduct—Attempts to seize on Amsterdam—His Death—Different Sensations caused by his Death—The Prerogatives of the Stadtholder assumed by the People—Naval War with England—English Act of Navigation—Irish Hostilities—Death of Tromp—A Peace with England—Disturbed State of the Republic—War with Denmark—Peace concluded—Charles II. restored to the English Throne—Declares War against Holland—Naval Actions—Charles endeavors to excite all Europe against the Dutch—His Failure—Renewed Hostilities—De Ruyter defeated—Peace of Breda—Invasion of Flanders by Louis XIV.—He overruns Brabant and Flanders—Triple League, 1668—Perfidious Conduct of Charles II.—He declares War against Holland, etc., as does Louis XIV.—Unprepared **State of** United Provinces—William III. **Prince of** Orange—Appointed Captain-General **and** High **Admiral—Battle of** Solebay—The French Invade the Republic—The States-General implore Peace—Terms demanded by Louis XIV. **and** by Charles II.—Desperation of the Dutch—The Prince of Orange proclaimed Stadtholder—Massacre of the De Witts—Fine Conduct of the Prince **of** Orange—He takes the Field—Is reinforced by **Spain,** the Emperor, and Brandenburg—Louis XIV. forced to **abandon his** Conquests—Naval Actions with the **English—A** Peace, 1674—Military Affairs—Battle of Senef—Death of De Ruyter—Congress **for Peace at Nimeguen—Battle** of Mont Cassel—Marriage of the **Prince of Orange—Peace of** Nimeguen. 290

CHAPTER XX

FROM THE PEACE OF NIMEGUEN TO THE PEACE OF UTRECHT

A.D. 1678—1713

State of Europe subsequently **to the Peace of Nimeguen—Arrogant** Conduct of Louis XIV.**—Truce for Twenty Years—Death of** Charles II. of England—League of Augsburg—**The Conduct of William**—He invades England—James II. deposed—**William III. proclaimed** King of England—King William puts **himself at the Head of the Confederacy against** Louis XIV., **and enters on** the War—Military Operations—Peace **of Ryswyk—Death of Charles** II. of Spain—War of Succession—**Death of William III.—His Character—** Duke of Marlborough—**Prince Eugene—Successes of the** Earl of Peterborough **in Spain and Portugal—Louis XIV.** solicits Peace—Conferences **for Peace—Peace of Utrecht—Treaty of the Barrier** 311

CHAPTER XXI

FROM THE PEACE OF UTRECHT TO THE INCORPORATION OF BELGIUM WITH THE FRENCH REPUBLIC

A.D. 1713—1794

Quadruple Alliance—General Peace of Europe—Wise Conduct of the Republic—Great Danger from the bad State of the Dikes—

Death of the Emperor Charles VI.—Maria Theresa Empress—Her heroic Conduct—Battle of Dettingen—Louis XV. invades the Netherlands—Conferences for Peace at Breda—Battle of Fontenoy—William IV. Stadtholder and Captain-General—Peace of Aix-la-Chapelle—Death of the Stadtholder, who is succeeded by his Son William V.—War of Seven Years—State of the Republic—William V. Stadtholder—Dismemberment of Poland—Joseph II. Emperor—His attempted Reforms in Religion—War with England—Sea-Fight on the Doggerbank—Peace with England, 1784—Progress of Public Opinion in Europe, in Belgium, and Holland—Violent Opposition to the Stadtholder—Arrest of the Princess of Orange—Invasion of Holland by the Prussian Army—Agitation in Belgium—Vander Noot—Prince Albert of Saxe-Teschen and the Archduchess Maria Theresa joint Governors-General—Succeeded by Count Murray—Riots—Meetings of the Provisional States-General Insurrection—Vonckists—Vander Mersch—Takes the Command of the Insurgents—His Skilful Conduct—He gains the Battle of Turnhout—Takes Possession of Flanders—Confederation of the Belgian Provinces—Death of Joseph II.—Leopold Emperor—Arrest of Vander Mersch—Arrogance of the States-General of Belgium—The Austrians overrun the Country—Convention at The Hague—Death of Leopold—Battle of Jemmappes—General Dumouriez—Conquest of Belgium by the French—Recovered by the Austrians—The Archduke Charles Governor-General—War in the Netherlands—Duke of York—The Emperor Francis—The Battle of Fleurus—Incorporation of Belgium with the French Republic—Peace of Leoben—Treaty of Campo-Formio 325

CHAPTER XXII

FROM THE INVASION OF HOLLAND BY THE FRENCH TO THE RETURN OF THE PRINCE OF ORANGE

A.D. 1794—1813.

Pichegru invades Holland—Winter Campaign—The Duke of York vainly resists the French Army—Abdication of the Stadtholder—Batavian Republic—War with England—Unfortunate Situation of Holland—Naval Fight—English Expedition to the Helder—Napoleon Bonaparte—Louis Bonaparte named King of Holland—His popular Conduct—He abdicates the Throne—Annexation of Holland to the French Empire—Ruinous to the Prosperity of the Republic—The People desire the Return of the Prince of Orange—Confederacy to effect this Purpose—The

Allied Armies advance toward Holland—The Nation rises to throw off the Yoke of France—Count Styrum and his Associates lead on that Movement, and proclaim the Prince of Orange, who lands from England—His first Proclamation—His second Proclamation 340

CHAPTER XXIII

FROM THE INSTALLATION OF WILLIAM I. AS PRINCE-SOVEREIGN OF THE NETHERLANDS TO THE BATTLE OF WATERLOO

A.D. 1813—1815

Rapid Organization of Holland—The Constitution formed—Accepted by the People—Objections made to it by some Individuals—Inauguration of the Prince-Sovereign—Belgium is occupied by the Allies—Treaty of Paris—Treaty of London—Formation of the Kingdom of the Netherlands—Basis of the Government—Relative Character and Situation of Holland and Belgium—The Prince-Sovereign of Holland arrives in Belgium as Governor-General—The fundamental Law—Report of the Commissioners by whom it was framed—Public Feeling in Holland, and in Belgium—The Emperor Napoleon invades France, and Belgium—The Prince of Orange takes the Field—The Duke of Wellington—Prince Blucher—Battle of Ligny—Battle of Quatre Bras—Battle of Waterloo—Anecdote of the Prince of Orange, who is wounded—Inauguration of the King 357

SUPPLEMENTARY CHAPTER (A.D. 1815—1899) 372

LIST OF ILLUSTRATIONS

HOLLAND

The Duke of Alva Deposes Margaret of Parma
Storming the Barricades at Brussels During the Revolution of 1848
William the Silent of Orange
A Holland Beauty

HISTORY OF THE NETHERLANDS

CHAPTER I

FROM THE INVASION OF THE NETHERLANDS BY THE ROMANS
TO THE INVASION BY THE SALIAN FRANKS

B.C. 50—A.D. 250

THE NETHERLANDS form a kingdom of moderate extent, situated on the borders of the ocean, opposite to the southeast coast of England, and stretching from the frontiers of France to those of Hanover. The country is principally composed of low and humid grounds, presenting a vast plain, irrigated by the waters from all those neighboring states which are traversed by the Rhine, the Meuse, and the Scheldt. This plain, gradually rising toward its eastern and southern extremities, blends on the one hand with Prussia, and on the other with France. Having, therefore, no natural or strongly marked limits on those sides, the extent of the kingdom could only be determined by convention; and it must be at all times subject to the arbitrary and varying influence of European policy. Its greatest length, from north to south, is about two hundred and twenty English miles; and its breadth, from east to west, is nearly one hundred and forty.

Two distinct kinds of men inhabit this kingdom. The one occupying the valleys of the Meuse and the Scheldt, and the high grounds bordering on France, speak a dialect of the language of that country, and evidently belong to the Gallic race. They are called Walloons, and are distinguished from the others by many peculiar qualities. Their most prominent characteristic is a propensity for war, and their principal source of subsistence the **working of** their mines. They form nearly one-fourth **of** the population **of** the whole king-**dom, or about one million** three hundred thousand persons. **All the rest of the nation** speak **Low** German, **in** its modifi-**cations of Dutch and** Flemish; **and they offer the** distinctive **characteristics of the** Saxon race—talents **for** agriculture, **navigation, and** commerce; perseverance rather **than vivac-ity; and more courage than** taste for the profession of **arms. They are subdivided into** Flemings—those who were the last **to submit to the House of** Austria; and Dutch—those who **formed the republic of the** United Provinces. **But** there is **no difference between these two** subdivisions, except **such as has been produced by political and** religious institutions. **The physical aspect of the people is** the same; and the soil, **equally low and moist, is at once** fertilized and menaced by **the waters.**

The history of this **last-mentioned portion of** the nation **is completely linked to that of the soil which** they occupy. In **remote times, when the inhabitants of this** plain were few and **uncivilized, the country formed but** one immense **morass, of which the chief part was incessan**tly inundated **and made sterile by the waters of the** sea. Pliny the natu-ralist, **who visited the northern** coasts, has left us a picture **of their state in his days.** "There," says he, "the ocean **pours in** its flood **twice every day,** and produces a perpetual **uncertainty** whether the **country** may be considered **as a part of the** continent **or of** the sea. The wretched inhabi-tants take refuge on the sand-hills, or in little huts, which **they construct** on the summits of lofty **stakes, whose eleva-tion is** conformable to that of **the highest tides.** When the **sea rises, they** appear like **navigators;** when it retires, they **seem as though** they had been shipwrecked. They subsist **on the fish** left by the refluent waters, and which they catch **in nets** formed of rushes or seaweed. Neither tree nor shrub is visible on these shores. The drink of the people is rain-water, which they preserve with great care; their fuel, a sort of turf, which they gather and form with the hand.

And yet these unfortunate beings dare to complain against their fate, when they fall under the power and are incorporated with the empire of Rome!"

The picture of poverty and suffering which this passage presents is heightened when joined to a description of the country. The coasts consisted only of sand-banks or slime, alternately overflowed or left imperfectly dry. A little further inland, trees were to be found, but on a soil so marshy that an inundation or a tempest threw down whole forests, such as are still at times discovered at either eight or ten feet depth below the surface. The sea had no limits; the rivers no beds nor banks; the earth no solidity; for, according to an author of the third century of our era, there was not, in the whole of the immense plain, a spot of ground that did not yield under the footsteps of man.—Eumenius.

It was not the same in the southern parts, which form at present the Walloon country. These high grounds suffered much less from the ravages of the waters. The ancient forest of the Ardennes, extending from the Rhine to the Scheldt, sheltered a numerous though savage population, which in all things resembled the Germans, from whom they derived their descent. The chase and the occupations of rude agriculture sufficed for the wants of a race less poor and less patient, but more unsteady and ambitious, than the fishermen of the low lands. Thus it is that history presents us with a tribe of warriors and conquerors on the southern frontier of the country; while the scattered inhabitants of the remaining parts seemed to have fixed there without a contest, and to have traced out for themselves, by necessity and habit, an existence which any other people must have considered insupportable.

This difference in the nature of the soil and in the fate of the inhabitants appears more striking when we consider the present situation of the country. The high grounds, formerly so preferable, are now the least valuable part of the kingdom, even as regards their agriculture; while the ancient marshes have been changed by human industry into rich and fertile tracts, the best parts of which are precisely those conquered from the grasp of the ocean. In order to form an idea of the solitude and desolation which once reigned where we now see the most richly cultivated fields, the most thriving villages, and the wealthiest towns of the continent, the imagination must go back to times which have not left one monument of antiquity and scarcely a vestige of fact.

The history of the Netherlands is, then, essentially that of a patient and industrious population struggling against every obstacle which nature could oppose to its well-being; and, in this contest, man triumphed most completely over the elements in those places where they offered the greatest resistance. This extraordinary result was due to the hardy stamp of character imprinted by suffering and danger on those who had the ocean for their foe; to the nature of their country, which presented no lure for conquest; and, finally, to the toleration, the justice, and the liberty nourished among men left to themselves, and who found resources in their social state which rendered change neither an object of their wants nor wishes.

About half a century before the Christian era, the obscurity which enveloped the north of Europe began to disperse; and the expedition of Julius Cæsar gave to the civilized world the first notions of the Netherlands, Germany, and England. Cæsar, after having subjugated the chief part of Gaul, turned his arms against the warlike tribes of the Ardennes, who refused to accept his alliance or implore his protection. They were called Belgæ by the Romans; and at once pronounced the least civilized and the bravest of the Gauls. Cæsar there found several ignorant and poor but intrepid clans of warriors, who marched fiercely to encounter him; and, notwithstanding their inferiority in numbers, in weapons, and in tactics, they nearly destroyed the disciplined armies of Rome. They were, however, defeated, and their country ravaged by the invaders, who found less success when they attacked the natives of the low grounds. The Menapians, a people who occupied the present provinces of Flanders and Antwerp, though less numerous than those whom the Romans had last vanquished, arrested their progress both by open fight and by that petty and harassing contest—that warfare of the people rather than of the soldiery—so well adapted to the nature of the country. The Roman legions retreated for the first time, and were contented to occupy the higher parts, which now form the Walloon provinces.

But the policy of Cæsar made greater progress than his arms. He had rather defeated than subdued those who had dared the contest. He consolidated his victories without new battles; he offered peace to his enemies, in proposing to them alliance; and he required their aid, as friends, to carry on new wars in other lands. He thus attracted toward him, and ranged under his banners, not only those people situated to the west of the Rhine and the Meuse, but several other nations more to the north, whose territory he had never seen; and particularly the Batavians—a valiant tribe, stated by various ancient authors, and particularly by Tacitus, as a fraction of the Catti, who occupied the space comprised between these rivers. The young men of these warlike people, dazzled by the splendor of the Roman armies, felt proud and happy in being allowed to identify themselves with them. Cæsar encouraged this disposition, and even went so far on some occasions as to deprive the Roman cavalry of their horses, on which he mounted those new allies, who managed them better than their Italian riders. He had no reason to repent these measures; almost all his subsequent victories, and particularly that of Pharsalia, being decided by the valor of the auxiliaries he obtained from the Low Countries.

These auxiliaries were chiefly drawn from Hainault, Luxemburg, and the country of the Batavians, and they formed the best cavalry of the Roman armies, as well as their choicest light infantry force. The Batavians also signalized themselves on many occasions, by the skill with which they swam across several great rivers without breaking their squadrons' ranks. They were amply rewarded for their military services and hazardous exploits, and were treated like stanch and valuable allies. But this unequal connection of a mighty empire with a few petty states must have been fatal to the liberty of the weaker party. Its first effect was to destroy all feeling of nationality in a great portion of the population. The young adventurer of this part of the Low Countries, after twenty years of service under the imperial eagles, returned to his native wilds a Roman. The generals of the empire pierced the forests of the Ardennes with causeways, and founded towns in the heart of the country. The result of such innovations was a total amalgamation of the Romans and their new allies; and little by little the national character of the latter became entirely obliterated. But to trace now the precise history of this gradual change would be as impossible as it will be one day to follow the progress of civilization in the woods of North America.

But it must be remarked that this metamorphosis affected only the inhabitants of the high grounds, and the Batavians (who were in their origin Germans) properly so called. The scanty population of the rest of the country, endowed with that fidelity to their ancient customs which characterizes the Saxon race, showed no tendency to mix with foreigners, rarely figured in their ranks, and seemed to revolt from the southern refinement which was so little in harmony with their manners and ways of life. It is astonishing, at the first view, that those beings, whose whole existence was a contest against famine or the waves, should show less inclination than their happier neighbors to receive from Rome an abundant recompense for their services. But the greater their difficulty to find subsistence in their native land, the stronger seemed their attachment; like that of the Switzer to his barren rocks, or of the mariner to the frail and hazardous home that bears him afloat on the ocean. This race of patriots was divided into two separate peoples. Those to the north of the Rhine were the Frisons; those to the west of the Meuse, the Menapians, already mentioned.

The Frisons differed little from those early inhabitants of the coast, who, perched on their high-built huts, fed on fish and drank the water of the clouds. Slow and successive improvements taught them to cultivate the beans which grew wild among the marshes, and to tend and feed a small and degenerate breed of horned cattle. But if these first steps toward civilization were slow, they were also sure; and they were made by a race of men who could never retrograde in a career once begun.

The Menapians, equally repugnant to foreign impressions, made, on their part, a more rapid progress. They were already a maritime people, and carried on a considerable commerce with England. It appears that they exported thither salt, the art of manufacturing which was well known to them; and they brought back in return marl, a most important commodity for the improvement of their land. They also understood the preparation of salting meat, with a perfection that made it in high repute even in Italy; and, finally, we are told by Ptolemy that they had established a colony on the eastern coast of Ireland, not far from Dublin.

The two classes of what forms at present the population of the Netherlands thus followed careers widely different, during the long period of the Roman power in these parts of Europe. While those of the high lands and the Batavians distinguished themselves by a long-continued course of military service or servitude, those of the plains improved by degrees their social condition, and fitted themselves for a place in civilized Europe. The former received from Rome great marks of favor in exchange for their freedom. The latter, rejecting the honors and distinctions lavished on their neighbors, secured their national independence, by trusting to their industry alone for all the advantages they gradually acquired.

Were the means of protecting themselves and their country from the inundations of the sea known and practiced by these ancient inhabitants of the coast? or did they occupy only those elevated points of land which stood out like islands in the middle of the floods? These questions are among the most important presented by their history; since it was the victorious struggle of man against the ocean that fixed the extent and form of the country. It appears almost certain that in the time of Cæsar they did not labor at the construction of dikes, but that they began to be raised during the obscurity of the following century; for the remains of ancient towns are even now discovered in places at present overflowed by the sea. These ruins often bring to light traces of Roman construction, and Latin inscriptions in honor of the Menapian divinities. It is, then, certain that they had learned to imitate those who ruled in the neighboring countries: a result by no means surprising; for even England, the mart of their commerce, and the nation with which they had the most constant intercourse, was at that period occupied by the Romans. But the nature of their country repulsed so effectually every attempt at foreign domination that the conquerors of the world left them unmolested, and established arsenals and formed communications with Great Britain only at Boulogne and in the island of the Batavians near Leyden.

This isolation formed in itself a powerful and perfect barrier between the inhabitants of the plain and those of the high grounds. The first held firm to their primitive customs and their ancient language; the second finished by speaking Latin, and borrowing all the manners and usages of Italy. The moral effect of this contrast was that the people, once so famous for their bravery, lost, with their liberty, their energy and their courage. One of the Batavian chieftains, named Civilis, formed an exception to this degeneracy, and, about the year 70 of our era, bravely took up arms for the expulsion of the Romans. He effected prodigies of valor and perseverance, and boldly met and defeated the enemy both by land and sea. Reverses followed his first success, and he finally concluded an honorable treaty, by which his countrymen once more became the allies of Rome. But after this expiring effort of valor, the Batavians, even though

FROM THE ROMANS TO THE SALIAN FRANKS 25

chosen from all nations for the bodyguards of the Roman emperors, became rapidly degenerate; and when Tacitus wrote, ninety years after Christ, they were already looked on as less brave than the Frisons and the other peoples beyond the Rhine. A century and a half later saw them confounded with the Gauls; and the barbarian conquerors said that "they were not a nation, but merely a *prey*."

Reduced into a Roman province, the southern portion of the Netherlands was at this period called Belgic Gaul; and the name of Belgium, preserved to our days, has until lately been applied to distinguish that part of the country situated to the south of the Rhine and the Meuse, or nearly that which formed the Austrian Netherlands.

During the establishment of the Roman power in the north of Europe, observation was not much excited toward the rapid effects of this degeneracy, compared with the fast-growing vigor of the people of the low lands. The fact of the Frisons having, on one occasion, near the year 47 of our era, beaten a whole army of Romans, had confirmed their character for intrepidity. But the long stagnation produced in these remote countries by the colossal weight of the empire was broken, about the year 250, by an irruption of Germans or Salian Franks, who, passing the Rhine and the Meuse, established themselves in the vicinity of the Menapians, near Antwerp, Breda and Bois-le-duc. All the nations that had been subjugated by the Roman power appear to have taken arms on this occasion and opposed the intruders. But the Menapians united themselves with these newcomers, and aided them to meet the shock of the imperial armies. Carausius, originally a Menapian pilot, but promoted to the command of a Roman fleet, made common cause with his fellow-citizens, and proclaimed himself emperor of Great Britain, where the naval superiority of the Menapians left him no fear of a competitor. In recompense of the assistance given him by the Franks, he crossed the sea again from his new empire, to aid them in their war with the Batavians, the allies of Rome; and having seized on their islands, and massacred nearly the whole of its inhabitants, he there established his faithful friends the Salians. Constantius and his son Constantine the Great vainly strove, even after the death of the brave Carausius, to regain possession of the country; but they were forced to leave the new inhabitants in quiet possession of their conquest.

CHAPTER II

FROM THE SETTLEMENT OF THE FRANKS TO THE SUBJUGATION OF FRIESLAND

A.D. 250—800

FROM this epoch we must trace the progress of a totally new and distinct population in the Netherlands. The Batavians being annihilated, almost without resistance, the low countries contained only the free people of the German race. But these people did not completely sympathize together so as to form one consolidated nation. The Salians, and the other petty tribes of Franks, their allies, were essentially warlike, and appeared precisely the same as the original inhabitants of the high grounds. The Menapians and the Frisons, on the contrary, lost nothing of their spirit of commerce and industry. The result of this diversity was a separation between the Franks and the Menapians. While the latter, under the name of Armoricans, joined themselves more closely with the people who bordered the Channel, the Frisons associated themselves with the tribes settled on the limits of the German Ocean, and formed with them a connection celebrated under the title of the Saxon League. Thus was formed on all points a union between the maritime races against the inland inhabitants; and their mutual antipathy became more and more developed as the decline of the Roman empire ended the former struggle between liberty and conquest.

The Netherlands now became the earliest theatre of an entirely new movement, the consequences of which were destined to affect the whole world. This country was occupied toward the sea by a people wholly maritime, excepting the narrow space between the Rhine and the Vahal, of which the Salian Franks had become possessed. The nature of this marshy soil, in comparison with the sands of Westphalia, Guelders, and North Brabant, was not more strikingly contrasted than was the character of their population. The Franks, who had been for a while under the Roman sway, showed a compound of the violence of savage life and the corruption of civilized society. They were covetous and treacherous, but made excellent soldiers; and at this epoch, which intervened between the power of imperial Rome and that of Germany, the Frank might be morally considered as a borderer on the frontiers of the Middle Ages. The Saxon (and this name comprehends all the tribes of the coast from the Rhine as far north as Denmark), uniting in himself the distinctive qualities of German and navigator, was moderate and sincere, but implacable in his rage. Neither of these two races of men was excelled in point of courage; but the number of Franks who still entered into the service of the empire diminished the real force of this nation, and naturally tended to disunite it. Therefore, in the subsequent shock of people against people, the Saxons invariably gained the final advantage.

They had no doubt often measured their strength in the most remote times, since the Franks were but the descendants of the ancient tribes of Sicambers and others, against whom the Batavians had offered their assistance to Cæsar. Under Augustus, the inhabitants of the coast had in the same way joined themselves with Drusus, to oppose these their old enemies. It was also after having been expelled by the Frisons from Guelders that the Salians had passed the Rhine and the Meuse; but, in the fourth century, the two peoples, recovering their strength, the struggle recommenced, never to terminate—at least between the direct descendants of each. It is believed that it was the Varni, a race of Saxons nearly connected with those of England (and coming, like them, from the coast of Denmark), who on this occasion struck the decisive blow on the side of the

Saxons. Embarking on board a numerous fleet, they made a descent in the ancient isle of the Batavians, at that time inhabited by the Salians, whom they completely destroyed. Julian the Apostate, who was then with a numerous army pursuing his career of early glory in these countries, interfered for the purpose of preventing the expulsion, or at least the utter destruction, of the vanquished; but his efforts were unavailing. The Salians appear to have figured no more in this part of the Low Countries.

The defeat of the Salians by a Saxon tribe is a fact on which no doubt rests. The name of the victors is, however, questionable. The Varni having remained settled near the mouths of the Rhine till near the year 500, there is strong probability that they were the people alluded to. But names and histories, which may on this point appear of such little importance, acquire considerable interest when we reflect that these Salians, driven from their settlement, became the conquerors of France; that those Saxons who forced them on their career of conquest were destined to become the masters of England; and that these two petty tribes, who battled so long for a corner of marshy earth, carried with them their reciprocal antipathy while involuntarily deciding the destiny of Europe.

The defeat of the Franks was fatal to those peoples who had become incorporated with the Romans; for it was from them that the exiled wanderers, still fierce in their ruin, and with arms in their hands, demanded lands and herds; all, in short, which they themselves had lost. From the middle of the fourth century to the end of the fifth, there was a succession of invasions in this spirit, which always ended by the subjugation of a part of the country; and which was completed about the year 490, by Clovis making himself master of almost the whole of Gaul. Under this new empire not a vestige of the ancient nations of the Ardennes was left. The civilized population either perished or was reduced to slavery, and all the high grounds were added to the previous conquests of the Salians.

But the maritime population, when once possessed of the whole coast, did not seek to make the slightest progress toward the interior. The element of their enterprise and the object of their ambition was the ocean; and when this hardy and intrepid race became too numerous for their narrow limits, expeditions and colonies beyond the sea carried off their redundant population. The Saxon warriors established themselves near the mouths of the Loire; others, conducted by Hengist and Horsa, settled in Great Britain. It will always remain problematical from what point of the coast these adventurers departed; but many circumstances tend to give weight to the opinion which pronounces those old Saxons to have started from the Netherlands.

Paganism not being yet banished from these countries, the obscurity which would have enveloped them is in some degree dispelled by the recitals of the monks who went among them to preach Christianity. We see in those records, and by the text of some of their early laws, that this maritime people were more industrious, prosperous, and happy, than those of France. The men were handsome and richly clothed; and the land well cultivated, and abounding in fruits, milk, and honey. The Saxon merchants carried their trade far into the southern countries. In the meantime, the parts of the Netherlands which belonged to France resembled a desert. The monasteries which were there founded were established, according to the words of their charters, amid immense solitudes; and the French nobles only came into Brabant for the sport of bear-hunting in its interminable forests. Thus, while the inhabitants of the low lands, as far back as the light of history penetrates, appear in a continual state of improvement, those of the high grounds, after frequent vicissitudes, seem to sink into utter degeneracy and subjugation. The latter wished to denaturalize themselves, and become as though they were foreigners even on their native soil; the former remained firm and faithful to their country and to each other.

But the growth of French power menaced utter ruin to

this interesting race. Clovis had succeeded, about the year 485 of our era, in destroying the last remnants of Roman domination in Gaul. The successors of these conquerors soon extended their empire from the Pyrenees to the Rhine. They had continual contests with the free population of the Low Countries, and their nearest neighbors. In the commencement of the seventh century, the French king, Clotaire II., exterminated the chief part of the Saxons of Hanover and Westphalia; and the historians of those barbarous times unanimously relate that he caused to be beheaded every inhabitant of the vanquished tribes who exceeded the height of his sword. The Saxon name was thus nearly extinguished in those countries; and the remnant of these various peoples adopted that of Frisons (Friesen), either because they became really incorporated with that nation, or merely that they recognized it for the most powerful of their tribes. Friesland, to speak in the language of that age, extended then from the Scheldt to the Weser, and formed a considerable state. But the ascendency of France was every year becoming more marked; and King Dagobert extended the limits of her power even as far as Utrecht. The descendants of the Menapians, known at that epoch by the different names of Menapians, Flemings, and Toxandirans, fell one after another directly or indirectly under the empire of the Merovingian princes; and the noblest family which existed among the French—that which subsequently took the name of Carlovingians—comprised in its dominions nearly the whole of the southern and western parts of the Netherlands.

Between this family, whose chief was called duke of the Frontier Marshes (*Dux Brabantiæ*), and the free tribes, united under the common name of Frisons, the same struggle was maintained as that which formerly existed between the Salians and the Saxons. Toward the year 700, the French monarchy was torn by anarchy, and, under "the lazy kings," lost much of its concentrated power; but every dukedom formed an independent sovereignty, and of all those that of Brabant was the most redoubtable. Nevertheless the Frisons, under their king, Radbod, assumed for a moment the superiority; and Utrecht, where the French had established Christianity, fell again into the power of the pagans. Charles Martell, at that time young, and but commencing his splendid career, was defeated by the hostile king in the forest of the Ardennes; and though, in subsequent conquests, he took an ample revenge, Radbod still remained a powerful opponent. It is related of this fierce monarch that he was converted by a Christian missionary; but, at the moment in which he put his foot in the water for the ceremony of baptism, he suddenly asked the priest where all his old Frison companions in arms had gone after their death? "To hell," replied the priest. "Well, then," said Radbod, drawing back his foot from the water, "I would rather go to hell with them, than to paradise with you and your fellow foreigners!" and he refused to receive the rite of baptism, and remained a pagan.

After the death of Radbod, in 719, Charles Martell, now become duke of the Franks, mayor of the palace, or by whatever other of his several titles he may be distinguished, finally triumphed over the long-resisting Frisons. He labored to establish Christianity among them; but they did not understand the French language, and the lot of converting them was consequently reserved for the English. St. Willebrod was the first missionary who met with any success, about the latter end of the seventh century; but it was not till toward the year 750 that this great mission was finally accomplished by St. Boniface, archbishop of Mayence, and the apostle of Germany. Yet the progress of Christianity, and the establishment of a foreign sway, still met the partial resistance which a conquered but not enervated people are always capable of opposing to their masters. St. Boniface fell a victim to this stubborn spirit. He perished a martyr to his zeal, but perhaps a victim as well to the violent measures of his colleagues, in Friesland, the very province which to this day preserves the name.

The last avenger of Friesland liberty and of the national idols was the illustrious Witikind, to whom the chronicles of his country give the title of first azing, or judge. This intrepid chieftain is considered as a compatriot, **not only by the** historians of Friesland, but by those **of** Saxony; both, it would appear, having equal claims to the honor; for the union between the two peoples **was** constantly strengthened by intermarriages **between the noblest** families of each. As long **as** Witikind **remained a pagan** and a freeman, some doubt existed as to **the final fate of** Friesland; but when by his conversion he became only a noble of the court of Charlemagne, the **slavery** of his country was consummated.

CHAPTER III

FROM THE CONQUEST OF FRIESLAND TO THE FORMATION OF HOLLAND

A.D. 800–1000

EVEN at this advanced epoch of foreign domination, there remained as great a difference as ever between the people of the high grounds and the inhabitants of the plain. The latter were, like the rest, incorporated with the great monarchy; but they preserved the remembrance of former independence, and even retained their ancient names. In Flanders, Menapians and Flemings were still found, and in the country of Antwerp the Toxandrians were not extinct. All the rest of the coast was still called Friesland. But in the high grounds the names of the old inhabitants were lost. Nations were designated by the names of their rivers, forests, or towns. They were classified as accessories to inanimate things; and having no monuments which reminded them of their origin, they became as it were without recollections or associations; and degenerated, as may be almost said, into a people without ancestry.

The physical state of the country had greatly changed from the times of Cæsar to those of Charlemagne. Many parts of the forest of the Ardennes had been cut down or cleared away. Civilization had only appeared for a while among these woods, to perish like a delicate plant in an ungenial clime; but it seemed to have sucked the very sap from the soil, and to have left the people no remains of the vigor of man in his savage state, nor of the desperate courage of the warriors of Germany. A race of serfs now culti-

TO THE FORMATION OF HOLLAND

vated the domains of haughty lords and imperious priests. The clergy had immense posessions in this country; an act of the following century recognizes fourteen thousand families of vassals as belonging to the single abbey of Nivelle. Tournay and Tongres, both Episcopal cities, were by that title somewhat less oppressed than the other ancient towns founded by the Romans; but they appear to have possessed only a poor and degraded population.

The low lands, on the other hand, announced a striking commencement of improvement and prosperity. The marshes and fens, which had arrested and repulsed the progress of imperial Rome, had disappeared in every part of the interior. The Meuse and the Scheldt no longer joined at their outlets, to desolate the neighboring lands; whether this change was produced by the labors of man, or merely by the accumulation of sand deposited by either stream and forming barriers to both. The towns of Courtraig, Bruges, Ghent, Antwerp, Berg-op-Zoom, and Thiel, had already a flourishing trade. The last-mentioned town contained in the following century fifty-five churches; a fact from which, in the absence of other evidence, the extent of the population may be conjectured. The formation of dikes for the protection of lands formerly submerged was already well understood, and regulated by uniform custom. The plains thus reconquered from the waters were distributed in portions, according to their labor, by those who reclaimed them, except the parts reserved for the chieftain, the church, and the poor. This vital necessity for the construction of dikes had given to the Frison and Flemish population a particular habit of union, goodwill, and reciprocal justice, because it was necessary to make common cause in this great work for their mutual preservation. In all other points, the detail of the laws and manners of this united people presents a picture similar to that of the Saxons of England, with the sole exception that the people of the Netherlands were milder than the Saxon race properly so called—their long habit of laborious industry exercising its happy influence on the martial spirit original to both. The manufacturing arts were also somewhat more advanced in this part of the continent than in Great Britain. The Frisons, for example, were the only people who could succeed in making the costly mantles in use among the wealthy Franks.

The government of Charlemagne admitted but one form, borrowed from that of the empire in the period of its decline—a mixture of the spiritual and temporal powers, exercised in the first place by the emperor, and at second-hand by the counts and bishops. The counts in those times were not the heads of noble families, as they afterward became, but officers of the government, removable at will, and possessing no hereditary rights. Their incomes did not arise from salaries paid in money, but consisted of lands, of which they had the revenues during the continuance of their authority. These lands being situated in the limits of their administration, each regarded them as his property only for the time being, and considered himself as a tenant at will. How unfavorable such a system was to culture and improvement may be well imagined. The force of possession was, however, frequently opposed to the seigniorial rights of the crown; and thus, though all civil dignity and the revenues attached to it were but personal and reclaimable at will, still many dignitaries, taking advantage of the barbarous state of the country in which their isolated cantons were placed, sought by every possible means to render their power and prerogatives inalienable and real. The force of the monarchical government, which consists mainly in its centralization, was necessarily weakened by the intervention of local obstacles, before it could pass from the heart of the empire to its limits. Thus it was only by perpetually interposing his personal efforts, and flying, as it were, from one end to the other of his dominions, that Charlemagne succeeded in preserving his authority. As for the people, without any sort of guarantee against the despotism of the government, they were utterly at the mercy of the nobles or of the sovereign. But this state of servitude was quite incompatible with the union of social powers necessary to a population that had to struggle against the tyranny of the ocean. To repulse its attacks with successful vigor, a spirit of complete concert was absolutely required; and the nation being thus united, and consequently strong, the **efforts of** foreign tyrants were shattered by its resistance, as the waves of the sea that broke against the dikes **by** which it was defied.

From the **time of Charlemagne, the people of the ancient** Menapia, **now become a** prosperous commonwealth, formed political associations **to** raise a barrier against the despotic violence of the Franks. These associations were called Gilden, and in the Latin of **the times** Gildonia. They **comprised, besides their covenants for** mutual protection, an obligation which bound every member **to give** succor to any other, in cases of illness, **conflagration, or shipwreck.** But **the** growing force of **these social compacts alarmed** the quick-sighted despotism **of Charlemagne, and they were,** consequently, prohibited **both by** him **and** his successors. To give a notion of the **importance of** this prohibition to the whole of Europe, **it is only necessary to state that the** most ancient corporations **(all which had** preceded and engendered the most valuable municipal rights) **were** nothing more than gilden. Thus, to draw **an** example from Great Britain, the corporative charter **of Berwick** still bears the title of Charta Gildoniæ. But the **ban of the** sovereigns was without efficacy, when **opposed to the popular** will. The gilden stood their **ground, and within a** century after the death of Charlemagne, **all Flanders was** covered with corporate towns.

This popular opposition **took,** however, another **form** in the northern parts **of** the country, which still bore the common name of Friesland; for there it was not merely local but national. The Frisons succeeded in obtaining the sanction of the monarch to consecrate, as it were, those rights which were established under the ancient forms of government. The fact is undoubted; but the means which they employed are uncertain. It appears most probable that this great privilege was the price of their military services; for they held a high place in the victorious armies of Charlemagne; and Turpin, the old French romancer, alluding to the popular traditions of his time, represents the warriors of Friesland as endowed with the most heroic valor.

These rights, which the Frisons secured, according to their own statements, from Charlemagne, but most undoubtedly from some one or other of the earliest emperors, consisted, first, in the freedom of every order of citizens; secondly, in the right of property—a right which admitted no authority of the sovereign to violate by confiscation, except in cases of downright treason; thirdly, in the privilege of trial by none but native judges, and according to their national usages; fourthly, in a very narrow limitation of the military services which they owed to the king; fifthly, in the hereditary title to feudal property, in direct line, on payment of certain dues or rents. These five principal articles sufficed to render Friesland, in its political aspect, totally different from the other portions of the monarchy. Their privileges secured, their property inviolable, their duties limited, the Frisons were altogether free from the servitude which weighed down France. It will soon be seen that these special advantages produced a government nearly analogous to that which Magna Charta was the means of founding at a later period in England.

The successors of Charlemagne chiefly signalized their authority by lavishing donations of all kinds on the church. By such means the ecclesiastical power became greater and greater, and, in those countries under the sway of France, was quite as arbitrary and enormous as that of the nobility. The bishops of Utrecht, Liege, and Tournay, became, in the course of time, the chief personages on that line of the frontier. They had the great advantage over the counts, of not being subjected to capricious or tyrannical removals. They therefore, even in civil affairs, played a more considerable part than the latter; and began to render themselves more and more independent in their episcopal cities, which were soon to become so many principalities. The counts, on their parts, used their best exertions to wear out, if they had not the strength to break, the chains which bound them to the footstool of the monarch. They were not all now dependent on the same sovereign; for the empire of Charlemagne was divided among his successors: France, properly so called, was bounded by the Scheldt; the country to the eastward of that river, **that is to say, nearly** the whole of the Netherlands, **belonged** to Lorraine and Germany.

In the state of things, it happened that in **the year 864,** Judith, daughter of Charles the Bald, king of France, having survived her husband Ethelwolf, **king** of England, became attached to a powerful Flemish **chieftain** called Baldwin. It is not quite certain **whether he was count, forester,** marquis, **or** protector of the **frontiers;** but **he certainly** enjoyed, no matter under what title, considerable authority in **the country;** since the pope on **one** occasion **wrote** to Charles **the** Bald to beware of **offending him, lest** he should join **the** Normans, and open to them **an** entrance into France. **He** carried off Judith to his possessions **in** Flanders. The king, her father, after many ineffectual **threats, was forced to consent** to their union; and confirmed to Baldwin, with the title of count, the hereditary government **of all** the country between the Scheldt and the Somme, a river of Picardy. This was the commencement of **the** celebrated **county** of Flanders; and this Baldwin **is designated** in history by **the** surname of Bras-de-fer (iron-handed), **to** which his courage had justly entitled him.

The Belgian historians are also desirous of placing about this epoch the first counts of Hainault, and even of Holland. But though it may be true that the chief families of each canton sought then, as at all times, to shake off the yoke, **the** epoch of their independence can only be fixed at the later period at which they obtained or enforced the privilege of not being deprived of their titles and their feudal estates. The counts of the high grounds, and those of Friesland, enjoyed at the utmost but a fortuitous privilege of continuance in their rank. Several foreigners had gained a footing and an authority in the country; among others Wickmand, from whom descended the chatelains of Ghent; and the counts of Holland, and Heriold, a Norman prince who had been banished from his own country. This name of Normans, hardly known before the time of Charlemagne, soon became too celebrated. It designated the pagan inhabitants of Denmark, Norway, and Sweden, who, driven by rapacity and want, infested the neighboring seas. The asylum allowed in the dominions of the emperors to some of those exiled outlaws, and the imprudent provocations given by these latter to their adventurous countrymen, attracted various bands of Norman pirates to the shores of Guelders; and from desultory descents upon the coast, they soon came to inundate the interior of the country. Flanders alone successfully resisted them during the life of Baldwin Bras-defer; but after the death of this brave chieftain there was not a province of the whole country that was not ravaged by these invaders. Their multiplied expeditions threw back the Netherlands at least two centuries, if, indeed, any calculation of the kind may be fairly formed respecting the relative state of population and improvement on the imperfect data that are left us. Several cantons became deserted. The chief cities were reduced to heaps of ruins. The German emperors vainly interposed for the relief of their unfortunate vassals. Finally, an agreement was entered into, in the year 882, with Godfrey the king or leader of the Normans, by which a peace was purchased on condition of paying him a large subsidy, and ceding to him the government of Friesland. But, in about two years from this period, the fierce barbarian began to complain that the country he had thus gained did not produce grapes, and the present inspiration of his rapacity seemed to be the blooming vineyards of France. The emperor Charles the Fat, anticipating the consequence of a rupture with Godfrey, enticed him to an interview, in which he caused him to be assassinated. His followers, attacked on all points by the people of

Friesland, perished almost to a man; and their destruction was completed, in 891, by Arnoul the Germanic. From that period, the scourge of Norman depredation became gradually less felt. They now made but short and desultory attempts on the coast; and their last expedition appears to have taken place about the year 1000, when they threatened, but did not succeed in seizing on, the city of Utrecht.

It is remarkable that, although for the space of one hundred and fifty years the Netherlands were continually the scene of invasion and devastation by these northern barbarians, the political state of the country underwent no important changes. The emperors of Germany were sovereigns of the whole country, with the exception of Flanders. These portions of the empire were still called Lorraine, as well as all which they possessed of what is now called France, and which was that part forming the appanage of Lothaire and of the Lotheringian kings. The great difficulty of maintaining subordination among the numerous chieftains of this country caused it, in 958, to be divided into two governments, which were called Higher and Lower Lorraine. The latter portion comprised nearly the whole of the Netherlands, which thus became governed by a lieutenant of the emperors. Godfrey count of Ardenne was the first who filled this place; and he soon felt all the perils of the situation. The other counts saw, with a jealous eye, their equal now promoted into a superior. Two of the most powerful, Lambert and Reginald, were brothers. They made common cause against the new duke; and after a desperate struggle, which did not cease till the year 985, they gained a species of imperfect independence—Lambert becoming the root from which sprang the counts of Louvain, and Reginald that of the counts of Hainault.

The emperor Othon II., who upheld the authority of his lieutenant, Godfrey, became convinced that the imperial power was too weak to resist singly the opposition of the nobles of the country. He had therefore transferred, about the year 980, the title of duke to a young prince of the royal house of France; and we thus see the duchy of Lower Lorraine governed, in the name of the emperor, by the last two shoots of the branch of Charlemagne, the dukes Charles and Othon of France, son and grandson of Louis d'Outremer. The first was a gallant prince: he may be looked on as the founder of the greatness of Brussels, where he fixed his residence. After several years of tranquil government, the death of his brother called him to the throne of France; and from that time he bravely contended for the crown of his ancestors, against the usurpation of Hugues Capet, whom he frequently defeated in battle; but he was at length treacherously surprised and put to death in 990. Othon, his son, did not signalize his name nor justify his descent by any memorable action; and in him ingloriously perished the name of the Carlovingians.

The death of Othon set the emperor and the great vassals once more in opposition. The German monarch insisted on naming some creature of his own to the dignity of duke; but Lambert II., count of Louvain, and Robert, count of Namur, having married the sisters of Othon, respectively claimed the right of inheritance to his title. Baldwin of the comely beard, count of Flanders, joined himself to their league, hoping to extend his power to the eastward of the Scheldt. And, in fact, the emperor, as the only means of disuniting his two powerful vassals, felt himself obliged to cede Valenciennes and the islands of Zealand to Baldwin. The imperial power thus lost ground at every struggle.

Amid the confusion of these events, a power well calculated to rival or even supplant that of the fierce counts was growing up. Many circumstances were combined to extend and consolidate the episcopal sway. It is true that the bishops of Tournay had no temporal authority since the period of their city being ruined by the Normans. But those of Liege and Utrecht, and more particularly the latter, had accumulated immense possessions; and their power being inalienable, they had nothing to fear from the caprices of sovereign favor, which so often ruined the families of the aristocracy. Those bishops, who were warriors and huntsmen rather than ecclesiastics, possessed, however, in addition to the lance and the sword, the terrible artillery of excommunication and anathema, which they thundered forth without mercy against every laic opponent; and when they had, by conquest or treachery, acquired new dominions and additional store of wealth, they could not portion it among their children, like the nobles, but it devolved to their successors, who thus became more and more powerful, and gained by degrees an authority almost royal, like that of the ecclesiastical elector of Germany.

Whenever the emperor warred against his lay vassals, he was sure of assistance from the bishops, because they were at all times jealous of the power of the counts, and had much less to gain from an alliance with them than with the imperial despots on whose donations they throve, and who repaid their efforts by new privileges and extended possessions. So that when the monarch, at length, lost the superiority in his contests with the counts, little was wanting to make his authority be merged altogether in the overgrown power of these churchmen. Nevertheless, a first effort of the bishop of Liege to seize on the rights of the count of Louvain in 1013 met with a signal defeat, in a battle which took place at the little village of Stongarde. And five years later, the count of the Friesland marshes (*comes Frisonum Morsatenorum*) gave a still more severe lesson to the bishop of Utrecht. This last merits a more particular mention, from the nature of the quarrel and the importance of its results.

CHAPTER IV

FROM THE FORMATION OF HOLLAND TO THE DEATH OF LOUIS DE MALE

A.D. 1018—1384

THE district in which Dordrecht is situated, and the grounds in its environs which are at present submerged, formed in those times an island just raised above the waters, and which was called Holland or Holtland (which means *wooded* land, or, according to some, *hollow* land). The formation of this island, or rather its recovery from the waters, being only of recent date, the right to its possession was more disputable than that of long-established countries. All the bishops and abbots whose states bordered the Rhine and the Meuse had, being equally covetous and grasping, and mutually resolved to pounce on the prey, made it their common property. A certain Count Thierry, descended from the counts of Ghent, governed about this period the western extremity of Friesland—the country which now forms the province of Holland; and with much difficulty maintained his power against the Frisons, by whom his right was not acknowledged. Beaten out of his own territories by these refractory insurgents, he sought refuge in the ecclesiastical island, where he intrenched himself, and founded a town which is believed to have been the origin of Dordrecht.

This Count Thierry, like all the feudal lords, took advantage of his position to establish and levy certain duties on all the vessels which sailed past his territory, dispossessing in the meantime some vassals of the church, and beating, as we have stated, the bishop of Utrecht himself.

Complaints and appeals without number were laid at the foot of the imperial throne. Godfrey of Eenham, whom the emperor had created duke of Lower Lorraine, was commanded to call the whole country to arms. The bishop of Liege, though actually dying, put himself at the head of the expedition, to revenge his brother prelate, and punish the audacious spoiler of the church property. But Thierry and his fierce Frisons took Godfrey prisoner, and cut his army in pieces. The victor had the good sense and moderation to spare his prisoners, and set them free without ransom. He received in return an imperial amnesty; and from that period the count of Holland and his posterity formed a barrier against which the ecclesiastical power and the remains of the imperial supremacy continually struggled, to be only shattered in each new assault. John Egmont, an old chronicler, says that the counts of Holland were "a sword in the flanks of the bishops of Utrecht."

As the partial independence of the great vassals became consolidated, the monarchs were proportionally anxious to prevent its perpetuation in the same families. In pursuance of this system, Godfrey of Eenham obtained the preference over the Counts Lambert and Robert; and Frederick of Luxemburg was named duke of Lower Lorraine in 1046, instead of a second Godfrey, who was nephew and expectant heir to the first. But this Godfrey, upheld by Baldwin of Flanders, forced the emperor to concede to him the inheritance of the dukedom. Baldwin secured for his share the country of Alost and Waas, and the citadel of Ghent; and he also succeeded in obtaining in marriage for his son the Countess Richilde, heiress of Hainault and Namur. Thus was Flanders incessantly gaining new aggrandizement, while the duchy of Lorraine was crumbling away on every side.

In the year 1066 this state of Flanders, even then flourishing and powerful, furnished assistance, both in men and ships, to William the Bastard of Normandy, for the conquest of England. William was son-in-law to Count Baldwin, and recompensed the assistance of his wife's father by an annual payment of three hundred silver marks. It was Mathilda, the Flemish princess and wife of the conqueror, who worked with her own hands the celebrated tapestry of Bayeux, on which is embroidered the whole history of the conquest, and which is the most curious monument of the state of the arts in that age.

Flanders acquired a positive and considerable superiority over all the other parts of the Netherlands, from the first establishment of its counts or earls. The descendants of Baldwin Bras-de-fer, after having valiantly repulsed the Normans toward the end of the ninth century, showed themselves worthy of ruling over an industrious and energetic people. They had built towns, cut down and cleared away forests, and reclaimed inundated lands: above all things, they had understood and guarded against the danger of parcelling out their states at every succeeding generation; and the county of Flanders passed entire into the hands of the first-born of the family. The stability produced by this state of things had allowed the people to prosper. The Normans now visited the coasts, not as enemies, but as merchants; and Bruges became the mart of the booty acquired by these bold pirates in England and on the high seas. The fisheries had begun to acquire an importance sufficient to establish the herring as one of the chief aliments of the population. Maritime commerce had made such strides that Spain and Portugal were well known to both sailors and traders, and the voyage from Flanders to Lisbon was estimated at fifteen days' sail. Woollen stuffs formed the principal wealth of the country; but salt, corn, and jewelry were also important branches of traffic; while the youth of Flanders were so famous for their excellence in all martial pursuits that foreign sovereigns were at all times desirous of obtaining bodies of troops from this nation.

The greatest part of Flanders was attached, as has been

seen, to the king of France, and not to Lorraine; but the dependence was little more than nominal. In 1071 the king of France attempted to exercise his authority over the country, by naming to the government the same Countess Richilde who had received Hainault and Namur for her dower, and who was **left** a widow, with sons still in their minority. The people **assembled** in the principal towns, and protested **against** this intervention of the French monarch. But **we must remark that it was** only the population of the low lands **(whose sturdy** ancestors had ever resisted foreign domination) **that now took** part in this opposition. **The vassals which the counts** of Flanders possessed in the Gallic provinces **(the high grounds),** and **in general all** the nobility, **pronounced strongly for submission** to France; **for the principles of political freedom had not** yet been fixed **in the minds of the inhabitants of** those parts of **the** country. But the lowlanders joined together under Robert, surnamed **the Frison, brother of the deceased count; and they** so completely defeated **the French,** the nobles and their **unworthy associates of the** high **ground,** that they despoiled the **usurping** Countess Richilde **of even** her hereditary possessions. In this **war** perished the celebrated Norman, William **Fitz-Osborn, who had flown to** the succor of the defeated **countess, of whom he was** enamored.

Robert **the Frison, not satisfied with** having beaten **the** king of France **and the bishop of** Liege, **reinstated in** 1076 the grandson of Thierry of Holland in the possessions which had been **forced from him** by the duke of Lower Lorraine, in the name **of the** emperor **and** the bishop of Utrecht; **so** that it was this valiant chieftain, who, above all others, is entitled to the praise of having successfully opposed the system of foreign domination on all the principal points of the country. Four years later, Othon of Nassau was the first to unite in one county the various cantons of Guelders. Finally, in 1086, Henry of Louvain, the direct descendant of Lambert, joined to his title that of count of Brabant;

and from this period the country was partitioned pretty nearly as it was destined to remain for several centuries.

In the midst of this gradual organization of the various counties, history for some time loses sight of those Frisons, the maritime people of the north, who took little part in the civil wars of two centuries. But still there was no portion of Europe which at that time offered a finer picture of social improvement than these damp and unhealthy coasts. The name of Frisons extended from the Weser to the westward of the Zuyder Zee, but not quite to the Rhine; and it became usual to consider no longer as Frisons the subjects of the counts of Holland, whom we may now begin to distinguish as Hollanders or Dutch. The Frison race alone refused to recognize the sovereign counts. They boasted of being self-governed; owning no allegiance but to the emperor, and regarding the counts of his nomination as so many officers charged to require obedience to the laws of the country, but themselves obliged in all things to respect them. But the counts of Holland, the bishops of Utrecht, and several German lords, dignified from time to time with the title of counts of Friesland, insisted that it carried with it a personal authority superior to that of the sovereign they represented. The descendants of the Count Thierry, a race of men remarkably warlike, were the most violent in this assumption of power. Defeat after defeat, however, punished their obstinacy; and numbers of those princes met death on the pikes of their Frison opponents. The latter had no regular leaders; but at the approach of the enemy the inhabitants of each canton flew to arms, like the members of a single family; and all the feudal forces brought against them failed to subdue this popular militia.

The frequent result of these collisions was the refusal of the Frisons to recognize any authority whatever but that of the national judges. Each canton was governed according to its own laws. If a difficulty arose, the deputies of the nation met together on the borders of the Ems, in a place called "the Trees of Upstal" (*Upstall-boomen*), where three old oaks stood in the middle of an immense plain. In this primitive council-place chieftains were chosen, who, on swearing to maintain the laws and oppose the common enemy, were invested with a limited and temporary authority.

It does not appear that Friesland possessed any large towns, with the exception of Staveren. In this respect the Frisons resembled those ancient Germans who had a horror of shutting themselves up within walls. They lived in a way completely patriarchal; dwelling in isolated cabins, and with habits of the utmost frugality. We read in one of their old histories that a whole convent of Benedictines was terrified at the voracity of a German sculptor who was repairing their chapel. They implored him to look elsewhere for his food; for that he and his sons consumed enough to exhaust the whole stock of the monastery.

In no part of Europe was the good sense of the people so effectively opposed to the unreasonable practices of Catholicism in those days. The Frisons successfully resisted the payment of tithes; and as a punishment (if the monks are to be believed) the sea inflicted upon them repeated inundations. They forced their priests to marry, saying that the man who had no wife necessarily sought for the wife of another. They acknowledged no ecclesiastical decree, if secular judges, double the number of the priests, did not bear a part in it. Thus the spirit of liberty burst forth in all their proceedings, and they were justified in calling themselves *Vri-Vriesen*, Free-Frisons.

No nation is more interested than England in the examination of all that concerns this remote corner of Europe, so resolute in its opposition to both civil and religious tyranny; for it was there that those Saxon institutions and principles were first developed without constraint, while the time of their establishment in England was still distant. Restrained by our narrow limits, we can merely indicate this curious state of things; nor may we enter on many mysteries of social government which the most learned find a difficulty in solving. What were the rights of the nobles in their connection with these freemen? What ties of reciprocal interest bound the different cantons to each other? What were the privileges of the towns?—These are the minute but important points of detail which are overshadowed by the grand and imposing figure of the national independence. But in fact the emperors themselves, in these distant times, had little knowledge of this province, and spoke of it vaguely, and as it were at random, in their diplomas, the chief monuments of the history of the Middle Ages. The counts of Holland and the apostolic nuncios addressed their acts and rescripts indiscriminately to the nobles, clergy, magistrates, judges, consuls, or commons of Friesland. Sometimes appeared in those documents the vague and imposing title of "the great Frison," applied to some popular leader. All this confusion tends to prove, on the authority of the historians of the epoch, and the charters so carefully collected by the learned, that this question, now so impossible to solve, was even then not rightly understood—what were really those fierce and redoubtable Frisons in their popular and political relations? The fact is, that liberty was a matter so difficult to be comprehended by the writers of those times that Froissart gave as his opinion, about the year 1380, that the Frisons were a most unreasonable race, for not recognizing the authority and power of the great lords.

The eleventh century had been for the Netherlands (with the exception of Friesland and Flanders) an epoch of organization; and had nearly fixed the political existence of the provinces, which were so long confounded in the vast possessions of the empire. It is therefore important to ascertain under what influence and on what basis these provinces became consolidated at that period. Holland and Zealand, animated by the spirit which we may fairly distinguish under the mingled title of Saxon and maritime, countries scarcely accessible, and with a vigorous population, possessed, in the descendants of Thierry I., a race of national chieftains who did not attempt despotic rule over so unconquerable a people. In Brabant, the maritime towns of Berg-op-Zoom and Antwerp formed, in the Flemish style, so many republics, small but not insignificant; while the southern parts of the province were under the sway of a nobility who crushed, trampled on, or sold their vassals at their pleasure or caprice. The bishopric of Liege offered also the same contrast; the domains of the nobility being governed with the utmost harshness, while those prince-prelates lavished on their plebeian vassals privileges which might have been supposed the fruits of generosity, were it not clear that the object was to create an opposition in the lower orders against the turbulent aristocracy, whom they found it impossible to manage single-handed. The wars of these bishops against the petty nobles, who made their castles so many receptacles of robbers and plunder, were thus the foundation of public liberty. And it appears tolerably certain that the Paladins of Ariosto were in reality nothing more than those brigand chieftains of the Ardennes, whose ruined residences preserve to this day the names which the poet borrowed from the old romance writers. But in all the rest of the Netherlands, excepting the provinces already mentioned, no form of government existed, but that fierce feudality which reduced the people into serfs, and turned the social state of man into a cheerless waste of bondage.

It was then that the Crusades, with wild and stirring fanaticism, agitated, in the common impulse given to all Europe, even those little states which seemed to slumber in their isolated independence. Nowhere did the voice of Peter the Hermit find a more sympathizing echo than in these lands, still desolated by so many intestine struggles. Godfrey of Bouillon, duke of Lower Lorraine, took the lead in this chivalric and religious frenzy. With him set out the counts of Hainault and Flanders; the latter of whom received from the English crusaders the honorable appellation of Fitz St. George. But although the valor of all these princes was conspicuous, from the foundation of the kingdom of Jerusalem by Godfrey of Bouillon in 1098, until that of the Latin empire of Constantinople by Baldwin of Flanders in 1203, still the simple gentlemen and peasants of Friesland did not less distinguish themselves. They were, on all occasions, the first to mount the breach or lead the charge; and the pope's nuncio found himself forced to prohibit the very women of Friesland from embarking for the Holy Land—so anxious were they to share the perils and glory of their husbands and brothers in combating the Saracens.

The outlet given by the crusaders to the overboiling ardor of these warlike countries was a source of infinite advantage to their internal economy; under the rapid progress of civilization, the population increased and the fields were cultivated. The nobility, reduced to moderation by the enfeebling consequences of extensive foreign wars, became comparatively impotent in their attempted efforts against domestic freedom. Those of Flanders and Brabant, also, were almost decimated in the terrible battle of Bouvines, fought between the Emperor Othon and Philip Augustus, king of France. On no occasion, however, had this reduced but not degenerate nobility shown more heroic valor. The Flemish knights, disdaining to mount their horses or form their ranks for the repulse of the French cavalry, composed of common persons, contemptuously received their shock on foot and in the disorder of individual resistance. The brave Buridan of Ypres led his comrades to the fight, with the chivalric war-cry, "Let each now think of her he loves!" But the issue of this battle was ruinous to the Belgians, in consequence of the bad generalship of the emperor, who had divided his army into small portions, which were defeated in detail.

While the nobility thus declined, the towns began rapidly to develop the elements of popular force. In 1120, a Flemish knight who might descend so far as to marry a woman of the plebeian ranks incurred the penalty of degradation and servitude. In 1220, scarcely a serf was to be found in all Flanders. The Countess Jane had enfranchised all those belonging to her as early as 1222. In 1300, the chiefs of the gilden, or trades, were more powerful than the nobles. These dates and these facts must suffice to mark the epoch at which the great mass of the nation arose from the wretchedness in which it was plunged by the Norman invasion, and acquired sufficient strength and freedom to form a real political force. But it is remarkable that the same results took place in all the counties or dukedoms of the Lowlands precisely at the same period. In fact, if we start from the year 1200 on this interesting inquiry, we shall see the commons attacking, in the first place, the petty feudal lords, and next the counts and the dukes themselves, as often as justice was denied them. In 1257, the peasants of Holland and the burghers of Utrecht proclaimed freedom and equality, drove out the bishop and the nobles, and began a memorable struggle which lasted full two hundred years. In 1260, the townspeople of Flanders appealed to the king of France against the decrees of their count, who ended the quarrel by the loss of his county. In 1303, Mechlin and Louvain, the chief towns of Brabant, expelled the patrician families. A coincidence like this cannot be attributed to trifling or partial causes, such as the misconduct of a single count, or other local evil; but to a great general movement in the popular mind, the progress of agriculture and industry in the whole country, superinducing an increase of wealth and intelligence, which, when unrestrained by the influence of a corrupt government, must naturally lead to the liberty and the happiness of a people.

The weaving of woollen and linen cloths was one of the chief sources of this growing prosperity. A prodigious quantity of cloth and linen was manufactured in all parts of the Netherlands. The maritime prosperity acquired an equal increase by the carrying trade, both in imports and exports. Whole fleets of Dutch and Flemish merchant ships repaired regularly to the coasts of Spain and Languedoc. Flanders was already become the great market for England and all the north of Europe. The great increase of population forced all parts of the country into cultivation; so much so, that lands were in those times sold at a high price, which are to-day left waste from imputed sterility.

Legislation naturally followed the movements of those positive and material interests. The earliest of the towns, after the invasion of the Normans, were in some degree but places of refuge. It was soon, however, established that the regular inhabitants of these bulwarks of the country should not be subjected to any servitude beyond their care and defence; but the citizen who might absent himself for a longer period than forty days was considered a deserter and deprived of his rights. It was about the year 1100 that the commons began to possess the privilege of regulating their internal affairs; they appointed their judges and magistrates, and attached to their authority the old custom of ordering all the citizens to assemble or march when the summons of the feudal lord sounded the signal for their assemblage or service. By this means each municipal magistracy had the disposal of a force far superior to those of the nobles, for the population of the towns exceeded both in number and discipline the vassals of the seigniorial lands. And these trained bands of the towns made war in a way very different from that hitherto practiced; for the chivalry of the country, making the trade of arms a profession for life, the feuds of the chieftains produced hereditary struggles, almost always slow, and mutually disastrous. But the townsmen, forced to tear themselves from every association of home and its manifold endearments, advanced boldly to the object of the contest; never shrinking from the dangers of war, from fear of that still greater to be found in a prolonged struggle. It is thus that it may be remarked, during the memorable conflicts of the thirteenth century, that when even the bravest of the knights advised their counts or dukes to grant or demand a truce, the citizen militia never knew but one cry—"To the charge!"

Evidence was soon given of the importance of this new nation, when it became forced to take up arms against enemies still more redoubtable than the counts. In 1301, the Flemings, who had abandoned their own sovereign to attach themselves to Philip the Fair, king of France, began to repent of their newly-formed allegiance, and to be weary of the master they had chosen. Two citizens of Bruges, Peter de Koning, a draper, and John Breydel, a butcher, put themselves at the head of their fellow-townsmen, and completely dislodged the French troops who garrisoned it. The following year the militia of Bruges and the immediate neighborhood sustained alone, at the battle of Courtrai, the shock of one of the finest armies that France ever sent into the field. Victory soon declared for the gallant men of Bruges; upward of three thousand of the French chivalry, besides common soldiers, were left dead on the field. In 1304, after a long contested battle, the Flemings forced the king of France to release their count, whom he had held prisoner. "I believe it rains Flemings!" said Philip, astonished to see them crowd on him from all sides of the field. But this multitude of warriors, always ready to meet the foe, were provided for the most part by the towns. In the seigniorial system a village hardly furnished more than four or five men, and these only on important occasions; but in that of the towns every citizen was enrolled as a soldier to defend the country at all times.

The same system established in Brabant forced the duke of that province to sanction and guarantee the popular privileges, and the superiority of the people over the nobility. Such was the result of the famous contract concluded in 1312 at Cortenbergh, by which the duke created a legislative and judicial assembly to meet every twenty-one days for the provincial business; and to consist of fourteen deputies, of whom only four were to be nobles, and ten were chosen from the people. The duke was bound by this act to hold himself in obedience to the legislative decisions of the council, and renounced all right of levying arbitrary taxes or duties on the state. Thus were the local privileges of the people by degrees secured and ratified; but the various towns, making common cause for general liberty, became strictly united together, and progressively extended their influence and power. The confederation between Flanders and Brabant was soon consolidated. The burghers of Bruges, who had taken the lead in the grand national union, and had been the foremost to expel the foreign force, took umbrage in 1323 at an arbitrary measure of their count, Louis (called of Cressy by posthumous nomination, from his having been killed at that celebrated fight), by which he ceded to the count of Namur, his great-uncle, the port of Ecluse, and authorized him to levy duties there in the style of the feudal lords of the high country. It was but the affair of a day to the intrepid citizens to attack the fortress of Ecluse, carry it by assault, and take prisoner the old count of Namur. They destroyed in a short time almost all the strong castles of the nobles throughout the province; and having been joined by all the towns of western Flanders, they finally made prisoners of Count Louis himself, with almost the whole of the nobility, who had taken refuge with him in the town of Courtrai. But Ghent, actuated by the jealousy which at all times existed between it and Bruges, stood aloof at this crisis. The latter town was obliged to come to a compromise with the count, who soon afterward, on a new quarrel breaking out, and supported by the king of France, almost annihilated his sturdy opponents at the battle of Cassel, where the Flemish infantry, commanded by Nicholas Zannekin and others, were literally cut to pieces by the French knights and men-at-arms.

This check proved the absolute necessity of union among the rival cities. Ten years after the battle of Cassel, Ghent set the example of general opposition; this example was promptly followed, and the chief towns flew to arms. The celebrated **James** d'Artaveldt, commonly called the brewer of Ghent, put himself at the head of this formidable insurrection. He was a man of a distinguished family, who had himself enrolled among the guild of brewers, to entitle him to occupy a place in the corporation **of Ghent, which** he soon succeeded **in managing** and **leading at** his **pleasure.** The tyranny **of the count, and the French party which** supported **him, became so intolerable to** Artaveldt, **that he** resolved **to assail them at all** hazards, unappalled **by the fate of his** father-in-law, Sohier **de** Courtrai, who **lost his** head for a similar attempt, and notwithstanding **the hitherto** devoted fidelity **of his** native **city to the count. One** only object seemed insurmountable. **The** Flemings **had sworn allegiance** to the crown **of France; and** they **revolted at the idea** of perjury, even **from an extorted oath. But to** overcome their scruples, Artaveldt proposed to acknowledge the claim of Edward III. **of** England **to the French crown.** The Flemings readily **acceded to this arrangement;** quickly overwhelmed Count Louis **of Cressy and his French partisans;** and then joined, **with an army of sixty thousand men, the** English monarch, who had landed **at Antwerp.** These numerous auxiliaries **rendered** Edward's army irresistible; and **soon afterward the** French and English fleets, both **of** formidable **power, but the** latter **of** inferior force, **met near** Sluys, **and engaged in a battle meant to be** decisive **of the war:** victory **remained** doubtful **during an entire day of** fighting, until **a Flemish squadron, hastening to** the **aid** of the English, **fixed the fate of the combat by the utter** defeat of the **enemy.**

A truce **between the two kings did not deprive Artaveldt** of his well-earned authority. **He was invested with the** title **of** ruward, or conservator **of** the peace, **of** Flanders, and governed the whole province **with** almost sovereign sway. It was said that King Edward used familiarly to call him "his dear gossip"; and it is certain **that** there was not **a** feudal lord of the time whose power was not eclipsed by this leader of the people. One of the principal motives which cemented the attachment of the Flemings to Artaveldt was the advantage obtained through his influence with Edward for facilitating the trade with England, whence they procured the chief supply of wool for their manufactories. Edward promised them seventy thousand sacks as the reward of their alliance. But though greatly influenced by the stimulus of general interest, the Flemings loved their domestic liberty better than English wool; and when they found that their ruward degenerated from a firm patriot into the partisan of a foreign prince, they became disgusted with him altogether; and he perished in 1345, in a tumult raised against him by those by whom he had been so lately idolized. The Flemings held firm, nevertheless, in their alliance with England, only regulating the connection by a steady principle of national independence.

Edward knew well how to conciliate and manage these faithful and important auxiliaries during all his continental wars. A Flemish army covered the siege of Calais in 1348; and, under the command of Giles de Rypergherste, a mere weaver of Ghent, they beat the dauphin of France in a pitched battle. But Calais once taken, and a truce concluded, the English king abandoned his allies. These, left wholly to their own resources, forced the French and the heir of their count, young Louis de Male, to recognize their right to self-government according to their ancient privileges, and of not being forced to give aid to France in any war against England. Flanders may therefore be pronounced as forming, at this epoch, both in right and fact, a truly independent principality.

But such struggles as these left a deep and immovable sentiment of hatred in the minds of the vanquished. Louis de Male longed for the re-establishment and extension of his authority; and had the art to gain over to his views not only all the nobles, but many of the most influential guilds or trades. Ghent, which long resisted his attempts, was at length reduced by famine; and the count projected the ruin, or at least the total subjection, of this turbulent town.

A son of Artaveldt started forth at this juncture, when the popular cause seemed lost, and joining with his fellow-citizens, John Lyons and Peter du Bois, he led seven thousand resolute burghers against forty thousand feudal vassals. He completely defeated the count, and took the town of Bruges, where Louis de Male only obtained safety by hiding himself under the bed of an old woman who gave him shelter. Thus once more feudality was defeated in a fresh struggle with civic freedom.

The consequences of this event were immense. They reached to the very heart of France, where the people bore in great discontent the feudal yoke; and Froissart declares that the success of the people of Ghent had nearly overthrown the superiority of the nobility over the people in France. But the king, Charles VI., excited by his uncle, Philip the Bold, duke of Burgundy, took arms in support of the defeated count, and marched with a powerful army against the rebellious burghers. Though defeated in four successive combats, in the latter of which, that of Roosbeke, Artaveldt was killed, the Flemings would not submit to their imperious count, who used every persuasion with Charles to continue his assistance for the punishment of these refractory subjects. But the duke of Burgundy was aware that a too great perseverance would end, either in driving the people to despair and the possible defeat of the French, or the entire conquest of the country and its junction to the crown of France. He, being son-in-law to Louis de Male, and consequently aspiring to the inheritance of Flanders, saw with a keen glance the advantage of a present compromise. On the death of Louis, who is stated to have been murdered by Philip's brother, the duke of Berri, he concluded a peace with the rebel burghers, and entered at once upon the sovereignty of the country.

CHAPTER V

FROM THE SUCCESSION OF PHILIP THE BOLD TO THE COUNTY OF FLANDERS, TO THE DEATH OF PHILIP THE FAIR

A.D. 1384—1506

THUS the house of Burgundy, which soon after became so formidable and celebrated, obtained this vast accession to its power. The various changes which had taken place in the neighboring provinces during the continuance of these civil wars had altered the state of Flanders altogether. John d'Avesnes, count of Hainault, having also succeeded in 1299 to the county of Holland, the two provinces, though separated by Flanders and Brabant, remained from that time under the government of the same chief, who soon became more powerful than the bishops of Utrecht, or even than their formidable rivals the Frisons.

During the wars which desolated these opposing territories, in consequence of the perpetual conflicts for superiority, the power of the various towns insensibly became at least as great as that of the nobles to whom they were constantly opposed. The commercial interests of Holland, also, were considerably advanced by the influx of Flemish merchants forced to seek refuge there from the convulsions which agitated their province. Every day confirmed and increased the privileges of the people of Brabant; while at Liege the inhabitants gradually began to gain the upper hand, and to shake off the former subjection to their sovereign bishops.

Although Philip of Burgundy became count of Flanders, by the death of his father-in-law, in the year 1384, it was not till the following year that he concluded a peace with the people of Ghent, and entered into quiet possession of the province. In the same year the duchess of Brabant, the last descendant of the duke of that province, died, leaving no nearer relative than the duchess of Burgundy; so that Philip obtained in right of his wife this new and important accession to his dominions. But the consequent increase of the sovereign's power was not, as is often the case, injurious to the liberties or happiness of the people. Philip continued to govern in the interest of the country, which he had the good sense to consider as identified with his own. He augmented the privileges of the towns, and negotiated for the return into Flanders of those merchants who had emigrated to Germany and Holland during the continuance of the civil wars. He thus by degrees accustomed his new subjects, so proud of their rights, to submit to his authority; and his peaceable reign was only disturbed by the fatal issue of the expedition of his son, John the Fearless, count of Nevers, against the Turks. This young prince, filled with ambition and temerity, was offered the command of the force sent by Charles III. of France to the assistance of Sigismund of Hungary in his war against Bajazet. Followed by a numerous body of nobles, he entered on the contest, and was defeated and taken prisoner by the Turks at the battle of Nicopolis. His army was totally destroyed, and himself only restored to liberty on the payment of an immense ransom.

John the Fearless succeeded in 1404 to the inheritance of all his father's dominions, with the exception of Brabant, of which his younger brother, Anthony of Burgundy, became duke. John, whose ambitious and ferocious character became every day more strongly developed, now aspired to the government of France during the insanity of his cousin Charles VI. He occupied himself little with the affairs of the Netherlands, from which he only desired to draw supplies of men. But the Flemings, taking no interest in his personal views or private projects, and equally indifferent to the rivalry of England and France, which now began so fearfully to afflict the latter kingdom, forced their ambitious count to declare their province a neutral country; so that the English merchants were admitted as usual to trade in all the ports of Flanders, and the Flemings equally well received in England, while the duke made open war against Great Britain in his quality of a prince of France and sovereign of Burgundy. This is probably the earliest well-established instance of such a distinction between the prince and the people.

Anthony, duke of Brabant, the brother of Philip, was not so closely restricted in his authority and wishes. He led all the nobles of the province to take part in the quarrels of France; and he suffered the penalty of his rashness in meeting his death in the battle of Agincourt. But the duchy suffered nothing by this event, for the militia of the country had not followed their duke and his nobles to the war; and a national council was now established, consisting of eleven persons, two of whom were ecclesiastics, three barons, two knights, and four commoners. This council, formed on principles so fairly popular, conducted the public affairs with great wisdom during the minority of the young duke. Each province seems thus to have governed itself upon principles of republican independence. The sovereigns could not at discretion, or by the want of it, play the bloody game of war for their mere amusement; and the emperor putting in his claim at this epoch to his ancient rights of sovereignty over Brabant, as an imperial fief, the council and the people treated the demand with derision.

The spirit of constitutional liberty and legal equality which now animated the various provinces is strongly marked in the history of the time by two striking and characteristic incidents. At the death of Philip the Bold, his widow deposited on his tomb her purse, and the keys which she carried at her girdle in token of marriage; and by this humiliating ceremony she renounced her rights to a succession overloaded with her husband's debts. In the same year (1404) the widow of Albert, count of Holland and Hainault, finding herself in similar circumstances, required of the bailiff of Holland and the judges of his court permission to make a like renunciation. The claim was granted; and, to fulfil the requisite ceremony, she walked at the head of the funeral procession, carrying in her hand a blade of straw, which she placed on the coffin. We thus find that in such cases the reigning families were held liable to follow the common usages of the country. From such instances there required but little progress in the principle of equality to reach the republican contempt for rank which made the citizens of Bruges in the following century arrest their count for his private debts.

The spirit of independence had reached the same point at Liege. The families of the counts of Holland and Hainault, which were at this time distinguished by the name of Bavaria, because they were only descended from the ancient counts of Netherland extraction in the female line, had sufficient influence to obtain the nomination to the bishopric for a prince who was at the period in his infancy. John of Bavaria—for so he was called, and to his name was afterward added the epithet of "the Pitiless" —on reaching his majority, did not think it necessary to cause himself to be consecrated a priest, but governed as a lay sovereign. The indignant citizens of Liege expelled him, and chose another bishop. But the Houses of Burgundy and Bavaria, closely allied by intermarriages, made common cause in his quarrel; and John, duke of Burgundy, and William IV., count of Holland and Hainault, brother of the bishop, replaced by force this cruel and unworthy prelate.

This union of the government over all the provinces in two families so closely connected rendered the preponderance of the rulers too strong for that balance hitherto kept steady by the popular force. The former could on each new quarrel join together, and employ against any particular town their whole united resources; whereas the latter could only act by isolated efforts for the maintenance of their separate rights. Such was the cause of a considerable decline in public liberty during the fifteenth century. It is true that John the Fearless gave almost his whole attention to his French political intrigues, and to the fierce quarrels which he maintained with the House of Orleans. But his nephew, John, duke of Brabant, having married, in 1416, his cousin Jacqueline, daughter and heiress of William IV., count of Holland and Hainault, this branch of the House of Burgundy seemed to get the start of the elder in its progressive influence over the provinces of the Netherlands. The dukes of Guelders, who had changed their title of counts for one of superior rank, acquired no accession of power proportioned to their new dignity. The bishops of Utrecht became by degrees weaker; private dissensions enfeebled Friesland; Luxemburg was a poor, unimportant dukedom; but Holland, Hainault, and Brabant formed the very heart of the Netherlands; while the elder branch of the same family, under whom they were united, possessed Flanders, Artois, and the two Burgundies. To complete the prosperity and power of this latter branch, it was soon destined to inherit the entire dominions of the other.

A fact the consequences of which were so important for the entire of Europe merits considerable attention; but it is most difficult to explain at once concisely and clearly the series of accidents, manœuvres, tricks, and crimes by which it was accomplished. It must first be remarked that this John of Brabant, become the husband of his cousin Jacqueline, countess of Holland and Hainault, possessed neither the moral nor physical qualities suited to mate with the most lovely, intrepid, and talented woman of her times; nor the vigor and firmness required for the maintenance of an increased, and for those days a considerable, dominion. Jacqueline thoroughly despised her insignificant husband; first in secret, and subsequently by those open avowals forced from her by his revolting combination of weakness, cowardice, and tyranny. He tamely allowed the province of Holland to be invaded by the same ungrateful bishop of Liege, John the Pitiless, whom his wife's father and his own uncle had re-established in his justly forfeited authority. But John of Brabant revenged himself for his wife's contempt by a series of domestic persecutions so odious that the states of Brabant interfered for her protection. Finding it, however, impossible to remain in a perpetual contest with a husband whom she hated and despised, she fled from Brussels, where he held his ducal court, and took refuge in England, under the protection of Henry V., at that time in the plenitude of his fame and power.

England at this epoch enjoyed the proudest station in European affairs. John the Fearless, after having caused the murder of his rival, the duke of Orleans, was himself assassinated on the bridge of Montereau by the followers of the dauphin of France, and in his presence. Philip, duke of Burgundy, the son and successor of John, had formed a close alliance with Henry V., to revenge his father's murder; and soon after the death of the king he married his sister, and thus united himself still more nearly to the celebrated John, duke of Bedford, brother of Henry, and regent of France, in the name of his infant nephew, Henry VI. But besides the share on which he reckoned in the spoils of France, Philip also looked with a covetous eye on the inheritance of Jacqueline, his cousin. As soon as he had learned that this princess, so well received in England, was taking measures for having her marriage annulled, to enable her to espouse the duke of Gloucester, also the brother of Henry V., and subsequently known by the appellation of "the good duke Humphrey," he was tormented by a double anxiety. He, in the first place, dreaded that Jacqueline might have children by her projected marriage with Gloucester (a circumstance neither likely nor even possible, in the opinion of some historians, to result from her union with John of Brabant: Hume, vol. iii., p. 133), and thus deprive him of his right of succession to her states; and in the next, he was jealous of the possible domination of England in the Netherlands as well as in France. He therefore soon became self-absolved from all his vows of revenge in the cause of his murdered father, and labored solely for the object of his personal aggrandizement. To break his connection with Bedford; to treat secretly with the dauphin, his father's assassin, or at least the witness and warrant for his assassination; and to shuffle from party to party as occasion required, were movements of no difficulty to Philip, surnamed "the Good." He openly espoused the cause of his infamous relative, John of Brabant; sent a powerful army into Hainault, which Gloucester vainly strove to defend in right of his affianced wife; and next seized on Holland and Zealand, where he met with a long but ineffectual resistance on the part of the courageous woman he so mercilessly oppressed. Jacqueline, deprived of the assistance of her stanch but ruined friends,¹ and abandoned by Gloucester (who, on the refusal of Pope Martin V. to sanction her divorce, had married another woman, and but feebly aided the efforts of the former to maintain her rights), was now left a widow by the death of John of Brabant. But Philip, without a shadow of justice, pursued his designs against her dominions, and finally despoiled her of her last possessions, and even of the title of countess, which she forfeited by her marriage with Vrank Van Borselen, a gentleman of Zealand, contrary to a compact to which Philip's tyranny had forced her to consent. After a career the most checkered

---

[1] We must not omit to notice the existence of two factions, which, for near two centuries, divided and agitated the whole population of Holland and Zealand. One bore the title of *Hoeks* (fishing-hooks); the other was called *Kaabeljauws* (cod-fish). The origin of these burlesque denominations was a dispute between two parties at a feast, as to whether the cod-fish took the hook or the hook the cod-fish? This apparently frivolous dispute was made the pretext for a serious quarrel; and the partisans of the nobles and those of the towns ranged themselves at either side, and assumed different badges of distinction. The *Hoeks*, partisans of the towns, wore red caps; the *Kaabeljauws* wore gray ones. In Jacqueline's quarrel with Philip of Burgundy, she was supported by the former; and it was not till the year 1492 that the extinction of that popular and turbulent faction struck a final blow to the dissensions of both.

and romantic which is recorded in history, the beautiful and hitherto unfortunate Jacqueline found repose and happiness in the tranquillity of private life, and her **death** in 1436, **at the age of thirty-six, removed all restraint from** Philip's thirst for aggrandizement, in the **indulgence of** which he drowned his remorse. **As if fortune had conspired** for the rapid consolidation **of his greatness, the death of** Philip, count of **St. Pol, who had succeeded his** brother John in the dukedom **of Brabant, gave him the sovereignty of that** extensive province; and his dominions **soon extended to the very limits of** Picardy, by the Peace **of Arras,** concluded with the dauphin, **now** become Charles **VII., and by** his finally contracting a **strict alliance with France.**

Philip of Burgundy, thus become sovereign of **dominions at once so extensive and compact, had the precaution and address to** obtain from the emperor **a formal** renunciation **of his existing, though almost** nominal, **rights as** lord **paramount.** He next purchased the title of **the duchess of Luxemburg to that duchy; and thus the states of the House of Burgundy gained an extent about equal** to that of **the existing kingdom of the Netherlands.** For although on the north and east they did not include Friesland, the bishopric of Utrecht, Guelders, or the **province of** Liege, still on the south and west **they comprised French** Flanders, the Boulonnais, Artois, **and a part of** Picardy, **besides** Burgundy. But it has been **already seen** how limited **an** authority was possessed by the rulers of the maritime **provinces.** Flanders in particular, **the most populous and** wealthy, strictly preserved its republican institutions. Ghent and Bruges were the two great towns of the province, and each maintained its individual authority **over** its **respective** territory, with great indifference to the will or the wishes **of** the sovereign duke. Philip, however, had the policy to divide most effectually these rival towns. After having fallen into the hands of the people of Bruges, whom he made a vain attempt to surprise, and who massacred numbers of his followers before **his** eyes, he forced them to submission by the assistance of the citizens of Ghent, who sanctioned the banishment of the chief men of the vanquished town. But some years later Ghent was in its turn oppressed and punished for having resisted the payment of some new tax. It found no support from the rest of Flanders. Nevertheless this powerful city singly maintained the war for the space of two years; but the intrepid burghers finally yielded to the veterans of the duke, formed to victory in the French wars. The principal privileges of Ghent were on this occasion revoked and annulled.

During these transactions the province of Holland, which enjoyed a degree of liberty almost equal to Flanders, had declared war against the Hanseatic towns on its own proper authority. Supported by Zealand, which formed a distinct country, but was strictly united to it by a common interest, Holland equipped a fleet against the pirates which infested their coasts and assailed their commerce, and soon forced them to submission. Philip in the meantime contrived to manage the conflicting elements of his power with great subtlety. Notwithstanding his ambitious and despotic character, he conducted himself so cautiously that his people by common consent confirmed his title of "the Good," which was somewhat inappropriately given to him at the very epoch when he appeared to deserve it least. Age and exhaustion may be adduced among the causes of the toleration which signalized his latter years; and if he was the usurper of some parts of his dominions, he cannot be pronounced a tyrant over any.

Philip had an only son, born and reared in the midst of that ostentatious greatness which he looked on as his own by divine right; whereas his father remembered that it had chiefly become his by fortuitous acquirement, and much of it by means not likely to look well in the sight of Heaven. This son was Charles, count of Charolois, afterward celebrated under the name of Charles the Rash. He gave, even in the lifetime of his father, a striking specimen of despotism to the people of Holland. Appointed stadtholder of that province in 1457, he appropriated to himself several important successions; forced the inhabitants to labor in the formation of dikes for the security of the property thus acquired; and, in a word, conducted himself as an absolute master. Soon afterward he broke out into open opposition to his father, who had complained of this undutiful and impetuous son to the states of the provinces, venting his grief in lamentations instead of punishing his people's wrongs. But his private rage burst forth one day in a manner as furious as his public expressions were tame. He went so far as to draw his sword on Charles and pursue him through his palace; and a disgusting yet instructive spectacle it was, to see this father and son in mutual and disgraceful discord, like two birds of prey quarrelling in the same eyry; the old count outrageous to find he was no longer undisputed sovereign, and the young one in feeling that he had not yet become so. But Philip was declining daily. Yet even when dying he preserved his natural haughtiness and energy; and being provoked by the insubordination of the people of Liege, he had himself carried to the scene of their punishment. The refractory town of Dinant, on the Meuse, was utterly destroyed by the two counts, and six hundred of the citizens drowned in the river, and in cold blood. The following year Philip expired, leaving to Charles his long-wished-for inheritance.

The reign of Philip had produced a revolution in Belgian manners; for his example and the great increase of wealth had introduced habits of luxury hitherto quite unknown. He had also brought into fashion romantic notions of military honor, love, and chivalry; which, while they certainly softened the character of the nobility, contained nevertheless a certain mixture of frivolity and extravagance. The celebrated order of the Golden Fleece, which was introduced by Philip, was less an institution based on grounds of rational magnificence than a puerile emblem of his passion for Isabella of Portugal, his third wife. The verses of a contemporary poet induced him to make a vow for the conquest of Constantinople from the Turks. He certainly never attempted to execute this senseless crusade; but he did not omit so fair an opportunity for levying new taxes on his people. And it is undoubted that the splendor of his court and the immorality of his example were no slight sources of corruption to the countries which he governed.

In this respect, at least, a totally different kind of government was looked for on the part of his son and successor, who was by nature and habit a mere soldier. Charles began his career by seizing on all the money and jewels left by his father; he next dismissed the crowd of useless functionaries who had fed upon, under the pretence of managing, the treasures of the state. But this salutary and sweeping reform was only effected to enable the sovereign to pursue uncontrolled the most fatal of all passions, that of war. Nothing can better paint the true character of this haughty and impetuous prince than his crest (a branch of holly), and his motto, "Who touches it, pricks himself." Charles had conceived a furious and not ill-founded hatred for his base yet formidable neighbor and rival, Louis XI. of France. The latter had succeeded in obtaining from Philip the restitution of some towns in Picardy; cause sufficient to excite the resentment of his inflammable successor, who, during his father's lifetime, took open part with some of the vassals of France in a temporary struggle against the throne. Louis, who had been worsted in a combat where both he and Charles bore a part, was not behindhand in his hatred. But inasmuch as one was haughty, audacious, and intemperate, the other was cunning, cool, and treacherous. Charles was the proudest, most daring, and most unmanageable prince that ever made the sword the type and the guarantee of greatness; Louis the most subtle, dissimulating, and treacherous king that ever wove in his closet a tissue of hollow diplomacy and bad faith in government. The struggle between these sovereigns was unequal only in respect to this difference of character; for France, subdivided as it still was, and exhausted by the wars with England, was not comparable, either as regarded men, money, or the other resources of the **state, to** the compact and prosperous dominions of Burgundy.

Charles showed some symptoms of good sense and greatness of mind, soon after his accession **to** power, that gave a false coloring **to** his disposition, and encouraged illusory hopes as **to his** future career. Scarcely was he proclaimed **count of** Flanders at Ghent, **when** the populace, surrounding his hotel, absolutely insisted **on** and extorted his consent to the restitution of their ancient privileges. Furious **as** Charles **was at this bold proof** of insubordination, he did not revenge **it; and** he **treated** with **equal** indulgence the city of Mechlin, which **had expelled its governor** and razed the citadel. The people **of Liege, having** revolted **against** their bishop, Louis **of Bourbon, who was closely** connected with the House of **Burgundy, were defeated by the duke in** 1467, but he **treated them with clemency; and** immediately after this event, **in February,** 1468, **he concluded** with Edward IV. of England **an alliance,** offensive **and** defensive, against France.

The real motive **of this** alliance was rivalry and hatred against Louis. The ostensible pretext **was** this monarch's having made war against the duke **of** Brittany, Charles's old ally in the short **contest in** which he, while yet but count, had measured **his** strength with his **rival** after he became king. The **present union** between England and Burgundy was too powerful not **to alarm** Louis; he demanded an explanatory conference with Charles, and the town of Peronne in Picardy was fixed on for their meeting. Louis, willing to imitate the boldness of his rival, who had formerly come to meet him in the very midst of his army, now came to the rendezvous almost alone. But he was severely mortified and near paying a greater penalty than fright for this hazardous conduct. The duke, having received intelligence of a new revolt at Liege excited by some of the agents of France, instantly made Louis prisoner, in defiance of every law of honor or fair dealing. The excess of his rage and hatred might have carried him to a more disgraceful extremity, had not Louis, by force of bribery, gained over some of his most influential counsellors, who succeeded in appeasing his rage. He contented himself with humiliating, when he was disposed to punish. He forced his captive to accompany him to Liege, and witness the ruin of this unfortunate town, which he delivered over to plunder; and having given this lesson to Louis, he set him at liberty.

From this period there was a marked and material change in the conduct of Charles. He had been previously moved by sentiments of chivalry and notions of greatness. But sullied by his act of public treachery and violence toward the monarch who had, at least in seeming, manifested unlimited confidence in his honor, a secret sense of shame embittered his feelings and soured his temper. He became so insupportable to those around him that he was abandoned by several of his best officers, and even by his natural brother, Baldwin of Burgundy, who passed over to the side of Louis. Charles was at this time embarrassed by the expense of entertaining and maintaining Edward IV. and numerous English exiles, who were forced to take refuge in the Netherlands by the successes of the earl of Warwick, who had replaced Henry VI. on the throne. Charles at the same time held out to several princes in Europe hopes of bestowing on them in marriage his only daughter and heiress Mary, while he privately assured his friends, if his courtiers and ministers may be so called, "that he never meant to have a son-in-law until he was disposed to make himself a monk." In a word, he was no longer guided by any principle but that of fierce and brutal selfishness.

In this mood he soon became tired of the service of his nobles and of the national militia, who only maintained toward him a forced and modified obedience founded on the usages and rights of their several provinces; and he took into his pay all sorts of adventurers and vagabonds who were willing to submit to him as their absolute master.

When the taxes necessary for the support and pay of these bands of mercenaries caused the people to murmur, Charles laughed at their complaints, and severely punished some of the most refractory. He then entered France at the head of his army, to assist the duke of Brittany; but at the moment when nothing seemed to oppose the most extensive views of his ambition he lost by his hot-brained caprice every advantage within his easy reach: he chose to sit down before Beauvais; and thus made of this town, which lay in his road, a complete stumbling-block on his path of conquest.

The time he lost before its walls caused the defeat and ruin of his unsupported, or as might be said his abandoned, ally, who made the best terms he could with Louis; and thus Charles's presumption and obstinacy paralyzed all the efforts of his courage and power. But he soon afterward acquired the duchy of Guelders from the old Duke Arnoul, who had been temporarily despoiled of it by his son Adolphus. It was almost a hereditary consequence in this family that the children should revolt and rebel against their parents. Adolphus had the effrontery to found his justification on the argument that his father having reigned forty-four years, he was fully entitled to his share—a fine practical authority for greedy and expectant heirs. The old father replied to this reasoning by offering to meet his son in single combat. Charles cut short the affair by making Adolphus prisoner and seizing on the disputed territory; for which he, however, paid Arnoul the sum of two hundred and twenty thousand florins.

After this acquisition Charles conceived and had much at heart the design of becoming king, the first time that the Netherlands were considered sufficiently important and consolidated to entitle their possessor to that title. To lead to this object he offered to the emperor of Germany the hand of his daughter Mary for his son Maximilian. The emperor acceded to this proposition, and repaired to the city of Treves to meet Charles and countenance his coronation. But the insolence and selfishness of the latter put an end to the project. He humiliated the emperor, who was of a niggardly and mean-spirited disposition, by appearing with a train so numerous and sumptuous as totally to eclipse the imperial retinue; and deeply offended him by wishing to postpone the marriage, from his jealousy of creating for himself a rival in a son-in-law who might embitter his old age as he had done that of his own father. The mortified emperor quitted the place in high dudgeon, and the projected kingdom was doomed to a delay of some centuries.

Charles, urged on by the double motive of thirst for aggrandizement and vexation at his late failure, attempted, under pretext of some internal dissensions, to gain possession of Cologne and its territory, which belonged to the empire; and at the same time planned the invasion of France, in concert with his brother-in-law Edward IV., who had recovered possession of England. But the town of Nuys, in the archbishopric of Cologne, occupied him a full year before its walls. The emperor, who came to its succor, actually besieged the besiegers in their camp; and the dispute was terminated by leaving it to the arbitration of the pope's legate, and placing the contested town in his keeping. This half triumph gained by Charles saved Louis wholly from destruction. Edward, who had landed in France with a numerous force, seeing no appearance of his Burgundian allies, made peace with Louis; and Charles, who arrived in all haste, but not till after the treaty was signed, upbraided and abused the English king, and turned a warm friend into an inveterate enemy.

Louis, whose crooked policy had so far succeeded on all occasions, now seemed to favor Charles's plans of aggrandizement, and to recognize his pretended right to Lorraine, which legitimately belonged to the empire, and the invasion of which by Charles would be sure to set him at variance with the whole of Germany. The infatuated duke, blind to the ruin to which he was thus hurrying, abandoned to Louis, in return for this insidious support, the constable of St. Pol; a nobleman who had long maintained his independence in Picardy, where he had large possessions, and who was fitted to be a valuable friend or formidable enemy to either. Charles now marched against, and soon overcame, Lorraine. Thence he turned his army against the Swiss, who were allies to the conquered province, but who sent the most submissive dissuasions to the invader. They begged for peace, assuring Charles that their romantic but sterile mountains were not altogether worth the bridles of his splendidly equipped cavalry. But the more they humbled themselves, the higher was his haughtiness raised. It appeared that he had at this period conceived the project of uniting in one common conquest the ancient dominions of Lothaire I., who had possessed the whole of the countries traversed by the Rhine, the Rhone, and the Po; and he even spoke of passing the Alps, like Hannibal, for the invasion of Italy.

Switzerland was, by moral analogy as well as physical fact, the rock against which these extravagant projects were shattered. The army of Charles, which engaged the hardy mountaineers in the gorges of the Alps near the town of Granson, were literally crushed to atoms by the stones and fragments of granite detached from the heights and hurled down upon their heads. Charles, after this defeat, returned to the charge six weeks later, having rallied his army and drawn reinforcements from Burgundy. But Louis had despatched a body of cavalry to the Swiss—a force in which they were before deficient; and thus augmented, their army amounted to thirty-four thousand men. They took up a position, skilfully chosen, on the borders of the Lake of Morat, where they were attacked by Charles at the head of sixty thousand soldiers of all ranks. The result was the total defeat of the latter, with the loss of ten thousand killed, whose bones, gathered into an immense heap, and bleaching in the winds, remained for above three centuries; a terrible monument of rashness and injustice on the one hand, and of patriotism and valor on the other.

Charles was now plunged into a state of profound melancholy; **but he** soon burst from this gloomy mood into **one of renewed** fierceness and fatal desperation. Nine **months after the battle of** Morat he re-entered Lorraine, **at the head of an army, not composed of** his **faithful** militia **of the Netherlands, but of those mercenaries in whom** it was **madness to place trust. The** reinforcements **meant to be despatched to him by** those provinces were kept back **by the artifices of the count of Campo** Basso, an Italian who commanded his cavalry, and who only gained his confidence basely to betray it. Rene, duke of Lorraine, at the head of the confederate forces, offered battle to Charles under the walls of Nancy; and the night before the combat Campo Basso went over to the enemy with the troops under his command. Still Charles had the way open for retreat. Fresh troops from Burgundy and Flanders were on their march to join him; but he would not be dissuaded from his resolution to fight, and he resolved to try his fortune once more with his dispirited and shattered army. On this occasion the fate of Charles was decided, and the fortune of Louis triumphant. The rash and ill-fated duke lost both the battle and his life. His body, mutilated with wounds, was found the next day, and buried with great pomp in the town of Nancy, by the orders of the generous victor, the duke of Lorraine.

Thus perished the last prince of the powerful House of Burgundy. Charles left to his only daughter, then eighteen **years of age, the inheritance of** his extensive dominions, and **with them that of the hatred** and jealousy which he had so largely **excited.** External spoliation immediately commenced, and **internal** disunion quickly followed. Louis **XI. seized on Burgundy** and a part of Artois, as fiefs devolving **to the crown in** default of male issue. Several of **the** provinces refused to pay the new subsidies commanded in the name of Mary; Flanders alone showing a disposition to uphold the rights of the young princess. The states were assembled at **Ghent, and** ambassadors sent to the king of

France, in the hopes of obtaining peace on reasonable terms. Louis, true to his system of subtle perfidy, placed before one of those ambassadors, the burgomaster of Ghent, a letter from the inexperienced princess, which proved her intention to govern by the counsel of her father's ancient ministers rather than by that of the deputies of the nation. This was enough to decide the indignant Flemings to render themselves at once masters of the government and get rid of the ministers whom they hated. Two Burgundian nobles, Hugonet and Imbercourt, were arrested, accused of treason, and beheaded under the very eyes of their agonized and outraged mistress, who threw herself before the frenzied multitude, vainly imploring mercy for these innocent men. The people having thus completely gained the upper hand over the Burgundian influence, Mary was sovereign of the Netherlands but in name.

It would have now been easy for Louis XI. to have obtained for the dauphin, his son, the hand of this hitherto unfortunate but interesting princess; but he thought himself sufficiently strong and cunning to gain possession of her states without such an alliance. Mary, however, thus in some measure disdained, if not actually rejected, by Louis, soon after married her first-intended husband, Maximilian of Austria, son of the emperor Frederick III.; a prince so absolutely destitute, in consequence of his father's parsimony, that she was obliged to borrow money from the towns of Flanders to defray the expenses of his suite. Nevertheless he seemed equally acceptable to his bride and to his new subjects. They not only supplied all his wants, but enabled him to maintain the war against Louis XI., whom they defeated at the battle of Guinegate in Picardy, and forced to make peace on more favorable terms than they had hoped for. But these wealthy provinces were not more zealous for the national defence than bent on the maintenance of their local privileges, which Maximilian little understood, and sympathized with less. He was bred in the school of absolute despotism; and his duchess having met with a too early death by a fall from her horse in the year 1484, he could not even succeed in obtaining the nomination of guardian to his own children without passing through a year of civil war. His power being almost nominal in the northern provinces, he vainly attempted to suppress the violence of the factions of Hoeks and Kaabeljauws. **In** Flanders his authority was **openly resisted.** The turbulent towns of that country, and particularly **Bruges, taking** umbrage at a government half **German, half Burgundian,** and altogether hateful to the **people, rose up** against Maximilian, seized on his person, **imprisoned him in a house which still** exists, and put to **death his most faithful followers. But** the fury of Ghent and other places becoming still more outrageous, Maximilian **asked as a favor** from his rebel subjects of Bruges to be guarded while a prisoner by them alone. He was then king of the Romans, and all Europe became interested in his fate. The pope addressed a brief to the town of Bruges, demanding his deliverance. **But the burghers were as** inflexible as factious; **and they at** length released him, but not until they **had concluded with him** and the assembled states a treaty which **most amply** secured the enjoyment of their privileges and the pardon of their rebellion.

But these **kind of compacts were** never observed by the **princes of those days** beyond the actual period of their capacity to **violate them. The emperor** having entered the **Netherlands at the** head of forty thousand men, Maximilian, so supported, **soon showed** his contempt for **the** obligations he had sworn to, **and had** recourse to force for the extension **of his authority.** The valor of the Flemings and the military **talents of** their leader, Philip of Cleves, thwarted all **his projects,** and a new compromise was entered into. Flanders **paid a** large subsidy, and held fast her rights. The German troops were sent into Holland, and employed for the extinction of the Hoeks; who, as they formed by far the weaker faction, were now soon destroyed. That province, which had been so long distracted by its intestine feuds, and which had consequently played but an insignificant part in the transactions of the Netherlands, now resumed its place; and acquired thenceforth new honor, till it at length came to figure in all the importance of historical distinction.

The situation of the Netherlands was now extremely precarious and difficult to manage, during the unstable sway of a government so weak as Maximilian's. But he having succeeded his father on the imperial throne in 1493, and his son Philip having been proclaimed the following year duke and count of the various provinces at the age of sixteen, a more pleasing prospect was offered to the people. Philip, young, handsome, and descended by his mother from the ancient sovereigns of the country, was joyfully hailed by all the towns. He did not belie the hopes so enthusiastically expressed. He had the good sense to renounce all pretensions to Friesland, the fertile source of many preceding quarrels and sacrifices. He re-established the ancient commercial relations with England, to which country Maximilian had given mortal offence by sustaining the imposture of Perkin Warbeck. Philip also consulted the states-general on his projects of a double alliance between himself and his sister with the son and daughter of Ferdinand, king of Aragon, and Isabella, queen of Castile; and from this wise precaution the project soon became one of national partiality instead of private or personal interest. In this manner complete harmony was established between the young prince and the inhabitants of the Netherlands. All the ills produced by civil war disappeared with immense rapidity in Flanders and Brabant, as soon as peace was thus consolidated. Even Holland, though it had particularly felt the scourge of these dissensions, and suffered severely from repeated inundations, began to recover. Yet for all this, Philip can be scarcely called a good prince: his merits were negative rather than real. But that sufficed for the nation; which found in the nullity of its sovereign no obstacle to the resumption of that prosperous career which had been checked by the despotism of the House of Burgundy, and the attempts of Maximilian to continue the same system.

The reign of Philip, unfortunately a short one, was rendered remarkable by two intestine quarrels; one in Friesland, the other in Guelders. The Frisons, who had been so isolated from the more important affairs of Europe that they were in a manner lost sight of by history for several centuries, had nevertheless their full share of domestic disputes; too long, too multifarious, and too minute, to allow us to give more than this brief notice of their existence. But finally, about the period of Philip's accession, eastern Friesland had chosen for its count a gentleman of the country surnamed Edzart, who fixed the headquarters of his military government at Embden. The sight of such an elevation in an individual whose pretensions he thought far inferior to his own induced Albert of Saxony, who had well served Maximilian against the refractory Flemings, to demand as his reward the title of stadtholder or hereditary governor of Friesland. But it was far easier for the emperor to accede to this request than for his favorite to put the grant into effect. The Frisons, true to their old character, held firm to their privileges, and fought for their maintenance with heroic courage. Albert, furious at this resistance, had the horrid barbarity to cause to be impaled the chief burghers of the town of Leuwaarden, which he had taken by assault. But he himself died in the year 1500, without succeeding in his projects of an ambition unjust in its principle and atrocious in its practice.

The war of Guelders was of a totally different nature. In this case it was not a question of popular resistance to a tyrannical nomination, but of patriotic fidelity to the reigning family. Adolphus, the duke who had dethroned his father, had died in Flanders, leaving a son who had been brought up almost a captive as long as Maximilian governed the states of his inheritance. This young man, called Charles of Egmont, and who is honored in the history of his country under the title of the Achilles of Guelders, fell into the hands of the French during the combat in which he made his first essay in arms. The town of Guelders unanimously joined to pay his ransom; and as soon as he was at liberty they one and all proclaimed him duke. The emperor Philip and the Germanic diet in vain protested against this measure, and declared Charles a usurper. The spirit of justice and of liberty spoke more loudly than the thunders of their ban; and the people resolved to support to the last this scion of an ancient race, glorious in much of its conduct, though often criminal in many of its members. Charles of Egmont found faithful friends in his devoted subjects; and he maintained his rights, sometimes with, sometimes without, the assistance of France—making up for his want of numbers by energy and enterprise. We cannot follow this warlike prince in the long series of adventures which consolidated his power; nor stop to depict his daring adherents on land, who caused the whole of Holland to tremble at their deeds; nor his pirates—the chief of whom, Long Peter, called himself king of the Zuyder Zee. But amid all the consequent troubles of such a struggle, it is marvellous to find Charles of Egmont upholding his country in a state of high prosperity, and leaving it at his death almost as rich as Holland itself.

The incapacity of Philip the Fair doubtless contributed to cause him the loss of this portion of his dominions. This prince, after his first acts of moderation and good sense, was remarkable only as being the father of Charles V. The remainder of his life was worn out in undignified pleasures; and he died almost suddenly, in the year 1506, at Burgos in Castile, whither he had repaired to pay a visit to his brother-in-law, the king of Spain.

CHAPTER VI

FROM THE GOVERNMENT OF MARGARET OF AUSTRIA TO THE ABDICATION OF THE EMPEROR CHARLES V.

A.D. 1506—1555

PHILIP being dead, and his wife, Joanna of Spain, having become mad from grief at his loss, after nearly losing her senses from jealousy during his life, the regency of the Netherlands reverted to Maximilian, who immediately named his daughter Margaret stadtholderess of the country. This princess, scarcely twenty-seven years of age, had been, like the celebrated Jacqueline of Bavaria, already three times married, and was now again a widow. Her first husband, Charles VIII. of France, had broken from his contract of marriage before its consummation; her second, the Infante of Spain, died immediately after their union; and her third, the duke of Savoy, left her again a widow after three years of wedded life. She was a woman of talent and courage; both proved by the couplet she composed for her own epitaph, at the very moment of a dangerous accident which happened during her journey into Spain to join her second affianced spouse.

"Ci-gît Margot la gente demoiselle,
Qui eut deux maris, et si mourut pucelle."

"Here gentle Margot quietly is laid,
Who had two husbands, and yet died a maid."

She was received with the greatest joy by the people of the Netherlands; and she governed them as peaceably as circumstances allowed. Supported by England, she firmly maintained her authority against the threats of France; and she carried on in person all the negotiations between Louis XII., Maximilian, the pope Julius II., and Ferdinand of Aragon, for the famous League of Venice. These negotiations took place in 1508, at Cambray; where Margaret, if we are to credit an expression to that effect in one of her letters, was more than once on the point of having serious differences with the cardinal of Amboise, minister of Louis XII. But, besides her attention to the interests of her father on this important occasion, she also succeeded in repressing the rising pretensions of Charles of Egmont; and, assisted by the interference of the king of France, she obliged him to give up some places in Holland which he illegally held.

From this period the alliance between England and Spain raised the commerce and manufactures of the southern provinces of the Netherlands to a high degree of prosperity, while the northern parts of the country were still kept down by their various dissensions. Holland was at war with the Hanseatic towns. The Frisons continued to struggle for freedom against the heirs of Albert of Saxony. Utrecht was at variance with its bishop, and finally recognized Charles of Egmont as its protector. The consequence of all these causes was that the south took the start in a course of prosperity, which was, however, soon to become common to the whole nation.

A new rupture with France, in 1513, united Maximilian, Margaret, and Henry VIII. of England, in one common cause. An English and Belgian army, in which Maximilian figured as a spectator (taking care to be paid by England), marched for the destruction of Therouenne, and defeated and dispersed the French at the battle of Spurs. But Louis XII. soon persuaded Henry to make a separate peace; and the unconquerable duke of Guelders made Margaret and the emperor pay the penalty of their success against France. He pursued his victories in Friesland, and forced the country to recognize him as stadtholder of Groningen, its chief town; while the duke of Saxony at length renounced to another his unjust claim on a territory which engulfed both his armies and his treasure.

About the same epoch (1515), young Charles, son of Philip the Fair, having just attained his fifteenth year, was inaugurated duke of Brabant and count of Flanders and Holland, having purchased the presumed right of Saxony to the sovereignty of Friesland. In the following year he was recognized as prince of Castile, in right of his mother, who associated him with herself in the royal power —a step which soon left her merely the title of queen. Charles procured the nomination of bishop of Utrecht for Philip, bastard of Burgundy, which made that province completely dependent on him. But this event was also one of general and lasting importance on another account. This Philip of Burgundy was deeply affected by the doctrines of the Reformation, which had burst forth in Germany. He held in abhorrence the superstitious observances of the Romish Church, and set his face against the celibacy of the clergy. His example soon influenced his whole diocese, and the new notions on points of religion became rapidly popular. It was chiefly, however, in Friesland that the people embraced the opinions of Luther, which were quite conformable to many of the local customs of which we have already spoken. The celebrated Edzard, count of eastern Friesland, openly adopted the Reformation. While Erasmus of Rotterdam, without actually pronouncing himself a disciple of Lutheranism, effected more than all its advocates to throw the abuses of Catholicism into discredit.

We may here remark that, during the government of the House of Burgundy, the clergy of the Netherlands had fallen into considerable disrepute. Intrigue and court favor alone had the disposal of the benefices; while the career of commerce was open to the enterprise of every spirited and independent competitor. The Reformation, therefore, in the first instance found but a slight obstacle in the opposition of a slavish and ignorant clergy, and its progress was all at once prodigious. The refusal of the dignity of emperor by Frederick "the Wise," duke of Saxony, to whom it was offered by the electors, was also an event highly favorable to the new opinions; for Francis I. of France, and Charles, already king of Spain and sovereign of the Netherlands, both claiming the succession to the empire, a sort of interregnum deprived the disputed dominions of a chief who might lay the heavy hand of power on the new-springing doctrines of Protestantism. At length the intrigues of Charles, and his pretensions as grandson of Maximilian, having caused him to be chosen emperor, a desperate rivalry resulted between him and the French king, which for a while absorbed his whole attention and occupied all his power.

From the earliest appearance of the Reformation, the young sovereign of so many states, having to establish his authority at the two extremities of Europe, could not efficiently occupy himself in resisting the doctrines which, despite their dishonoring epithet of heresy, were doomed so soon to become orthodox for a great part of the Continent. While Charles vigorously put down the revolted Spaniards, Luther gained new proselytes in Germany; so that the very greatness of the sovereignty was the cause of his impotency; and while Charles's extent of dominion thus fostered the growing Reformation, his sense of honor proved the safeguard of its apostle. The intrepid Luther, boldly venturing to appear and plead its cause before the representative power of Germany assembled at the Diet of Worms, was protected by the guarantee of the emperor; unlike the celebrated and unfortunate John Huss, who fell a victim to his own confidence and the bad faith of Sigismund, in the year 1415.

Charles was nevertheless a zealous and rigid Catholic; and in the Low Countries, where his authority was undisputed, he proscribed the heretics, and even violated the privileges of the country by appointing functionaries for the express purpose of their pursuit and punishment. This imprudent stretch of power fostered a rising spirit of opposition; for, though entertaining the best disposition to their young prince, the people deeply felt and loudly complained of the government; and thus the germs of a mighty revolution gradually began to be developed.

Charles V. and Francis I. had been rivals for dignity and power, and they now became implacable personal enemies. Young, ambitious, and sanguine, they could not, without reciprocal resentment, pursue in the same field objects essential to both. Charles, by a short but timely visit to England in 1520, had the address to gain over to his cause and secure for his purpose the powerful interest of Cardinal Wolsey, and to make a most favorable impression on Henry VIII.; and thus strengthened, he entered on the struggle against his less wily enemy with infinite advantage. War was declared on frivolous pretexts in 1521. The French sustained it for some time with great valor; but Francis being obstinately bent on the conquest of the Milanais, his reverses secured the triumph of his rival, and he fell into the hands of the imperial troops at the battle of Pavia in 1525. Charles's dominions in the Netherlands suffered severely from the naval operations during the war; for the French cruisers having, on repeated occasions, taken, pillaged, and almost destroyed the principal resources of the herring fishery, Holland and Zealand felt considerable distress, which was still further augmented by the famine which desolated these provinces in 1524.

While such calamities afflicted the northern portion of the Netherlands, Flanders and Brabant continued to flourish, in spite of temporary embarrassments. The bishop of Utrecht having died, his successor found himself engaged in a hopeless quarrel with his new diocese, already more than half converted to Protestantism; and to gain a triumph over these enemies, even by the sacrifice of his dignity, he ceded to the emperor in 1527 the whole of his temporal power. The duke of Guelders, who then occupied the city

TO THE ABDICATION OF CHARLES V.   87

of Utrecht, redoubled his hostility at this intelligence; and after having ravaged the neighboring country, he did not lay down his arms till the subsequent year, having first procured an honorable and advantageous peace. One year more saw the term of this long-continued state of warfare by the Peace of Cambray, between Charles and Francis, which was signed on the 5th of August, 1529.

This peace once concluded, the industry and perseverance of the inhabitants of the Netherlands repaired in a short time the evils caused by so many wars, excited by the ambition of princes, but in scarcely any instance for the interest of the country. Little, however, was wanting to endanger this tranquillity, and to excite the people against each other on the score of religious dissension. The sect of Anabaptists, whose wild opinions were subversive of all principles of social order and every sentiment of natural decency, had its birth in Germany, and found many proselytes in the Netherlands. John Bokelszoon, a tailor of Leyden, one of the number, caused himself to be proclaimed king of Jerusalem; and making himself master of the town of Munster, sent out his disciples to preach in the neighboring countries. Mary, sister of Charles V., and queen-dowager of Hungary, the stadtholderess of the Netherlands, proposed a crusade against this fanatic; which was, however, totally discountenanced by the states. Encouraged by impunity, whole troops of these infuriate sectarians, from the very extremities of Hainault, put themselves into motion for Munster; and notwithstanding the colds of February, they marched along, quite naked, according to the system of their sect. The frenzy of these fanatics being increased by persecution, they projected attempts against several towns, and particularly against Amsterdam. They were easily defeated, and massacred without mercy; and it was only by multiplied and horrible executions that their numbers were at length diminished. John Bokelszoon held out at Munster, which was besieged by the bishop and the neighboring princes. This profligate fanatic, who had married no less than seventeen women, had gained considerable influence over the insensate multitude; but he was at length taken and imprisoned in an iron cage—an event which undeceived the greater number of those whom he had persuaded of his superhuman powers.

The prosperity of the southern provinces proceeded rapidly and uninterruptedly, in consequence of the great and valuable traffic of the merchants of Flanders and Brabant, who exchanged their goods of native manufacture for the riches drawn from America and India by the Spaniards and Portuguese. Antwerp had succeeded to Bruges as the general mart of commerce, and was the most opulent town of the north of Europe. The expenses, estimated at one hundred and thirty thousand golden crowns, which this city voluntarily incurred, to do honor to the visit of Philip, son of Charles V., are cited as a proof of its wealth. The value of the wool annually imported for manufacture into the Low Countries from England and Spain was calculated at four million pieces of gold. Their herring fishery was unrivalled; for even the Scotch, on whose coasts these fish were taken, did not attempt a competition with the Zealanders. But the chief seat of prosperity was the south. Flanders alone was taxed for one-third of the general burdens of the state. Brabant paid only one-seventh less than Flanders. So that these two rich provinces contributed thirteen out of twenty-one parts of the general contribution; and all the rest combined but eight. A search for further or minuter proofs of the comparative state of the various divisions of the country would be superfluous.

The perpetual quarrels of Charles V. with Francis I. and Charles of Guelders led, as may be supposed, to a repeated state of exhaustion, which forced the princes to pause, till the people recovered strength and resources for each fresh encounter. Charles rarely appeared in the Netherlands; fixing his residence chiefly in Spain, and leaving to his sister the regulation of those distant provinces. One of his occasional visits was for the purpose of inflicting a terrible example upon them. The people of Ghent, suspecting an improper or improvident application of the funds they had furnished for a new campaign, offered themselves to march against the French, instead of being forced to pay their quota of some further subsidy. The government having rejected this proposal, a sedition was the result, at the moment when Charles and Francis already negotiated one of their temporary reconciliations. On this occasion, Charles formed the daring resolution of crossing the kingdom of France, to promptly take into his own hands the settlement of this affair—trusting to the generosity of his scarcely reconciled enemy not to abuse the confidence with which he risked himself in his power. Ghent, taken by surprise, did not dare to oppose the entrance of the emperor, when he appeared before the walls; and the city was punished with extreme severity. Twenty-seven leaders of the sedition were beheaded; the principal privileges of the city were withdrawn, and a citadel built to hold it in check for the future. Charles met with neither opposition nor complaint. The province had so prospered under his sway, and was so flattered by the greatness of the sovereign, who was born in the town he so severely punished, that his acts of despotic harshness were borne without a murmur. But in the north the people did not view his measures so complacently; and a wide separation in interests and opinions became manifest in the different divisions of the nation.

Yet the Dutch and the Zealanders signalized themselves beyond all his other subjects on the occasion of two expeditions which Charles undertook against Tunis and Algiers. The two northern provinces furnished a greater number of ships than the united quotas of all the rest of his states. But though Charles's gratitude did not lead him to do anything in return as peculiarly favorable to these provinces, he obtained for them, nevertheless, a great advantage in making himself master of Friesland and Guelders on the death of Charles of Egmont. His acquisition of the latter, which took place in 1543, put an end to the domestic wars of the northern provinces. From that period they might fairly look for a futurity of union and peace; and thus the latter years of Charles promised better for his country than his early ones, though he obtained less success in his new wars with France, which were not, however, signalized by any grand event on either side.

Toward the end of his career, Charles redoubled his severities against the Protestants, and even introduced a modified species of inquisition into the Netherlands, but with little effect toward the suppression of the reformed doctrines. The misunderstandings between his only son Philip and Mary of England, whom he had induced him to marry, and the unamiable disposition of this young prince, tormented him almost as much as he was humiliated by the victories of Henry II. of France, the successor of Francis I., and the successful dissimulation of Maurice, elector of Saxony, by whom he was completely outwitted, deceived, and defeated. Impelled by these motives, and others, perhaps, which are and must ever remain unknown, Charles at length decided on abdicating the whole of his immense possessions. He chose the city of Brussels as the scene of the solemnity, and the day fixed for it was the 25th of October, 1555. It took place accordingly, in the presence of the king of Bohemia, the duke of Savoy, the dowager queens of France and Hungary, the duchess of Lorraine, and an immense assemblage of nobility from various countries. Charles resigned the empire to his brother Ferdinand, already king of the Romans; and all the rest of his dominions to his son. Soon after the ceremony, Charles embarked from Zealand on his voyage to Spain. He retired to the monastery of St. Justus, near the town of Placentia, in Estremadura. He entered this retreat in February, 1556, and died there on the 21st of September, 1558, in the fifty-ninth year of his age. The last six months of his existence, contrasted with the daring vigor of his former life, formed a melancholy picture of timidity and superstition.

The whole of the provinces of the Netherlands being now

for the first time united under one sovereign, such a junction marks the limits of a second epoch in their history. It would be a presumptuous and vain attempt to trace, in a compass so confined as ours, the various changes in manners and customs which arose in these countries during a period of one thousand years. The extended and profound remarks of many celebrated writers on the state of Europe from the decline of the Roman power to the epoch at which we are now arrived must be referred to, to judge of the gradual progress of civilization through the gloom of the dark ages, till the dawn of enlightenment which led to the grand system of European politics commenced during the reign of Charles V. The amazing increase of commerce was, above all other considerations, the cause of the growth of liberty in the Netherlands. The Reformation opened the minds of men to that intellectual freedom without which political enfranchisement is a worthless privilege. The invention of printing opened a thousand channels to the flow of erudition and talent, and sent them out from the reservoirs of individual possession to fertilize the whole domain of human nature. War, which seems to be an instinct of man, and which particular instances of heroism often raise to the dignity of a passion, was reduced to a science, and made subservient to those great principles of policy in which society began to perceive its only chance of durable good. Manufactures attained a state of high perfection, and went on progressively with the growth of wealth and luxury. The opulence of the towns of Brabant and Flanders was without any previous example in the state of Europe. A merchant of Bruges took upon himself alone the security for the ransom of John the Fearless, taken at the battle of Nicopolis, amounting to two hundred thousand ducats. A provost of Valenciennes repaired to Paris at one of the great fairs periodically held there, and purchased on his own account every article that was for sale. At a repast given by one of the counts of Flanders to the Flemish magistrates the seats they occupied were unfurnished with cushions. These proud burghers folded their sumptuous cloaks and sat on them. After the feast they were retiring without retaining these important and **costly** articles of **dress**; and on a **courtier** reminding **them of their** apparent neglect, the burgomaster of Bruges **replied, "We** Flemings **are not in the habit of** carrying **away the** cushions after dinner!" The meetings of the different towns for the sports of archery were signalized by **the most splendid** display of **dress** and decoration. The archers were habited in silk, **damask, and** the finest linen, **and carried chains of gold of great weight** and **value.** Luxury **was at its height among women. The queen of** Philip **the Fair of France, on a visit to Bruges, exclaimed, with astonishment not unmixed** with envy, **"I thought myself the only queen here; but I** see six hundred others who appear **more so than I."**

The court of Philip the Good seemed to carry magnificence **and splendor to their** greatest possible height. The **dresses of both men and** women at this chivalric epoch **were of almost** incredible expense. Velvet, satin, gold, and **precious stones seemed the** ordinary materials for the dress of **either sex; while the very housings of the** horses sparkled **with brilliants and cost immense sums.** This absurd **extravagance was carried so far** that **Charles** V. found himself **forced at length to proclaim** sumptuary laws for its **repression.**

The **style of** the banquets given on grand occasions **was regulated on a scale** of almost puerile splendor. The Banquet **of Vows given** at Lille, in the **year** 1453, and so called **from the obligations entered** into by some of the nobles to **accompany Philip in a new** crusade against the infidels, showed a succession of costly fooleries, most amusing in the **detail** given by an eye-witness (Olivier de la Marche), the minutest of the chroniclers, but unluckily too long to find a place in our pages.

Such excessive luxury naturally led **to** great corruption of manners and the commission of terrible crimes. During the reign of Philip de Male, there were committed in the city of Ghent and its outskirts, in less than a year, above fourteen hundred murders in gambling-houses and other resorts of debauchery. As early as the tenth century, the petty sovereigns established on the ruins of the empire of Charlemagne began the independent coining of money; and the various provinces were during the rest of this epoch inundated with a most embarrassing variety of gold, silver, and copper. Even in ages of comparative darkness, literature made feeble efforts to burst through the entangled weeds of superstition, ignorance, and war. In the fourteenth and fifteenth centuries, history was greatly cultivated; and Froissart, Monstrelet, Olivier de la Marche, and Philip de Comines, gave to their chronicles and memoirs a charm of style since their days almost unrivalled. Poetry began to be followed with success in the Netherlands, in the Dutch, Flemish, and French languages; and even before the institution of the Floral Games in France, Belgium possessed its chambers of rhetoric (*rederykkamers*) which labored to keep alive the sacred flame of poetry with more zeal than success. In the fourteenth and fifteenth centuries, these societies were established in almost every burgh of Flanders and Brabant; the principal towns possessing several at once.

The arts in their several branches made considerable progress in the Netherlands during this epoch. Architecture was greatly cultivated in the thirteenth and fourteenth centuries; most of the cathedrals and town houses being constructed in that age. Their vastness, solidity, and beauty of design and execution, make them still speaking monuments of the stern magnificence and finished taste of the times. The patronage of Philip the Good, Charles the Rash, and Margaret of Austria, brought music into fashion, and led to its cultivation in a remarkable degree. The first musicians of France were drawn from Flanders; and other professors from that country acquired great celebrity in Italy for their scientific improvements in their delightful art.

Painting, which had languished before the fifteenth century, sprung at once into a new existence from the invention of John Van Eyck, known better by the name of John of Bruges. His accidental discovery of the art of painting in oil quickly spread over Europe, and served to perpetuate to all time the records of the genius which has bequeathed its vivid impressions to the world. Painting on glass, polishing diamonds, the Carillon, lace, and tapestry, were among the inventions which owed their birth to the Netherlands in these ages, when the faculties of mankind sought so many new channels for mechanical development. The discovery of a new world by Columbus and other eminent navigators gave a fresh and powerful impulse to European talent, by affording an immense reservoir for its reward. The town of Antwerp was, during the reign of Charles V., the outlet for the industry of Europe, and the receptacle for the productions of all the nations of the earth. Its port was so often crowded with vessels that each successive fleet was obliged to wait long in the Scheldt before it could obtain admission for the discharge of its cargoes. The university of Louvain, that great nursery of science, was founded in 1425, and served greatly to the spread of knowledge, although it degenerated into the hotbed of those fierce disputes which stamped on theology the degradation of bigotry, and drew down odium on a study that, if purely practiced, ought only to inspire veneration.

Charles V. was the first to establish a solid plan of government, instead of the constant fluctuations in the management of justice, police, and finance. He caused the edicts of the various sovereigns, and the municipal usages, to be embodied into a system of laws; and thus gave stability and method to the enjoyment of the prosperity in which he left his dominions.

CHAPTER VII

FROM THE ACCESSION OF PHILIP II. OF SPAIN TO THE ESTABLISHMENT OF THE INQUISITION IN THE NETHERLANDS

A.D. 1555–1566

IT has been shown that the Netherlands were never in a more flourishing state than at the accession of Philip II. The external relations of the country presented an aspect of prosperity and peace. England was closely allied to it by Queen Mary's marriage with Philip; France, fatigued with war, had just concluded with it a five years' truce; Germany, paralyzed by religious dissensions, exhausted itself in domestic quarrels; the other states were too distant or too weak to inspire any uneasiness; and nothing appeared wanting for the public weal. Nevertheless there was something dangerous and alarming in the situation of the Low Countries; but the danger consisted wholly in the connection between the monarch and the people, and the alarm was not sounded till the mischief was beyond remedy.

From the time that Charles V. was called to reign over Spain, he may be said to have been virtually lost to the country of his birth. He was no longer a mere duke of Brabant or Limberg, a count of Flanders or Holland; he was also king of Castile, Aragon, Leon, and Navarre, of Naples, and of Sicily. These various kingdoms had interests evidently opposed to those of the Low Countries, and forms of government far different. It was scarcely to be doubted that the absolute monarch of so many peoples would look with a jealous eye on the institutions of those provinces which placed limits to his power; and the natural consequence was that he who was a legitimate king in the south soon degenerated into a usurping master in the north.

But during the reign of Charles the danger was in some measure lessened, or at least concealed from public view, by the apparent facility with which he submitted to and observed the laws and customs of his native country. With Philip, the case was far different, and the results too obvious. Uninformed on the Belgian character, despising the state of manners, and ignorant of the language, no sympathy attached him to the people. He brought with him to the throne all the hostile prejudices of a foreigner, without one of the kindly or considerate feelings of a compatriot.

Spain, where this young prince had hitherto passed his life, was in some degree excluded from European civilization. A contest of seven centuries between the Mohammedan tribes and the descendants of the Visigoths, cruel, like all civil wars, and, like all those of religion, not merely a contest of rulers, but essentially of the people, had given to the manners and feelings of this unhappy country a deep stamp of barbarity. The ferocity of military chieftains had become the basis of the government and laws. The Christian kings had adopted the perfidious and bloody system of the despotic sultans they replaced. Magnificence and tyranny, power and cruelty, wisdom and dissimulation, respect and fear, were inseparably associated in the minds of a people so governed. They comprehended nothing in religion but a God armed with omnipotence and vengeance, or in politics but a king as terrible as the deity he represented.

Philip, bred in this school of slavish superstition, taught that he was the despot for whom it was formed, familiar with the degrading tactics of eastern tyranny, was at once the most contemptible and unfortunate of men. Isolated from his kind, and wishing to appear superior to those beyond whom his station had placed him, he was insensible to the affections which soften and ennoble human nature. He was perpetually filled with one idea—that of his greatness; he had but one ambition—that of command; but one enjoyment—that of exciting fear. Victim to this revolting selfishness, his heart was never free from care; and the bitter melancholy of his character seemed to nourish a desire of evil-doing, which irritated suffering often produces in man. Deceit and blood were his greatest, if not his only, delights. The religious zeal which he affected, or felt, showed itself but in acts of cruelty; and the fanatic bigotry which inspired him formed the strongest contrast to the divine spirit of Christianity.

Nature had endowed this ferocious being with wonderful penetration and unusual self-command; the first revealing to him the views of others, and the latter giving him the surest means of counteracting them, by enabling him to control himself. Although ignorant, he had a prodigious instinct of cunning. He wanted courage, but its place was supplied by the harsh obstinacy of wounded pride. All the corruptions of intrigue were familiar to him; yet he often failed in his most deep-laid designs, at the very moment of their apparent success, by the recoil of the bad faith and treachery with which his plans were overcharged.

Such was the man who now began that terrible reign which menaced utter ruin to the national prosperity of the Netherlands. His father had already sapped its foundations, by encouraging foreign manners and ideas among the nobility, and dazzling them with the hope of the honors and wealth which he had at his disposal abroad. His severe edicts against heresy had also begun to accustom the nation to religious discords and hatred. Philip soon enlarged on what Charles had commenced, and he unmercifully sacrificed the well-being of a people to the worst objects of his selfish ambition.

Philip had only once visited the Netherlands before his accession to sovereign power. Being at that time twenty-two years of age, his opinions were formed and his prejudices deeply rooted. Everything that he observed on this visit was calculated to revolt both. The frank cordiality of the people appeared too familiar. The expression of popular rights sounded like the voice of rebellion. Even the magnificence displayed in his honor offended his jealous vanity. From that moment he seems to have conceived an implacable aversion to the country, in which alone, of all his vast possessions, he could not display the power or inspire the terror of despotism.

The sovereign's dislike was fully equalled by the disgust of his subjects. His haughty severity and vexatious etiquette revolted their pride as well as their plain dealing; and the moral qualities of their new sovereign were considered with loathing. The commercial and political connection between the Netherlands and Spain had given the two people ample opportunities for mutual acquaintance. The dark, vindictive dispositions of the latter inspired a deep antipathy in those whom civilization had softened and liberty rendered frank and generous; and the new sovereign seemed to embody all that was repulsive and odious in the nation of which he was the type. Yet Philip did not at first act in a way to make himself more particularly hated. He rather, by an apparent consideration for a few points of political interest and individual privilege, and particularly by the revocation of some of the edicts against heretics, removed the suspicions his earlier conduct had excited; and his intended victims did not perceive that the despot sought to lull them to sleep, in the hopes of making them an easier prey.

Philip knew well that force alone was insufficient to reduce such a people to slavery. He succeeded in persuading the states to grant him considerable subsidies, some of which were to be paid by instalments during a period of nine years. That was gaining a great step toward his designs, as it superseded the necessity of a yearly application to the three orders, the guardians of the public liberty. At the same time he sent secret agents to Rome, to obtain the approbation of the pope to his insidious but most effective plan for placing the whole of the clergy in dependence upon the crown. He also kept up the army of Spaniards and Germans which his father had formed on the frontiers of

France; and although he did not remove from their employments the functionaries already in place, he took care to make no new appointments to office among the natives of the Netherlands.

In the midst of these cunning preparations for tyranny, Philip was suddenly attacked in two quarters at once; by Henry II. of France, and by Pope Paul IV. A prince less obstinate than Philip would in such circumstances have renounced, or at least postponed, his designs against the liberties of so important a part of his dominions, as those to which he was obliged to have recourse for aid in support of this double war. But he seemed to make every foreign consideration subservient to the object of domestic aggression which he had so much at heart.

He, however, promptly met the threatened dangers from abroad. He turned his first attention toward his contest with the pope; and he extricated himself from it with an adroitness that proved the whole force and cunning of his character. Having first publicly obtained the opinion of several doctors of theology, that he was justified in taking arms against the pontiff (a point on which there was really no doubt), he prosecuted the war with the utmost vigor, by the means of the afterward notorious duke of Alva, at that time viceroy of his Italian dominions. Paul soon yielded to superior skill and force, and demanded terms of peace, which were granted with a readiness and seeming liberality that astonished no one more than the defeated pontiff. But Philip's moderation to his enemy was far outdone by his perfidy to his allies. He confirmed Alva's consent to the confiscation of the domains of the noble Romans who had espoused his cause; and thus gained a stanch and powerful supporter to all his future projects in the religious authority of the successor of St. Peter.

His conduct in the conclusion of the war with France was not less base. His army, under the command of Philibert Emmanuel, duke of Savoy, consisting of Belgians, Germans, and Spaniards, with a considerable body of English, sent by Mary to the assistance of her husband, penetrated into Picardy, and gained a complete victory over the French forces. The honor of this brilliant affair, which took place near St. Quintin, was almost wholly due to the count d'Egmont, a Belgian noble, who commanded the light cavalry; but the king, unwilling to let any one man enjoy the glory of the day, piously pretended that he owed the entire obligation to St. Lawrence, on whose festival the battle was fought. His gratitude or hypocrisy found a fitting monument in the celebrated convent and palace of the Escurial, which he absurdly caused to be built in the form of a gridiron, the instrument of the saint's martyrdom. When the news of the victory reached Charles V. in his retreat, the old warrior inquired if Philip was in Paris? but the cautious victor had no notion of such prompt manœuvring; nor would he risk against foreign enemies the exhaustion of forces destined for the enslavement of his people.

The French in some measure retrieved their late disgrace by the capture of Calais, the only town remaining to England of all its French conquests, and which, consequently, had deeply interested the national glory of each people. In the early part of the year 1558, one of the generals of Henry II. made an irruption into western Flanders; but the gallant count of Egmont once more proved his valor and skill by attacking and totally defeating the invaders near the town of Gravelines.

A general peace was concluded in April, 1559, which bore the name of Câteau-Cambresis, from that of the place where it was negotiated. Philip secured for himself various advantages in the treaty; but he sacrificed the interests of England, by consenting to the retention of Calais by the French king—a cession deeply humiliating to the national pride of his allies; and, if general opinion be correct, a proximate cause of his consort's death. The alliance of France and the support of Rome, the important results of the two wars now brought to a close, were counterbalanced by the well-known hostility of Elizabeth, who had succeeded to the throne of England; and **this latter consideration was an** additional motive with Philip **to push forward the design of** consolidating his despotism in the Low Countries.

To lead his **already** deceived subjects **the** more surely into the snare, **he** announced his intended departure **on a** short visit **to Spain;** and **created** for the period of his absence **a provisional government,** chiefly composed **of** the leading **men among the Belgian** nobility. He flattered himself **that** the states, **dazzled by the** illustrious illusion thus prepared, **would cheerfully grant to this** provisional government the **right of levying taxes during the** temporary absence of **the sovereign.** He also reckoned on the influence of the **clergy in the national** assembly, **to procure** the revival of the edicts against heresy, which he **had gained** the merit of suspending. These, **with many minor details** of profound duplicity, formed **the principal features of a** plan, which, if successful, **would have reduced the Netherlands** to the wretched state **of colonial dependence by which** Naples and Sicily were held in **the tenure of Spain.**

As soon as the states had consented **to** place the whole powers of government in the hands **of the new** administration for the period of **the king's absence,** the royal hypocrite believed **his scheme secure, and flattered** himself he had established **an instrument of durable despotism.** The composition of **this new** government **was a** masterpiece of political machinery. **It** consisted of several councils, in which the most distinguished citizens were entitled to a place, in sufficient numbers **to deceive the people with a** show of representation, **but not enough to command a** majority, which was sure on any important question **to rest with** the titled creatures of the court. The edicts **against heresy,** soon adopted, gave to the clergy an almost **unlimited** power over **the** lives and fortunes of the people. But almost all the dignitaries of the church being men **of** great respectability **and** moderation, chosen by **the** body of the inferior clergy, these extraordinary powers excited little alarm.

Philip's project was suddenly to replace these virtuous ecclesiastics by others of his own choice, as soon as the states broke up from their annual meeting; and for this intention he had procured the secret consent and authority of the court of Rome.

In support of these combinations, the Belgian troops were completely broken up and scattered in small bodies over the country. The whole of this force, so redoubtable to the fears of despotism, consisted of only three thousand cavalry. It was now divided into fourteen companies (or squadrons in the modern phraseology), under the command of as many independent chiefs, so as to leave little chance of any principle of union reigning among them. But the German and Spanish troops in Philip's pay were cantoned on the frontiers, ready to stifle any incipient effort in opposition to his plans. In addition to these imposing means for their execution, he had secured a still more secret and more powerful support: a secret article in the treaty of Câteau-Cambresis obliged the king of France to assist him with the whole armies of France against his Belgian subjects, should they prove refractory. Thus the late war, of which the Netherlands had borne all the weight, and earned all the glory, only brought about the junction of the defeated enemy with their own king for the extinction of their national independence.

To complete the execution of this system of perfidy, Philip convened an assembly of all the states at Ghent, in the month of July, 1559. This meeting of the representatives of the three orders of the state offered no apparent obstacle to Philip's views. The clergy, alarmed at the progress of the new doctrines, gathered more closely round the government of which they required the support. The nobles had lost much of their ancient attachment to liberty; and had become, in various ways, dependent on the royal favor. Many of the first families were then represented by men possessed rather of courage and candor than of foresight and sagacity. That of Nassau, the most distinguished of all, seemed the least interested in the national cause. A great part of its possessions were in Germany and France, where it had recently acquired the sovereign principality of Orange. It was only from the third order—that of the commons—that Philip had to expect any opposition. Already, during the war, it had shown some discontent, and had insisted on the nomination of commissioners to control the accounts and the disbursements of the subsidies. But it seemed improbable that among this class of men any would be found capable of penetrating the manifold combinations of the king, and disconcerting his designs.

Anthony Perrenotte de Granvelle, bishop of Arras, who was considered as Philip's favorite counsellor, but who was in reality no more than his docile agent, was commissioned to address the assembly in the name of his master, who spoke only Spanish. His oration was one of cautious deception, and contained the most flattering assurances of Philip's attachment to the people of the Netherlands. It excused the king for not having nominated his only son, Don Carlos, to reign over them in his name; alleging, as a proof of his royal affection, that he preferred giving them as stadtholderess a Belgian princess, Madame Marguerite, duchess of Parma, the natural daughter of Charles V. by a young lady, a native of Audenarde. Fair promises and fine words were thus lavished in profusion to gain the confidence of the deputies.

But notwithstanding all the talent, the caution, and the mystery of Philip and his minister, there was among the nobles one man who saw through all. This individual, endowed with many of the highest attributes of political genius, and pre-eminently with judgment, the most important of all, entered fearlessly into the contest against tyranny—despising every personal sacrifice for the country's good. Without making himself suspiciously prominent, he privately warned some members of the states of the coming danger. Those in whom he confided did not betray the trust. They spread among the other deputies the alarm, and pointed out the danger to which they had been so judiciously awakened. The consequence was a reply to Philip's demand, in vague and general terms, without binding the nation by any pledge; and a unanimous entreaty that he would diminish the taxes, withdraw the foreign troops, and intrust no official employments to any but natives of the country. The object of this last request was the removal of Granvelle, who was born in Franche-Comte.

Philip was utterly astounded at all this. In the first moment of his vexation he imprudently cried out, "Would ye, then, also bereave *me* of my place; I, who am a Spaniard?" But he soon recovered his self-command, and resumed his usual mask; expressed his regret at not having sooner learned the wishes of the states; promised to remove the foreign troops within three months; and set off for Zealand, with assumed composure, but filled with the fury of a discovered traitor and a humiliated despot.

A fleet under the command of Count Horn, the admiral of the United Provinces, waited at Flessingue to form his escort to Spain. At the very moment of his departure, William of Nassau, prince of Orange and governor of Zealand, waited on him to pay his official respects. The king, taking him apart from the other attendant nobles, recommended him to hasten the execution of several gentlemen and wealthy citizens attached to the newly introduced religious opinions. Then, quite suddenly, whether in the random impulse of suppressed rage, or that his piercing glance discovered William's secret feelings in his countenance, he accused him with having been the means of thwarting his designs. "Sire," replied Nassau, "it was the work of the national states."—"No!" cried Philip, grasping him furiously by the arm; "it was not done by the states, but by you, and you alone!"—Schiller. The words of Philip were: "*No, no los estados; ma vos, vos, vos!*" *Vos* thus used in Spanish is a term of contempt, equivalent to *toi* in French.

This glorious accusation was not repelled. He who had saved his country in unmasking the designs of its tyrant admitted by his silence his title to the hatred of the one and the gratitude of the other. On the 20th of August, Philip embarked and set sail; turning his back forever on the country which offered the first check to his despotism; and, after a perilous voyage, he arrived in that which permitted a free indulgence to his ferocious and sanguinary career.

For some time after Philip's departure, the Netherlands continued to enjoy considerable prosperity. From the period of the Peace of Câteau-Cambresis, commerce and navigation had acquired new and increasing activity. The fisheries, but particularly that of herrings, became daily more important; that one alone occupying two thousand boats. While Holland, Zealand and Friesland made this progress in their peculiar branches of industry, the southern provinces were not less active or successful. Spain and the colonies offered such a mart for the objects of their manufacture that in a single year they received from Flanders fifty large ships filled with articles of household furniture and utensils. The exportation of woollen goods amounted to enormous sums. Bruges alone sold annually to the amount of four million florins of stuffs of Spanish, and as much of English, wool; and the least value of the florin then was quadruple its present worth. The commerce with England, though less important than that with Spain, was calculated yearly at twenty-four million florins, which was chiefly clear profit to the Netherlands, as their exportations consisted almost entirely of objects of their own manufacture. Their commercial relations with France, Germany, Italy, Portugal, and the Levant, were daily increasing. Antwerp was the centre of this prodigious trade. Several sovereigns, among others Elizabeth of England, had recognized agents in that city, equivalent to consuls of the present times; and loans of immense amount were frequently negotiated by them with wealthy merchants, who furnished them, not in negotiable bills or for unredeemable debentures, but in solid gold, and on a simple acknowledgment.

Flanders and Brabant were still the richest and most flourishing portions of the state. Some municipal fêtes given about this time afford a notion of their opulence. On one of these occasions the town of Mechlin sent a deputation to Antwerp, consisting of three hundred and twenty-six horsemen dressed in velvet and satin with gold and silver ornaments; while those of Brussels consisted of three hundred and forty, as splendidly equipped, and accompanied by seven huge triumphal chariots and seventy-eight carriages of various constructions—a prodigious number for those days.

But the splendor and prosperity which thus sprung out of the national industry and independence, and which a wise or a generous sovereign would have promoted, or at least have established on a permanent basis, was destined speedily to sink beneath the bigoted fury of Philip II. The new government which he had established was most ingeniously adapted to produce every imaginable evil to the state. The king, hundreds of leagues distant, could not himself issue an order but with a lapse of time ruinous to any object of pressing importance. The stadtholderess, who represented him, having but a nominal authority, was forced to follow her instructions, and liable to have all her acts reversed; besides which, she had the king's orders to consult her private council on all affairs whatever, and the council of state on any matter of paramount importance. These two councils, however, contained the elements of a serious opposition to the royal projects, in the persons of the patriot nobles sprinkled among Philip's devoted creatures. Thus the influence of the crown was often thwarted, if not actually balanced; and the proposals which emanated from it frequently opposed by the stadtholderess herself. She, although a woman of masculine appearance and habits,[1] was

---

[1] Strada.

possessed of no strength of mind. Her prevailing sentiment seemed to be dread of the king; yet she was at times influenced by a sense of justice, and by the remonstrances of the well-judging members of her councils. But these were not all the difficulties that clogged the machinery of the state. After the king, the government, and the councils, had deliberated on any measure, its execution rested with the provincial governors or stadtholders, or the magistrates of the towns. Almost every one of these, being strongly attached to the laws and customs of the nation, hesitated, or refused to obey the orders conveyed to them, when those orders appeared illegal. Some, however, yielded to the authority of the government; so it often happened that an edict, which in one district was carried into full effect, was in others deferred, rejected, or violated, in a way productive of great confusion in the public affairs.

Philip was conscious that he had himself to blame for the consequent disorder. In nominating the members of the two councils, he had overreached himself in his plan for silently sapping the liberty that was so obnoxious to his designs. But to neutralize the influence of the restive members, he had left Granvelle the first place in the administration. This man, an immoral ecclesiastic, an eloquent orator, a supple courtier, and a profound politician, bloated with pride, envy, insolence, and vanity, was the real head of the government.[1] Next to him among the royalist party was Viglius, president of the privy council, an erudite schoolman, attached less to the broad principles of justice than to the letter of the laws, and thus carrying pedantry into the very councils of the state. Next in order came the count de Berlaimont, head of the financial department—a stern and intolerant satellite of the court, and a furious enemy to those national institutions which operated as checks upon

---

[1] Strada, a royalist, a Jesuit, and therefore a fair witness on this point, uses the following words in portraying the character of this odious minister: *Animum avidum invidumque, ac simultates inter principem et populos occulti foventum.*

fraud. These three individuals formed the stadtholderess's privy council. The remaining creatures of the king were mere subaltern agents.

A government so composed could scarcely fail to excite discontent and create danger to the public weal. The first proof of incapacity was elicited by the measures required for the departure of the Spanish troops. The period fixed by the king had already expired, and these obnoxious foreigners were still in the country, living in part on pillage, and each day committing some new excess. Complaints were carried in successive gradation from the government to the council, and from the council to the king. The Spaniards were removed to Zealand; but instead of being embarked at any of its ports, they were detained there on various pretexts. Money, ships, or, on necessity, a wind, was professed to be still wanting for their final removal, by those who found excuses for delay in every element of nature or subterfuge of art. In the meantime those ferocious soldiers ravaged a part of the country. The simple natives at length declared they would open the sluices of their dikes; preferring to be swallowed by the waters rather than remain exposed to the cruelty and rapacity of those Spaniards. Still the embarkation was postponed; until the king, requiring his troops in Spain for some domestic project, they took their long-desired departure in the beginning of the year 1561.

The public discontent at this just cause was soon, however, overwhelmed by one infinitely more important and lasting. The Belgian clergy had hitherto formed a free and powerful order in the state, governed and represented by four bishops, chosen by the chapters of the towns or elected by the monks of the principal abbeys. These bishops, possessing an independent territorial revenue, and not directly subject to the influence of the crown, had interests and feelings in common with the nation. But Philip had prepared, and the pope had sanctioned, the new system of ecclesiastical organization before alluded to, and the provisional government now put it into execution. Instead of four bishops, it was intended to appoint eighteen, their nomination being vested in the king. By a wily system of trickery, the subserviency of the abbeys was also aimed at. The new prelates, on a pretended principle of economy, were endowed with the title of abbots of the chief monasteries of their respective dioceses. Thus not only would they enjoy the immense wealth of these establishments, but the political rights of the abbots whom they were to succeed; and the whole of the ecclesiastical order become gradually represented (after the death of the then living abbots) by the creatures of the crown.

The consequences of this vital blow to the integrity of the national institutions were evident; and the indignation of both clergy and laity was universal. Every legal means of opposition was resorted to, but the people were without leaders; the states were not in session. While the authority of the pope and the king combined, the reverence excited by the very name of religion, and the address and perseverance of the government, formed too powerful a combination, and triumphed over the national discontents which had not yet been formed into resistance. The new bishops were appointed; Granvelle securing for himself the archiepiscopal see of Mechlin, with the title of primate of the Low Countries. At the same time Paul IV. put the crowning point to the capital of his ambition, by presenting him with a cardinal's hat.

The new bishops were to a man most violent, intolerant, and it may be conscientious, opponents to the wide-spreading doctrines of reform. The execution of the edicts against heresy was confided to them. The provincial governors and inferior magistrates were commanded to aid them with a strong arm; and the most unjust and frightful persecution immediately commenced. But still some of these governors and magistrates, considering themselves not only the officers of the prince, but the protectors of the people, and the defenders of the laws rather than of the faith, did not blindly conform to those harsh and illegal commands. The Prince of Orange, stadtholder of Holland, Zealand, and Utrecht, and the count of Egmont, governor of Flanders and Artois, permitted no persecutions in those five provinces. But in various places the very people, even when influenced by their superiors, openly opposed it. Catholics as well as Protestants were indignant at the atrocious spectacles of cruelty presented on all sides. The public peace was endangered by isolated acts of resistance, and fears of a general insurrection soon became universal.

The apparent temporizing or seeming uncertainty of the champions of the new doctrines formed the great obstacle to the reformation, and tended to prolong the dreadful struggle which was now only commencing in the Low Countries. It was a matter of great difficulty to convince the people that popery was absurd, and at the same time to set limits to the absurdity. Had the change been from blind belief to total infidelity, it would (as in a modern instance) have been much easier, though less lasting. Men might, in a time of such excitement, have been persuaded that *all* religion productive of abuses such as then abounded was a farce, and that common sense called for its abolition. But when the boundaries of belief became a question; when the world was told it ought to reject some doctrines, and retain others which seemed as difficult of comprehension; when one tenet was pronounced idolatry, and to doubt another declared damnation—the world either exploded or recoiled: it went too far or it shrank back; plunged into atheism, or relapsed into popery. It was thus the reformation was checked in the first instance. Its supporters were the strong-minded and intelligent; and they never, and least of all in those days, formed the mass. Superstition and bigotry had enervated the intellects of the majority; and the high resolve of those with whom the great work commenced was mixed with a severity that materially retarded its progress. For though personal interests, as with Henry VIII. of England, and rigid enthusiasm, as with Calvin, strengthened the infant reformation; the first led to violence which irritated

TO ESTABLISHMENT OF THE INQUISITION

many, the second to austerity which disgusted them; and it was soon discovered that the change was almost confined to forms of practice, and that the essentials of abuse were likely to be carefully preserved. All these, **and other** arguments, artfully modified to distract the **people, were urged** by the new bishops **in the** Netherlands, **and by those whom** they employed to **arrest the progress of reform.**

Among the various **causes** of the general confusion, **the** situation **of Brabant gave to that province** a peculiar **share** of suffering. **Brussels,** its capital, **being the seat** of **government, had no particular** chief magistrate, like **the** other **provinces. The executive** power **was** therefore **wholly** confided **to the** municipal authorities **and the** territorial proprietors. But these, **though** generally **patriotic in their views, were** divided **into a** multiplicity **of different opinions. Rivalry and** resentment produced **a total want of union, ended in anarchy, and** prepared **the way for civil war.** William **of** Nassau penetrated **the cause, and proposed the remedy** in moving for the appointment **of a provincial governor. This proposition terrified Granvelle, who saw, as clearly as** did his sagacious **opponent in the council, that the nomination of a special protector** between **the people and the government would have paralyzed all his efforts for hurrying on the** discord and resistance which **were meant to be the** plausible **excuses for the introduction of** arbitrary **power. He therefore** energetically **dissented from the proposed measure, and** William **immediately desisted from his demand. But he at** the **same** time claimed, **in** the name **of the whole country,** the convocation of **the** states-general. This assembly **alone was competent to** decide what **was** just, **legal, and** obligatory for **each province and** every town. **Governors, magistrates, and** simple citizens, would thus have some rule for their common conduct; and the government would be at least endowed with **the** dignity of uniformity and steadiness. The ministers endeavored to evade a demand which they were at first unwilling openly to refuse. But the firm demeanor and persuasive eloquence of the Prince of Orange carried before them all who were not actually bought by the crown; and Granvelle found himself at length forced to avow that an express order from the king forbade the convocation of the states, on any pretext, during his absence.

The veil was thus rent asunder which had in some measure concealed the deformity of Philip's despotism. The result was a powerful confederacy, among all who held it odious, for the overthrow of Granvelle, to whom they chose to attribute the king's conduct; thus bringing into practical result the sound principle of ministerial responsibility, without which, except in some peculiar case of local urgency or political crisis, the name of constitutional government is but a mockery. Many of the royalist nobles united for the national cause; and even the stadtholderess joined her efforts to theirs, for an object which would relieve her from the tyranny which none felt more than she did. Those who composed this confederacy against the minister were actuated by a great variety of motives. The duchess of Parma hated him, as a domestic spy robbing her of all real authority; the royalist nobles, as an insolent upstart at every instant mortifying their pride. The counts Egmont and Horn, with nobler sentiments, opposed him as the author of their country's growing misfortunes. But it is doubtful if any of the confederates except the Prince of Orange clearly saw that they were putting themselves in direct and personal opposition to the king himself. William alone, clear-sighted in politics and profound in his views, knew, in thus devoting himself to the public cause, the adversary with whom he entered the lists.

This great man, for whom the national traditions still preserve the sacred title of "father" (Vader-Willem), and who was in truth not merely the parent but the political creator of the country, was at this period in his thirtieth year. He already joined the vigor of manhood to the wisdom of age. Brought up under the eye of Charles V., whose sagacity soon discovered his precocious talents, he was admitted to the councils of the emperor at a time of life which was little advanced beyond mere boyhood. He alone was chosen by this powerful **sovereign** to be present at the audiences which he gave **to foreign** ambassadors, which proves that in early **youth he well deserved by his discretion** the surname of "the **taciturn." It was on the arm of** William, then twenty years of **age, and already named** by him to **the command of the Belgian troops, that** this powerful monarch **leaned for support on the memorable day of** his abdication; **and he immediately afterward employed him on** the **important mission of bearing the imperial crown to** his **brother** Ferdinand, **in whose favor he had resigned it. William's** grateful **attachment to Charles did not blind him** to the **demerits of** Philip. **He repaired to France, as one** of **the hostages on the part of the latter monarch for the fulfilment of the peace of** Câteau **Cambresis; and he then learned from the lips of** Henry **II., who soon conceived a high esteem for** him, the measures **reciprocally agreed on** by **the two sovereigns for the oppression of their subjects. From that moment his mind was made up on the character of Philip, and on** the part which he **had himself to perform; and he never felt a** doubt on the **first point, nor swerved** from **the latter.**

But **even before his patriotism was openly displayed,** Philip had taken a **dislike to one in whom his shrewdness** quickly discovered **an intellect of which he was jealous.** He **could not actually remove William from all interference with** public **affairs; but he refused him the government of** Flanders, **and** opposed, in secret, his projected **marriage with a** princess of the House of Lorraine, which was calculated **to** bring him a considerable accession of **fortune, and** consequently **of influence. It** may **be therefore said that William, in** his **subsequent** conduct, **was urged** by **motives of** personal **enmity against** Philip. **Be it so.** We do **not seek to raise him** above the **common** feelings **of** humanity; **and we should risk the** sinking him below them, if **we supposed him insensible to the** natural effects of **just resentment.**

The secret impulses of conduct can never be known beyond the individual's **own** breast; but actions must, however questionable, **be taken as** the tests of motives. In all those of William's illustrious career we can detect none that might be **supposed to spring** from vulgar or base feelings. If his **hostility to Philip was** indeed increased by private dislike, **he has at least set an** example of unparalleled dignity in his **method of revenge; but in calmly** considering and weighing, without **deciding on** the question, we see nothing that **should deprive William of an** unsullied title to pure and perfect patriotism. The injuries done **to** him **by** Philip at this period were not of a nature to excite any violent hatred. Enough of public wrong was inflicted to arouse the patriot, but not of private ill to inflame the man. Neither was William of a vindictive disposition. He was never known to turn the knife of an assassin against his royal rival, even when the blade hired by the latter glanced from him reeking with his blood. And though William's **enmity may have been kept alive or strengthened by the** provocations he received, it is certain that, if a foe to the king, **he was,** as long as it was possible, the faithful **counsellor** of the crown. **He spared no pains to impress on the** monarch who hated **him the real means for preventing the** coming evils; and **had not a revolution been absolutely** inevitable, it is he who **would have prevented it.**

Such was the chief of the patriot party, chosen by the **silent election of general** opinion, and by that involuntary **homage to genius which** leads individuals in the train of those **master-minds who take the lead in** public affairs. Counts **Egmont and Horn, and some** others, largely shared with him the popular favor. The multitude could not for some time distinguish **the** uncertain and capricious opposi**tion of an** offended courtier from the determined resistance **of a** great man. William was still comparatively young; he had lived long out of the country; and it was little by little that his eminent public virtues were developed and understood.

The great object of immediate **good** was the removal of Cardinal Granvelle. William boldly put himself **at** the head of the confederacy. He wrote to the **king**, conjointly with Counts Egmont and Horn, faithfully portraying **the state of** affairs. The duchess of Parma backed this remonstrance with a strenuous request for Granvelle's dismissal. Philip's reply to the three noblemen was a mere tissue of duplicity to obtain delay, accompanied by an invitation to Count Egmont **to repair to Madrid, to hear** his sentiments at large by word **of mouth. His only** answer to the stadtholderess was a positive recommendation to use every possible means **to** disunite and breed ill-will among the three confederate **lords. It was** difficult to deprive William of the confidence of his friends, and impossible to **deceive** him. **He** saw **the** trap prepared by the royal intrigues, restrained **Egmont for a** while **from** the fatal step **he** was but **too well inclined to take, and persuaded him and Horn to renew with him their** firm but respectful representations; **at the same time begging permission** to resign their various **employments,** and **simultaneously** ceasing to appear at **the court of** the stadtholderess.

In the meantime **every possible** indignity **was** offered to the cardinal **by private pique and** public satire. Several **lords, following Count Egmont's example, had** a kind **of capuchon or fool's-cap embroidered on the liveries of their varlets; and it was generally known that this was meant as a practical parody on the cardinal's hat.** The crowd **laughed heartily at this** stupid pleasantry; and **the coarse satire of the times may be judged** by a caricature, which was **forwarded to the cardinal's** own hands, representing him in **the act of** hatching a **nest** full of eggs, from which a crowd of bishops escaped, while overhead was the devil *in propriâ personâ*, with **the** following scroll: "This is my well-beloved son—listen to him!"

Philip, thus driven before the popular voice, found himself forced to the choice of throwing off the mask at once, or of sacrificing Granvelle. An invincible inclination for manœuvring and deceit decided him on the latter measure;

and the cardinal, recalled but not disgraced, quitted the Netherlands on the 10th of March, 1564. The secret instructions to the stadtholderess remained unrevoked; the president Viglius succeeded to the post which Granvelle had occupied; and it was clear that the projects of the king had suffered no change.

Nevertheless some good resulted from the departure of the unpopular minister. The public fermentation subsided; the patriot lords reappeared at court; and the Prince of Orange acquired an increasing influence in the council and over the stadtholderess, who by his advice adopted a conciliatory line of conduct—a fallacious but still a temporary hope for the nation. But the calm was of short duration. Scarcely was this moderation evinced by the government, when Philip, obstinate in his designs, and outrageous in his resentment, sent an order to have the edicts against heresy put into most rigorous execution, and to proclaim throughout the seventeen provinces the furious decree of the Council of Trent.

The revolting cruelty and illegality of the first edicts were already admitted. As to the decrees of this memorable council, they were only adapted for countries in submission to an absolute despotism. They were received in the Netherlands with general reprobation. Even the new bishops loudly denounced them as unjust innovations; and thus Philip found zealous opponents in those on whom he had reckoned as his most servile tools. The stadtholderess was not the less urged to implicit obedience to the orders of the king by Viglius and De Berlaimont, who took upon themselves an almost menacing tone. The duchess assembled a council of state, and asked its advice as to her proceedings. The Prince of Orange at once boldly proposed disobedience to measures fraught with danger to the monarchy and ruin to the nation. The council could not resist his appeal to their best feelings. His proposal that fresh remonstrances should be addressed to the king met with almost general support. The president Viglius, who had spoken in the opening of the council in favor of the king's orders, was overwhelmed by William's reasoning, and demanded time to prepare his reply. His agitation during the debate, and his despair of carrying the measures against the patriot party, brought on in the night an attack of apoplexy.

It was resolved to despatch a special envoy to Spain, to explain to Philip the views of the council, and to lay before him a plan proposed by the Prince of Orange for forming a junction between the two councils and that of finance, and forming them into one body. The object of this measure was at once to give greater union and power to the provisional government, to create a central administration in the Netherlands, and to remove from some obscure and avaricious financiers the exclusive management of the national resources. The Count of Egmont, chosen by the council for this important mission, set out for Madrid in the month of February, 1565. Philip received him with profound hypocrisy; loaded him with the most flattering promises; sent him back in the utmost elation: and when the credulous count returned to Brussels, he found that the written orders, of which he was the bearer, were in direct variance with every word which the king had uttered.

These orders were chiefly concerning the reiterated subject of the persecution to be inflexibly pursued against the religious reformers. Not satisfied with the hitherto established forms of punishment, Philip now expressly commanded that the more revolting means decreed by his father in the rigor of his early zeal, such as burning, living burial, and the like, should be adopted; and he somewhat more obscurely directed that the victims should be no longer publicly immolated, but secretly destroyed. He endeavored, by this vague phraseology, to avoid the actual utterance of the word "inquisition"; but he thus virtually established that atrocious tribunal, with attributes still more terrific than even in Spain; for there the condemned had at least the consolation of dying in open day, and of displaying the fortitude which is rarely proof against the horror of a private execution. Philip had thus consummated his treason against the principles of justice and the practices of jurisprudence, which had heretofore characterized the country; and against the most vital of those privileges which he had solemnly sworn to maintain.

His design of establishing this horrible tribunal, so impiously named "holy" by its founders, had been long suspected by the people of the Netherlands. The expression of those fears had reached him more than once. He as often replied by assurances that he had formed no such project, and particularly to Count d'Egmont during his recent visit to Madrid. But at that very time he assembled a conclave of his creatures, doctors of theology, of whom he formally demanded an opinion as to whether he could conscientiously tolerate two sorts of religion in the Netherlands. The doctors, hoping to please him, replied, that "he might, for the avoidance of a greater evil." Philip trembled with rage, and exclaimed, with a threatening tone, "I ask not if I *can*, but if I *ought*." The theologians read in this question the nature of the expected reply; and it was amply conformable to his wish. He immediately threw himself on his knees before a crucifix, and raising his hands toward heaven, put up a prayer for strength in his resolution to pursue as deadly enemies all who viewed that effigy with feelings different from his own. If this were not really a sacrilegious farce, it must be that the blaspheming bigot believed the Deity to be a monster of cruelty like himself.

Even Viglius was terrified by the nature of Philip's commands; and the patriot lords once more withdrew from all share in the government, leaving to the duchess of Parma and her ministers the whole responsibility of the new measures. They were at length put into actual and vigorous execution in the beginning of the year 1566. The inquisitors of the faith, with their familiars, stalked abroad boldly in the devoted provinces, carrying persecution and death in their train. Numerous but partial insurrections opposed these odious intruders. Every district and town became the scene of frightful executions or tumultuous resistance. The converts to the new doctrines multiplied, as usual, under the effects of persecution. "There was nowhere to be seen," says a contemporary author, "the meanest mechanic who did not find a weapon to strike down the murderers of his compatriots." Holland, Zealand and Utrecht alone escaped from those fast accumulating horrors. William of Nassau was there.

CHAPTER VIII

COMMENCEMENT OF THE REVOLUTION

A.D. 1566

THE stadtholderess and her ministers now began to tremble. Philip's favorite counsellors advised him to yield to the popular despair; but nothing could change his determination to pursue his bloody game to the last chance. He had foreseen the impossibility of reducing the country to slavery as long as it maintained its tranquillity, and that union which forms in itself the elements and the cement of strength. It was from deep calculation that he had excited the troubles, and now kept them alive. He knew that the structure of illegal power could only be raised on the ruins of public rights and national happiness; and the materials of desolation found sympathy in his congenial mind.

And now in reality began the awful revolution of the Netherlands against their tyrant. In a few years this so lately flourishing and happy nation presented a frightful picture; and in the midst of European peace, prosperity, and civilization, the wickedness of one prince drew down on the country he misgoverned more evils than it had suffered for centuries from the worst effects of its foreign foes.

William of Nassau has been accused of having at length urged on the stadtholderess to promulgate the final edicts and the resolutions of the Council of Trent, and then retiring from the council of state. This line of conduct may be safely admitted and fairly defended by his admirers. He had seen the uselessness of remonstrance against the intentions of the king. Every possible means had been tried, without effect, to soften his pitiless heart to the sufferings of the country. At length the moment came when the people had reached that pitch of despair which is the great force of the oppressed, and William felt that their strength was now equal to the contest he had long foreseen. It is therefore absurd to accuse him of artifice in the exercise of that wisdom which rarely failed him on any important crisis. A change of circumstances gives a new name to actions and motives; and it would be hard to blame William of Nassau for the only point in which he bore the least resemblance to Philip of Spain—that depth of penetration, which the latter turned to every base and the former to every noble purpose.

Up to the present moment the Prince of Orange and the Counts Egmont and Horn, with their partisans and friends, had sincerely desired the public peace, and acted in the common interest of the king and the people. But all the nobles had not acted with the same constitutional moderation. Many of those, disappointed on personal accounts, others professing the new doctrines, and the rest variously affected by manifold motives, formed a body of violent and sometimes of imprudent malcontents. The marriage of Alexander, prince of Parma, son of the stadtholderess, which was at this time celebrated at Brussels, brought together an immense number of these dissatisfied nobles, who became thus drawn into closer connection, and whose national candor was more than usually brought out in the confidential intercourse of society. Politics and patriotism were the common subjects of conversation in the various convivial meetings that took place. Two German nobles, Counts Holle and Schwarzemberg, at that period in the Netherlands, loudly proclaimed the favorable disposition of the princes of the empire toward the Belgians. It was supposed even thus early that negotiations had been opened with several of those sovereigns. In short, nothing seemed wanting but a leader, to give consistency and weight to the confederacy which was as yet but in embryo. This was doubly furnished in the persons of Louis of Nassau and

Henry de **Brederode**. The former, brother of the Prince of **Orange, was possessed** of many of those brilliant qualities which **mark men as** worthy of distinction in times of peril. Educated at Geneva, he was passionately attached to the reformed religion, and identified in his hatred the Catholic Church and the tyranny of Spain. Brave and impetuous, he was, to his elder brother, but as an adventurous partisan compared with a sagacious general. He loved William as well as he did their common cause, and his life was devoted to both.

Henry de Brederode, lord of Vienen and marquis of Utrecht, was descended from the ancient counts of Holland. This illustrious origin, which in his own eyes formed a high claim to distinction, had not procured him any of those employments or dignities which he considered his due. He was presumptuous and rash, and rather a fluent speaker than an eloquent orator. Louis of Nassau was thoroughly inspired by the justice of the cause he espoused; De Brederode espoused it for the glory of becoming its champion. The first only wished for action; the latter longed for distinction. But neither the enthusiasm of Nassau, nor the vanity of De Brederode, was allied with those superior attributes required to form a hero.

The confederation acquired its perfect organization in the month of February, 1566, **on** the **tenth of which** month its **celebrated manifesto was** signed **by its numerous** adherents. The first name affixed to this document was that of **Philip de Marnix,** lord **of St. Aldegonde, from** whose pen **it emanated; a man of great talents** both as soldier and writer. **Numbers of the nobility** followed him on this **muster-roll of** patriotism, and many of the most zealous **royalists** were among them. This remarkable proclamation of general feeling consisted chiefly in a powerful reprehension of the illegal establishment of the Inquisition in the Low Countries, and a solemn obligation on the members of the confederacy to unite in the common cause against this **detested nuisance.** Men of all ranks and classes offered their signatures, and several Catholic priests among the rest. The Prince of Orange, and the Counts Egmont, Horn, and Meghem, declined becoming actual parties to this bold measure; and when the question was debated as to the most appropriate way of presenting an address to the stadtholderess these noblemen advised the mildest and most respectful demeanor on the part of the purposed deputation.

At the first intelligence of these proceedings, the duchess of Parma, absorbed by terror, had no resource but to assemble hastily such members of the council of state as were at Brussels; and she entreated, by the most pressing letters, the Prince of Orange and Count Horn to resume their places at this council. But three courses of conduct seemed applicable to the emergency: to take up arms; to grant the demands of the confederates; or to temporize and to amuse them with a feint of moderation, until the orders of the king might be obtained from Spain. It was not, however, till after a lapse of four months that the council finally met to deliberate on these important questions; and during this long interval at such a crisis the confederates gained constant accessions to their numbers, and completely consolidated their plans. The opinions in the council were greatly divided as to the mode of treatment toward those whom one party considered as patriots acting in their constitutional rights, and the other as rebels in open revolt against the king. The Prince of Orange and De Berlaimont were the principal leaders and chief speakers on either side. But the reasonings of the former, backed by the urgency of events, carried the majority of the suffrages; and a promised redress of grievances was agreed on beforehand as the anticipated answer to the coming demands.

Even while the council of state held its sittings, the report was spread through Brussels that the confederates were approaching. And at length they did enter the city, to the amount of some hundreds of the representatives of the first families in the country. On the following day, the 5th of April, 1566, they walked in solemn procession to the palace.

Their demeanor was highly imposing, from their mingled air of forbearance and determination. All Brussels thronged out to gaze and sympathize with this extraordinary spectacle of men whose resolute step showed they were no common suppliants, but whose modest bearing had none of the seditious air of faction. The stadtholderess received the distinguished petitioners with courtesy, listened to their detail of grievances, and returned a moderate, conciliatory, but evasive answer.

The confederation, which owed its birth to, and was cradled in social enjoyments, was consolidated in the midst of a feast. The day following this first deputation to the stadtholderess, De Brederode gave a grand repast to his associates in the Hotel de Culembourg. Three hundred guests were present. Inflamed by joy and hope, their spirits rose high under the influence of wine, and temperance gave way to temerity. In the midst of their carousing, some of the members remarked that when the stadtholderess received the written petition, Count Berlaimont observed to her that "she had nothing to fear from such a band of beggars" (*las de* GUEUX). The fact was that many of the confederates were, from individual extravagance and mismanagement, reduced to such a state of poverty as to justify in some sort the sarcasm. The chiefs of the company being at that very moment debating on the name which they should choose for this patriotic league, the title of Gueux was instantly proposed, and adopted with acclamation. The reproach it was originally intended to convey became neutralized, as its general application to men of all ranks and fortunes concealed its effect as a stigma on many to whom it might be seriously applied. Neither were examples wanting of the most absurd and apparently dishonoring nicknames being elsewhere adopted by powerful political parties. "Long live the Gueux!" was the toast given and tumultuously drunk by this mad-brained company; and Brederode, setting no bounds to the boisterous excitement which followed, procured immediately, and slung across his shoulders, a wallet such as was worn by pilgrims and beggars; drank to the health of all present, in a wooden cup or porringer; and loudly swore that he was ready to sacrifice his fortune and life for the common cause. Each man passed round the bowl, which he first put to his lips, repeated the oath, and thus pledged himself to the compact. The wallet next went the rounds of the whole assembly, and was finally hung upon a nail driven into the wall for the purpose; and gazed on with such enthusiasm as the emblems of political or religious faith, however worthless or absurd, never fail to inspire in the minds of enthusiasts.

The tumult caused by this ceremony, so ridiculous in itself, but so sublime in its results, attracted to the spot the Prince of Orange and Counts Egmont and Horn, whose presence is universally attributed by the historians to accident, but which was probably that kind of chance that leads medical practitioners in our days to the field where a duel is fought. They entered; and Brederode, who did the honors of the mansion, forced them to be seated, and to join in the festivity. The following was Egmont's account of their conduct: "We drank a single glass of wine each, to shouts of 'Long live the king! Long live the Gueux!' It was the first time I had heard the confederacy so named, and I avow that it displeased me; but the times were so critical that people were obliged to tolerate many things contrary to their inclinations, and I believed myself on this occasion to act with perfect innocence." The appearance of three such distinguished personages heightened the general excitement; and the most important assemblage that had for centuries met together in the Netherlands mingled the discussion of affairs of state with all the burlesque extravagance of a débauch. But this frantic scene did not finish the affair. What they resolved on while drunk, they prepared to perform when sober. Rallying signs and watchwords were adopted and soon displayed. It was thought that nothing better suited the occasion than the immediate adoption of the costume as well as the title of beggary. In a very few days the city streets were filled with men in gray cloaks, fashioned on the model of those used by mendicants and pilgrims. Each confederate caused this uniform to be worn by every member of his family, and replaced with it the livery of his servants. Several fastened to their girdles or their sword-hilts small wooden drinking-cups, clasp-knives, and other symbols of the begging fraternity; while all soon wore on their breasts a medal of gold or silver, representing on one side the effigy of Philip, with the words, "Faithful to the king"; and on the reverse, two hands clasped, with the motto, "Jusqu' à la besace" (Even to the wallet). From this origin arose the application of the word Gueux, in its political sense, as common to all the inhabitants of the Netherlands who embraced the cause of the Reformation and took up arms against their tyrant. Having presented two subsequent remonstrances to the stadtholderess, and obtained some consoling promises of moderation, the chief confederates quitted Brussels, leaving several directors to sustain their cause in the capital; while they themselves spread into the various provinces, exciting the people to join the legal and constitutional resistance with which they were resolved to oppose the march of bigotry and despotism.

A new form of edict was now decided on by the stadtholderess and her council; and after various insidious and illegal but successful tricks, the consent of several of the provinces was obtained to the adoption of measures that, under a guise of comparative moderation, were little less abominable than those commanded by the king. These were formally signed by the council, and despatched to Spain to receive Philip's sanction, and thus acquire the force of law. The embassy to Madrid was confided to the marquis of Bergen and the baron de Montigny; the latter of whom was brother to Count Horn, and had formerly been employed on a like mission. Montigny appears to have had some qualms of apprehension in undertaking this new office. His good genius seemed for a while to stand between him and **the fate** which awaited him. **An** accident which happened to his colleague allowed an excuse **for** retarding his journey. But the stadtholderess urged him away; he set out, and reached his **destination;** not to defend the cause of his **country at** the foot of the **throne, but to** perish a victim **to his patriotism.**

The situation **of the** patriot lords was at this crisis peculi**arly** embarrassing. **The conduct of the** confederates was **so essentially tantamount to open** rebellion, **that** the Prince **of Orange and his friends found it** almost impossible **to preserve a neutrality between the court and the** people. All their wishes **urged them to join at once in the** public cause; but they were restrained by **a lingering sense of loyalty to** the **king, whose employments they still held, and whose confidence they were, therefore, nominally supposed to share. They seemed reduced to the necessity of coming to an explanation, and, perhaps, a premature rupture with the government; of joining in the harsh measures it was** likely to adopt against **those with whose proceedings they** sympathized; **or,** as **a last alternative, to withdraw, as** they had done before, wholly from **all interference in** public affairs. Still their presence in **the council of** state **was, even though** their influence **had greatly decreased, of vast service to the patriots, in checking the hostility of** the court; and the confederates, on **the other hand, were** restrained from acts of open violence, **by fear of the** disapprobation of these their best and most powerful friends. Be their individual motives **of** reasoning what they might, they at length adopted the alternative above **alluded** to, and resigned their places. Count Horn retired to his estates; Count Egmont repaired to Aix-la-Chapelle, under the pretext of being ordered thither by his physicians; the **Prince of** Orange remained for a while at Brussels.

In the meanwhile, the confederation gained ground every day. Its measures had totally changed the face of affairs in all parts of the nation. The general discontent now acquired stability, and consequent importance. The chief merchants of many of the towns enrolled themselves in the patriot band. Many active and ardent minds, hitherto withheld by the doubtful construction of the association, now freely entered into it when it took the form of union and respectability. Energy, if not excess, seemed legitimatized. The vanity of the leaders was flattered by the consequence they acquired; and weak minds gladly embraced an occasion of mixing with those whose importance gave both protection and concealment to their insignificance.

An occasion so favorable for the rapid promulgation of the new doctrines was promptly taken advantage of by the French Huguenots and their Protestant brethren of Germany. The disciples of reform poured from all quarters into the Low Countries, and made prodigious progress, with all the energy of proselytes, and too often with the fury of fanatics. The three principal sects into which the reformers were divided, were those of the Anabaptists, the Calvinists, and the Lutherans. The first and least numerous were chiefly established in Friesland. The second were spread over the eastern provinces. Their doctrines being already admitted into some kingdoms of the north, they were protected by the most powerful princes of the empire. The third, and by far the most numerous and wealthy, abounded in the southern provinces, and particularly in Flanders. They were supported by the zealous efforts of French, Swiss, and German ministers; and their dogmas were nearly the same with those of the established religion of England. The city of Antwerp was the central point of union for the three sects; but the only principle they held in common was their hatred against popery, the Inquisition, and Spain.

The stadtholderess had now issued orders to the chief magistrates to proceed with moderation against the heretics; orders which were obeyed in their most ample latitude by those to whose sympathies they were so congenial. Until then, the Protestants were satisfied to meet by stealth at night; but under this negative protection of the authorities they now boldly assembled in public. Field-preachings commenced in Flanders; and the minister who first set this example was Herman Stricker, a **converted** monk, a native of Overyssel, a powerful speaker, **and a** bold enthusiast. He soon drew **together an audience of seven** thousand **persons.** A furious **magistrate** rushed among this crowd, **and** hoped **to disperse them sword in hand;** but he was **soon struck down,** mortally wounded, **with a** shower of stones. Irritated and emboldened **by** this **rash** attempt, **the Protestants** assembled in still **greater numbers near Alost; but on** this occasion **they** appeared **with poniards, guns, and halberds. They** intrenched **themselves under the protection of** wagons and all sorts of obstacles to a sudden **attack; placed** outposts and videttes; and thus took **the** field **in the** doubly dangerous aspect of fanaticism and war. **Similar assemblies** soon spread over the whole **of** Flanders, **inflamed by the** exhortations of Stricker and another **preacher, called Peter** Dathen, of Poperingue. It was calculated that fifteen thousand men attended at some of these preachings; **while a** third apostle of Calvinism, Ambrose Ville, **a** Frenchman, successfully excited the inhabitants **of Tournay,** Valenciennes, **and Antwerp, to** form a **common league for** the promulgation of **their faith.** The sudden appearance of De Brederode at **the latter place** decided their plan, and gave the courage **to fix on a day for its execution.** An immense assemblage simultaneously quitted **the** three cities at a preconcerted **time;** and when they united **their** forces at the appointed rendezvous, the preachings, exhortations, and psalm-singing commenced, **under** the auspices **of** several Huguenot and German ministers, and continued for several days in all the zealous extravagance which **may** be well imagined to characterize such a scene.

The citizens of Antwerp were terrified for the safety of the place, and courier after courier was despatched to the stadtholderess at Brussels to implore her presence. The duchess, not daring to take such a step without the authority of the king, sent Count Meghem as her representative, with proposals to the magistrates to call out the garrison. The populace soon understood the object of this messenger; and assailing him with a violent outcry, forced him to fly from the city. Then the Calvinists petitioned the magistrates for permission to openly exercise their religion, and for the grant of a temple in which to celebrate its rites. The magistrates in this conjuncture renewed their application to the stadtholderess, and entreated her to send the Prince of Orange, as the only person capable of saving the city from destruction. The duchess was forced to adopt this bitter alternative; and the prince, after repeated refusals to mix again in public affairs, yielded, at length, less to the supplications of the stadtholderess than to his own wishes to do another service to the cause of his country. At half a league from the city he was met by De Brederode, with an immense concourse of people of all sects and opinions, who hailed him as a protector from the tyranny of the king, and a savior from the dangers of their own excess. Nothing could exceed the wisdom, the firmness, and the benevolence, with which he managed all conflicting interests, and preserved tranquillity amid a chaos of opposing prejudices and passions.

From the first establishment of the field-preachings the stadtholderess had implored the confederate lords to aid her for the re-establishment of order. De Brederode seized this excuse for convoking a general meeting of the associates, which consequently took place at the town of St. Trond, in the district of Liege. Full two thousand of the members appeared on the summons. The language held in this assembly was much stronger and less equivocal than that formerly used. The delay in the arrival of the king's answer presaged ill as to his intentions; while the rapid growth of the public power seemed to mark the present as the time for successfully demanding all that the people required. Several of the Catholic members, still royalists at heart, were shocked to hear a total liberty of conscience spoken of as one of the privileges sought for. The young count of Mansfield, among others, withdrew immediately from the confederation; and thus the first stone seemed to be removed from this imperfectly constructed edifice.

The Prince of Orange and Count Egmont were applied to, and appointed by the stadtholderess, with full powers to treat with the confederates. Twelve of the latter, among whom were Louis of Nassau, De Brederode, and De Culembourg, met them by appointment at Duffle, a village not far from Mechlin. The result of the conference was a respectful but firm address to the stadtholderess, repelling her accusations of having entered into foreign treaties; declaring their readiness to march against the French troops, should they set foot in the country; and claiming, with the utmost force of reasoning, the convocation of the states-general. This was replied to by an entreaty that they would still wait patiently for twenty-four days, in hopes of an answer from the king; and she sent the marquess of Bergen in all speed to Madrid, to support Montigny in his efforts to obtain some prompt decision from Philip. The king, who was then at Segovia, assembled his council, consisting of the duke of Alva and eight other grandees. The two deputies from the Netherlands attended at the deliberations, which were held for several successive days; but the king was never present. The whole state of affairs being debated with what appears a calm and dispassionate view, considering the hostile prejudices of this council, it was decided to advise the king to adopt generally a more moderate line of conduct in the Netherlands, and to abolish the inquisition; at the same time prohibiting under the most awful threats all confederation, assemblage, or public preachings, under any pretext whatever.

The king's first care on receiving this advice was to order, in all the principal towns of Spain and the Netherlands, prayer and processions to implore the divine approbation on the resolutions which he had formed. He appeared then in person at the council of state, and issued a decree, by which he refused his consent to the convocation of the states-general, and bound himself to take several German regiments into his pay. He ordered the duchess of Parma, by a private letter, to immediately cause to be raised three thousand cavalry and ten thousand foot, and he remitted to her for this purpose three hundred thousand florins in gold. He next wrote with his own hand to several of his partisans in the various towns, encouraging them in their fidelity to his purpose, and promising them his support. He rejected the adoption of the moderation recommended to him; but he consented to the abolition of the inquisition in its most odious sense, re-establishing that modified species of ecclesiastical tyranny which had been introduced into the Netherlands by Charles V. The people of that devoted country were thus successful in obtaining one important concession from the king, and in meeting unexpected consideration from this Spanish council. Whether these measures had been calculated with a view to their failure, it is not now easy to determine; at all events they came too late. When Philip's letters reached Brussels, the iconoclasts or image-breakers were abroad.

It requires no profound research to comprehend the impulse which leads a horde of fanatics to the most monstrous excesses. That the deeds of the iconoclasts arose from the spontaneous outburst of mere vulgar fury, admits of no doubt. The aspersion which would trace those deeds to the meeting of St. Trond, and fix the infamy on the body of nobility there assembled, is scarcely worthy of refutation. The very lowest of the people were the actors as well as the authors of the outrages, which were at once shocking to every friend of liberty, and injurious to that sacred cause. Artois and western Flanders were the scenes of the first exploits of the iconoclasts. A band of peasants, intermixed with beggars and various other vagabonds, to the amount of about three hundred, urged by fanaticism and those baser passions which animate every lawless body of men, armed with hatchets, clubs, and hammers, forced open the doors of some of the village churches in the neighborhood of St. Omer, and tore down and destroyed not only the images and relics of saints, but those very ornaments which Christians of all sects hold sacred, and essential to the most simple rites of religion.

The cities of Ypres, Lille, and other places of importance, were soon subject to similar visitations; and the whole of Flanders was in a few days ravaged by furious multitudes, whose frantic energy spread terror and destruction on their route. Antwerp was protected for a while by the presence of the Prince of Orange; but an order from the stadtholderess having obliged him to repair to Brussels, a few nights after his departure the celebrated cathedral shared the fate of many a minor temple, and was utterly pillaged. The blind fury of the spoilers was not confined to the mere effigies which they considered the types of idolatry, nor even to the pictures, the vases, the sixty-six altars, and their richly wrought accessories; but it was equally fatal to the splendid organ, which was considered the finest at that time in existence. The rapidity and the order with which this torch-light scene was acted, without a single accident among the numerous doers, has excited the wonder of almost all its early historians. One of them does not hesitate to ascribe the "miracle" to the absolute agency of demons. For three days and nights these revolting scenes were acted, and every church in the city shared the fate of the cathedral, which next to St. Peter's at Rome was the most magnificent in Christendom.

Ghent, Tournay, Valenciennes, Mechlin, and other cities, were next the theatres of similar excesses; and in an incredibly short space of time above four hundred churches were pillaged in Flanders and Brabant. Zealand, Utrecht, and others of the northern provinces, suffered more or less; Friesland, Guelders, and Holland alone escaped, and even the latter but in partial instances.

These terrible scenes extinguished every hope of reconciliation with the king. An inveterate and interminable hatred was now established between him and the people; for the whole nation was identified with deeds which were in reality only shared by the most base, and were loathsome to all who were enlightened. It was in vain that the patriot nobles might hope or strive to exculpate themselves; they were sure to be held criminal either in fact or by implication. No show of loyalty, no efforts to restore order, no personal sacrifice, could save them from the hatred or screen them from the vengeance of Philip.

The affright of the stadtholderess during the short reign of anarchy and terror was without bounds. She strove to make her escape from Brussels, and was restrained from so doing only by the joint solicitations of Viglius and the various knights of the order of the Golden Fleece, consisting of the first among the nobles of all parties. But, in fact, a species of violence was used to restrain her from this most fatal step; for Viglius gave orders that the gates of the city should be shut, and egress refused to any one belonging to the court. The somewhat less terrified duchess now named Count Mansfield governor of the town, reinforced the garrison, ordered arms to be distributed to all her adherents, and then called a council to deliberate on the measures to be adopted. A compromise with the confederates and the reformers was unanimously agreed to. The Prince of Orange and Counts Egmont and Horn were once more appointed to this arduous arbitration between the court and the people. Necessity now extorted almost every concession which had been so long denied to justice and prudence. The confederates were declared absolved from all responsibility relative to their proceedings. The suppression of the Inquisition, the abolition of the edicts against heresy, and a permission for the preachings, were simultaneously published.

The confederates on their side undertook to remain faithful to the service of the king, to do their best for the establishment of order, and to punish the iconoclasts. A regular treaty to this effect was drawn up and executed by the respective plenipotentiaries, and formally approved by the stadtholderess, who affixed her sign-manual to the instrument. She only consented to this measure after a long struggle, and with tears in her eyes; and it was with a trembling hand that she wrote an account of these transactions to the king.

Soon after this the several governors repaired to their respective provinces, and their efforts for the re-establishment of tranquillity were attended with various degrees of success. Several of the ringleaders in the late excesses were executed; and this severity was not confined to the partisans of the Catholic Church. The Prince of Orange and Count Egmont, with others of the patriot lords, set the example of this just severity. John Casambrot, lord of Beckerzeel, Egmont's secretary, and a leading member of the confederation, put himself at the head of some others of the associated gentlemen, fell upon a refractory band of iconoclasts near Gramont, in Flanders, and took thirty prisoners, of whom he ordered twenty-eight to be hanged on the spot.

CHAPTER IX

TO THE ADMINISTRATION OF REQUESENS

A.D. 1566—1573

ALL the services just related in the common cause of the country and the king produced no effect on the vindictive spirit of the latter. Neither the lapse of time, the proofs of repentance, nor the fulfilment of their duty, could efface the hatred excited by a conscientious opposition to even one design of despotism.

Philip was ill at Segovia when he received accounts of the excesses of the image-breakers, and of the convention concluded with the heretics. Despatches from the stadtholderess, with private advices from Viglius, Egmont, Mansfield, Meghem, De Berlaimont, and others, gave him ample information as to the real state of things, and they thus strove to palliate their having acceded to the convention. The emperor even wrote to his royal nephew, imploring him to treat his wayward subjects with moderation, and offered his mediation between them. Philip, though severely suffering, gave great attention to the details of this correspondence, which he minutely examined, and laid before his council of state, with notes and observations taken by himself. But he took special care to send to them only such parts as he chose them to be well informed upon; his natural distrust not suffering him to have any confidential communication with men.

Again the Spanish council appears to have interfered between the people of the Netherlands and the enmity of the monarch; and the offered mediation of the emperor was recommended to his acceptance, to avoid the appearance of a forced concession to the popular will. Philip was also strongly urged to repair to the scene of the disturbances; and a main question of debate was, whether he should march at the head of an army or confide himself to the loyalty and good faith of his Belgian subjects. But the indolence or the pride of Philip was too strong to admit of his taking so vigorous a measure; and all these consultations ended in two letters to the stadtholderess. In the first he declared his firm intention to visit the Netherlands in person; refused to convoke the states-general; passed in silence the treaties concluded with the Protestants and the confederates; and finished by a declaration that he would throw himself wholly on the fidelity of the country. In his second letter, meant for the stadtholderess alone, he authorized her to assemble the states-general if public opinion became too powerful for resistance, but on no account to let it transpire that he had under any circumstances given his consent.

During these deliberations in Spain, the Protestants in the Netherlands amply availed themselves of the privileges they had gained. They erected numerous wooden churches with incredible activity. Young and old, noble and plebeian, of these energetic men, assisted in the manual labors of these occupations; and the women freely applied the produce of their ornaments and jewels to forward the pious work. But the furious outrages of the iconoclasts had done infinite mischief to both political and religious freedom; many of the Catholics, and particularly the priests, gradually withdrew themselves from the confederacy, which thus lost some of its most firm supporters. And, on the other hand, the severity with which some of its members pursued the guilty offended and alarmed the body of the people, who could not distinguish the shades of difference between the love of liberty and the practice of licentiousness.

The stadtholderess and her satellites adroitly took advantage of this state of things to sow dissension among the patriots. Autograph letters from Philip to the principal lords were distributed among them with such artful and mysterious precautions as to throw the rest into perplexity, and give each suspicions of the other's fidelity. The report of the immediate arrival of Philip had also considerable effect over the less resolute or more selfish; and the confederation was dissolving rapidly under the operations of intrigue, self-interest, and fear. Even the Count of Egmont was not proof against the subtle seductions of the wily monarch, whose severe yet flattering letters half frightened and half soothed him into a relapse of royalism. But with the Prince of Orange Philip had no chance of success. It is unquestionable that, be his means of acquiring information what they might, he did succeed in procuring minute intelligence of all that was going on in the king's most secret council. He had from time to time procured copies of the stadtholderess's despatches; but the document which threw the most important light upon the real intentions of Philip was a confidential epistle to the stadtholderess from D'Alava, the Spanish minister at Paris, in which he spoke in terms too clear to admit any doubt as to the terrible example which the king was resolved to make among the patriot lords. Bergen and Montigny confirmed this by the accounts they sent home from Madrid of the alteration in the manner with which they were treated by Philip and his courtiers; and the Prince of Orange was more firmly decided in his opinions of the coming vengeance of the tyrant.

William summoned his brother Louis, the Counts Egmont, Horn, and Hoogstraeten, to a secret conference at Termonde; and he there submitted to them this letter of Alava's, with others which he had received from Spain, confirmatory of his worst fears. Louis of Nassau voted for open and instant rebellion; William recommended a cautious observance of the projects of government, not doubting but a fair pretext would be soon given to justify the most vigorous overt acts of revolt; but Egmont at once struck a death-blow to the energetic project of one brother, and the cautious amendment of the other, by declaring his present resolution to devote himself wholly to the service of the king, and on no inducement whatever to risk the perils of rebellion. He expressed his perfect reliance on the justice and the goodness of Philip when once he should see the determined loyalty of those whom he had hitherto had so much reason to suspect; and he exhorted the others to follow his example. The two brothers and Count Horn implored him in their turn to abandon this blind reliance on the tyrant; but in vain. His new and unlooked-for profession of faith completely paralyzed their plans. He possessed too largely the confidence of both the soldiery and the people to make it possible to attempt any serious measure of resistance in which he would not take a part. The meeting broke up without coming to any decision. All those who bore a part in it were expected at Brussels to attend the council of state; Egmont alone repaired thither. The stadtholderess questioned him on the object of the conference at Termonde: he only replied by an indignant glance, at the same time presenting a copy of Alava's letter.

The stadtholderess now applied her whole efforts to destroy the union among the patriot lords. She, in the meantime, ordered levies of troops to the amount of some thousands, the command of which was given to the nobles on whose attachment she could reckon. The most vigorous measures were adopted. Noircarmes, governor of Hainault, appeared before Valenciennes, which, being in the power of the Calvinists, had assumed a most determined attitude of resistance. He vainly summoned the place to submission, and to admit a royalist garrison; and on receiving an obstinate refusal, he commenced the siege in form. An undisciplined rabble of between three thousand and four thousand Gueux, under the direction of John de Sereas, gathered together in the neighborhood of Lille and Tournay, with a show of attacking these places. But the governor of the former town dispersed one party of them; and Noircarmes surprised and almost destroyed the main body—their leader falling in the action. These were the first encounters of the civil war, which raged without cessation for upward of forty years in these devoted countries, and which is universally allowed to be the most remarkable that ever desolated any isolated portion of Europe. The space which we have already given to the causes which produced this memorable revolution, now actually commenced, will not allow us to do more than rapidly sketch the fierce events that succeeded each other with frightful rapidity.

While Valenciennes prepared for a vigorous resistance, a general synod of the Protestants was held at Antwerp, and De Brederode undertook an attempt to see the stadtholderess, and lay before her the complaints of this body; but she refused to admit him into the capital. He then addressed to her a remonstrance in writing, in which he reproached her with her violation of the treaties, on the faith of which the confederates had dispersed, and the majority of the Protestants laid down their arms. He implored her to revoke the new proclamations, by which she prohibited them from the free exercise of their religion; and, above all things, he insisted on the abandonment of the siege of Valenciennes, and the disbanding of the new levies. The stadtholderess's reply was one of haughty reproach and defiance. The gauntlet was now thrown down; no possible hope of reconciliation remained; and the whole country flew to arms. A sudden attempt on the part of the royalists, under Count Meghem, against Bois-le-duc, was repulsed by eight hundred men, commanded by an officer named Bomberg, in the immediate service of De Brederode, who had fortified himself in his garrison town of Vienen.

The Prince of Orange maintained at Antwerp an attitude of extreme firmness and caution. His time for action had not yet arrived; but his advice and protection were of infinite importance on many occasions. John de Marnix, lord of Toulouse, brother of Philip de St. Aldegonde, took possession of Osterweel on the Scheldt, a quarter of a league from Antwerp, and fortified himself in a strong position. But he was impetuously attacked by the Count de Lannoy with a considerable force, and perished, after a desperate defence, with full one thousand of his followers. Three hundred who laid down their arms were immediately after the action butchered in cold blood. Antwerp was on this occasion saved from the excesses of its divided and furious citizens, and preserved from the horrors of pillage, by the calmness and **intrepidity of the** Prince of Orange. Valenciennes **at length capitulated to** the royalists, disheartened by the **defeat and death of De** Marnix, and terrified by a bombardment **of thirty-six hours.** The governor, two preachers, **and about forty of the citizens** were hanged by the victors, **and the reformed** religion prohibited. Noircarmes promptly **followed up his** success. **Maestricht,** Turnhout, **and Bois-le-duc submitted at his approach;** and the insurgents **were soon driven from all** the provinces, Holland alone **excepted. Brederode fled** to Germany, where he died **the following year.**

The stadtholderess showed, **in her success,** no small proofs of decision. She and **her** counsellors, acting under orders from the king, **were** resolved on embarrassing **to** the utmost the patriot **lords; and a new oath of** allegiance, **to be** proposed to **every functionary of the** state, was considered as a certain means **for** attaining **this object** without the violence **of an unmerited** dismissal. **The** terms of this oath were **strongly opposed to** every principle of patriotism and toleration. **Count Mansfield was** the first **of** the nobles who took it. **The duke of Arschot,** Counts Meghem, **Berlaimont, and Egmont followed his** example. The counts of Horn, **Hoogstraeten, De Brederode,** and others, refused on various pretexts. **Every** artifice and persuasion **was** tried to induce the Prince of Orange to subscribe **to** this new test; but his resolution had been for some time formed. He saw that every chance **of** constitutional resistance to tyranny was for the present at an end. The time for petitioning was gone by. The confederation was dissolved. A royalist army was in the field; the Duke of Alva was notoriously approaching **at** the head of another, more numerous. It was worse than useless to conclude a hollow convention with the stadtholderess of mock loyalty on his part and mock confidence on hers. Many other important considerations convinced William that his only honorable, safe, and wise course was to exile himself from the Netherlands altogether, until more propitious circumstances allowed of his acting openly, boldly, and with effect.

Before he put this plan of voluntary banishment into execution, he and Egmont had a parting interview at the village of Willebrock, between Antwerp and Brussels. Count Mansfield, and Berti, secretary to the stadtholderess, were present at this memorable meeting. The details of what passed were reported to the confederates by one of their party, who contrived to conceal himself in the chimney of the chamber. Nothing could exceed the energetic warmth with which the two illustrious friends reciprocally endeavored to turn each other from their respective line of conduct; but in vain. Egmont's fatal confidence in the king was not to be shaken; nor was Nassau's penetrating mind to be deceived by the romantic delusion which led away his friend. They separated with most affectionate expressions; and Nassau was even moved to tears. His parting words were to the following effect: "Confide, then, since it must be so, in the gratitude of the king; but a painful presentiment (God grant it may prove a false one!) tells me that you will serve the Spaniards as the bridge by which they will enter the country, and which they will destroy as soon as they have passed over it!"

On the 11th of April, a few days after this conference, the Prince of Orange set out for Germany, with his three brothers and his whole family, with the exception of his eldest son Philip William, count de Beuren, whom he left behind a student in the University of Louvain. He believed that the privileges of the college and the franchises of Brabant would prove a sufficient protection to the youth; and this appears the only instance in which William's vigilant prudence was deceived. The departure of the prince

TO THE ADMINISTRATION OF REQUESENS

seemed to remove all hope of protection or support from the unfortunate Protestants, now left the prey of their implacable tyrant. The confederation of the nobles was completely broken up. The counts of Hoogstraeten, Bergen, and Culembourg followed the example of the Prince of Orange, and escaped to Germany; and the greater number of those who remained behind took the new oath of allegiance, and became reconciled to the government.

This total dispersion of the confederacy brought all the towns of Holland into obedience to the king. But the emigration which immediately commenced threatened the country with ruin. England and Germany swarmed with Dutch and Belgian refugees; and all the efforts of the stadtholderess could not restrain the thousands that took to flight. She was not more successful in her attempts to influence the measures of the king. She implored him, in repeated letters, to abandon his design of sending a foreign army into the country, which she represented as being now quite reduced to submission and tranquillity. She added that the mere report of this royal invasion (so to call it) had already deprived the Netherlands of many thousands of its best inhabitants; and that the appearance of the troops would change it into a desert. These arguments, meant to dissuade, were the very means of encouraging Philip in his design. He conceived his project to be now ripe for the complete suppression of freedom; and Alva soon began his march.

On the 5th of May, 1567, this celebrated captain, whose reputation was so quickly destined to sink into the notoriety of an executioner, began his memorable march; and on the 22d of August he, with his two natural sons, and his veteran army consisting of about fifteen thousand men, arrived at the walls of Brussels. The discipline observed on this march was a terrible forewarning to the people of the Netherlands of the influence of the general and the obedience of the troops. They had little chance of resistance against such soldiers so commanded.

Several of the Belgian nobility went forward to meet Alva, to render him the accustomed honors, and endeavor thus early to gain his good graces. Among them was the infatuated Egmont, who made a present to Alva of two superb horses, which the latter received with a disdainful air of condescension. Alva's first care was the distribution of his troops—several thousands of whom were placed in Antwerp, Ghent, and other important towns, and the remainder reserved under his own immediate orders at Brussels. His approach was celebrated by universal terror; and his arrival was thoroughly humiliating to the duchess of Parma. He immediately produced his commission as commander-in-chief of the royal armies in the Netherlands; but he next showed her another, which confided to him powers infinitely more extended than any Marguerite herself had enjoyed, and which proved to her that the almost sovereign power over the country was virtually vested in him.

Alva first turned his attention to the seizure of those patriot lords whose pertinacious infatuation left them within his reach. He summoned a meeting of all the members of the council of state and the knights of the order of the Golden Fleece, to deliberate on matters of great importance. Counts Egmont and Horn attended, among many others; and at the conclusion of the council they were both arrested (some historians assert by the hands of Alva and his eldest son), as was also Van Straeten, burgomaster of Antwerp, and Casambrot, Egmont's secretary. The young count of Mansfield appeared for a moment at this meeting; but, warned by his father of the fate intended him, as an original member of the confederation, he had time to fly. The count of Hoogstraeten was happily detained by illness, and thus escaped the fate of his friends. Egmont and Horn were transferred to the citadel of Ghent, under an escort of three thousand Spanish soldiers. Several other persons of the first families were arrested; and those who had originally been taken in arms were executed without delay.

The next measures of the new governor were the re-

STORMING THE BARRICADES AT BRUSSELS DURING THE REVOLUTION OF 1848

Hellard.

establishment of the Inquisition, the promulgation of the decrees of the Council of Trent, the revocation of the duchess of Parma's edicts, and the royal refusal to recognize the terms of her treaties with the Protestants. He immediately established a special tribunal, composed of twelve members, with full powers to inquire into and pronounce judgment on every circumstance connected with the late troubles. He named himself president of this council, and appointed a Spaniard, named Vargas, as vice-president—a wretch of the most diabolical cruelty. Several others of the judges were also Spaniards, in direct infraction of the fundamental laws of the country. This council, immortalized by its infamy, was named by the new governor (for so Alva was in fact, though not yet in name), the Council of Troubles. By the people it was soon designed the Council of Blood. In its atrocious proceedings no respect was paid to titles, contracts, or privileges, however sacred. Its judgments were without appeal. Every subject of the state was amenable to its summons; clergy and laity, the first individuals of the country, as well as the most wretched outcasts of society. Its decrees were passed with disgusting rapidity and contempt of form. Contumacy was punished with exile and confiscation. Those who, strong in innocence, dared to brave a trial were lost without resource. The accused were forced to its bar without previous warning. Many a wealthy citizen was dragged to trial four leagues' distance, tied to a horse's tail. The number of victims was appalling. On one occasion, the town of Valenciennes alone saw fifty-five of its citizens fall by the hands of the executioner. Hanging, beheading, quartering and burning were the every-day spectacles. The enormous confiscations only added to the thirst for gold and blood by which Alva and his satellites were parched. History offers no example of parallel horrors; for while party vengeance on other occasions has led to scenes of fury and terror, they arose, in this instance, from the vilest cupidity and the most cold-blooded cruelty.

After three months of such atrocity, Alva, fatigued rather than satiated with butchery, resigned his hateful functions wholly into the hands of Vargas, who was chiefly aided by the members Delrio and Dela Torre. Even at this remote period we cannot repress the indignation excited by the mention of those monsters, and it is impossible not to feel satisfaction in fixing upon their names the brand of historic execration. One of these wretches, called Hesselts, used at length to sleep during the mock trials of the already doomed victims; and as often as he was roused up by his colleagues, he used to cry out mechanically, "To the gibbet! to the gibbet!" so familiar was his tongue with the sounds of condemnation.

The despair of the people may be imagined from the fact that, until the end of the year 1567, their only consolation was the prospect of the king's arrival! He never dreamed of coming. Even the delight of feasting in horrors like these could not conquer his indolence. The good duchess of Parma—for so she was in comparison with her successor—was not long left to oppose the feeble barrier of her prayers between Alva and his victims. She demanded her dismissal from the nominal dignity, which was now but a title of disgrace. Philip granted it readily, accompanied by a hypocritical letter, a present of thirty thousand crowns, and the promise of an annual pension of twenty thousand more. She left Brussels in the month of April, 1568, raised to a high place in the esteem and gratitude of the people, less by any actual claims from her own conduct than by its fortuitous contrast with the infamy of her successor. She retired to Italy, and died at Naples in the month of February, 1586.

Ferdinand Alvarez de Toledo, duke of Alva, was of a distinguished family in Spain, and even boasted of his descent from one of the Moorish monarchs who had reigned in the insignificant kingdom of Toledo. When he assumed the chief command in the Netherlands, he was sixty years of age; having grown old and obdurate in pride, ferocity, and avarice. His deeds must stand instead of a more detailed portrait, which, to be thoroughly striking, should be traced with a pen dipped in blood. He was a fierce and clever soldier, brought up in the school of Charles V., and trained to his profession in the wars of that monarch in Germany, and subsequently in that of Philip II. against France. In addition to the horrors acted by the Council of Blood, Alva committed many deeds of collateral but minor tyranny; among others, he issued a decree forbidding, under severe penalties, any inhabitant of the country to marry without his express permission. His furious edicts against emigration were attempted to be enforced in vain. Elizabeth of England opened all the ports of her kingdom to the Flemish refugees, who carried with them those abundant stores of manufacturing knowledge which she wisely knew to be the elements of national wealth.

Alva soon summoned the Prince of Orange, his brothers, and all the confederate lords, to appear before the council and answer to the charge of high treason. The prince gave a prompt and contemptuous answer, denying the authority of Alva and his council, and acknowledging for his judges only the emperor, whose vassal he was, or the king of Spain in person, as president of the order of the Golden Fleece. The other lords made replies nearly similar. The trials of each were, therefore, proceeded on, by contumacy; confiscation of property being an object almost as dear to the tyrant viceroy as the death of his victims. Judgments were promptly pronounced against those present or absent, alive or dead. Witness the case of the unfortunate marquess of Bergues, who had previously expired at Madrid, as was universally believed, by poison; and his equally ill-fated colleague in the embassy, the Baron Montigny, was for a while imprisoned at Segovia, where he was soon after secretly beheaded, on the base pretext of former disaffection.

The departure of the duchess of Parma having left Alva undisputed as well as unlimited authority, he proceeded rapidly in his terrible career. The count of Beuren was seized at Louvain, and sent prisoner to Madrid; and wherever it was possible to lay hands on a suspected patriot, the occasion was not neglected. It would be a revolting task to enter into a minute detail of all the horrors committed, and impossible to record the names of the victims who so quickly fell before Alva's insatiate cruelty. The people were driven to frenzy. Bands of wretches fled to the woods and marshes; whence, half famished and perishing for want, they revenged themselves with pillage and murder. Pirates infested and ravaged the coast; and thus, from both sea and land, the whole extent of the Netherlands was devoted to carnage and ruin. The chronicles of Brabant and Holland, chiefly written in Flemish by contemporary authors, abound in thrilling details of the horrors of this general desolation, with long lists of those who perished. Suffice it to say, that, on the recorded boast of Alva himself, he caused eighteen thousand inhabitants of the Low Countries to perish by the hands of the executioner, during his less than six years' sovereignty in the Netherlands.

The most important of these tragical scenes was now soon to be acted. The Counts Egmont and Horn, having submitted to some previous interrogatories by Vargas and others, were removed from Ghent to Brussels, on the 3d of June, under a strong escort. The following day they passed through the mockery of a trial before the Council of Blood; and on the 5th they were both beheaded in the great square of Brussels, in the presence of Alva, who gloated on the spectacle from a balcony that commanded the execution. The same day Van Straeten and Casambrot shared the fate of their illustrious friends, in the castle of Vilvorde; with many others whose names only find a place in the local chronicles of the times. Egmont and Horn met their fate with the firmness expected from their well-proved courage.

These judicial murders excited in the Netherlands an agitation without bounds. It was no longer hatred or aversion that filled men's minds, but fury and despair. The outbursting of a general revolt was hourly watched for.

The foreign powers, without exception, expressed their disapproval of these executions. The emperor Maximilian II., and all the Catholic princes, condemned them. The former sent his brother expressly to the king of Spain, to warn him that without a cessation of his cruelties he could not restrain a general declaration from the members of the empire, which would, in all likelihood, deprive him of every acre of land in the Netherlands. The princes of the Protestant states held no terms in the expression of their disgust and resentment; and everything seemed now ripe, both at home and abroad, to favor the enterprise on which the Prince of Orange was determined to risk his fortune and his life. But his principal resources were to be found in his genius and courage, and in the heroic devotion partaken by his whole family in the cause of their country. His brother, Count John, advanced him a considerable sum of money; the Flemings and Hollanders, in England and elsewhere, subscribed largely; the prince himself, after raising loans in every possible way on his private means, sold his jewels, his plate, and even the furniture of his houses, and threw the amount into the common fund.

Two remarkable events took place this year in Spain, and added to the general odium entertained against Philip's character throughout Europe. The first was the death of his son Don Carlos, whose sad story is too well known in connection with the annals of his country to require a place here; the other was the death of the queen. Universal opinion assigned poison as the cause; and Charles IX. of France, her brother, who loved her with great tenderness, seems to have joined in this belief. Astonishment and horror filled all minds on the double denouement of this romantic tragedy; and the enemies of the tyrant reaped all the advantages it was so well adapted to produce them.

The Prince of Orange, having raised a considerable force in Germany, now entered on the war with all the well-directed energy by which he was characterized. The queen of England, the French Huguenots, and the Protestant princes of Germany, all lent him their aid in money or in men; and he opened his first campaign with great advantage. He formed his army into four several corps, intending to enter the country on as many different points, and by a sudden irruption on that most vulnerable to rouse at once the hopes and the co-operation of the people. His brothers **Louis** and **Adolphus, at the head** of one of these divisions, penetrated into **Friesland**, and there commenced the **contest.** The count of Aremberg, governor of this province, assisted by the Spanish troops under Gonsalvo de Bracamonte, quickly opposed the invaders. They met on the 24th of May near the abbey of Heiligerlee, which gave its **name** to the battle; and after a short contest the royalists were defeated with great loss. The **count of** Aremberg **and Adolphus of Nassau encountered in single** combat, and fell by each other's hands. The victory was dearly purchased by the loss of this gallant prince, the first of his illustrious family who have on so many occasions, down to these very days, freely shed their blood for the freedom and happiness of the country which may be so emphatically called their own.

Alva immediately hastened to the scene of this first action, and soon forced Count Louis to another at a place called Jemminghem, near the town of Embden, on the 21st of July. Their forces were nearly equal, about fourteen thousand on either side; but all the advantage of discipline and skill was in favor of Alva; and the consequence was, the total rout of the patriots with a considerable loss in killed and the whole of the cannon and baggage. The entire province of Friesland was thus again reduced to obedience, and Alva **hastened** back to Brabant to make head against the Prince of Orange. The latter had now under his command an **army** of twenty-eight thousand men—an imposing force in point of numbers, being double that which his rival was able to muster. He soon made himself master of the towns of Tongres and St. Trond, and the whole province of Liege was in his power. He advanced boldly against

TO THE ADMINISTRATION OF REQUESENS 151

Alva, and for several months did all that manœuvring could do to force him to a battle. But the wily veteran knew his trade too well; he felt sure that in time the prince's force would disperse for want of pay and supplies; and he managed his resources so ably that with little risk and scarcely any loss he finally succeeded in his object. In the month of October the prince found himself forced to disband his large but undisciplined force; and he retired into France to recruit his funds and consider on the best measures for some future enterprise.

The insolent triumph of Alva knew no bounds. The rest of the year was consumed in new executions. The hotel of Culembourg, the early cradle of De Brederode's confederacy, was razed to the ground, and a pillar erected on the spot commemorative of the deed; while Alva, resolved to erect a monument of his success as well as of his hate, had his own statue in brass, formed of the cannons taken at Jemminghem, set up in the citadel of Antwerp, with various symbols of power and an inscription of inflated pride.

The following year was ushered in by a demand of unwonted and extravagant rapacity; the establishment of two taxes on property, personal and real, to the amount of the hundredth penny (or denier) on each kind; and at every transfer or sale ten per cent on personal and five per cent for real property. The states-general, of whom this demand was made, were unanimous in their opposition, as well as the ministers; but particularly De Berlaimont and Viglius. Alva was so irritated that he even menaced the venerable president of the council, but could not succeed in intimidating him. He obstinately persisted in his design for a considerable period; resisting arguments and prayers, and even the more likely means tried for softening his cupidity, by furnishing him with sums from other sources equivalent to those which the new taxes were calculated to produce. To his repeated threats against Viglius the latter replied, that "he was convinced the king would not condemn him unheard; but that at any rate his gray hairs saved him from any ignoble fear of death."

A deputation was sent from the states-general to Philip explaining the impossibility of persevering in the attempted taxes, which were incompatible with every principle of commercial liberty. But Alva would not abandon his design till he had forced every province into resistance, and the king himself commanded him to desist. The events of this and the following year, 1570, may be shortly summed up; none of any striking interest or eventual importance having occurred. The sufferings of the country were increasing from day to day under the intolerable tyranny which bore it down. The patriots attempted nothing on land; but their naval force began from this time to acquire that consistency and power which was so soon to render it the chief means of resistance and the great source of wealth. The privateers or corsairs, which began to swarm from every port in Holland and Zealand, and which found refuge in all those of England, sullied many gallant exploits by instances of culpable excess; so much so that the Prince of Orange was forced to withdraw the command which he had delegated to the lord of Dolhain, and to replace him by Gislain de Fiennes: for already several of the exiled nobles and ruined merchants of Antwerp and Amsterdam had joined these bold adventurers; and purchased or built, with the remnant of their fortunes, many vessels, in which they carried on a most productive warfare against Spanish commerce through the whole extent of the English Channel, from the mouth of the Embs to the harbor of La Rochelle.

One of those frightful inundations to which the northern provinces were so constantly exposed occurred this year, carrying away the dikes, and destroying lives and property to a considerable amount. In Friesland alone twenty thousand men were victims to this calamity. But no suffering could affect the inflexible sternness of the duke of Alva; and to such excess did he carry his persecution that Philip himself began to be discontented, and thought his representative was overstepping the bounds of delegated tyranny. He even reproached him sharply in some of his despatches. The governor replied in the same strain; **and such was** the effect of this correspondence that Philip **resolved to** remove him from his command. But the king's **marriage** with Anne of Austria, daughter of **the** emperor Maximilian, obliged him **to defer** his intentions for a while; and he at length named **John de la** Cerda, duke of Medina-Celi, **for** Alva's **successor. Upward of a** year, however, elapsed before this **new** governor **was** finally appointed; **and he made** his appearance on the **coast of** Flanders with a **considerable** fleet, on the 11th **of** May, 1572. He **was afforded on this** very day a specimen **of** the sort of **people he came to contend** with; for his fleet **was suddenly attacked by that of** the patriots, and **many of his vessels burned and taken before** his eyes, with their **rich cargoes and considerable treasures** intended for the service **of the state.**

The duke of Medina-Celi **proceeded rapidly to Brussels,** where he was ceremoniously **received by Alva, who,** however, refused to resign the government, **under the** pretext that the term of his appointment **had not expired,** and that he was resolved first to completely **suppress** all symptoms of revolt in the northern **provinces. He succeeded in** effectually disgusting La **Cerda, who** almost immediately demanded and **obtained his own** recall **to Spain.** Alva, left once more in **undisputed** possession of **his power,** turned it with increased **vigor** into new channels of oppression. He was **soon** again **employed** in efforts **to** effect the levying of his favorite **taxes; and** such was the resolution **of** the tradesmen of Brussels, **that,** sooner than submit, they almost universally closed their shops altogether. Alva, furious at this measure, caused sixty of the citizens to be seized, and ordered them to be hanged opposite their **own** doors. The gibbets were actually erected, when, **on the** very morning of the day fixed for the executions, he received despatches that wholly disconcerted him and stopped their completion.

To avoid an open rupture with Spain, the queen of England had just at this time interdicted the Dutch and Flemish privateers from taking shelter in her ports. William de la Marck, count of Lunoy, had now the chief command of this adventurous force. He was distinguished by an inveterate hatred against the Spaniards, and had made a wild and romantic **vow never to cut** his hair or beard till he had **avenged the murders** of Egmont and Horn. He was impetuous and terrible in all his actions, and bore the surname of "**the wild boar of the Ardennes.**" Driven out of **the harbors of England, he resolved** on **some** desperate enterprise; and on the 1st of April he **succeeded in** surprising the little town of Brille, **in the island of Voorn,** situate between Zealand and Holland. This insignificant **place** acquired **great celebrity from this** event, which **may** be considered the **first successful step toward** the establishment **of** liberty and the republic.

Alva was confounded by the news of this exploit, but with his usual activity he immediately turned his whole attention toward the point of greatest danger. His embarrassment, however, became every day more considerable. Lunoy's success was the signal of a general revolt. In a few days every **town in** Holland and Zealand declared for **liberty,** with the **exception** of Amsterdam and Middleburg, where the Spanish **garrisons were** too strong for the people to attempt their **expulsion.**

The Prince of Orange, who had been on the **watch** for a favorable moment, now entered Brabant at the head of **twenty thousand men,** composed of French, German, and **English, and made** himself **master of** several important **places;** while his indefatigable brother Louis, with **a** minor **force,** suddenly appeared in Hainault, and, joined by a large **body** of French Huguenots under De Genlis, **he** seized on **Mons,** the capital of the province, on the 25th **of May.**

Alva turned first toward the recovery of this important place, and gave the command of the siege to his son Frederic of Toledo, who was assisted by the counsels of Noircarmes and Vitelli; but Louis of Nassau held out for upward of three months, and only **surrendered on an honorable** capitulation in the month of September; his French allies having been first entirely defeated, **and** their brave leader De Genlis taken prisoner. The **Prince of** Orange had in the meantime secured **possession** of Louvain, Ruremonde, Mechlin, and **other** towns, carried Termonde and Oudenarde **by assault, and** made demonstrations **which** seemed **to court Alva once more to try the** fortune of the campaign **in a pitched battle.** But such were not William's **real** intentions, nor did the cautious tactics of his able opponent allow him to **provoke such a risk.** He, however, ordered his son Frederic to **march with all his force into Holland, and he soon** undertook **the siege of Haerlem. By the time that** Mons **fell again into the power of the Spaniards,** sixty-five **towns and their territories,** chiefly **in the northern** provinces, had thrown off the **yoke.** The single port of Flessingue contained one **hundred and fifty patriot vessels, well** armed and equipped; and **from that epoch may be dated the** rapid growth of the first **naval power in Europe, with the** single exception of Great **Britain.**

It is here worthy of remark, **that all the horrors of which** the people of Flanders **were the victims, and in their full** proportion, had not the effect of **exciting them to revolt; but they rose** up with fury against the payment **of the new taxes.** They sacrificed everything **sooner** than pay these unjust exactions—*Omnia dabant,* **ne** *decimam darant.* The next important **event in these wars was** the siege of Haerlem, before which place **the** Spaniards **were arrested in their progress for** seven months, and which they at length succeeded in taking with a loss **of ten** thousand men.

The details of this memorable siege **are** calculated to arouse every feeling of pity for the heroic defenders, and of execration against the cruel assailants. A widow, named Kenau Hasselaer, gained a niche in history by her remarkable valor at the head of a battalion of three hundred of her townswomen, who bore a part in all the labors and perils of the siege. After the surrender, and in pursuance of Alva's common system, his ferocious son caused the governor and the other chief officers to be beheaded; and upward of two thousand of the worn-out garrison and burghers were either put to the sword, or tied two and two and drowned in the lake which gives its name to the town. Tergoes in South Beveland, Mechlin, Naerden, and other towns, were about the same period the scenes of gallant actions, and of subsequent cruelties of the most revolting nature as soon as they fell into the power of the Spaniards. Strada, with all his bigotry to the Spanish cause, admits that these excesses were atrocious crimes rather than just punishments: *non pœna, sed flagitium*. Horrors like these were sure to force reprisals on the part of the maddened patriots. De la Marck carried on his daring exploits with a cruelty which excited the indignation of the Prince of Orange, by whom he was removed from his command. The contest was for a while prosecuted with a decrease of vigor proportioned to the serious losses on both sides; money and the munitions of war began to fail; and though the Spaniards succeeded in taking The Hague, they were repulsed before Alkmaer with great loss, and their fleet was almost entirely destroyed in a naval combat on the Zuyder Zee. The count Bossu, their admiral, was taken in this fight, with about three hundred of his best sailors.

Holland was now from one end to the other the theatre of the most shocking events. While the people performed deeds of the greatest heroism, the perfidy and cruelty of the Spaniards had no bounds. The patriots saw more danger in submission than in resistance; each town, which was in succession subdued, endured the last extremities of suffering before it yielded, and victory was frequently the consequence of despair. This unlooked-for turn in affairs decided the king to remove Alva, whose barbarous and rapacious conduct was now objected to even by Philip, when it produced results disastrous to his cause. Don Luis Zanega y Requesens, commander of the order of Malta, was named to the government of the Netherlands. He arrived at Brussels on the 17th of November, 1573; and on the 18th of the following month, the monster whom he succeeded set out for Spain, loaded with the booty to which he had waded through oceans of blood, and with the curses of the country, which, however, owed its subsequent freedom to the impulse given by his intolerable cruelty. He repaired to Spain; and after various fluctuations of favor and disgrace at the hands of his congenial master, he died in his bed, at Lisbon, in 1582, at the advanced age of seventy-four years.

CHAPTER X

TO THE PACIFICATION OF GHENT

A.D. 1573–1576

THE character of Requesens was not more opposed to that of his predecessor, than were the instructions given to him for his government. He was an honest, well-meaning, and moderate man, and the king of Spain hoped that by his influence and a total change of measures he might succeed in recalling the Netherlands to obedience. But, happily for the country, this change was adopted too late for success; and the weakness of the new government completed the glorious results which the ferocity of the former had prepared.

Requesens performed all that depended on him, to gain the confidence of the people. He caused Alva's statue to be removed; and hoped to efface the memory of the tyrant by dissolving the Council of Blood and abandoning the obnoxious taxes which their inventor had suspended rather than abolished. A general amnesty was also promulgated against the revolted provinces; they received it with contempt and defiance. Nothing then was left to Requesens but to renew the war; and this he found to be a matter of no easy execution. The finances were in a state of the greatest confusion; and the Spanish troops were in many places seditious, in some openly mutinous, Alva having left large arrears of pay due to almost all, notwithstanding the immense amount of his pillage and extortion. Middleburg, which had long sustained a siege against all the efforts of the patriots, was now nearly reduced by famine, notwithstanding the gallant efforts of its governor, Mondragon. Requesens turned his immediate attention to the relief of this important place; and he soon assembled, at Antwerp and Berg-op-Zoom, a fleet of sixty vessels for that purpose. But Louis Boisot, admiral of Zealand, promptly repaired to attack this force; and after a severe action he totally defeated it, and killed De Glimes, one of its admirals, under the eyes of Requesens himself, who, accompanied by his suite, stood during the whole affair on the dike of Schakerloo. This action took place the 29th of January, 1574; and, on the 19th of February following, Middleburg surrendered, after a resistance of two years. The Prince of Orange granted such conditions as were due to the bravery of the governor; and thus set an example of generosity and honor which greatly changed the complexion of the war. All Zealand was now free; and the intrepid Admiral Boisot gained another victory on the 30th of May—destroying several of the Spanish vessels, and taking some others, with their Admiral Von Haemstede. Frequent naval enterprises were also undertaken against the frontiers of Flanders; and while the naval forces thus harassed the enemy on every vulnerable point, the unfortunate provinces of the interior were ravaged by the mutinous and revolted Spaniards, and by the native brigands, who pillaged both royalists and patriots with atrocious impartiality.

To these manifold evils was now added one more terrible, in the appearance of the plague, which broke out at Ghent in the month of October, and devastated a great part of the Netherlands; not, however, with that violence with which it rages in more southern climates.

Requesens, overwhelmed by difficulties, yet exerted himself to the utmost to put the best face on the affairs of government. His chief care was to appease the mutinous soldiery: he even caused his plate to be melted, and freely gave the produce toward the payment of their arrears. The patriots, well informed of this state of things, labored to turn it to their best advantage. They opened the campaign in the province of Guelders, where Louis of Nassau, with his younger brother Henry, and the prince Palatine, son of the elector Frederick III., appeared at the head of eleven thousand men; the Prince of Orange prepared to join him with an equal number; but Requesens promptly despatched Sanchez d'Avila to prevent this junction. The Spanish commander quickly passed the Meuse near Nimeguen; and on the 14th of April he forced Count Louis to a battle, on the great plain called Mookerheyde, close to the village of Mook. The royalists attacked with their usual valor; and, after two hours of hard fighting, the confederates were totally defeated. The three gallant princes were among the slain, and their bodies were never afterward discovered. It has been stated, on doubtful authority, that Louis of Nassau, after having lain some time among the heaps of dead, dragged himself to the side of the river Meuse, and while washing his wounds was inhumanly murdered by some straggling peasants, to whom he was unknown. The unfortunate fate of this enterprising prince was a severe blow to the patriot cause, and a cruel affliction to the Prince of Orange. He had now already lost three brothers in the war; and remained alone, to revenge their fate and sustain the cause for which they had perished.

D'Avila soon found his victory to be as fruitless as it was brilliant. The ruffian troops, by whom it was gained, became immediately self-disbanded; threw off all authority; hastened to possess themselves of Antwerp; and threatened to proceed to the most horrible extremities if their pay was longer withheld. The citizens succeeded with difficulty in appeasing them, by the sacrifice of some money in part payment of their claims. Requesens took advantage of their temporary calm, and despatched them promptly to take part in the siege of Leyden.

This siege formed another of those numerous instances which became so memorable from the mixture of heroism and horror. Jean Vanderdoes, known in literature by the name of Dousa, and celebrated for his Latin poems, commanded the place. Valdez, who conducted the siege, urged

Dousa to surrender; when the latter replied, in the name of the inhabitants, "that when provisions failed them, they would devour their left hands, reserving the right to defend their liberty." A party of the inhabitants, driven to disobedience and revolt by the excess of misery to which they were shortly reduced, attempted to force the burgomaster, Vanderwerf, to supply them with bread, or yield up the place. But he sternly made the celebrated answer, which cannot be remembered without shuddering—"Bread I have none; but if my death can afford you relief, tear my body in pieces, and let those who are most hungry devour it!"

But in this extremity relief at last was afforded by the decisive measures of the Prince of Orange, who ordered all the neighboring dikes to be opened and the sluices raised, thus sweeping away the besiegers on the waves of the ocean: the inhabitants of Leyden were apprised of this intention by means of letters intrusted to the safe carriage of pigeons trained for the purpose. The inundation was no sooner effected than hundreds of flat-bottomed boats brought abundance of supplies to the half-famished town; while a violent storm carried the sea across the country for twenty leagues around, and destroyed the Spanish camp, with above one thousand soldiers, who were overtaken by the flood. This deliverance took place on the 3d of October, on which day it is still annually celebrated by the descendants of the grateful citizens.

It was now for the first time that Spain would consent to listen to advice or mediation, which had for its object the termination of this frightful war. The emperor Maximilian II. renewed at this epoch his efforts with Philip; and under such favorable auspices conferences commenced at Breda, where the counts Swartzenberg and Hohenloe, brothers-in-law of the Prince of Orange, met, on the part of the emperor, the deputies from the king of Spain and the patriots; and hopes of a complete pacification were generally entertained. But three months of deliberation proved their fallacy. The patriots demanded toleration for the reformed religion. The king's deputies obstinately refused it. The congress was therefore broken up; and both oppressors and oppressed resumed their arms with increased vigor and tenfold desperation.

Requesens had long fixed his eyes on Zealand as the scene of an expedition by which he hoped to repair the failure before Leyden; and he caused an attempt to be made on the town of Zuriczee, in the island of Scauwen, which merits record as one of the boldest and most original enterprises of the war.

The little islands of Zealand are separated from each other by narrow branches of the sea, which are fordable at low water; and it was by such a passage, two leagues in breadth, and till then untried, that the Spanish detachment of one thousand seven hundred and fifty men, under Ulloa and other veteran captains, advanced to their exploit in the midst of dangers greatly increased by a night of total darkness. Each man carried round his neck two pounds of gunpowder, with a sufficient supply of biscuit for two days; and holding their swords and muskets high over their heads, they boldly waded forward, three abreast, in some places up to their shoulders in water. The alarm was soon given; and a shower of balls was poured upon the gallant band, from upward of forty boats which the Zealanders sent rapidly toward the spot. The only light afforded to either party was from the flashes of their guns; and while the adventurers advanced with undaunted firmness, their equally daring assailants, jumping from their boats into the water, attacked them with oars and hooked handspikes, by which many of the Spaniards were destroyed. The rearguard, in this extremity, cut off from their companions, was obliged to retreat; but the rest, after a considerable loss, at length reached the land, and thus gained possession of the island, on the night of the 28th of September, 1575.

Requesens quickly afterward repaired to the scene of this gallant exploit, and commenced the siege of Zuriczee, which he did not live to see completed. After having passed the winter months in preparations for the success of this object which he had so **much at heart, he was recalled to Brussels** by accounts of new mutinies in the Spanish cavalry; and the very evening before he reached the city he was attacked by a violent fever, which **carried him** off five days afterward, on the 5th **of March, 1576.**

The suddenness of Requesen's illness **had not** allowed time for even **the** nomination of **a** successor, **to which he was** authorized **by letters** patent from **the** king. **It is believed that his intention was to appoint** Count Mansfield **to the command of the army, and De** Berlaimont **to the administration of civil affairs. The government, however, now** devolved **entirely** into the **hands of the** council **of state, which was at that period composed of nine members. The principal of these was Philip de Croi, duke of Arschot; the other leading members were Viglius, Counts Mansfield and Berlaimont; and the council was degraded by numbering, among the rest, Debris and De Roda, two of the notorious** Spaniards **who had formed part of the Council of Blood.**

The king resolved to **leave the authority in the hands of this** incongruous mixture, **until the arrival of Don John of Austria,** his natural **brother, whom he had already named to the office of** governor-general. **But in the** interval the government assumed an **aspect of** unprecedented disorder; and widespread anarchy **embraced the whole** country. The royal troops openly revolted, **and** fought against each other like deadly enemies. **The** nobles, divided **in** their views, arrogated to themselves in different places the titles and powers **of command.** Public faith and private probity seemed alike **destroyed.** Pillage, violence and ferocity were the commonplace characteristics **of** the times.

Circumstances like **these** may be well **supposed to have** revived the hopes of the Prince of Orange, **who** quickly saw amid this chaos the elements of order, strength, and liberty. Such had been his previous affliction at the harrowing events which he witnessed and despaired of being able to relieve, that he had proposed to the patriots of Holland and Zealand to destroy the dikes, submerge the whole country, and abandon to the waves the soil which refused security to freedom. But Providence destined him to be the savior, instead of the destroyer, of his country. The chief motive of this excessive desperation had been the apparent desertion by Queen Elizabeth of the cause which she had hitherto so mainly assisted. Offended at the capture of some English ships by the Dutch, who asserted that they carried supplies for the Spaniards, she withdrew from them her protection; but by timely submission they appeased her wrath; and it is thought by some historians that even thus early the Prince of Orange proposed to place the revolted provinces wholly under her protection. This, however, she for the time refused; but she strongly solicited Philip's mercy for these unfortunate countries, through the Spanish ambassador at her court.

In the meantime the council of state at Brussels seemed disposed to follow up as far as possible the plans of Requesens. The siege of Zuriczee was continued; but speedy dissensions among the members of the government rendered their authority contemptible, if not utterly extinct, in the eyes of the people. The exhaustion of the treasury deprived them of all power to put an end to the mutinous excesses of the Spanish troops, and the latter carried their licentiousness to the utmost bounds. Zuriczee, admitted to a surrender, and saved from pillage by the payment of a large sum, was lost to the royalists within three months, from the want of discipline in its garrison; and the towns and burghs of Brabant suffered as much from the excesses of their nominal protectors as could have been inflicted by the enemy. The mutineers at length, to the number of some thousands, attacked and carried by force the town of Alost, at equal distances between Brussels, Ghent, and Antwerp, imprisoned the chief citizens, and levied contributions on all the country round. It was then that the council of state found itself forced to proclaim them rebels, traitors, and enemies to the king and the country, and called on all loyal subjects to pursue and exterminate them wherever they were found in arms.

This proscription of the Spanish mutineers was followed by the convocation of the states-general, and the government thus hoped to maintain some show of union and some chance of authority. But a new scene of intestine violence completed the picture of executive inefficiency. On the 4th of September, the grand bailiff of Brabant, as lieutenant of the Baron de Hesse, governor of Brussels, entered the council chamber by force, and arrested all the members present, on suspicion of treacherously maintaining intelligence with the Spaniards. Counts Mansfield and Berlaimont were imprisoned, with some others. Viglius escaped this indignity by being absent from indisposition. This bold measure was hailed by the people with unusual joy, as the signal for that total change in the government which they reckoned on as the prelude to complete freedom.

The states-general were all at this time assembled, with the exception of those of Flanders, who joined the others with but little delay. The general reprobation against the Spaniards procured a second decree of proscription; and their desperate conduct justified the utmost violence with which they might be pursued. They still held the citadels of Ghent and Antwerp, as well as Maestricht, which they had seized on, sacked, and pillaged with all the fury which a barbarous enemy inflicts on a town carried by assault. On the 3d of November, the other body of mutineers, in possession of Alost, marched to the support of their fellow brigands in the citadel of Antwerp; and both, simultaneously attacking this magnificent city, became masters of it in all points, in spite of a vigorous resistance on the part of the citizens. They then began a scene of rapine and destruction unequalled in the annals of these desperate wars. More than five hundred private mansions and the splendid town-house were delivered to the flames: seven thousand citizens perished by the sword or in the waters of the Scheldt. For three days the carnage and the pillage went on with unheard-of fury; and the most opulent town in Europe was thus reduced to ruin and desolation by a few thousand frantic ruffians. The loss was valued at above two million golden crowns. Vargas and Romero were the principal leaders of this infernal exploit; and De Roda gained a new title to his immortality of shame by standing forth as its apologist.

The states-general, assembled at Ghent, were solemnly opened on the 14th of September. Being apprehensive of a sudden attack from the Spanish troops in the citadel, they proposed a negotiation, and demanded a protecting force from the Prince of Orange, who immediately entered into a treaty with their envoy, and sent to their assistance eight companies of infantry and seventeen pieces of cannon, under the command of the English colonel, Temple. In the midst of this turmoil and apparent insecurity, the states-general proceeded in their great work, and assumed the reins of government in the name of the king. They allowed the council of state still nominally to exist, but they restricted its powers far within those it had hitherto exercised; and the government, thus absolutely assuming the form of a republic, issued manifestoes in justification of its conduct, and demanded succor from all the foreign powers. To complete the union between the various provinces, it was resolved to resume the negotiations commenced the preceding year at Breda; and the 10th of October was fixed for this new congress to be held in the town-house of Ghent.

On the day appointed, the congress opened its sittings; and rapidly arriving at the termination of its important object, the celebrated treaty known by the title of "The Pacification of Ghent" was published on the 8th of November, to the sound of bells and trumpets; while the ceremony was rendered still more imposing by the thunder of the artillery which battered the walls of the besieged citadel. It was even intended to have delivered a general assault against the place at the moment of the proclamation; but the mutineers demanded a capitulation and finally surrendered three days afterward. It was the wife of the famous Mondragon who commanded the place in her husband's absence; and by her heroism gave a new proof of the capability of the sex to surpass the limits which nature seems to have fixed for their conduct.

The Pacification contained twenty-five articles. Among others, it was agreed:

That a full amnesty should be passed for all offences whatsoever.

That the estates of Brabant, Flanders, Hainault, Artois, and others, on the one part; the Prince of Orange, and the states of Holland and Zealand and their associates, on the other; promised to maintain good faith, peace, and friendship, firm and inviolable; to mutually assist each other, at all times, in council and action; and to employ life and fortune, above all things, to expel from the country the Spanish soldiers and other foreigners.

That no one should be allowed to injure or insult, by word or deed, the exercise of the Catholic religion, on pain of being treated as a disturber of the public peace.

That the edicts against heresy and the proclamations of the duke of Alva should be suspended.

That all confiscations, sentences, and judgments rendered since 1566 should be annulled.

That the inscriptions, monuments, and trophies erected by the duke of Alva should be demolished.

Such were the general conditions of the treaty; the remaining articles chiefly concerned individual interests. The promulgation of this great charter of union, which was considered as the fundamental law of the country, was hailed in all parts of the Netherlands with extravagant demonstrations of joy.

CHAPTER XI

TO THE RENUNCIATION OF THE SOVEREIGNTY OF SPAIN AND THE DECLARATION OF INDEPENDENCE

A.D. 1576—1580

ON the very day of the sack of Antwerp, Don John of Austria arrived at Luxemburg. This ominous commencement of his viceregal reign was not belied by the events which followed; and the hero of Lepanto, the victor of the Turks, the idol of Christendom, was destined to have his reputation and well-won laurels tarnished in the service of the insidious despotism to which he now became an instrument. Don John was a natural son of Charles V., and to fine talents and a good disposition united the advantages of hereditary courage and a liberal education. He was born at Ratisbon on the 24th of February, 1543. His reputed mother was a young lady of that place named Barbara Blomberg; but one historian states that the real parent was of a condition too elevated to have her rank betrayed; and that, to conceal the mystery, Barbara Blomberg had voluntarily assumed the distinction, or the dishonor, according to the different constructions put upon the case. The prince, having passed through France, disguised, for greater secrecy or in a youthful frolic, as a negro valet to Prince Octavo Gonzaga, entered on the limits of his new government, and immediately wrote to the council of state in the most condescending terms to announce his arrival.

Nothing could present a less promising aspect to the prince than the country at the head of which he was now placed. He found all its provinces, with the sole exception of Luxemburg, in the anarchy attendant on a ten years' civil war, and apparently resolved on a total breach of their allegiance to Spain. He found his best, indeed his only, course to be that of moderation and management; and it is most probable that at the outset his intentions were really honorable and candid.

The states-general were not less embarrassed than the prince. His sudden arrival threw them into great perplexity, which was increased by the conciliatory tone of his letter. They had now removed from Ghent to Brussels; and first sending deputies to pay the honors of a ceremonious welcome to Don John, they wrote to the Prince of Orange, then in Holland, for his advice in this difficult conjuncture. The prince replied by a memorial of considerable length, dated Middleburg, the 30th of November, in which he gave them the most wise and prudent advice; the substance of which was to receive any propositions coming from the wily and perfidious Philip with the utmost suspicion, and to refuse all negotiation with his deputy, if the immediate withdrawal of the foreign troops was not at once conceded, and the acceptance of the Pacification guaranteed in its most ample extent.

This advice was implicitly followed; the states in the meantime taking the precaution of assembling a large body of troops at Wavre, between Brussels and Namur, the command of which was given to the count of Lalain. A still more important measure was the despatch of an envoy to England, to implore the assistance of Elizabeth. She acted on this occasion with frankness and intrepidity; giving a distinguished reception to the envoy, De Sweveghem, and advancing a loan of one hundred thousand pounds sterling, on condition that the states made no treaty without her knowledge or participation.

To secure still more closely the federal union that now bound the different provinces, a new compact was concluded by the deputies on the 9th of January, 1577, known by the title of The Union of Brussels, and signed by the prelates, ecclesiastics, lords, gentlemen, magistrates, and others, representing the estates of the Netherlands. A copy of this act of union was transmitted to Don John, to enable him thoroughly to understand the present state of feeling among those with whom he was now about to negotiate. He maintained a general tone of great moderation throughout the conference which immediately took place; and after some months of cautious parleying, in the latter part of which the candor of the prince seemed doubtful, and which the native historians do not hesitate to stigmatize as merely assumed, a treaty was signed at Marche-en-Famenne, a place between Namur and Luxemburg, in which every point insisted on by the states was, to the surprise and delight of the nation, fully consented to and guaranteed. This important document is called The Perpetual Edict, bears date the 12th of February, 1577, and contains nineteen articles. They were all based on the acceptance of the Pacification; but one expressly stipulated that the count of Beuren should be set at liberty as soon as the Prince of Orange, his father, had on his part ratified the treaty.

Don John made his solemn entry into Brussels on the 1st of May, and assumed the functions of his limited authority. The conditions of the treaty were promptly and regularly fulfilled. The citadels occupied by the Spanish soldiers were given up to the Flemish and Walloon troops; and the departure of these ferocious foreigners took place at once. The large sums required to facilitate this measure made it necessary to submit for a while to the presence of the German mercenaries. But Don John's conduct soon destroyed the temporary delusion which had deceived the country. Whether his projects were hitherto only concealed, or that they were now for the first time excited by the disappointment of those hopes of authority held out to him by Philip, and which his predecessors had shared, it is certain that he very early displayed his ambition, and very imprudently attempted to put it in force. He at once demanded from the council of state the command of the troops and the disposal of the revenues. The answer was a simple reference to the Pacification of Ghent; and the prince's rejoinder was an apparent submission, and the immediate despatch of letters in **cipher** to the king, **demand**ing a supply of troops sufficient **to** restore his ruined authority. These letters **were** intercepted by the king of Navarre, afterward **Henry IV. of** France, who immediately transmitted **them to the Prince of** Orange, his old friend and **fellow-soldier.**

Public **opinion, to** the suspicions **of** which **Don John** had been from **the** first obnoxious, was now unanimous in attributing to design all **that** was unconstitutional and un**fair.** His **impetuous character could no longer** submit to **the restraint of dissimulation, and he resolved to take some** bold and decided **measure. A very** favorable opportunity was presented in **the arrival of the queen of Navarre, Mar**guerite of Valois, **at Namur, on her way to** Spa. The prince, numerously **attended, hastened to the former town** under pretence of **paying** his **respects to the queen. As** soon as she left the place, he repaired **to the glacis of the** town, as if for the mere **enjoyment of a** walk, admired **the** external appearance **of the citadel, and** expressed **a desire** to be admitted inside. **The young** count of Berlaimont, **in** the absence of **his** father, the governor of the place, **and an** accomplice in the plot with Don John, freely admitted him. The prince immediately drew forth a pistol, and exclaimed that "that was the first moment of his government"; took possession of **the place** with his immediate guard, and in**stantly formed them into a** devoted garrison.

The Prince of **Orange** immediately made public the intercepted letters; **and, at** the solicitation of the states-general, repaired to Brussels; into which city he made a truly triumphant entry on the 23d of September, **and was** immediately nominated governor, protector or *ruward* of Brabant—a dignity which had fallen into disuse, but was revived on this occasion, and which was little inferior in power to that of the dictators of Rome. His authority, now almost unlimited, extended over every province of the Netherlands, except Namur and Luxemburg, both of which acknowledged Don John.

The first care of the liberated nation was to demolish the various citadels rendered celebrated and odious by the excesses of the Spaniards. This was done with an enthusiastic industry in which every age and sex bore a part, and which promised well for liberty. Among the ruins of that of Antwerp the statue of the duke of Alva was discovered; dragged through the filthiest streets of the town; and, with all the indignity so well merited by the original, it was finally broken into a thousand pieces.

The country, in conferring such extensive powers on the Prince of Orange, had certainly gone too far, not for his desert, but for its own tranquillity. It was impossible that such an elevation should not excite the discontent and awaken the enmity of the haughty aristocracy of Flanders and Brabant; and particularly of the House of Croi, the ancient rivals of that of Nassau. The then representative of that family seemed the person most suited to counterbalance William's excessive power. The duke of Arschot was therefore named governor of Flanders; and he immediately put himself at the head of a confederacy of the Catholic party, which quickly decided to offer the chief government of the country, still in the name of Philip, to the archduke Mathias, brother of the emperor Rodolf II., and cousin-german to Philip of Spain, a youth but nineteen years of age. A Flemish gentleman named Maelsted was intrusted with the proposal. Mathias joyously consented; and, quitting Vienna with the greatest secrecy, he arrived at Maestricht, without any previous announcement, and expected only by the party that had invited him, at the end of October, 1577.

The Prince of Orange, instead of showing the least symptom of dissatisfaction at this underhand proceeding aimed at his personal authority, announced his perfect approval of the nomination, and was the foremost in recommending measures for the honor of the **archduke and** the security of the country. He drew up **the basis of a** treaty **for** Mathias's acceptance, **on** terms which guaranteed **to the** council of state **and the** states-general the virtual sovereignty, and left **to the young prince little beyond the** fine title which had dazzled **his boyish vanity. The Prince** of Orange **was** appointed his lieutenant, in all the branches of the **administration, civil,** military, **or** financial; and the duke **of Arschot, who** had hoped **to** obtain an entire domination **over the** puppet he had brought upon **the stage, saw himself** totally foiled in **his project, and left without a chance or a** pretext **for the least increase to his influence.**

But a still **greater disappointment attended this ambitious** nobleman **in the very stronghold of his power. The** Flemings, **driven by persecution to a state of fury almost** unnatural, **had, in their antipathy to Spain, adopted a** hatred against **Catholicism, which had its source only in** political frenzy, **while the converts imagined it to arise from reason and conviction. Two men had taken advantage of this state of the public mind and gained over it an** unbounded ascendency. **They were Francis de** Kethulle, **lord of Ryhove, and John Hembyse, who each** seemed **formed to realize the beau-ideal of a** factious demagogue. They had acquired supreme power **over the people** of Ghent, and had at their command **a body of twenty thousand resolute and well-armed** supporters. **The duke of Arschot vainly attempted to** oppose his authority **to that of these men;** and he on one occasion imprudently exclaimed that "he would **have them** hanged, even though they were protected by the Prince of Orange himself." The same night Ryhove summoned **the leaders** of his bands; and quickly assembling a considerable force, they **repaired to the** duke's hotel, made him prisoner, and, without allowing him time to dress, carried him away in triumph. **At the** same time the bishops of Bruges and Ypres, the high bailiffs of Ghent **and** Courtrai, the governor of Oudenarde, and other important magistrates, were arrested—accused of complicity with the duke, but of what particular offence the lawless demagogues did not deign to specify. The two tribunes immediately divided the whole honors and authority of administration; **Ryhove** as military, and **Hembyse** as civil, chief.

The latter of these legislators completely changed the forms of the government; he revived the ancient privileges destroyed by Charles **V.**, **and** took all preliminary measures for forcing the various provinces to join with the city of Ghent in forming a federative republic. The states-general and the Prince of Orange were alarmed, lest these troubles might lead to a renewal of the anarchy from the effects of which the country had but just obtained breathing-time. Ryhove consented, at the remonstrance of the Prince of Orange, to release the duke of Arschot; but William was obliged to repair to Ghent in person, in the hope of establishing order. He arrived on the 29th of December, and entered on a strict inquiry with his usual calmness and decision. He could not succeed in obtaining the liberty of the other prisoners, though he pleaded for them strongly. Having severely reprimanded the factious leaders, and pointed out the dangers of their illegal course, he returned to Brussels, leaving the factious city in a temporary tranquillity which his firmness and discretion could alone have obtained.

The archduke Mathias, having visited Antwerp, and acceded to all the conditions required of him, made his public entry into Brussels on the 18th of January, 1578, and was installed in his dignity of governor-general amid the usual fetes and rejoicings. Don John of Austria was at the same time declared an enemy to the country, with a public order to quit it without delay; and a prohibition was issued against any inhabitant acknowledging his forfeited authority.

War was now once more openly declared; some fruitless negotiations having afforded a fair pretext for hostilities. The rapid appearance of a numerous army under the orders of Don John gave strength to the suspicions of his former dissimulation. It was currently believed that large bodies of the Spanish troops had remained concealed in the forests of Luxemburg and Lorraine; while several regiments, which had remained in France in the service of the League, immediatly re-entered the Netherlands. Alexander Farnese, prince of Parma, son of the former stadtholderess, came to the aid of his uncle, Don John, at the head of a large force of Italians; and these several reinforcements, with the German auxiliaries still in the country, composed an army of twenty thousand men. The army of the states-general was still larger; but far inferior in point of discipline. It was commanded by Antoine de Goignies, a gentleman of Hainault, and an old soldier of the school of Charles V.

After a sharp affair at the village of Riminants, in which the royalists had the worst, the two armies met at Gemblours, on the 31st of January, 1578; and the prince of Parma gained a complete victory, almost with his cavalry only, taking De Goignies prisoner, with the whole of his artillery and baggage. The account of his victory is almost miraculous. The royalists, if we are to credit their most minute but not impartial historian, had only one thousand two hundred men engaged; by whom six thousand were put to the sword, with the loss of but twelve men and little more than an hour's labor.

The news of this battle threw the states into the utmost consternation. Brussels being considered insecure, the archduke Mathias and his council retired to Antwerp; but the victors did not feel their forces sufficient to justify an attack upon the capital. They, however, took Louvain, Tirlemont, and several other towns; but these conquests were of little import in comparison with the loss of Amsterdam, which declared openly and unanimously for the patriot cause. The states-general recovered their courage, and prepared for a new contest. They sent deputies to the diet of Worms, to ask succor from the princes of the empire. The count palatine John Casimir repaired to their assistance with a considerable force of Germans and English, all equipped and paid by Queen Elizabeth. The duke of Alençon, brother of

Henry III. of France, hovered on the frontiers of Hainault with a respectable army; and the cause of liberty seemed not quite desperate.

But all the various chiefs had separate interests and opposite views; while the fanatic violence of the people of Ghent sapped the foundations of the pacification to which the town had given its name. The Walloon provinces, deep-rooted in their attachment to religious bigotry, which they loved still better than political freedom, gradually withdrew from the common cause; and without yet openly becoming reconciled with Spain, they adopted a neutrality which was tantamount to it. Don John was, however, deprived of all chance of reaping any advantage from these unfortunate dissensions. He was suddenly taken ill in his camp at Bougy; and died, after a fortnight's suffering, on the 1st of October, 1578, in the thirty-third year of his age.

This unlooked-for close to a career which had been so brilliant, and to a life from which so much was yet to be expected, makes us pause to consider for a moment the different opinions of his times and of history on the fate of a personage so remarkable. The contemporary Flemish memoirs say that he died of the plague; those of Spain call his disorder the purple fever. The examination of his corpse caused an almost general belief that he was poisoned. "He lost his life," says one author, "with great suspicion of poison." "Acabo su vida, con gran sospecho de veneno."—Herrera. Another speaks of the suspicious state of his intestines, but without any direct opinion. An English historian states the fact of his being poisoned, without any reserve. Flemish writers do not hesitate to attribute his murder to the jealousy of Philip II., who, they assert, had discovered a secret treaty of marriage about to be concluded between Don John and Elizabeth of England, securing them the joint sovereignty of the Netherlands. An Italian historian of credit asserts that this ambitious design was attributed to the prince; and admits that his death was not considered as having arisen from natural causes. "E quindi nacque l'opinione dispersa allora, ch'egli mancasse di morte aiutata più tosto che naturale."—Bentivoglio. It was also believed that Escovedo, his confidential secretary, being immediately called back to Spain, was secretly assassinated by Antonio Perez, Philip's celebrated minister, and by the special orders of the king. Time has, however, covered the affair with impenetrable mystery; and the death of Don John was of little importance to the affairs of the country he governed so briefly and so ingloriously, if it be not that it added another motive to the natural hatred for his assumed murderer.

The prince of Parma, who now succeeded, by virtue of Don John's testament, to the post of governor-general in the name of the king, remained intrenched in his camp. He expected much from the disunion of his various opponents; and what he foresaw very quickly happened. The duke of Alençon disbanded his troops and retired to France; and the prince Palatine, following his example, withdrew to Germany, having first made an unsuccessful attempt to engage the queen of England as a principal in the confederacy. In this perplexity, the Prince of Orange saw that the real hope for safety was in uniting still more closely the northern provinces of the union; for he discovered the fallacy of reckoning on the cordial and persevering fidelity of the Walloons. He therefore convoked a new assembly at Utrecht; and the deputies of Holland, Guelders, Zealand, Utrecht, and Groningen, signed, on the 29th of January, 1579, the famous act called the Union of Utrecht, the real basis or fundamental pact of the republic of the United Provinces. It makes no formal renunciation of allegiance to Spain, but this is virtually done by the omission of the king's name. The twenty-six articles of this act consolidate the indissoluble connection of the United Provinces; each preserving its separate franchises, and following its own good pleasure on the subject of religion. The towns of Ghent, Antwerp, Bruges, and Ypres, soon after acceded to and joined the union.

The prince of Parma now assumed the offensive, and marched against Maestricht with his whole army. He took the place in the month of June, 1579, after a gallant resistance, and delivered it to sack and massacre for three entire days. About the same time Mechlin and Bois-le-duc returned to their obedience to the king. Hembyse having renewed his attempts against the public peace at Ghent, the Prince of Orange repaired to that place, re-established order, frightened the inveterate demagogue into secret flight, and Flanders was once more restored to tranquillity.

An attempt was made this year at a reconciliation between the king and the states. The emperor Rodolf II. and Pope Gregory XIII. offered their mediation; and on the 5th of April a congress assembled at Cologne, where a number of the most celebrated diplomatists in Europe were collected. But it was early seen that no settlement would result from the apparently reciprocal wish for peace. One point—that of religion, the main, and indeed the only one in debate—was now maintained by Philip's ambassador in the same unchristian spirit as if torrents of blood and millions of treasure had never been sacrificed in the cause. Philip was inflexible in his resolution never to concede the exercise of the reformed worship; and after nearly a year of fruitless consultation, and the expenditure of immense sums of money, the congress separated on the 17th of November, without having effected anything. There were several other articles intended for discussion, had the main one been adjusted, on which Philip was fully as determined to make no concession; but his obstinacy was not put to these new tests.

The time had now arrived for the execution of the great and decisive step for independence, the means of effecting which had been so long the object of exertion and calculation on the part of the Prince of Orange. He now resolved to assemble the states of the United Provinces, solemnly abjure the dominion of Spain, and depose King Philip from the sovereignty he had so justly forfeited. Much has been written both for and against this measure, which involved every argument of natural rights and municipal privilege. The natural rights of man may seem to comprise only those which he enjoys in a state of nature; but he carries several of those with him into society, which is based upon the very principle of their preservation. The great precedent which so many subsequent revolutions have acknowledged and confirmed is that which we now record. The states-general assembled at Antwerp early in the year 1580; and, in spite of all the opposition of the Catholic deputies, the authority of Spain was revoked forever, and the United Provinces declared a free and independent state. At the same time was debated the important question as to whether the protection of the new state should be offered to England or to France. Opinions were divided on this point; but that of the Prince of Orange being in favor of the latter country, from many motives of sound policy, it was decided to offer the sovereignty to the duke of Alençon. The archduke Mathias, who was present at the deliberations, was treated with little ceremony; but he obtained the promise of a pension when the finances were in a situation to afford it. The definite proposal to be made to the duke of Alençon was not agreed upon for some months afterward; and it was in the month of August following that St. Aldegonde and other deputies waited on the duke at the chateau of Plessis-le-Tours, when he accepted the offered sovereignty on the proposed conditions, which set narrow bounds to his authority, and gave ample security to the United Provinces. The articles were formally signed on the 29th day of September; and the duke not only promised quickly to lead a numerous army to the Netherlands, but he obtained a letter from his brother, Henry III., dated December 26th, by which the king pledged himself to give further aid, as soon as he might succeed in quieting his own disturbed and unfortunate country. The states-general, assembled at Delft, ratified the treaty on the 30th of December; and the year which was about to open seemed to promise the consolidation of freedom and internal peace.

CHAPTER XII

TO THE MURDER OF THE PRINCE OF ORANGE

A.D. 1580—1584

PHILIP might be well excused the utmost violence of resentment on this occasion, had it been bounded by fair and honorable efforts for the maintenance of his authority. But every general principle seemed lost in the base inveteracy of private hatred. The ruin of the Prince of Orange was his main object, and his industry and ingenuity were taxed to the utmost to procure his murder. Existing documents prove that he first wished to accomplish this in such a way as that the responsibility and odium of the act might rest on the prince of Parma; but the mind of the prince was at that period too magnanimous to allow of a participation in the crime. The correspondence on the subject is preserved in the archives, and the date of Philip's first letter (30th of November, 1579) proves that even before the final disavowal of his authority by the United Provinces he had harbored his diabolical design. The prince remonstrated, but with no effect. It even appears that Philip's anxiety would not admit of the delay necessary for the prince's reply. The infamous edict of proscription against William bears date the 15th of March; and the most pressing letters commanded the prince of Parma to make it public. It was not, however, till the 15th of June that he sent forth the fatal ban.

This edict, under Philip's own signature, is a tissue of invective and virulence. The illustrious object of its abuse is accused of having engaged the heretics to profane the churches and break the images; of having persecuted and massacred the Catholic priests; of hypocrisy, tyranny, and perjury; and, as the height of atrocity, of having introduced liberty of conscience into his country! For these causes, and many others, the king declares him "proscribed and banished as a public pest"; and it is permitted to all persons to assail him "in his fortune, person, and life, as an enemy to human nature." Philip also, "for the recompense of virtue and the punishment of crime," promises to whoever will deliver up William of Nassau, dead or alive, "in lands or money, at his choice, the sum of twenty-five thousand golden crowns; to grant a free pardon to such person for all former offences of what kind soever, and to invest him with letters patent of nobility."

In reply to this brutal document of human depravity, William published all over Europe his famous "Apology," of which it is enough to say that language could not produce a more splendid refutation of every charge or a more terrible recrimination against the guilty tyrant. It was attributed to the pen of Peter de Villiers, a Protestant minister. It is universally pronounced one of the noblest monuments of history. William, from the hour of his proscription, became at once the equal in worldly station, as he had ever been the superior in moral worth, of his royal calumniator. He took his place as a prince of an imperial family, not less ancient or illustrious than that of the House of Austria; and he stood forward at the supreme tribunal of public feeling and opinion as the accuser of a king who disgraced his lineage and his throne.

By a separate article in the treaty with the states, the duke of Alençon secured to William the sovereignty of Holland and Zealand, as well as the lordship of Friesland, with his title of stadtholder, retaining to the duke his claim on the prince's faith and homage. The exact nature of William's authority was finally ratified on the 24th of July, 1581; on which day he took the prescribed oath, and entered on the exercise of his well-earned rights.

Philip now formed the design of sending back the duchess of Parma to resume her former situation as stadtholderess, and exercise the authority conjointly with her son. But the latter positively declined this proposal of divided power; and he, consequently, was left alone to its entire exercise. Military affairs made but slow progress this year. The most remarkable event was the capture of La Noue, a native of Bretagne, one of the bravest, and certainly the cleverest, officers in the service of the states, into which he had passed after having given important aid to the Huguenots of France. He was considered so important a prize that Philip refused all proposals for his exchange, and detained him in the castle of Limburg for five years.

The siege of Cambray was now undertaken by the prince of Parma in person; while the duke of Alençon, at the head of a large army and the flower of the French nobility, advanced to its relief, and soon forced his rival to raise the siege. The new sovereign of the Netherlands entered the town, and was received with tumultuous joy by the half-starved citizens and garrison. The prince of Parma sought an equivalent for this check in the attack of Tournay, which he immediately afterward invested. The town was but feebly garrisoned; but the Protestant inhabitants prepared for a desperate defence, under the exciting example of the princess of Epinoi, wife of the governor, who was himself absent. This remarkable woman furnishes another proof of the female heroism which abounded in these wars. Though wounded in the arm, she fought in the breach sword in hand, braving peril and death. And when at length it was impossible to hold out longer, she obtained an honorable capitulation, and marched out, on the 29th of November, on horseback, at the head of the garrison, with an air of triumph rather than of defeat.

The duke of Alençon, now created duke of Anjou, by which title we shall hereafter distinguish him, had repaired to England, in hopes of completing his project of marriage with Elizabeth. After three months of almost confident expectation, the virgin queen, at this time fifty years of age, with a caprice not quite justifiable, broke all her former engagements; and, happily for herself and her country, declined the marriage. Anjou burst out into all the violence of his turbulent temper, and set sail for the Netherlands. Elizabeth made all the reparation in her power, by the honors paid him on his dismissal. She accompanied him as far as Canterbury, and sent him away under the convoy of the earl of Leicester, her chief favorite; and with a brilliant suite and a fleet of fifteen sail. Anjou was received at Antwerp with equal distinction; and was inaugurated there on the 19th of February as duke of Brabant, Lothier, Limburg, and Guelders, with many other titles, of which he soon proved himself unworthy. When the Prince of Orange, at the ceremony, placed the ducal mantle on his shoulders, Anjou said to him, "Fasten it so well, prince, that they cannot take it off again!"

During the rejoicings which followed this inauspicious ceremony, Philip's proscription against the Prince of Orange put forth its first fruits. The latter gave a grand dinner in the chateau of Antwerp, which he occupied, on the 18th of March, the birthday of the duke of Anjou; and, as he was quitting the dining-room, on his way to his private chamber, a young man stepped forward and offered a pretended petition, William being at all times of easy access for such an object. While he read the paper, the treacherous suppliant discharged a pistol at his head: the ball struck him under the left ear, and passed out at the right cheek. As he tottered and fell, the assassin drew a poniard to add suicide to the crime, but he was instantly put to death by the attendant guards. The young Count Maurice, William's second son, examined the murderer's body; and the papers found on him, and subsequent inquiries, told fully who and what he was. His name was John Jaureguay, his age twenty-three years; he was a native of Biscay, and clerk to a Spanish merchant of Antwerp, called Gaspar Anastro. This man had instigated him to the crime; having received a promise signed by King Philip, engaging to give him twenty-eight thousand ducats and other advantages, if he would undertake to assassinate the Prince of Orange. The inducements held out by Anastro to his simple dupe, were backed strongly by the persuasions of Antony Timmerman, a Dominican monk; and by Venero, Anastro's cashier, who had from fear declined becoming himself the murderer. Jaureguay had duly heard mass, and received the sacrament, before executing his attempt; and in his pockets were found a catechism of the Jesuits, with tablets filled with prayers in the Spanish language; one in particular being addressed to the Angel Gabriel, imploring his intercession with God and the Virgin, to aid him in the consummation of his object. Other accompanying absurdities seem to pronounce this miserable wretch to be as much an instrument in the hands of others as the weapon of his crime was in his own. Timmerman and Venero made a full avowal of their criminality, and suffered death in the usual barbarous manner of the times. The Jesuits, some years afterward, solemnly gathered the remains of these three pretended martyrs, and exposed them as holy relics for public veneration. Anastro effected his escape.

The alarm and indignation of the people of Antwerp knew no bounds. Their suspicions at first fell on the duke of Anjou and the French party; but the truth was soon discovered; and the rapid recovery of the Prince of Orange from his desperate wound set everything once more to rights. But a premature report of his death flew rapidly abroad; and he had anticipated proofs of his importance in the eyes of all Europe, in the frantic delight of the base, and the deep affliction of the good. Within three months, William was able to accompany the duke of Anjou in his visits to Ghent, Bruges, and the other chief towns of Flanders; in each of which the ceremony of inauguration was repeated. Several military exploits now took place, and various towns fell into the hands of the opposing parties; changing masters with a rapidity, as well as a previous endurance of suffering, that must have carried confusion and change on the contending principles of allegiance into the hearts and heads of the harassed inhabitants.

The duke of Anjou, intemperate, inconstant, and unprincipled, saw that his authority was but the shadow of power, compared to the deep-fixed practices of despotism which governed the other nations of Europe. The French officers, who formed his suite and possessed all his confidence, had no difficulty in raising his discontent into treason against the people with whom he had made a solemn compact. The result of their councils was a deep-laid plot against Flemish liberty; and its execution was ere-long attempted. He sent secret orders to the governors of Dunkirk, Bruges, Termonde, and other towns, to seize on and hold them in his name; reserving for himself the infamy of the enterprise against Antwerp. To prepare for its execution, he caused his numerous army of French and Swiss to approach the city; and they were encamped in the neighborhood, at a place called Borgerhout.

On the 17th of January, 1583, the duke dined somewhat earlier than usual, under the pretext of proceeding afterward to review his army in their camp. He set out at noon, accompanied by his guard of two hundred horse; and when he reached the second drawbridge, one of his officers gave the preconcerted signal for an attack on the Flemish guard, by pretending that he had fallen and broken his leg. The duke called out to his followers, "Courage, courage! the town is ours!" The guard at the gate was all soon despatched; and the French troops, which waited outside to the number of three thousand, rushed quickly in, furiously shouting the war-cry, "Town taken! town taken! kill! kill!" The astonished but intrepid citizens, recovering from their confusion, instantly flew to arms. All differences in religion or politics were forgotten in the common danger to their freedom. Catholics and Protestants, men and women, rushed alike to the conflict. The ancient spirit of Flanders seemed to animate all. Workmen, armed with the instruments of their various trades, started from their shops and flung themselves upon the enemy. A baker sprang from the cellar where he was kneading his dough, and with his oven shovel struck a French dragoon to the ground. Those who had firearms, after expending their bullets, took from their pouches and pockets pieces of money, which they bent between their teeth, and used for charging their arquebuses. The French were driven successively from the streets and ramparts, and the cannons planted on the latter were immediately turned against the reinforcements which attempted to enter the town. The French were everywhere beaten; the duke of Anjou saved himself by flight, and reached Termonde, after the perilous necessity of passing through a large tract of inundated country. His loss in this base enterprise amounted to one thousand five hundred; while that of the citizens did not exceed eighty men. The attempts simultaneously made on the other towns succeeded at Dunkirk and Termonde; but all the others failed.

The character of the Prince of Orange never appeared so thoroughly great as at this crisis. With wisdom and magnanimity rarely equalled and never surpassed, he threw himself and his authority between the indignation of the country and the guilt of Anjou; saving the former from excess, and the latter from execration. The disgraced and discomfited duke proffered to the states excuses as mean as they were hypocritical; and his brother, the king of France, sent a special envoy to intercede for him. But it was the influence of William that screened the culprit from public reprobation and ruin, and regained for him the place and power which he might easily have secured for himself, had he not prized the welfare of his country far above all objects of private advantage. A new treaty was negotiated, confirming Anjou in his former station, with renewed security against any future treachery on his part. He in the meantime retired to France, to let the public indignation subside; but before he could assume sufficient confidence again to face the country he had so basely injured his worthless existence was suddenly terminated, some thought by poison—the common solution of all such doubtful questions in those days—in the month of June in the following year. He expired in his twenty-ninth year.

A disgusting proof of public ingratitude and want of judgment was previously furnished by the conduct of the people of Antwerp against him who had been so often their deliverer from such various dangers. Unable to comprehend the greatness of his mind, they openly accused the Prince of Orange of having joined with the French for their subjugation, and of having concealed a body of that detested nation in the citadel. The populace rushed to the place, and having minutely examined it, were convinced of their own absurdity and the prince's innocence. He scorned to demand their punishment for such an outrageous calumny; but he was not the less afflicted at it. He took the resolution of quitting Flanders, as it turned out, forever; and he retired into Zealand, where he was better known and consequently better trusted.

In the midst of the consequent confusion in the former of these provinces, the prince of Parma, with indefatigable vigor, made himself master of town after town; and turned his particular attention to the creation of a naval force, which was greatly favored by the possession of Dunkirk, Nieuport, and Gravelines. Native treachery was not idle in this time of tumult and confusion. The count of Renneberg, governor of Friesland and Groningen, had set the basest example, and gone over to the Spaniards. The prince of Chimay, son of the duke of Arschot, and governor of Bruges, yielded to the persuasions of his father, and gave up the place to the prince of Parma. Hembyse also, amply confirming the bad opinion in which the Prince of Orange always held him, returned to Ghent, where he regained a great portion of his former influence, and immediately commenced a correspondence with the prince of Parma, offering to deliver up both Ghent and Termonde. An attempt was consequently made by the Spaniards to surprise the former town; but the citizens were prepared for this, having intercepted some of the letters of Hembyse;

and the traitor was seized, tried, condemned, and executed on the 4th of August, 1584. He was upward of seventy years of age. Ryhove, his celebrated colleague, died in Holland some years later.

But the fate of so insignificant a person as Hembyse passed almost unnoticed, in the agitation caused by an event which shortly preceded his death.

From the moment of their abandonment by the duke of Anjou, the United Provinces considered themselves independent; and although they consented to renew his authority over the country at large, at the solicitation of the Prince of Orange, they were resolved to confirm the influence of the latter over their particular interests, which they were now sensible could acquire stability only by that means. The death of Anjou left them without a sovereign; and they did not hesitate in the choice which they were now called upon to make. On whom, indeed, could they fix but William of Nassau, without the utmost injustice to him, and the deepest injury to themselves? To whom could they turn, in preference to him who had given consistency to the early explosion of their despair; to him who first gave the country political existence, then nursed it into freedom, and now beheld it in the vigor and prime of independence? He had seen the necessity, but certainly overrated the value, of foreign support, to enable the new state to cope with the tremendous tyranny from which it had broken. He had tried successively Germany, England and France. From the first and the last of these powers he had received two governors, to whom he cheerfully resigned the title. The incapacity of both, and the treachery of the latter, proved to the states that their only chance for safety was in the consolidation of William's authority; and they contemplated the noblest reward which a grateful nation could bestow on a glorious liberator. And is it to be believed that he who for twenty years had sacrificed his repose, lavished his fortune, and risked his life, for the public cause, now aimed at absolute dominion, or coveted a despotism which all his actions prove him to have abhorred? Defeated bigotry has put forward such vapid accusations. He has been also held responsible for the early cruelties which, it is notorious, he used every means to avert, and frequently punished. But while these revolting acts can only be viewed in the light of reprisals against the bloodiest persecution that ever existed, by exasperated men driven to vengeance by a bad example, not one single act of cruelty or bad faith has ever been made good against William, who may be safely pronounced one of the wisest and best men that history has held up as examples to the species.

The authority of one author has been produced to prove that, during the lifetime of his brother Louis, offers were made to him by France of the sovereignty of the northern provinces, on condition of the southern being joined to the French crown. That he ever accepted those offers is without proof; that he never acted on them is certain. But he might have been justified in purchasing freedom for those states which had so well earned it, at the price even of a qualified independence under another power, to the exclusion of those which had never heartily struggled against Spain. The best evidence, however, of William's real views is to be found in the Capitulation, as it is called; that is to say, the act which was on the point of being executed between him and the states, when a base fanatic, instigated by a bloody tyrant, put a period to his splendid career. This capitulation exists at full length, but was never formally executed. Its conditions are founded on the same principles, and conceived in nearly the same terms, as those accepted by the duke of Anjou; and the whole compact is one of the most thoroughly liberal that history has on record. The prince repaired to Delft for the ceremony of his inauguration, the price of his long labors; but there, instead of anticipated dignity, he met the sudden stroke of death.

On the 10th of July, as he left his dining-room, and

while he placed his foot on the first step of the great stair leading to the upper apartments of his house, a man named Balthazar Gerard (who, like the former assassin, waited for him at the moment of convivial relaxation), discharged a pistol at his body. Three balls entered it. He fell into the arms of an attendant, and cried out faintly, in the French language, "God pity me! I am sadly wounded—God have mercy on my soul, and on this unfortunate nation!" His sister, the countess of Swartzenberg, who now hastened to his side, asked him in German if he did not recommend his soul to God? He answered, "Yes," in the same language, but with a feeble voice. He was carried into the dining-room, where he immediately expired. His sister closed his eyes; his wife, too, was on the spot—Louisa, daughter of the illustrious Coligny, and widow of the gallant count of Teligny, both of whom were also murdered almost in her sight, in the frightful massacre of St. Bartholomew. We may not enter on a description of the afflicting scene which followed; but the mind is pleased in picturing the bold solemnity with which Prince Maurice, then eighteen years of age, swore—not vengeance or hatred against his father's murderers—but that he would faithfully and religiously follow the glorious example he had given him.

Whoever would really enjoy the spirit of historical details should never omit an opportunity of seeing places rendered memorable by associations connected with the deeds, and especially with the death, of great men; the spot, for instance, where William was assassinated at Delft; the old staircase he was just on the point of ascending; the narrow pass between that and the dining-hall whence he came out, of scarcely sufficient extent for the murderer to hold forth his arm and his pistol, two and a half feet long. This weapon, and its fellow, are both preserved in the museum of The Hague, together with two of the fatal bullets, and the very clothes which the victim wore. The leathern doublet, pierced by the balls and burned by the powder, lies beside the other parts of the dress, the simple gravity of which, in fashion and color, irresistibly brings the wise, great man before us, and adds a hundred-fold to the interest excited by a recital of his murder.

There is but one important feature in the character of William which we have hitherto left untouched, but which the circumstances of his death seemed to sanctify, and point out for record in the same page with it. We mean his religious opinions; and we shall despatch a subject which is, in regard to all men, so delicate, indeed so sacred, in a few words. He was born a Lutheran. When he arrived, a boy, at the court of Charles V., he was initiated into the Catholic creed, in which he was thenceforward brought up. Afterward, when he could think for himself and choose his profession of faith, he embraced the doctrine of Calvin. His whole public conduct seems to prove that he viewed sectarian principles chiefly in the light of political instruments; and that, himself a conscientious Christian, in the broad sense of the term, he was deeply imbued with the spirit of universal toleration, and considered the various shades of belief as subservient to the one grand principle of civil and religious liberty, for which he had long devoted and at length laid down his life. His assassin was taken alive, and four days afterward executed with terrible circumstances of cruelty, which he bore as a martyr might have borne them. He was a native of Burgundy, and had for some months lingered near his victim, and insinuated himself into his confidence by a feigned attachment to liberty, and an apparent zeal for the reformed faith. He was nevertheless a bigoted Catholic and, by his own confession, he had communicated his design to, and received encouragement to its execution from, more than one minister of the sect to which he belonged. But his avowal criminated a more important accomplice, and one whose character stands so high in history that it behooves us to examine thoroughly the truth of the accusation, and the nature of the collateral proofs by which it is supported. Most writers on this question have leaned to the side which all would wish to adopt, for the honor of human nature and the integrity of a celebrated name. But an original letter exists in the archives of Brussels, from the prince of Parma himself to Philip of Spain, in which he admits that Balthazar Gerard had communicated to him his intention of murdering the Prince of Orange some months before the deed was done; and he mixes phrases of compassion for "the poor man" (the murderer) and of praise for the act; which, if the document be really authentic, sinks Alexander of Parma as low as the wretch with whom he sympathized.

CHAPTER XIII

TO THE DEATH OF ALEXANDER, PRINCE OF PARMA

A.D. 1584—1592

THE death of William of Nassau not only closes the scene of his individual career, but throws a deep gloom over the history of a revolution that was sealed by so great a sacrifice. The animation of the story seems suspended. Its events lose for a time their excitement. The last act of the political drama is performed. The great hero of the tragedy is no more. The other most memorable actors have one by one passed away. A whole generation has fallen in the contest; and it is with exhausted interest, and feelings less intense, that we resume the details of war and blood, which seem no longer sanctified by the grander movements of heroism. The stirring impulse of slavery breaking its chains yields to the colder inspiration of independence maintaining its rights. The men we have now to depict were born free; and the deeds they did were those of stern resolve rather than of frantic despair. The present picture may be as instructive as the last, but it is less thrilling. Passion gives place to reason; and that which wore the air of fierce romance is superseded by what bears the stamp of calm reality.

The consternation caused by the news of William's death soon yielded to the firmness natural to a people inured to suffering and calamity. The United Provinces rejected at once the overtures made by the prince of Parma to induce them to obedience. They seemed proud to show that their fate did not depend on that of one man. He therefore turned his attention to the most effective means of obtaining results by force which he found it impossible to secure by persuasion. He proceeded vigorously to the reduction of the chief towns of Flanders, the conquest of which would give him possession of the entire province, no army now remaining to oppose him in the field. He soon obliged Ypres and Termonde to surrender; and Ghent, forced by famine, at length yielded on reasonable terms. The most severe was the utter abolition of the reformed religion; by which a large portion of the population was driven to the alternative of exile; and they passed over in crowds to Holland and Zealand, not half of the inhabitants remaining behind. Mechlin, and finally Brussels, worn out by a fruitless resistance, followed the example of the rest; and thus, within a year after the death of William of Nassau, the power of Spain was again established in the whole province of Flanders, and the others which comprise what is in modern days generally denominated Belgium.

But these domestic victories of the prince of Parma were barren in any of those results which humanity would love to see in the train of conquest. The reconciled provinces presented the most deplorable spectacle. The chief towns were almost depopulated. The inhabitants had in a great measure fallen victims to war, pestilence and famine. Little inducement existed to replace by marriage the ravages caused by death, for few men wished to propagate a race which divine wrath seemed to have marked for persecution. The thousands of villages which had covered the face of the country were absolutely abandoned to the wolves, which had so rapidly increased that they attacked not merely cattle and children, but grown-up persons. The dogs, driven abroad by hunger, had become as ferocious as other beasts of prey, and joined in large packs to hunt down brutes and men. Neither fields, nor woods, nor roads, were now to be distinguished by any visible limits. All was an entangled mass of trees, weeds, and grass. The prices of the necessaries of life were so high that people of rank, after selling everything to buy bread, were obliged to have recourse to open beggary in the streets of the great towns.

From this frightful picture, and the numerous details which imagination may readily supply, we gladly turn to the contrast afforded by the northern states. Those we have just described have a feeble hold upon our sympathies; we cannot pronounce their sufferings to be unmerited. The want of firmness or enlightenment, which preferred such an existence to the risk of entire destruction, only heightens the glory of the people whose unyielding energy and courage gained them so proud a place among the independent nations of Europe.

The murder of William seemed to carry to the United Provinces conviction of the weakness as well as the atrocity of Spain; and the indecent joy excited among the royalists added to their courage. An immediate council was created, composed of eighteen members, at the head of which was unanimously placed Prince Maurice of Nassau (who even then gave striking indications of talent and prudence); his elder brother, the count of Beuren, now Prince of Orange, being still kept captive in Spain. Count Hohenloe was appointed lieutenant-general; and several other measures were promptly adopted to consolidate the power of the infant republic. The whole of its forces amounted but to five thousand five hundred men. The prince of Parma had eighty thousand at his command. With such means of carrying on his conquests, he sat down regularly before Antwerp, and commenced the operations of one of the most celebrated among the many memorable sieges of those times. He completely surrounded the city with troops; placing a large portion of his army on the left bank of the Scheldt, the other on the right; and causing to be attacked at the same time the two strong forts of Liefkinshoek and Lillo. Repulsed on the latter important point, his only hope of gaining the command of the navigation of the river, on which the success of the siege depended, was by throwing a bridge across the stream. Neither its great rapidity, nor its immense width, nor the want of wood and workmen, could deter him from this vast undertaking. He was assisted, if not guided, in all his projects on the occasion, by Barroccio, a celebrated Italian engineer sent to him by Philip; and the merit of all that was done ought fairly to be, at least, divided between the general and the engineer. If enterprise and perseverance belonged to the first, science and skill were the portion of the latter. They first caused two strong forts to be erected at opposite sides of the river; and adding to their resources by every possible means, they threw forward a pier on each side of, and far into, the stream. The stakes, driven firmly into the bed of the river and cemented with masses of earth and stones, were at a proper height covered with planks and defended by parapets. These estoccades, as they were called, reduced the river to half its original breadth; and the cannon with which they were mounted rendered the passage extremely dangerous to hostile vessels. But to fill up this strait a considerable number of boats were fastened together by chain-hooks and anchors; and being manned and armed with cannon, they were moored in the interval between the estoccades. During these operations, a canal was cut between the Moer and Calloo; by which means a communication was formed with Ghent, which insured a supply of ammunition and provisions. The works of the bridge, which was two thousand four hundred feet in length, were constructed with such strength and solidity that they braved the winds, the floods, and the ice of the whole winter.

The people of Antwerp at first laughed to scorn the whole of these stupendous preparations; but when they found that the bridge resisted the natural elements, by which they doubted not it would have been destroyed, they began to tremble in the anticipation of famine; yet they vigorously prepared for their defence, and rejected the overtures made by the prince of Parma even at this advanced stage of his proceedings. Ninety-seven pieces of cannon now defended the bridge; besides which thirty large barges at each side of the river guarded its extremities; and forty ships of war formed a fleet of protection,

constantly ready to meet any attack from the besieged. **They,** seeing the Scheldt thus really closed **up,** and all communication with Zealand impossible, felt **their** whole safety to depend on the destruction **of the** bridge. The states of Zealand **now sent** forward **an expedition,** which, joined with some ships **from** Lillo, **gave new courage to** the besieged; **and everything was** prepared for their great attempt. **An Italian** engineer named Giambelli was at this time **in Antwerp, and by** his talents **had long** protracted the **defence. He has the chief merit of being the** inventor **of** those terrible fire-ships **which gained the title of** "infernal machines"; **and with some of these formidable instruments** and the Zealand **fleet, the long-projected attack was at** length made.

Early on the **night of the 4th of April, the prince of** Parma and his army **were amazed by the spectacle of three** huge masses of **flame floating down the river, accompanied** by numerous lesser **appearances of a similar kind, and bearing** directly against the prodigious **barrier, which had cost** months of labor to him **and** his **troops, and immense** sums of money to the state. **The whole surface of the** Scheldt presented one **sheet** of **fire; the country all** round was as visible as **at noon;** the **flags, the arms of** the soldiers, and every object **on the** bridge, **in the fleet, or** the **forts,** stood out clearly **to view; and the** pitchy **darkness of** the sky gave increased **effect to the marked** distinctness of all. **Astonishment was soon succeeded** by consternation, when one **of the three machines burst with** a terrific noise before they reached **their intended mark,** but time enough **to** offer a sample of their **nature. The** prince of Parma, **with numerous** officers **and soldiers rushed to** the bridge, to witness the effects of this explosion; and just then a second and still larger fire-ship, having burst **through** the flying bridge of boats, struck against one of the estoccades. Alexander, unmindful of danger, used every exertion of his authority to stimulate the sailors in their attempts to clear away the monstrous machine which threatened destruction to all within its reach. Happily for him, an ensign who was near, forgetting in his general's peril all rules of discipline and forms of ceremony, actually forced him from the estoccade. He had not put his foot on the river bank when the machine blew up. The effects were such as really baffle description. The bridge was burst through; the estoccade was shattered almost to atoms, and, with all that it supported—men, cannon, and the huge machinery employed in the various works—dispersed in the air. The cruel marquis of Roubais, many other officers, and eight hundred soldiers, perished in all varieties of death—by flood, or flame, or the horrid wounds from the missiles with which the terrible machine was overcharged. Fragments of bodies and limbs were flung far and wide; and many gallant soldiers were destroyed, without a vestige of the human form being left to prove that they had ever existed. The river, forced from its bed at either side, rushed into the forts and drowned numbers of their garrisons; while the ground far beyond shook as in an earthquake. The prince was struck down by a beam, and lay for some time senseless, together with two generals, Delvasto and Gajitani, both more seriously wounded than he; and many of the soldiers were burned and mutilated in the most frightful manner. Alexander soon recovered; and by his presence of mind, humanity, and resolution, he endeavored with incredible quickness to repair the mischief, and raised the confidence of his army as high as ever. Had the Zealand fleet come in time to the spot, the whole plan might have been crowned with success; but by some want of concert, or accidental delay, it did not appear; and consequently the beleaguered town received no relief.

One last resource was left to the besieged; that which had formerly been resorted to at Leyden, and by which the place was saved. To enable them to inundate the immense plain which stretched between Lillo and Strabroek up to the walls of Antwerp, it was necessary to cut through the dike which defended it against the irruptions of the eastern

Scheldt. This plain was traversed by a high and wide counter-dike, called the dike of Couvestien; and Alexander, knowing its importance, had early taken possession of and strongly defended it by several forts. Two attacks were made by the garrison of Antwerp on this important construction; the latter of which led to one of the most desperate encounters of the war. The prince, seeing that on the results of this day depended the whole consequences of his labors, fought with a valor that even he had never before displayed, and he was finally victorious. The confederates were forced to abandon the attack, leaving three thousand dead upon the dike or at its base; and the Spaniards lost full eight hundred men.

One more fruitless attempt was made to destroy the bridge and raise the siege, by means of an enormous vessel bearing the presumptuous title of The End of the War. But this floating citadel ran aground, without producing any effect; and the gallant governor of Antwerp, the celebrated Philip de Saint Aldegonde, was forced to capitulate on the 16th of August, after a siege of fourteen months. The reduction of Antwerp was considered a miracle of perseverance and courage. The prince of Parma was elevated by his success to the highest pinnacle of renown; and Philip, on receiving the news, displayed a burst of joy such as rarely varied his cold and gloomy reserve.

Even while the fate of Antwerp was undecided, the United Provinces, seeing that they were still too weak to resist alone the undivided force of the Spanish monarchy, had opened negotiations with France and England at once, in the hope of gaining one or the other for an ally and protector. Henry III. gave a most honorable reception to the ambassadors sent to his court, and was evidently disposed to accept their offers, had not the distracted state of his own country, still torn by civil war, quite disabled him from any effective co-operation. The deputies sent to England were also well received. Elizabeth listened to the proposals of the states, sent them an ambassador in return, and held out the most flattering hopes of succor. But her cautious policy would not suffer her to accept the sovereignty; and she declared that she would in nowise interfere with the negotiations, which might end in its being accepted by the king of France. She gave prompt evidence of her sincerity by an advance of considerable sums of money, and by sending to Holland a body of six thousand troops, under the command of her favorite, Robert Dudley, earl of Leicester; and as security for the repayment of her loan, the towns of Flushing and Brille, and the castle of Rammekins, were given up to her.

The earl of Leicester was accompanied by a splendid retinue of noblemen, and a select troop of five hundred followers. He was received at Flushing by the governor, Sir Philip Sidney, his nephew, the model of manners and conduct for the young men of his day. But Leicester possessed neither courage nor capacity equal to the trust reposed in him; and his arbitrary and indolent conduct soon disgusted the people whom he was sent to assist. They had, in the first impulse of their gratitude, given him the title of governor and captain-general of the provinces, in the hope of flattering Elizabeth. But this had a far contrary effect: she was equally displeased with the states and with Leicester; and it was with difficulty that, after many humble submissions, they were able to appease her.

To form a counterpoise to the power so lavishly conferred on Leicester, Prince Maurice was, according to the wise advice of Olden Barnevelt, raised to the dignity of stadtholder, captain-general, and admiral of Holland and Zealand. This is the first instance of these states taking on themselves the nomination to the dignity of stadtholder, for even William has held his commission from Philip, or in his name; but Friesland, Groningen, and Guelders had already appointed their local governors, under the same title, by the authority of the states-general, the archduke Mathias, or even of the provincial states. Holland had now also at the head of its civil government a citizen full of talent and probity, who was thus able to contend with the insidious designs of Leicester against the liberty he nominally came to protect. This was Barnevelt, who was promoted from his office of pensionary of Rotterdam to that of Holland, and who accepted the dignity only on condition of being free to resign it if any accommodation of differences should take place with Spain.

Alexander of Parma had, by the death of his mother, in February, 1586, exchanged his title of prince for the superior one of duke of Parma, and soon resumed his enterprises with his usual energy and success; various operations took place, in which the English on every opportunity distinguished themselves; particularly in an action near the town of Grave, in Brabant; and in the taking of Axel by escalade, under the orders of Sir Philip Sidney. A more important affair occurred near Zutphen, at a place called Warnsfeld, both of which towns have given names to the action. On this occasion the veteran Spaniards, under the marquis of Guasto, were warmly attacked and completely defeated by the English; but the victory was dearly purchased by the death of Sir Philip Sidney, who was mortally wounded in the thigh, and expired a few days afterward, at the early age of thirty-two years. In addition to the valor, talent, and conduct, which had united to establish his fame, he displayed, on this last opportunity of his short career, an instance of humanity that sheds a new lustre on even a character like his. Stretched on the battlefield, in all the agony of his wound, and parched with thirst, his afflicted followers brought him some water, procured with difficulty at a distance, and during the heat of the fight. But Sidney, seeing a soldier lying near, mangled like himself, and apparently expiring, refused the water, saying, "Give it to that poor man; his sufferings are greater than mine."

Leicester's conduct was now become quite intolerable to the states. His incapacity and presumption were every day more evident and more revolting. He seemed to consider himself in a province wholly reduced to English authority, and paid no sort of attention to the very opposite character of the people. An eminent Dutch author accounts for this, in terms which may make an Englishman of this age not a little proud of the contrast which his character presents to what it was then considered. "The Englishman," says Grotius, "obeys like a slave, and governs like a tyrant; while the Belgian knows how to serve and to command with equal moderation." The dislike between Leicester and those he insulted and misgoverned soon became mutual. He retired to the town of Utrecht; and pushed his injurious conduct to such an extent that he became an object of utter hatred to the provinces. All the friendly feelings toward England were gradually changed into suspicion and dislike. Conferences took place at The Hague between Leicester and the states, in which Barnevelt overwhelmed his contemptible shuffling by the force of irresistible eloquence and well-deserved reproaches; and after new acts of treachery, still more odious than his former, this unworthy favorite at last set out for England, to lay an account of his government at the feet of the queen.

The growing hatred against England was fomented by the true patriots, who aimed at the liberty of their country; and may be excused, from the various instances of treachery displayed, not only by the commander-in-chief, but by several of his inferiors in command. A strong fort, near Zutphen, **under the** government of Roland York, the town of Deventer, under that of William **Stanly**, and subsequently **Guelders**, under a Scotchman named Pallot, were delivered up to **the Spaniards by** these men; and about the **same time** the **English cavalry** committed some excesses in **Guelders and Holland, which** added to the prevalent prejudice against the nation in general. This enmity was no longer to be concealed. The partisans of Leicester were, one by one, under plausible pretexts, removed from the council of state; and Elizabeth having required from Holland the exportation into England of a large quantity of rye, it was firmly but respectfully refused, as inconsistent with the wants of the provinces.

Prince Maurice, from the caprice and jealousy of Leicester, now united in himself the whole power of command, and commenced that brilliant course of conduct which consolidated the independence of his country and elevated him to the first rank of military glory. His early efforts were turned to the suppression of the partiality which in some places existed for English domination; and he never allowed himself to be deceived by the hopes of peace held out by the emperor and the kings of Denmark and Poland. Without refusing their mediation, he labored incessantly to organize every possible means for maintaining the war. His efforts were considerably favored by the measures of Philip for the support of the league formed by the House of Guise against Henry III. and Henry IV. of France; but still more by the formidable enterprise which the Spanish monarch was now preparing against England.

Irritated and mortified by the assistance which Elizabeth had given to the revolted provinces, Philip resolved to employ his whole power in attempting the conquest of England itself; hoping afterward to effect with ease the subjugation of the Netherlands. He caused to be built, in almost every port of Spain and Portugal, galleons, carricks, and other ships of war of the largest dimensions; and at the same time gave orders to the duke of Parma to assemble in the harbors of Flanders as many vessels as he could collect together.

The Spanish fleet, consisting of more than one hundred and forty ships of the line, and manned by twenty thousand sailors, assembled at Lisbon under the orders of the duke of Medina Sidonia; while the duke of Parma, uniting his forces, held himself ready on the coast of Flanders, with an army of thirty thousand men and four hundred transports. This prodigious force obtained, in Spain, the ostentatious title of the Invincible Armada. Its destination was for a while attempted to be concealed, under pretext that it was meant for India, or for the annihilation of the United Provinces; but the mystery was soon discovered. At the end of May, the principal fleet sailed from the port of Lisbon; and being reinforced off Corunna by a considerable squadron, the whole armament steered its course for the shores of England.

The details of the progress and the failure of this celebrated attempt are so thoroughly the province of English history that they would be in this place superfluous. But it must not be forgotten that the glory of the proud result was amply shared by the new republic, whose existence depended on it. While Howard and Drake held the British fleet in readiness to oppose the Spanish Armada, that of Holland, consisting of but twenty-five ships, under the command of Justin of Nassau, prepared to take a part in the conflict. This gallant though illegitimate scion of the illustrious house, whose name he upheld on many occasions, proved himself on the present worthy of such a father as William, and such a brother as Maurice. While the duke of Medina Sidonia, ascending the Channel as far as Dunkirk, there expected the junction of the duke of Parma with his important reinforcement, Justin of Nassau, by a constant activity, and a display of intrepid talent, contrived to block up the whole expected force in the ports of Flanders from Lillo to Dunkirk. The duke of Parma found it impossible to force a passage on any one point; and was doomed to the mortification of knowing that the attempt was frustrated, and the whole force of Spain frittered away, discomfited, and disgraced, from the want of a co-operation, which he could not, however, reproach himself for having withheld. The issue of the memorable expedition, which cost Spain years of preparation, thousands of men, and millions of treasure, was received in the country which sent it forth with consternation and rage. Philip alone possessed or affected an apathy which he covered with a veil of mock devotion that few were deceived by. At the news of the disaster, he fell on his knees, and rendering thanks for that gracious dispensation of Providence, expressed his joy that the calamity was not greater.

The people, the priests, and the commanders of the expedition were not so easily appeased, or so clever as their hypocritical master in concealing their mortification. The priests accounted for this triumph of heresy as a punishment on Spain for suffering the existence of the infidel Moors in some parts of the country. The defeated admirals threw the whole blame on the duke of Parma. He, on his part, sent an ample remonstrance to the king; and Philip declared that he was satisfied with the conduct of his nephew. Leicester died four days after the final defeat and dispersion of the Armada.

The war in the Netherlands had been necessarily suffered to languish, while every eye was fixed on the progress of the Armada, from formation to defeat. But new efforts were soon made by the duke of Parma to repair the time he had lost, and soothe, by his successes, the disappointed pride of Spain. Several officers now came into notice, remarkable for deeds of great gallantry and skill. None among those was so distinguished as Martin Schenck, a soldier of fortune, a man of ferocious activity, who began his career in the service of tyranny, and ended it by chance in that of independence. He changed sides several times, but, no matter who he fought for, he did his duty well, from that unconquerable principle of pugnacity which seemed to make his sword a part of himself.

Schenck had lately, for the last time, gone over to the side of the states, and had caused a fort to be built in the isle of Betewe—that possessed of old by the Batavians—which was called by his name, and was considered the key to the passage of the Rhine. From this stronghold he constantly harassed the archbishop of Cologne, and had as his latest exploit surprised and taken the strong town of Bonn. While the duke of Parma took prompt measures for the relief of the prelate, making himself master in the meantime of some places of strength, the indefatigable Schenck resolved to make an attempt on the important town of Nimeguen. He with great caution embarked a chosen body of troops on the Wahal, and arrived under the walls of Nimeguen at sunrise on the morning chosen for the attack. His enterprise seemed almost crowned with success; when the inhabitants, recovering from their fright, precipitated themselves from the town; forced the assailants to retreat to their boats; and, carrying the combat into those overcharged and fragile vessels, upset several, and among others that which contained Schenck himself, who, covered with wounds, and fighting to the last gasp, was drowned with the greater part of his followers. His body, when recovered, was treated with the utmost indignity, quartered, and hung in portions over the different gates of the city.

The following year was distinguished by another daring attempt on the part of the Hollanders, but followed by a different result. A captain named Haranguer concerted with one Adrien Vandenberg a plan for the surprise of Breda, on the possession of which Prince Maurice had set a great value. The associates contrived to conceal in a boat laden with turf (which formed the principal fuel of the inhabitants of that part of the country), and of which Vandenberg was master, eighty determined soldiers, and succeeded in arriving close to the city without any suspicion being excited. One of the soldiers, named Matthew Helt, being suddenly affected with a violent cough, implored his comrades to put him to death, to avoid the risk of a discovery. But a corporal of the city guard having inspected the cargo with unsuspecting carelessness, the immolation of the brave soldier became unnecessary, and the boat was dragged into the basin by the assistance of some of the very garrison who were so soon to fall victims to the stratagem. At midnight the concealed soldiers quitted their hiding-places, leaped on shore, killed the sentinels, and easily became masters of the citadel. Prince Maurice, following close with his army, soon forced the town to submit, and put it into so good a state of defence that Count Mansfield, who was sent to retake it, was obliged to retreat after useless efforts to fulfil his mission.

The duke of Parma, whose constitution was severely injured by the constant fatigues of war and the anxieties attending on the late transactions, had snatched a short interval for the purpose of recruiting his health at the waters of Spa. While at that place he received urgent orders from Philip to abandon for a while all his proceedings in the Netherlands, and to hasten into France with his whole disposable force, to assist the army of the League. The battle of Yvri (in which the son of the unfortunate Count Egmont met his death while fighting in the service of his father's royal murderer) had raised the prospects and hopes of Henry IV. to a high pitch; and Paris, which he closely besieged, was on the point of yielding to his arms. The duke of Parma received his uncle's orders with great repugnance; and lamented the necessity of leaving the field of his former exploits open to the enterprise and talents of Prince Maurice. He nevertheless obeyed; and leaving Count Mansfield at the head of the government, he conducted his troops against the royal opponent, who alone seemed fully worthy of coping with him.

The attention of all Europe was now fixed on the exciting spectacle of a contest between those two greatest captains of the age. The glory of success, the fruit of consummate skill, was gained by Alexander; who, by an admirable manœuvre, got possession of the town of Lagny-sur-Seine, under the very eyes of Henry and his whole army, and thus acquired the means of providing Paris with everything requisite for its defence. The French monarch saw all his projects baffled, and his hopes frustrated; while his antagonist, having fully completed his object, drew off his army through Champagne, and made a fine retreat through an enemy's country, harassed at every step, but with scarcely any loss.

But while this expedition added greatly to the renown

of the general, it considerably injured the cause of Spain in the Low Countries. Prince Maurice, taking prompt advantage of the absence of his great rival, had made himself master of several fortresses; and some Spanish regiments having mutinied against the commanders left behind by the duke of Parma, others, encouraged by the impunity they enjoyed, were ready on the slightest pretext to follow their example. Maurice did not lose a single opportunity of profiting by circumstances so favorable; and even after the return of Alexander he seized on Zutphen, Deventer, and Nimeguen, despite all the efforts of the Spanish army. The duke of Parma, daily breaking down under the progress of disease, and agitated by these reverses, repaired again to Spa, taking at once every possible means for the recruitment of his army and the recovery of his health, on which its discipline and the chances of success now so evidently depended.

But all his plans were again frustrated by a renewal of Philip's peremptory orders to march once more into France, to uphold the failing cause of the League against the intrepidity and talent of Henry IV. At this juncture the emperor Rodolf again offered his mediation between Spain and the United Provinces. But it was not likely that the confederated States, at the very moment when their cause began to triumph, and their commerce was every day becoming more and more flourishing, would consent to make any compromise with the tyranny they were at length in a fair way of crushing.

The duke of Parma again appeared in France in the beginning of the year 1592; and, having formed his communications with the army of the League, marched to the relief of the city of Rouen, at that period pressed to the last extremity by the Huguenot forces. After some sharp skirmishes—and one in particular, in which Henry IV. suffered his valor to lead him into a too rash exposure of his own and his army's safety—a series of manœuvres took place, which displayed the talents of the rival generals in the most brilliant aspect. Alexander at length succeeded in raising the siege of Rouen, and made himself master of Condebec, which commanded the navigation of the Seine. Henry, taking advantage of what appeared an irreparable fault on the part of the duke, invested his army in the hazardous position he had chosen; but while believing that he had the whole of his enemies in his power, he found that Alexander had passed the Seine with his entire force—raising his military renown to the utmost possible height by a retreat which it was deemed utterly impossible to effect.

On his return to the Netherlands, the duke found himself again under the necessity of repairing to Spa, in search of some relief from the suffering which was considerably increased by the effects of a wound received in this last campaign. In spite of his shattered constitution, he maintained to the latest moment the most active endeavors for the reorganization of his army; and he was preparing for a new expedition into France, when, fortunately for the good cause in both countries, he was surprised by death on the 3d of December, 1592, at the abbey of St. Vaast, near Arras, at the age of forty-seven years. As it was hard to imagine that Philip would suffer any one who had excited his jealousy to die a natural death, that of the duke of Parma was attributed to slow poison.

Alexander of Parma was certainly one of the most remarkable, and, it may be added, one of the greatest, characters of his day. Most historians have upheld him even higher perhaps than he should be placed on the scale; asserting that he can be reproached with very few of the vices of the age in which he lived. Others consider this judgment too favorable, and accuse him of participation in all the crimes of Philip, whom he served so zealously. His having excited the jealousy of the tyrant, or even had he been put to death by his orders, would little influence the question; for Philip was quite capable of ingratitude or murder, to either an accomplice or an opponent of his baseness. But even allowing that Alexander's fine qualities were sullied by his complicity in these odious measures, we must still in justice admit that they were too much in the spirit of the times, and particularly of the school in which he was trained; and while we lament that his political or private faults place him on so low a level, we must rank him as one of the very first masters in the art of war in his own or any other age.

CHAPTER XIV

TO THE INDEPENDENCE OF BELGIUM AND THE DEATH OF PHILIP II.

A.D. 1592—1599

THE duke of Parma had chosen the count of Mansfield for his successor, and the nomination was approved by the king. He entered on his government under most disheartening circumstances. The rapid conquests of Prince Maurice in Brabant and Flanders were scarcely less mortifying than the total disorganization into which those two provinces had fallen. They were ravaged by bands of robbers called Picaroons, whose audacity reached such a height that they opposed in large bodies the forces sent for their suppression by the government. They on one occasion killed the provost of Flanders, and burned his lieutenant in a hollow tree; and on another they mutilated a whole troop of the national militia, and their commander, with circumstances of most revolting cruelty.

The authority of governor-general, though not the title, was now fully shared by the count of Fuentes, who was sent to Brussels by the king of Spain; and the ill effects of this double viceroyalty was soon seen, in the brilliant progress of Prince Maurice, and the continual reverses sustained by the royalist armies. The king, still bent on projects of bigotry, sacrificed without scruple men and treasure for the overthrow of Henry IV. and the success of the League. The affairs of the Netherlands seemed now a secondary object; and he drew largely on his forces in that country for reinforcements to the ranks of his tottering allies. A final blow was, however, struck against the hopes of intolerance in France, and to the existence of the League, by the conversion of Henry IV. to the Catholic religion;

he deeming theological disputes, which put the happiness of a whole kingdom in jeopardy, as quite subordinate to the public good.

Such was the prosperity of the United Provinces, that they had been enabled to send a large supply, both of money and men, to the aid of Henry, their constant and generous ally. And notwithstanding this, their armies and fleets, so far from suffering diminution, were augmented day by day. Philip, resolved to summon up all his energy for the revival of the war against the republic, now appointed the archduke Ernest, brother of the emperor Rodolf, to the post which the disunion of Mansfield and Fuentes rendered as embarrassing as it had become inglorious. This prince, of a gentle and conciliatory character, was received at Brussels with great magnificence and general joy; his presence reviving the deep-felt hopes of peace entertained by the suffering people. Such were also the cordial wishes of the prince; but more than one design, formed at this period against the life of Prince Maurice, frustrated every expectation of the kind. A priest of the province of Namur, named Michael Renichon, disguised as a soldier, was the new instrument meant to strike another blow at the greatness of the House of Nassau, in the person of its gallant representative, Prince Maurice; as also in that of his brother, Frederic Henry, then ten years of age. On the confession of the intended assassin, he was employed by Count Berlaimont to murder the two princes. Renichon happily mismanaged the affair, and betrayed his intention. He was arrested at Breda, conducted to The Hague, and there tried and executed on the 3d of June, 1594. This miserable wretch accused the archduke Ernest of having countenanced his attempt; but nothing whatever tends to criminate, while every probability acquits, that prince of such a participation.

In this same year a soldier named Peter Dufour embarked in a like atrocious plot. He, too, was seized and executed before he could carry it into effect; and to his dying hour persisted in accusing the archduke of being his instigator. But neither the judges who tried, nor the best historians who record, his intended crime, gave any belief to this accusation. The mild and honorable disposition of the prince held a sufficient guarantee against its likelihood; and it is not less pleasing to be able fully to join in the prevalent opinion, than to mark a spirit of candor and impartiality break forth through the mass of bad and violent passions which crowd the records of that age.

But all the esteem inspired by the personal character of Ernest could not overcome the repugnance of the United Provinces to trust to the apparent sincerity of the tyrant in whose name he made his overtures for peace. They were all respectfully and firmly rejected; and Prince Maurice, in the meantime, with his usual activity, passed the Meuse and the Rhine, and invested and quickly took the town of Groningen, by which he consummated the establishment of the republic, and secured its rank among the principal powers of Europe.

The archduke Ernest, finding all his efforts for peace frustrated, and all hopes of gaining his object by hostility to be vain, became a prey to disappointment and regret, and died, from the effects of a slow fever, on the 21st of February, 1595; leaving to the count of Fuentes the honors and anxieties of the government, subject to the ratification of the king. This nobleman began the exercise of his temporary functions by an irruption into France, at the head of a small army; war having been declared against Spain by Henry IV., who, on his side, had despatched the Admiral de Villars to attack Philip's possessions in Hainault and Artois. This gallant officer lost a battle and his life in the contest; and Fuentes, encouraged by the victory, took some frontier towns, and laid siege to Cambray, the great object of his plans. The citizens, who detested their governor, the marquis of Bologni, who had for some time assumed an independent tyranny over them, gave up the place to the besiegers; and the citadel surrendered some days later. After this exploit Fuentes returned to Brussels, where, notwithstanding his success, he was extremely unpopular. He had placed a part of his forces under the command of Mondragon, one of the oldest and cleverest officers in the service of Spain. Some trifling affairs took place in Brabant; but the arrival of the archduke Albert, whom the king had appointed to succeed his brother Ernest in the office of governor-general, deprived Fuentes of any further opportunity of signalizing his talents for supreme command. Albert arrived at Brussels on the 11th of February, 1596, accompanied by the Prince of Orange, who, when count of Beuren, had been carried off from the university of Louvain, twenty-eight years previously, and held captive in Spain during the whole of that period.

The archduke Albert, fifth son of the emperor Maximilian II., and brother of Rodolf, stood high in the opinion of Philip, his uncle, and merited his reputation for talents, bravery, and prudence. He had been early made archbishop of Toledo, and afterward cardinal; but his profession was not that of these nominal dignities. He was a warrior and politician of considerable capacity; and had for some years faithfully served the king, as viceroy of Portugal. But Philip meant him for the more independent situation of sovereign of the Netherlands, and at the same time destined him to be the husband of his daughter Isabella. He now sent him, in the capacity of governor-general, to prepare the way for the important change; at once to gain the good graces of the people, and soothe, by this removal from Philip's too close neighborhood, the jealousy of his son, the hereditary prince of Spain. Albert brought with him to Brussels a small reinforcement for the army, with a large supply of money, more wanting at this conjuncture than men. He highly praised the conduct of Fuentes in the operations just finished; and resolved to continue the war on the same plan, but with forces much superior.

He opened his first campaign early; and, by a display of clever manœuvring, which threatened an attempt to force the French to raise the siege of La **Fere**, in the heart of Picardy, he concealed his real design—the capture of Calais; and he succeeded in its completion almost before it was suspected. The Spanish and Walloon troops, led on by **Rone**, a distinguished officer, carried the first **defences**: after nine days of siege the place was forced to **surrender**; and in a few more the **citadel** followed **the example.** The archduke soon **after took the towns of Ardres and** Hulst; and by **prudently avoiding a battle, to which he was** constantly **provoked by Henry IV., who commanded the French army in person, he** established **his character for** military **talent of no ordinary degree.**

He at the same time made **overtures of reconciliation to the United Provinces, and** hoped **that the return of the Prince of Orange would be a means of effecting so desirable a** purpose. **But the Dutch were not to be deceived by** the apparent sincerity **of Spanish negotiation. They even** doubted the **sentiments of the Prince of** Orange, whose attachments and principles **had been formed in so** hated **a** school; and nothing passed **between them and him but mutual** civilities. **They** clearly **evinced their** disapprobation of his intended visit **to Holland; and he** consequently fixed **his** residence **in Brussels, passing his life in an** inglorious neutrality.

A naval expedition formed in this year by the English and **Dutch against Cadiz, commanded by the earl of** Essex, and Counts **Louis and William of Nassau,** cousins of Prince **Maurice, was crowned with** brilliant success, and somewhat consoled **the provinces for the** contemporary exploits **of** the archduke. **But the following year** opened with an affair which at once proved his unceasing activity, and added largely to the reputation **of his** rival, Prince Maurice. The former had detached the count of Varas, with about six thousand men, for the purpose of invading the province of Holland; but Maurice, with **equal energy and superior talent, followed his movements, came up with him near Turnhout, on the 24th of** January, 1597; and after a sharp action, of which the Dutch cavalry bore the whole brunt, **Varas was killed,** and his troops defeated with considerable loss.

This action may be taken as a fair sample of the difficulty with which any estimate can be formed of the relative losses on such occasions. The Dutch historians state the loss of the royalists, in killed, at upward of **two** thousand. Meteren, a good authority, says the peasants buried **two thousand two hundred and** fifty; while Bentivoglio, an Italian writer in the interest of Spain, **makes** the number exactly half that amount. Grotius says that the loss of the Dutch was four men killed. Bentivoglio states it at **one hundred.** But, at either computation, it is clear that **the affair was a brilliant one on the part of Prince** Maurice.

This was in its consequences a most disastrous affair to the archduke. His army was disorganized, and his finances exhausted; while the confidence of the states in their troops and their general was considerably raised. But the taking of Amiens by Portocarrero, one of the most enterprising of the Spanish captains, gave a new turn to the failing fortunes of Albert. This gallant officer, whose greatness of mind, according to some historians, was much **disproportioned to the smallness of his person,** gained possession of that important town by a well-conducted stratagem, and maintained his conquest valiantly till he **was killed in its defence.** Henry IV. made prodigious efforts to recover the place, the chief bulwark on that side of France; and having forced Montenegro, the worthy successor of Portocarrero, to capitulate, granted him and his garrison most honorable conditions. **Henry, having secured** Amiens against any new attack, **returned** to Paris and made a triumphal entry into the city.

During this year Prince Maurice took a number of towns in rapid succession; and the states, according to their custom, caused various medals, in gold, silver, and copper, to be struck, to commemorate the victories which had signalized their arms.

Philip II., feeling himself approaching the termination of his long and agitating career, now wholly occupied himself in negotiations for peace with France. Henry IV. desired it as anxiously. The pope, Clement VIII., encouraged by his exhortations this mutual inclination. The king of Poland sent ambassadors to The Hague and to London, to induce the states and Queen Elizabeth to become parties in a general pacification. These overtures led to no conclusion; but the conferences between France and Spain went on with apparent cordiality and great promptitude, and a peace was concluded between these powers at Vervins, on the 2d of May, 1598.

Shortly after the publication of this treaty, another important act was made known to the world, by which Philip ceded to Albert and Isabella, on their being formally affianced—a ceremony which now took place—the sovereignty of Burgundy and the Netherlands. This act bears date the 6th of May, and was proclaimed with all the solemnity due to so important a transaction. It contained thirteen articles; and was based on the misfortunes which the absence of the sovereign had hitherto caused to the Low Countries. The Catholic religion was declared that of the state, in its full integrity. The provinces were guaranteed against dismemberment. The archdukes, by which title the joint sovereigns were designated without any distinction of sex, were secured in the possession, with right of succession to their children; and a provision was added, that in default of posterity their possessions should revert to the Spanish crown. The infanta Isabella soon sent her procuration to the archduke, her affianced husband, giving him full power and authority to take possession of the ceded dominions in her name as in his own; and Albert was inaugurated with great pomp at Brussels, on the 22d of August. Having put everything in order for the regulation of the government during his absence, he set out for Spain for the purpose of accomplishing his spousals, and bringing back his bride to the chief seat of their joint power. But before his departure he wrote to the various states of the republic, and to Prince **Maurice himself,** strongly recommending submission and **reconciliation.** These letters **received no** answer; a new plot against the life **of Prince Maurice,** by a wretched individual named Peter Pann, having **aroused the** indignation **of the country, and determined it to treat with** suspicion **and contempt every insidious** proposition from the tyranny **it defied.**

Albert placed his uncle, the cardinal Andrew of Austria, **at the head of the temporary** government, and set **out on his journey; taking the** little **town of** Halle in his **route, and placing at the altar of the Virgin, who** is there **held in particular honor,** his cardinal**'s hat as a token of his veneration.** He had not made much progress when he **received accounts of the demise of** Philip II., who died, **after long suffering, and with great** resignation, on the **13th of September,** 1598, **at the age of seventy-two.** Albert **was several months on his** journey through Germany; **and the ceremonials of his union with the** infanta did not **take place till the 18th** of **April, 1599,** when it was finally **solemnized in the city of Valencia in** Spain.

This transaction, by which the Netherlands **were positively erected into a separate** sovereignty, **seems** naturally **to make the limits of another** epoch in their history. It **completely decided the** division between **the northern and southern** provinces, which, although it had **virtually taken place** long **previous to** this period, **could** scarcely be **considered as formally consummated until now.** Here then **we shall** pause **anew, and take a** rapid review of the social **state of** the Netherlands during **the** last half century, **which was** beyond all doubt the most important period of their **history,** from the earliest times till the present.

It has been seen that when Charles V. resigned his throne and the possession of his vast dominions to his son, arts, commerce, and manufactures **had** risen to a state of considerable perfection throughout the Netherlands. The revolution, of which we have traced the rise and progress, naturally produced to those provinces which relapsed into slavery a most lamentable change in every branch of industry, and struck a blow at the general prosperity, the effects of which are felt to this very day. Arts, science, and literature were sure to be checked and withered in the blaze of civil war; and we have now to mark the retrograde movements of most of those charms and advantages of civilized life, in which Flanders and the other southern states were so rich.

The rapid spread of enlightenment on religious subjects soon converted the manufactories and workshops of Flanders into so many conventicles of reform; and the clear-sighted artisans fled in thousands from the tyranny of Alva into England, Germany, and Holland—those happier countries, where the government adopted and went hand in hand with the progress of rational belief. Commerce followed the fate of manufactures. The foreign merchants one by one abandoned the theatre of bigotry and persecution; and even Antwerp, which had succeeded Bruges as the great mart of European traffic, was ruined by the horrible excesses of the Spanish soldiery, and never recovered from the shock. Its trade, its wealth, and its prosperity, were gradually transferred to Amsterdam, Rotterdam, and the towns of Holland and Zealand; and the growth of Dutch commerce attained its proud maturity in the establishment of the India Company in 1596, the effects of which we shall have hereafter more particularly to dwell on.

The exciting and romantic enterprises of the Portuguese and Spanish navigators in the fifteenth and sixteenth centuries roused all the ardor of other nations for those distant adventures; and the people of the Netherlands were early influenced by the general spirit of Europe. If they were not the discoverers of new worlds, they were certainly the first to make the name of European respected and venerated by the natives.

Animated by the ardor which springs from the spirit of freedom and the enthusiasm of success, the United

Provinces labored for the discovery of new outlets for their commerce and navigation. The government encouraged the speculations of individuals, which promised fresh and fertile sources of revenue, so necessary for the maintenance of the war. Until the year 1581 the merchants of Holland and Zealand were satisfied to find the productions of India at Lisbon, which was the mart of that branch of trade ever since the Portuguese discovered the passage by the Cape of Good Hope. But Philip II., having conquered Portugal, excluded the United Provinces from the ports of that country; and their enterprising mariners were from that period driven to those efforts which rapidly led to private fortune and general prosperity. The English had opened the way in this career; and the states-general having offered a large reward for the discovery of a northwest passage, frequent and most adventurous voyages took place. Houtman, Le Maire, Heemskirk, Ryp, and others, became celebrated for their enterprise, and some for their perilous and interesting adventures.

The United Provinces were soon without any rival on the seas. In Europe alone they had one thousand two hundred merchant ships in activity, and upward of seventy thousand sailors constantly employed. They built annually two thousand vessels. In the year 1598, eighty ships sailed from their ports for the Indies or America. They carried on, besides, an extensive trade on the coast of Guinea, whence they brought large quantities of gold-dust; and found, in short, in all quarters of the globe the reward of their skill, industry, and courage.

The spirit of conquest soon became grafted on the habits of trade. Expedition succeeded to expedition Failure taught wisdom to those who did not want bravery. The random efforts of individuals were succeeded by organized plans, under associations well constituted and wealthy; and these soon gave birth to those eastern and western companies before alluded to. The disputes between the English and the Hanseatic towns were carefully observed by the Dutch, and turned to their own advantage. The English manufacturers, who quickly began to flourish, from the influx of Flemish workmen under the encouragement of Elizabeth, formed companies in the Netherlands, and sent their cloths into those very towns of Germany which formerly possessed the exclusive privilege of their manufacture. These towns naturally felt dissatisfied, and their complaints were encouraged by the king of Spain. The English adventurers received orders to quit the empire; and, invited by the states-general, many of them fixed their residence in Middleburg, which became the most celebrated woollen market in Europe.

The establishment of the Jews in the towns of the republic forms a remarkable epoch in the annals of trade. This people, so outraged by the loathsome bigotry which Christians have not blushed to call religion, so far from being depressed by the general persecution, seemed to find it a fresh stimulus to the exertion of their industry. To escape death in Spain and Portugal they took refuge in Holland, where toleration encouraged and just principles of state maintained them. They were at first taken for Catholics, and subjected to suspicion; but when their real faith was understood they were no longer molested.

Astronomy and geography, two sciences so closely allied with and so essential to navigation, flourished now throughout Europe. Ortilius of Antwerp, and Gerard Mercator of Rupelmonde, were two of the greatest geographers of the sixteenth century; and the reform in the calendar at the end of that period gave stability to the calculations of time, which had previously suffered all the inconvenient fluctuations attendant on the old style.

Literature had assumed during the revolution in the Netherlands the almost exclusive and repulsive aspect of controversial learning. The university of Douay, installed in 1562 as a new screen against the piercing light of reform, quickly became the stronghold of intolerance. That of Leyden, established by the efforts of the Prince of Orange, soon after the famous siege of that town in 1574, was on a less exclusive plan—its professors being in the first instance drawn from Germany. Many Flemish historians succeeded in this century to the ancient and uncultivated chroniclers of preceding times; the civil wars drawing forth many writers, who recorded what they witnessed, but often in a spirit of partisanship and want of candor, which seriously embarrasses him who desires to learn the truth on both sides of an important question. Poetry declined and drooped in these times of tumult and suffering; and the chambers of rhetoric, to which its cultivation had been chiefly due, gradually lost their influence, and finally ceased to exist.

In fixing our attention on the republic of the United Provinces during the epoch now completed, we feel the desire, and lament the impossibility, of entering on the details of government in that most remarkable state. For these we must refer to what appears to us the best authority for clear and ample information on the prerogative of the stadtholder, the constitution of the states-general, the privileges of the tribunals and local assemblies, and other points of moment concerning the principles of the Belgic confederation.[1]

---

[1] See Cerisier, Hist. Gen. des Prov. Unies.

CHAPTER XV

TO THE CAMPAIGN OF PRINCE MAURICE AND SPINOLA

A.D. 1599—1604

PREVIOUS to his departure for Spain, the archduke Albert had placed the government of the provinces which acknowledged his domination in the hands of his uncle, the cardinal Andrew of Austria, leaving in command of the army Francisco Mendoza, admiral of Aragon. The troops at his disposal amounted to twenty-two thousand fighting men—a formidable force, and enough to justify the serious apprehensions of the republic. Albert, whose finances were exhausted by payments made to the numerous Spanish and Italian mutineers, had left orders with Mendoza to secure some place on the Rhine, which might open a passage for free quarters in the enemy's country. But this unprincipled officer forced his way into the neutral districts of Cleves and Westphalia; and with a body of executioners ready to hang up all who might resist, and of priests to prepare them for death, he carried such terror on his march that no opposition was ventured. The atrocious cruelties of Mendoza and his troops baffle all description: on one occasion they murdered, in cold blood, the count of Walkenstein, who surrendered his castle on the express condition of his freedom; and they committed every possible excess that may be imagined of ferocious soldiery encouraged by a base commander.

Prince Maurice soon put into motion, to oppose this army of brigands, his small disposable force of about seven thousand men. With these, however, and a succession of masterly manœuvres, he contrived to preserve the republic

(223)

from invasion, and to paralyze and almost destroy an army three times superior in numbers to his own. The horrors committed by the Spaniards, in the midst of peace, and without the slightest provocation, could not fail to excite the utmost indignation in a nation so fond of liberty and so proud as Germany. The duchy of Cleves felt particularly aggrieved; and Sybilla, the sister of the duke, a real heroine in a glorious cause, so worked on the excited passions of the people by her eloquence and her tears that she persuaded all the orders of the state to unite against the odious enemy. Some troops were suddenly raised; and a league was formed between several princes of the empire to revenge the common cause. The count de la Lippe was chosen general of their united forces; and the choice could not have fallen on one more certainly incapable or more probably treacherous.

The German army, with their usual want of activity, did not open the campaign till the month of June. It consisted of fourteen thousand men; and never was an army so badly conducted. Without money, artillery, provisions, or discipline, it was at any moment ready to break up and abandon its incompetent general; and on the very first encounter with the enemy, and after a loss of a couple of hundred men, it became self-disbanded; and, flying in every direction, not a single man could be rallied to clear away this disgrace.

The states-general, cruelly disappointed at this result of measures from which they had looked for so important a diversion in their favor, now resolved on a vigorous exertion of their own energies, and determined to undertake a naval expedition of a magnitude greater than any they had hitherto attempted. The force of public opinion was at this period more powerful than it had ever yet been in the United Provinces; for a great number of the inhabitants, who, during the life of Philip II., conscientiously believed that they could not lawfully abjure the authority once recognized and sworn to, became now liberated from those respectable, al-

CAMPAIGN OF MAURICE AND SPINOLA

though absurd, scruples; and the death of one unfeeling despot gave thousands of new citizens to the state.

A fleet of seventy-three vessels, carrying eight thousand men, was soon equipped, under the order of Admiral Vander Goes; and, after a series of attempts on the coasts of Spain, Portugal, Africa, and the Canary Isles, this expedition, from which the most splendid results were expected, was shattered, dispersed, and reduced to nothing by a succession of unheard-of mishaps.

To these disappointments were now added domestic dissensions in the republic, in consequence of the new taxes absolutely necessary for the exigencies of the state. The conduct of Queen Elizabeth greatly added to the general embarrassment: she called for the payment of her former loans; insisted on the recall of the English troops, and declared her resolution to make peace with Spain. Several German princes promised aid in men and money, but never furnished either; and in this most critical juncture, Henry IV. was the only foreign sovereign who did not abandon the republic. He sent them one thousand Swiss troops, whom he had in his pay; allowed them to levy three thousand more in France; and gave them a loan of two hundred thousand crowns—a very convenient supply in their exhausted state.

The archdukes Albert and Isabella arrived in the Netherlands in September, and made their entrance into Brussels with unexampled magnificence. They soon found themselves in a situation quite as critical as was that of the United Provinces, and both parties displayed immense energy to remedy their mutual embarrassments. The winter was extremely rigorous; so much so as to allow of military operations being undertaken on the ice. Prince Maurice soon commenced a Christmas campaign by taking the town of Wachtendonck; and he followed up his success by obtaining possession of the important forts of Crevecœur and St. Andrew, in the island of Bommel. A most dangerous mutiny at the same time broke out in the army of

HOLLAND (8)

the archdukes; and Albert seemed left without troops or money at the very beginning of his sovereignty.

But these successes of Prince Maurice were only the prelude to an expedition of infinitely more moment, arranged with the utmost secrecy, and executed with an energy scarcely to be looked for from the situation of the states. This was nothing less than an invasion poured into the very heart of Flanders, thus putting the archdukes on the defence of their own most vital possessions, and changing completely the whole character of the war. The whole disposable troops of the republic, amounting to about seventeen thousand men, were secretly assembled in the island of Walcheren, in the month of June; and setting sail for Flanders, they disembarked near Ghent, and arrived on the 20th of that month under the walls of Bruges. Some previous negotiations with that town had led the prince to expect that it would have opened its gates at his approach. In this he was, however, disappointed; and after taking possession of some forts in the neighborhood, he continued his march to Nieuport, which place he invested on the 1st of July.

At the news of this invasion the archdukes, though taken by surprise, displayed a promptness and decision that proved them worthy of the sovereignty which seemed at stake. With incredible activity they mustered, in a few days, an army of twelve thousand men, which they passed in review near Ghent. On this occasion Isabella, proving her title to a place among those heroic women with whom the age abounded, rode through the royalist ranks, and harangued them in a style of inspiring eloquence that inflamed their courage and secured their fidelity. Albert, seizing the moment of this excitement, put himself at their head, and marched to seek the enemy, leaving his intrepid wife at Bruges, the nearest town to the scene of the action he was resolved on. He gained possession of all the forts taken and garrisoned by Maurice a few days before; and pushing forward with his apparently irresistible troops, he came up on the morning of the 2d of July with a large body of those of the states, consisting of about three thousand men, sent forward under the command of Count Ernest of Nassau to reconnoitre and judge of the extent of this most unexpected movement: for Prince Maurice was, in his turn, completely surprised; and not merely by one of those manœuvres of war by which the best generals are sometimes deceived, but by an exertion of political vigor and capacity of which history offers few more striking examples. Such a circumstance, however, served only to draw forth a fresh display of those uncommon talents which in so many various accidents of war had placed Maurice on the highest rank for military talent. The detachment under Count Ernest of Nassau was chiefly composed of Scottish infantry; and this small force stood firmly opposed to the impetuous attack of the whole royalist army—thus giving time to the main body under the prince to take up a position, and form in order of battle. Count Ernest was at length driven back, with the loss of eight hundred men killed, almost all Scottish; and being cut off from the rest of the army, was forced to take refuge in Ostend, which town was in possession of the troops of the states.

The army of Albert now marched on, flushed with this first success and confident of final victory. Prince Maurice received them with the courage of a gallant soldier and the precaution of a consummate general. He had caused the fleet of ships of war and transports, which had sailed along the coast from Zealand, and landed supplies of ammunition and provisions, to retire far from the shore, so as to leave to his army no chance of escape but in victory. The commissioners from the states, who always accompanied the prince as a council of observation rather than of war, had retired to Ostend in great consternation, to wait the issue of the battle which now seemed inevitable. A scene of deep feeling and heroism was the next episode of this memorable day, and throws the charm of natural affection over those circumstances in which glory too seldom leaves a place for

the softer emotions of the heart. When the patriot army
was in its position, and firmly waiting the advance of the
foe, Prince Maurice turned to his brother, Frederick Henry,
then sixteen years of age, and several young noblemen, English, French, and German, who like him attended on the
great captain to learn the art of war: he pointed out in a
few words the perilous situation in which he was placed;
declared his resolution to conquer or perish on the battlefield, and recommended the boyish band to retire to Ostend,
and wait for some less desperate occasion to share his renown or revenge his fall. Frederick Henry spurned the
affectionate suggestion, and swore to stand by his brother
to the last; and all his young companions adopted the same
generous resolution.

The army of the states was placed in order of battle,
about a league in front of Nieuport, in the sand hills with
which the neighborhood abounds, its left wing resting on the
seashore. Its losses of the morning, and of the garrisons left
in the forts near Bruges, reduced it to an almost exact equality with that of the archduke. Each of these armies was
composed of that variety of troops which made them respectively an epitome of the various nations of Europe.
The patriot force contained Dutch, English, French, German, and Swiss, under the orders of Count Louis of Nassau,
Sir Francis and Sir Horace Vere, brothers and English officers of great celebrity, with other distinguished captains.
The archduke mustered Spaniards, Italians, Walloons, and
Irish in his ranks, led on by Mendoza, La Berlotta, and
their fellow-veterans. Both armies were in the highest
state of discipline, trained to war by long service, and enthusiastic in the several causes which they served; the two
highest principles of enthusiasm urging them on—religious
fanaticism on the one hand, and the love of freedom on the
other. The rival generals rode along their respective lines,
addressed a few brief sentences of encouragement to their
men, and presently the bloody contest began.

It was three o'clock in the afternoon when the archduke

commenced the attack. His advanced guard, commanded by Mendoza and composed of those former mutineers who now resolved to atone for their misconduct, marched across the sand-hills with desperate resolution. They soon came into contact with the English contingent under Francis Vere, who was desperately wounded in the shock. The assault was almost irresistible. The English, borne down by numbers, were forced to give way; but the main body pressed on to their support. Horace Vere stepped forward to supply his brother's place. Not an inch of ground more was gained or lost; the firing ceased, and pikes and swords crossed each other in the resolute conflict of man to man. The action became general along the whole line. The two commanders-in-chief were at all points. Nothing could exceed their mutual display of skill and courage. At length the Spanish cavalry, broken by the well-directed fire of the patriot artillery, fell back on their infantry and threw it into confusion. The archduke at the same instant was wounded by a lance in the cheek, unhorsed, and forced to quit the field. The report of his death, and the sight of his war-steed galloping alone across the field, spread alarm through the royalist ranks. Prince Maurice saw and seized on the critical moment. He who had so patiently maintained his position for three hours of desperate conflict now knew the crisis for a prompt and general advance. He gave the word and led on to the charge, and the victory was at once his own.

The defeat of the royalist army was complete. The whole of the artillery, baggage, standards, and ammunition, fell into the possession of the conquerors. Night coming on saved those who fled, and the nature of the ground prevented the cavalry from consummating the destruction of the whole. As far as the conflicting accounts of the various historians may be compared and calculated on, the royalists had three thousand killed, and among them several officers of rank; while the patriot army, including those who fell in the morning action, lost something more than half the number. The archduke, furnished with a fresh horse, gained Bruges in safety; but he only waited there long enough to join his heroic wife, with whom he proceeded rapidly to Ghent, and thence to Brussels. Mendoza was wounded and taken prisoner, and with difficulty saved by Prince Maurice from the fury of the German auxiliaries.

The moral effect produced by this victory on the vanquishers and vanquished, and on the state of public opinion throughout Europe, was immense; but its immediate consequences were incredibly trifling. Not one result in a military point of view followed an event which appeared almost decisive of the war. Nieuport was again invested three days after the battle; but a strong reinforcement entering the place saved it from all danger, and Maurice found himself forced for want of supplies to abandon the scene of his greatest exploit. He returned to Holland, welcomed by the acclamations of his grateful country, and exciting the jealousy and hatred of all who envied his glory or feared his power. Among the sincere and conscientious republicans who saw danger to the public liberty in the growing influence of a successful soldier, placed at the head of affairs and endeared to the people by every hereditary and personal claim, was Olden Barneveldt, the pensionary; and from this period may be traced the growth of the mutual antipathy which led to the sacrifice of the most virtuous statesman of Holland, and the eternal disgrace of its hitherto heroic chief.

The states of the Catholic provinces assembled at Brussels now gave the archdukes to understand that nothing but peace could satisfy their wishes or save the country from exhaustion and ruin. Albert saw the reasonableness of their remonstrances, and attempted to carry the great object into effect. The states-general listened to his proposals. Commissioners were appointed on both sides to treat of terms. They met at Berg-op-Zoom; but their conferences were broken up almost as soon as commenced. The Spanish deputies insisted on the submission of the republic to its ancient masters. Such a proposal was worse than insulting; it proved the inveterate insincerity of those with whom it originated, and who knew it could not be entertained for a moment. Preparations for hostilities were therefore commenced on both sides, and the whole of the winter was thus employed.

Early in the spring Prince Maurice opened the campaign at the head of sixteen thousand men, chiefly composed of English and French, who seemed throughout the contest to forget their national animosities, and to know no rivalry but that of emulation in the cause of liberty. The town of Rhinberg soon fell into the hands of the prince. His next attempt was against Bois-le-duc; and the siege of this place was signalized by an event that flavored of the chivalric contests now going out of fashion. A Norman gentleman of the name of Breaute, in the service of Prince Maurice, challenged the royalist garrison to meet him and twenty of his comrades in arms under the walls of the place. The cartel was accepted by a Fleming named Abramzoom, but better known by the epithet Leckerbeetje (savory bit), who, with twenty more, met Breaute and his friends. The combat was desperate. The Flemish champion was killed at the first shock by his Norman challenger; but the latter falling into the hands of the enemy, they treacherously and cruelly put him to death, in violation of the strict conditions of the fight. Prince Maurice was forced to raise the siege of Bois-le-duc, and turn his attention in another direction.

The archduke Albert had now resolved to invest Ostend, a place of great importance to the United Provinces, but little worth to either party in comparison with the dreadful waste of treasure and human life which was the consequence of its memorable siege. Sir Francis Vere commanded in the place at the period of its final investment; but governors, garrisons, and besieging forces, were renewed and replaced with a rapidity which gives one of the most frightful instances of the ravages of war. The siege of Ostend lasted upward of three years. It became a school for the young nobility of all Europe, who repaired to either one or the other party to learn the principles and the practice of attack and defence. Everything that the art of strategy could devise was resorted to on either side. The slaughter in the various assaults, sorties, and bombardments was enormous. Squadrons at sea gave a double interest to the land operations; and the celebrated brothers Frederick and Ambrose Spinola founded their reputation on these opposing elements. Frederick was killed in one of the naval combats with the Dutch galleys, and the fame of reducing Ostend was reserved for Ambrose. This afterward celebrated general had undertaken the command at the earnest entreaties of the archduke and the king of Spain, and by the firmness and vigor of his measures he revived the courage of the worn-out assailants of the place. Redoubled attacks and multiplied mines at length reduced the town to a mere mass of ruin, and scarcely left its still undaunted garrison sufficient footing on which to prolong their desperate defence. Ostend at length surrendered, on the 22d of September, 1604, and the victors marched in over its crumbled walls and shattered batteries. Scarcely a vestige of the place remained beyond those terrible evidences of destruction. Its ditches, filled up with the rubbish of ramparts, bastions, and redoubts, left no distinct line of separation between the operations of its attack and its defence. It resembled rather a vast sepulchre than a ruined town, a mountain of earth and rubbish, without a single house in which the wretched remnant of the inhabitants could hide their heads—a monument of desolation on which victory might have sat and wept.

During the progress of this memorable siege Queen Elizabeth of England had died, after a long and, it must be pronounced, a glorious reign; though the glory belongs rather to the nation than to the monarch, whose memory is marked with indelible stains of private cruelty, as in the cases of Essex and Mary Queen of Scots, and of public wrongs, as in that of her whole system of tyranny in Ireland. With respect to the United Provinces she was a harsh protectress and a capricious ally. She in turns advised them to remain faithful to the old impurities of religion and to their intolerable king; refused to incorporate them with her own states; and then used her best efforts for subjecting them to her sway. She seemed to take pleasure in the uncertainty to which she reduced them, by constant demands for payment of her loans, and threats of making peace with Spain. Thus the states-general were not much affected by the news of her death; and so rejoiced were they at the accession of James I. to the throne of England that all the bells of Holland rang out merry peals; bonfires were set blazing all over the country; a letter of congratulation was despatched to the new monarch; and it was speedily followed by a solemn embassy composed of Prince Frederick Henry, the grand pensionary De Barneveldt, and others of the first dignitaries of the republic. These ambassadors were grievously disappointed at the reception given to them by James, who treated them as little better than rebels to their lawful king. But this first disposition to contempt and insult was soon overcome by the united talents of Barneveldt and the great duke of Sully, who were at the same period ambassadors from France at the English court. The result of the negotiations was an agreement between those two powers to take the republic under their protection, and use their best efforts for obtaining the recognition of its independence by Spain.

The states-general considered themselves amply recompensed for the loss of Ostend by the taking of Ecluse, Rhinberg, and Grave, all of which had in the interval surrendered to Prince Maurice; but they were seriously alarmed on finding themselves abandoned by King James, who concluded a separate peace with Philip III of Spain in the month of August this year.

This event gives rise to a question very important to the honor of James, and consequently to England itself, as the acts of the absolute monarchs of those days must be considered as those of the nations which submitted to such a form of government. Historians of great authority have asserted that it appeared that, by a secret agreement, the king had expressly reserved the power of sending assistance to Holland. Others deny the existence of this secret article; and lean heavily on the reputation of James for his conduct in the transaction. It must be considered a very doubtful point, and is to be judged rather by subsequent events than by any direct testimony.

The two monarchs stipulated in the treaty that "neither was to give support of any kind to the revolted subjects of the other." It is nevertheless true that James did not withdraw his troops from the service of the states; but he authorized the Spaniards to levy soldiers in England. The United Provinces were at once afflicted and indignant at this equivocal conduct. Their first impulse was to deprive the English of the liberty of navigating the Scheldt. They even arrested the progress of several of their merchant-ships. But soon after, gratified at finding that James received their deputy with the title of ambassador, they resolved to dissimulate their resentment.

Prince Maurice and Spinola now took the field with their respective armies; and a rapid series of operations placing them in direct contact, displayed their talents in the most striking points of view. The first steps on the part of the prince were a new invasion of Flanders, and an attempt on Antwerp, which he hoped to carry before the Spanish army could arrive to its succor. But the promptitude and sagacity of Spinola defeated this plan, which Maurice was obliged to abandon after some loss; while the royalist general resolved to signalize himself by some important movement, and, ere his design was suspected, he had penetrated into the province of Overyssel, and thus retorted his rival's favorite measure of carrying the war into the enemy's country. Several towns were rapidly reduced; but Maurice flew toward the threatened provinces, and by his active measures forced Spinola to fall back on the Rhine and take up a position near Roeroord, where he was impetuously attacked by the Dutch army. But the cavalry having followed up too slowly the orders of Maurice, his hope of surprising the royalists was frustrated; and the Spanish forces, gaining time by this hesitation, soon **changed** the fortune of the **day**. The Dutch cavalry shamefully took to flight, despite **the** gallant endeavors **of** both Maurice and his brother Frederick Henry; **and at** this juncture a large reinforcement of Spaniards **arrived under** the command of **Velasco**. Maurice **now** brought forward some companies of English and **French infantry** under Horatio **Vere** and D'Omerville, **also a** distinguished officer. The battle was again fiercely **renewed**; and the Spaniards now gave way, and **had been** completely defeated, had not Spinola put in **practice an old and generally** successful stratagem. He **caused almost all** the drums of his army to beat in one **direction, so as to** give the impression that a still larger **reinforcement was** approaching. Maurice, apprehensive **that the former** panic might find a parallel in a fresh one, **prudently** ordered **a retreat,** which he was able to effect **in** good **order, in** preference to risking the total disorganization of his troops. The **loss** on **each** side was nearly the **same; but the** glory **of** this hard-fought day remained on the side **of** Spinola, who proved himself **a** worthy successor of **the great duke** of Parma, and an antagonist with whom **Maurice might** contend without dishonor.

The naval transactions of this **year** restored the balance which Spinola's successes had begun to turn in favor of the royalist **cause. A squadron** of ships, commanded by Hautain, admiral **of Zealand,** attacked a superior force of Spanish vessels close to Dover, and defeated them with considerable loss. But the victory was sullied by an act of great barbarity. All the soldiers found on board the captured ships were tied two and two and mercilessly flung into the sea. Some contrived to extricate themselves, and gained the shore by swimming; others were picked up by the English boats, whose crews witnessed the scene and hastened to their relief. The generous British seamen could not remain neuter in such a moment, nor repress their indignation against those whom they had hitherto so long considered as friends. The Dutch vessels pursuing those of Spain which fled into Dover harbor, were fired on by the cannon of the castle and forced to give up the chase. The English loudly complained that the Dutch had on this occasion violated their territory; and this transaction laid the foundation of the quarrel which subsequently broke out between England and the republic, and which the jealousies of rival merchants in either state unceasingly fomented. In this year also the Dutch succeeded in capturing the chief of the Dunkirk privateers, which had so long annoyed their trade; and they cruelly ordered sixty of the prisoners to be put to death. But the people, more humane than the authorities, rescued them from the executioners and set them free.

But these domestic instances of success and inhumanity were trifling in comparison with the splendid train of distant events, accompanied by a course of wholesale benevolence, that redeemed the traits of petty guilt. The maritime enterprises of Holland, forced by the imprudent policy of Spain to seek a wider career than in the narrow seas of Europe, were day by day extended in the Indies. To ruin if possible their increasing trade, Philip III. sent out the admiral Hurtado, with a fleet of eight galleons and thirty-two galleys. The Dutch squadron of five vessels, commanded by Wolfert Hermanszoon, attacked them off the coast of Malabar, and his temerity was crowned with great success. He took two of their vessels, and completely drove the remainder from the Indian seas. He then concluded a treaty with the natives of the isle of Banda, by which he promised to support them against the Spaniards and Portuguese, on condition that they were to give his fellow-countrymen the exclusive privilege of purchasing the spices of the island. This treaty was the foundation of the influence which the Dutch so soon succeeded in forming in the East Indies; and they established it by a candid, mild, and tolerant conduct, strongly contrasted with the pride and bigotry which had signalized every act of the Portuguese and Spaniards.

The prodigious success of the Indian trade occasioned numerous societies to be formed all through the republic. But by their great number they became at length injurious to each other. The spirit of speculation was pushed too far; and the merchants, who paid enormous prices for India goods, found themselves forced to sell in Europe at a loss. Many of those societies were too weak, in military force as well as in capital, to resist the armed competition of the Spaniards, and to support themselves in their disputes with the native princes. At length the states-general resolved to unite the whole of these scattered partnerships into one grand company, which was soon organized on a solid basis that led ere long to incredible wealth at home and a rapid succession of conquests in the East.

CHAPTER XVI

TO THE SYNOD AT DORT AND THE EXECUTION OF BARNEVELDT

A.D. 1606—1619

THE states-general now resolved to confine their military operations to a war merely defensive. Spinola had, by his conduct during the late campaign, completely revived the spirits of the Spanish troops, and excited at least the caution of the Dutch. He now threatened the United Provinces with invasion; and he exerted his utmost efforts to raise the supplies necessary for the execution of his plan. He not only exhausted the resources of the king of Spain and the archduke, but obtained money on his private account from all those usurers who were tempted by his confident anticipations of conquest. He soon equipped two armies of about twelve thousand men each. At the head of one of those he took the field; the other, commanded by the count of Bucquoi, was destined to join him in the neighborhood of Utrecht; and he was then resolved to push forward with the whole united force into the very heart of the republic.

Prince Maurice in the meantime concentrated his army, amounting to twelve thousand men, and prepared to make head against his formidable opponents. By a succession of the most prudent manœuvres he contrived to keep Spinola in check, disconcerted all his projects, and forced him to content himself with the capture of two or three towns—a comparatively insignificant conquest. Desiring to wipe away the disgrace of this discomfiture, and to risk everything for the accomplishment of his grand design, Spinola used every method to provoke the prince to a battle, even though a serious mutiny among his troops, and the impossibility of forming a junction with Bucquoi, had reduced his force below that of Maurice; but the latter, to the surprise of all who expected a decisive blow, retreated from before the Italian general—abandoning the town of Groll, which immediately fell into Spinola's power, and giving rise to manifold conjectures and infinite discontent at conduct so little in unison with his wonted enterprise and skill. Even Henry IV. acknowledged it did not answer the expectation he had formed from Maurice's splendid talents for war. The fact seems to be that the prince, much as he valued victory, dreaded peace more; and that he was resolved to avoid a decisive blow, which, in putting an end to the contest, would at the same time have decreased the individual influence in the state which his ambition now urged him to augment by every possible means.

The Dutch naval expeditions this year were not more brilliant than those on land. Admiral Hautain, with twenty ships, was surprised off Cape St. Vincent by the Spanish fleet. The formidable appearance of their galleons inspired on this occasion a perfect panic among the Dutch sailors. They hoisted their sails and fled, with the exception of one ship, commanded by Vice-Admiral Klaazoon, whose desperate conduct saved the national honor. Having held out until his vessel was quite unmanageable, and almost his whole crew killed or wounded, he prevailed on the rest to agree to the resolution he had formed, knelt down on the deck, and putting up a brief prayer for pardon for the act, thrust a light into the powder-magazine, and was instantly blown up with his companions. Only two men were snatched from the sea by the Spaniards; and even these, dreadfully burned and mangled, died in the utterance of curses on the enemy.

This disastrous occurrence was soon, however, forgotten in the rejoicings for a brilliant victory gained the following year by Heemskirk, so celebrated for his voyage to Nova

Zembla, and by his conduct in the East. He set sail from the ports of Holland in the month of March, determined to signalize himself by some great exploit, now necessary to redeem the disgrace which had begun to sully the reputation of the Dutch navy. He soon got intelligence that the Spanish fleet lay at anchor in the bay of Gibraltar, and he speedily prepared to offer them battle. Before the combat began he held a council of war, and addressed the officers in an energetic speech, in which he displayed the imperative call on their valor to conquer or die in the approaching conflict. He led on to the action in his own ship; and, to the astonishment of both fleets, he bore right down against the enormous galleon in which the flag of the Spanish admiral-in-chief was hoisted. D'Avila could scarcely believe the evidence of his eyes at this audacity: he at first burst into laughter at the notion; but as Heemskirk approached, he cut his cables and attempted to escape under the shelter of the town. The heroic Dutchman pursued him through the whole of the Spanish fleet, and soon forced him to action. At the second broadside Heemskirk had his left leg carried off by a cannon-ball, and he almost instantly died, exhorting his crew to seek for consolation in the defeat of the enemy. Verhoef, the captain of the ship, concealed the admiral's death; and the whole fleet continued the action with a valor worthy the spirit in which it was commenced. The victory was soon decided: four of the Spanish galleons were sunk or burned, the remainder fled; and the citizens of Cadiz trembled with the apprehension of sack and pillage. But the death of Heemskirk, when made known to the surviving victors, seemed completely to paralyze them. They attempted nothing further; but sailing back to Holland with the body of their lamented chief, thus paid a greater tribute to his importance than was to be found in the mausoleum erected to his memory in the city of Amsterdam.

The news of this battle reaching Brussels before it was known in Holland, contributed not a little to quicken the

WILLIAM THE SILENT OF ORANGE   Holland.

anxiety of the archdukes for peace. The king of Spain, worn out by the war which drained his treasury, had for some time ardently desired it. The Portuguese made loud complaints of the ruin that threatened their trade and their East Indian colonies. The Spanish ministers were fatigued with the apparently interminable contest which baffled all their calculations. Spinola, even in the midst of his brilliant career, found himself so overwhelmed with debts and so oppressed by the reproaches of the numerous creditors who were ruined by his default of payment, that he joined in the general demand for repose. In the month of May, 1607, proposals were made by the archdukes, in compliance with the general desire; and their two plenipotentiaries, Van Wittenhorst and Gevaerts, repaired to The Hague.

Public opinion in the United Provinces was divided on this important question. An instinctive hatred against the Spaniards, and long habits of warfare, influenced the great mass of the people to consider any overture for peace as some wily artifice aimed at their religion and liberty. War seemed to open inexhaustible sources of wealth; while peace seemed to threaten the extinction of the courage which was now as much a habit as war appeared to be a want. This reasoning was particularly convincing to Prince Maurice, whose fame, with a large portion of his authority and revenues, depended on the continuance of hostilities: it was also strongly relished and supported in Zealand generally, and in the chief towns, which dreaded the rivalry of Antwerp. But those who bore the burden of the war saw the subject under a different aspect. They feared that the present state of things would lead to their conquest by the enemy, or to the ruin of their liberty by the growing power of Maurice. They hoped that peace would consolidate the republic and cause the reduction of the debt, which now amounted to twenty-six million florins. At the head of the party who so reasoned was De Barneveldt; and his name is a guarantee with posterity for the wisdom of the opinion.

To allow the violent opposition to subside, and to prevent

any explosion of **party feuds,** the prudent Barneveldt **suggested** a mere suspension of arms, during which the permanent interests of both states might be calmly discussed. He even undertook to obtain Maurice's consent **to the** armistice. The prince listened to his arguments, and **was** apparently convinced **by them. He, at any rate,** sanctioned the proposal; but he afterward complained that Barneveldt had deceived him, in representing the negotiation as a feint **for the purpose of persuading the** kings of France and England **to give greater aid to the republic.** It is more than likely **that Maurice reckoned on the improbability of** Spain's **consenting to the terms of the** proposed **treaty;** and, on that **chance, withdrew an** opposition **which could** scarcely **be ascribed to any but motives of personal** ambition. **It is, however, certain that his discontent at this** transaction, **either with himself or Barneveldt, laid the** foundation of **that bitter enmity which proved fatal to the** life of the **latter, and covered his own name, otherwise** glorious, with **undying reproach.**

The **United Provinces** positively refused to admit even **the commencement of a negotiation without** the absolute **recognition of their independence by the** archdukes. A **new ambassador was accordingly chosen on** the part of **these sovereigns, and empowered** to concede this important **admission. This person** attracted considerable attention, **from his well-known** qualities as an **able diplomatist. He was a monk of the** order of St. **Francis,** named John de **Neyen, a native of** Antwerp, **and a person as** well versed in court intrigue **as in the studies of the** cloister. **He, in the first instance, repaired** secretly **to** The Hague; and **had** several private interviews with Prince Maurice and **Barneveldt, before he was regularly introduced to the states-general** in his official character. Two different journeys were undertaken by this agent between The Hague and Brussels, before he could succeed in obtaining a perfect understanding as **to** the specific views of the archdukes. The suspicions of the states-general seem fully justified by the dubious tone of the various communications, which avoided the direct admission of the required preliminary as to the independence of the United Provinces. It was at length concluded in explicit terms; and a suspension of arms for eight months was the immediate consequence.

But the negotiation for peace was on the point of being completely broken, in consequence of the conduct of Neyen, who justified every doubt of his sincerity by an attempt to corrupt Aarsens the greffier of the states-general, or at least to influence his conduct in the progress of the treaty. Neyen presented him, in the name of the archdukes, and as a token of his esteem, with a diamond of great value and a bond for fifty thousand crowns. Aarsens accepted these presents with the approbation of Prince Maurice, to whom he had confided the circumstance, and who was no doubt delighted at what promised a rupture to the negotiations. Verreiken, a councillor of state, who assisted Neyen in his diplomatic labors, was formally summoned before the assembled states-general, and there Barneveldt handed to him the diamond and the bond; and at the same time read him a lecture of true republican severity on the subject. Verreiken was overwhelmed by the violent attack: he denied the authority of Neyen for the measure he had taken; and remarked, "that it was not surprising that monks, naturally interested and avaricious, judged others by themselves." This repudiation of Neyen's suspicious conduct seems to have satisfied the stern resentment of Barneveldt, and the party which so earnestly labored for peace. In spite of all the opposition of Maurice and his partisans, the negotiation went on.

In the month of January, 1608, the various ambassadors were assembled at The Hague. Spinola was the chief of the plenipotentiaries appointed by the king of Spain; and Jeannin, president of the parliament of Dijon, a man of rare endowments, represented France. Prince Maurice, accompanied by his brother Frederick Henry, the various counts of Nassau his cousins, and a numerous escort, advanced some distance to meet Spinola, conveyed him to The Hague in his own carriage, and lavished on him all the attentions reciprocally due between two such renowned captains during the suspension of their rivalry. The president Richardot was, with Neyen and Verreiken, ambassador from the archdukes; but Barneveldt and Jeannin appear to have played the chief parts in the important transaction which now filled all Europe with anxiety. Every state was more or less concerned in the result; and the three great monarchies of England, France, and Spain, had all a vital interest at stake. The conferences were therefore frequent; and the debates assumed a great variety of aspects, which long kept the civilized world in suspense.

King James was extremely jealous of the more prominent part taken by the French ambassadors, and of the subaltern consideration held by his own envoys, Winwood and Spencer, in consequence of the disfavor in which he himself was held by the Dutch people. It appears evident that, whether deservedly or the contrary, England was at this period unpopular in the United Provinces, while France was looked up to with the greatest enthusiasm. This is not surprising, when we compare the characters of Henry IV. and James I., bearing in mind how much of national reputation at the time depended on the personal conduct of kings; and how political situations influence, if they do not create, the virtues and vices of a people. Independent of the suspicions of his being altogether unfavorable to the declaration required by the United Provinces from Spain, to which James's conduct had given rise, he had established some exactions which greatly embarrassed their fishing expeditions on the coasts of England.

The main points for discussion, and on which depended the decision for peace or war, were those which concerned religion; and the demand, on the part of Spain, that the United Provinces should renounce all claims to the navigation of the Indian seas. Philip required for the Catholics of the United Provinces the free exercise of their religion; this was opposed by the states-general: and the archduke

Albert, seeing the impossibility of carrying that point, despatched his confessor, **Fra** Inigo de Briznella, **to** Spain. This Dominican was furnished **with the written** opinion **of** several theologians, that the king might conscientiously **slur over the article of religion; and** he was the more successful with Philip, **as the** duke of **Lerma,** his **prime** minister, **was** resolved **to** accomplish **the peace at any** price. **The** conferences **at The Hague were therefore not** interrupted **on this question; but they went on slowly, months** being **consumed in discussions on articles of trifling importance.** They **were, however,** resumed **in the month of August with greater vigor. It was announced that the king of Spain abandoned the question respecting religion; but that it was in the certainty that his moderation would be recompensed by ample concessions on that of the Indian trade, on which he was inexorable. This article became the rock on which the whole** negotiation **eventually split. The court of Spain on the one hand, and** the **states-general on the other, inflexibly maintained their opposing claims. It was in vain that the ambassadors turned and twisted the subject with all the subtleties of** diplomacy. **Every possible expedient was used to** shake the determination **of the Dutch. But the** influence of the East India **Company, the islands of Zealand, and the** city of Amsterdam, **prevailed over all. Reports** of **the avowal on the part of the** king of Spain, that he would never renounce **his title to the sovereignty** of **the United** Provinces, unless **they abandoned the** Indian navigation and granted the free **exercise of religion, threw the** whole diplomatic **corps into** confusion**; and, on the 25th** of August, the states-general announced to the marquis **of** Spinola and **the** other ambassadors that the **congress was** dissolved, **and that** all hopes of peace were abandoned.

Nothing seemed now likely **to prevent** the immediate renewal of hostilities, when the ambassadors of France and England proposed the mediation **of** their respective masters for **the** conclusion of a truce for several years. The king of Spain and the archdukes were well satisfied to obtain even this temporary cessation of the war; but Prince Maurice and a portion of the Provinces strenuously opposed the proposition. The French and English ambassadors, however, in concert with Barneveldt, who steadily maintained his influence, labored incessantly to overcome those difficulties; and finally succeeded in overpowering all opposition to the truce. A new congress was agreed on, to assemble at Antwerp for the consideration of the conditions; and the states-general agreed to remove from The Hague to Bergop-Zoom, to be more within reach, and ready to co-operate in the negotiation.

But, before matters assumed this favorable turn, discussions and disputes had intervened on several occasions to render fruitless every effort of those who so incessantly labored for the great causes of humanity and the general good. On one occasion, Barneveldt, disgusted with the opposition of Prince Maurice and his partisans, had actually resigned his employments; but brought back by the solicitations of the states-general, and reconciled to Maurice by the intervention of Jeannin, the negotiations for the truce were resumed; and, under the auspices of the ambassadors, they were happily terminated. After two years' delay, this long-wished-for truce was concluded, and signed on the 9th of April, 1609, to continue for the space of twelve years.

This celebrated treaty contained thirty-two articles; and its fulfilment on either side was guaranteed by the kings of France and England. Notwithstanding the time taken up in previous discussions, the treaty is one of the most vague and unspecific state papers that exists. The archdukes, in their own names and in that of the king of Spain, declared the United Provinces to be free and independent states, on which they renounced all claim whatever. By the third article each party was to hold respectively the places which they possessed at the commencement of the armistice. The fourth and fifth articles grant to the republic, but in a phraseology obscure and even doubtful, the right of navigation and free trade to the Indies. The eighth contains all that regards the exercise of religion; and the remaining clauses are wholly relative to points of internal trade, custom-house regulations, and matters of private interest.

Ephemeral and temporary as this peace appeared, it was received with almost universal demonstrations of joy by the population of the Netherlands in their two grand divisions. Every one seemed to turn toward the enjoyment of tranquillity with the animated composure of tired laborers looking forward to a day of rest and sunshine. This truce brought a calm of comparative happiness upon the country, which an almost unremitting tempest had desolated for nearly half a century; and, after so long a series of calamity, all the national advantages of social life seemed about to settle on the land. The attitude which the United Provinces assumed at this period was indeed a proud one. They were not now compelled to look abroad and solicit other states to become their masters. They had forced their old tyrants to acknowledge their independence; to come and ask for peace on their own ground; and to treat with them on terms of no doubtful equality. They had already become so flourishing, so powerful, and so envied, that they who had so lately excited but compassion from the neighboring states were now regarded with such jealousy as rivals, unequivocally equal, may justly inspire in each other.

The ten southern provinces, now confirmed under the sovereignty of the House of Austria, and from this period generally distinguished by the name of Belgium, immediately began, like the northern division of the country, to labor for the great object of repairing the dreadful sufferings caused by their long and cruel war. Their success was considerable. Albert and Isabella, their sovereigns, joined, to considerable probity of character and talents for government, a fund of humanity which led them to unceasing acts of benevolence. The whole of their dominions quickly began to recover from the ravages of war. Agriculture and the minor operations of trade resumed all their wonted activity. But the manufactures of Flanders were no more;

and the grander exercise of commerce seemed finally removed to Amsterdam and the other chief towns of Holland.

This tranquil course of prosperity in the Belgian provinces was only once interrupted during the whole continuance of the twelve years' truce, and that was in the year following its commencement. The death of the duke of Cleves and Juliers, in this year, gave rise to serious disputes for the succession to his states, which was claimed by several of the princes of Germany. The elector of Brandenburg and the duke of Neuburg were seconded both by France and the United Provinces; and a joint army of both nations, commanded by Prince Maurice and the marshal de la Chatre, was marched into the county of Cleves. After taking possession of the town of Juliers, the allies retired, leaving the two princes above mentioned in a partnership possession of the disputed states. But this joint sovereignty did not satisfy the ambition of either, and serious divisions arose between them, each endeavoring to strengthen himself by foreign alliances. The archdukes Albert and Isabella were drawn into the quarrel; and they despatched Spinola at the head of twenty thousand men to support the duke of Neuburg, whose pretensions they countenanced. Prince Maurice, with a Dutch army, advanced on the other hand to uphold the claims of the elector of Brandenburg. Both generals took possession of several towns; and this double expedition offered the singular spectacle of two opposing armies, acting in different interests, making conquests, and dividing an important inheritance, without the occurrence of one act of hostility to each other. But the interference of the court of Madrid had nearly been the cause of a new rupture. The greatest alarm was excited in the Belgic provinces; and nothing but the prudence of the archdukes and the forbearance of the states-general could have succeeded in averting the threatened evil.

With the exception of this bloodless mimicry of war, the United Provinces presented for the space of twelve years a long-continued picture of peace, as the term is generally received; but a peace so disfigured by intestine troubles, and so stained by actions of despotic cruelty, that the period which should have been that of its greatest happiness becomes but an example of its worst disgrace.

The assassination of Henry IV., in the year 1609, was a new instance of the bigoted atrocity which reigned paramount in Europe at the time; and while robbing France of one of its best monarchs, it deprived the United Provinces of their truest and most powerful friend. Henry has, from his own days to the present, found a ready eulogy in all who value kings in proportion as they are distinguished by heroism, without ceasing to evince the feelings of humanity. Henry seems to have gone as far as man can go, to combine wisdom, dignity and courage with all those endearing qualities of private life which alone give men a prominent hold upon the sympathies of their kind. We acknowledge his errors, his faults, his follies, only to love him the better. We admire his valor and generosity, without being shocked by cruelty or disgusted by profusion. We look on his greatness without envy; and in tracing his whole career we seem to walk hand in hand beside a dear companion, rather than to follow the footsteps of a mighty monarch.

But the death of this powerful supporter of their efforts for freedom, and the chief guarantee for its continuance, was a trifling calamity to the United Provinces, in comparison with the rapid fall from the true point of glory so painfully exhibited in the conduct of their own domestic champion. It had been well for Prince Maurice of Nassau that the last shot fired by the defeated Spaniards in the battle of Nieuport had struck him dead in the moment of his greatest victory and on the summit of his fame. From that celebrated day he had performed no deed of war that could raise his reputation as a soldier, and all his acts as stadtholder were calculated to sink him below the level of civil virtue and just government. His two campaigns against Spinola had redounded more to the credit of his rival than to his own; and his whole conduct during the negotiation for the truce too plainly betrayed the unworthy nature of his ambition, founded on despotic principles. It was his misfortune to have been completely thrown out of the career for which he had been designed by nature and education. War was his element. By his genius, he improved it as a science: by his valor, he was one of those who raised it from the degradation of a trade to the dignity of a passion. But when removed from the camp to the council room, he became all at once a common man. His frankness degenerated into roughness; his decision into despotism; his courage into cruelty. He gave a new proof of the melancholy fact that circumstances may transform the most apparent qualities of virtue into those opposite vices between which human wisdom is baffled when it attempts to draw a decided and invariable line.

Opposed to Maurice in almost every one of his acts, was, as we have already seen, Barneveldt, one of the truest patriots of any time or country; and, with the exception of William the Great, prince of Orange, the most eminent citizen to whom the affairs of the Netherlands have given celebrity. A hundred pens have labored to do honor to this truly virtuous man. His greatness has found a record in every act of his life; and his death, like that of William, though differently accomplished, was equally a martyrdom for the liberties of his country. We cannot enter minutely into the train of circumstances which for several years brought Maurice and Barneveldt into perpetual concussion with each other. Long after the completion of the truce, which the latter so mainly aided in accomplishing, every minor point in the domestic affairs of the republic seemed merged in the conflict between the stadtholder and the pensionary. Without attempting to specify these, we may say, generally, that almost every one redounded to the disgrace of the prince and the honor of the patriot. But the main question of agitation was the fierce dispute which soon broke out between two professors of theology of the university of Leyden,

Francis Gomar and James Arminius. We do not regret on this occasion that our confined limits spare us the task of recording in detail controversies on points of speculative doctrine far beyond the reach of the human understanding, and therefore presumptuous, and the decision of which cannot be regarded as of vital importance by those who justly estimate the grand principles of Christianity. The whole strength of the intellects which had long been engaged in the conflict for national and religious liberty, was now directed to metaphysical theology, and wasted upon interminable disputes about predestination and grace. Barneveldt enrolled himself among the partisans of Arminius; Maurice became a Gomarist.

It was, however, scarcely to be wondered at that a country so recently delivered from slavery both in church and state should run into wild excesses of intolerance, before sectarian principles were thoroughly understood and definitively fixed. Persecutions of various kinds were indulged in against Papists, Anabaptists, Socinians, and all the shades of doctrine into which Christianity had split. Every minister who, in the milder spirit of Lutheranism, strove to moderate the rage of Calvinistic enthusiasm, was openly denounced by its partisans; and one, named Gaspard Koolhaas, was actually excommunicated by a synod, and denounced in plain terms to the devil. Arminius had been appointed professor at Leyden in 1603, for the mildness of his doctrines, which were joined to most affable manners, a happy temper, and a purity of conduct which no calumny could successfully traduce.

His colleague Gomar, a native of Bruges, learned, violent, and rigid in sectarian points, soon became jealous of the more popular professor's influence. A furious attack on the latter was answered by recrimination; and the whole battery of theological authorities was reciprocally discharged by one or other of the disputants. The states-general interfered between them: they were summoned to appear before the council of state; and grave politicians listened for hours to the dispute. Arminius obtained the advantage, by the apparent reasonableness of his creed, and the gentleness and moderation of his conduct. He was meek, while Gomar was furious; and many of the listeners declared that they would rather die with the charity of the former than in the faith of the latter. A second hearing was allowed them before the states of Holland. Again Arminius took the lead; and the controversy went on unceasingly, till this amiable man, worn out by his exertions and the presentiment of the evil which these disputes were engendering for his country, expired in his forty-ninth year, piously persisting in his opinions.

The Gomarists now loudly called for a national synod, to regulate the points of faith. The Arminians remonstrated on various grounds, and thus acquired the name of Remonstrants, by which they were soon generally distinguished. The most deplorable contests ensued. Serious riots occurred in several of the towns of Holland; and James I. of England could not resist the temptation of entering the polemical lists, as a champion of orthodoxy and a decided Gomarist. His hostility was chiefly directed against Vorstius, the successor and disciple of Arminius. He pretty strongly recommended to the states-general to have him burned for heresy. His inveterate intolerance knew no bounds; and it completed the melancholy picture of absurdity which the whole affair presents to reasonable minds.

In this dispute, which occupied and agitated all, it was impossible that Barneveldt should not choose the congenial temperance and toleration of Arminius. Maurice, with probably no distinct conviction or much interest in the abstract differences on either side, joined the Gomarists. His motives were purely temporal; for the party he espoused was now decidedly as much political as religious. King James rewarded him by conferring on him the ribbon of the Order of the Garter, vacant by the death of Henry IV. of France. The ceremony of investment was performed with great pomp by the English ambassador at The Hague;

and James and Maurice entered from that time into a closer and more uninterrupted correspondence than before.

During the long continuance of the theological disputes, the United Provinces had nevertheless made rapid strides toward commercial greatness; and the year 1616 witnessed the completion of an affair which was considered the consolidation of their independence. This important matter was the recovery of the towns of Brille and Flessingue, and the fort of Rammekins, which had been placed in the hands of the English as security for the loan granted to the republic by Queen Elizabeth. The whole merit of the transaction was due to the perseverance and address of Barneveldt acting on the weakness and the embarrassments of King James. Religious contention did not so fully occupy Barneveldt but that he kept a constant eye on political concerns. He was well informed on all that passed in the English court; he knew the wants of James, and was aware of his efforts to bring about the marriage of his son with the infanta of Spain. The danger of such an alliance was evident to the penetrating Barneveldt, who saw in perspective the probability of the wily Spaniards obtaining from the English monarch possession of the strong places in question. He therefore resolved on obtaining their recovery; and his great care was to get them back with a considerable abatement of the enormous debt for which they stood pledged, and which now amounted to eight million florins.

Barneveldt commenced his operations by sounding the needy monarch through the medium of Noel Caron, the ambassador from the states-general; and he next managed so as that James himself should offer to give up the towns, thereby allowing a fair pretext to the states for claiming a diminution of the debt. The English garrisons were unpaid and their complaints brought down a strong remonstrance from James, and excuses from the states, founded on the poverty of their financial resources. The negotiation rapidly went on, in the same spirit of avidity on the part of the king, and of good management on that of his debtors. It was finally agreed that the states should pay in full of the demand two million seven hundred and twenty-eight thousand florins (about two hundred and fifty thousand pounds sterling), being about one-third of the debt. Prince Maurice repaired to the cautionary towns in the month of June, and received them at the hands of the English governors; the garrisons at the same time entering into the service of the republic.

The accomplishment of this measure afforded the highest satisfaction to the United Provinces. It caused infinite discontent in England; and James, with the common injustice of men who make a bad bargain (even though its conditions be of their own seeking and suited to their own convenience), turned his own self-dissatisfaction into bitter hatred against him whose watchful integrity had successfully labored for his country's good. Barneveldt's leaning toward France and the Arminians filled the measure of James's unworthy enmity. Its effects were soon apparent, on the arrival at The Hague of Carleton, who succeeded Winwood as James's ambassador. The haughty pretensions of this diplomatist, whose attention seemed turned to theological disputes rather than politics, gave great disgust; and he contributed not a little to the persecution which led to the tragical end of Barneveldt's valuable life.

While this indefatigable patriot was busy in relieving his country from its dependence on England, his enemies accused him of the wish to reduce it once more to Spanish tyranny. Francis Aarsens, son to him who proved himself so incorruptible when attempted to be bribed by Neyen, was one of the foremost of the faction who now labored for the downfall of the pensionary. He was a man of infinite dissimulation; versed in all the intrigues of courts; and so deep in all their tortuous tactics that Cardinal Richelieu, well qualified to prize that species of talent, declared that he knew only three great political geniuses, of whom Francis Aarsens was one.

Prince Maurice now almost openly avowed his pretensions to absolute sovereignty; he knew that his success wholly depended on the consent of Barneveldt. To seduce him to favor his designs he had recourse to the dowager princess of Orange, his mother-in-law, whose gentle character and exemplary conduct had procured her universal esteem and the influence naturally attendant on it. Maurice took care to make her understand that her interest in his object was not trifling. Long time attached to Gertrude van Mechlen, his favorite mistress, who had borne him several children, he now announced his positive resolution to remain unmarried; so that his brother Frederick Henry, the dowager's only son, would be sure to succeed to the sovereignty he aimed at. The princess, not insensible to this appeal, followed the instructions of Maurice, and broached the affair to Barneveldt; but he was inexorable. He clearly explained to her the perilous career on which the prince proposed to enter; he showed how great, how independent, how almost absolute, he might continue, without shocking the principles of republicanism by grasping at an empty dignity, which could not virtually increase his authority, and would most probably convulse the state to its foundation and lead to his own ruin. The princess, convinced by his reasoning, repaired to Maurice; but instead of finding him as ready a convert as she herself had been, she received as cold an answer as was compatible with a passionate temper, wounded pride, and disappointed ambition. The princess and Barneveldt recounted the whole affair to Maurier, the French ambassador; and his son has transmitted it to posterity.

We cannot follow the misguided prince in all the winding ways of intrigue and subterfuge through which he labored to reach his object. Religion, the holiest of sentiments, and Christianity, the most sacred of its forms, were perpetually degraded by being made the pretexts for that unworthy object. He was for a while diverted from its direct pursuit by the preparation made to afford assistance to some of the allies of the republic. Fifty thousand florins a month were granted to the duke of Savoy, who was at war with Spain;

and seven thousand men, with nearly forty ships, were despatched to the aid of the republic of Venice, in its contest with Ferdinand, archduke of Gratz, who was afterward elected emperor. The honorary empire of the seas seems at this time to have been successfully claimed by the United Provinces. They paid back with interest the haughty conduct with which they had been long treated by the English; and they refused to pay the fishery duties to which the inhabitants of Great Britain were subject. The Dutch sailors had even the temerity, under pretext of pursuing pirates, to violate the British territory. They set fire to the town of Crookhaven, in Ireland, and massacred several of the inhabitants. King James, immersed in theological studies, appears to have passed slightly over this outrage. More was to have been expected from his usual attention to the affairs of Ireland; his management of which ill-fated country is the best feature of his political character, and ought, to Irish feelings at least, to be considered to redeem its many errors. But he took fire at the news that the states had prohibited the importation of cloth dyed and dressed in England. It required the best exertion of Barneveldt's talents to pacify him; and it was not easy to effect this through the jaundiced medium of the ambassador Carleton. But it was unanswerably argued by the pensionary that the manufacture of cloth was one of those ancient and natural sources of wealth which England had ravished from the Netherlands, and which the latter was justified in recovering by every effort consistent with national honor and fair principles of government.

The influence of Prince Maurice had gained complete success for the Calvinist party, in its various titles of Gomarists, non-remonstrants, etc. The audacity and violence of these ferocious sectarians knew no bounds. Outrages, too many to enumerate, became common through the country; and Arminianism was on all sides assailed and persecuted. Barreveldt frequently appealed to Maurice without effect; and all the efforts of the former to obtain justice by means of the civil authorities were paralyzed by the inaction in which the prince retained the military force. In this juncture, the magistrates of various towns, spurred on by Barneveldt, called out the national militia, termed Waardegelders, which possessed the right of arming at its own expense for the protection of the public peace. Schism upon schism was the consequence, and the whole country was reduced to that state of anarchy so favorable to the designs of an ambitious soldier already in the enjoyment of almost absolute power. Maurice possessed all the hardihood and vigor suited to such an occasion. At the head of two companies of infantry, and accompanied by his brother Frederick Henry, he suddenly set out at night from The Hague; arrived at the Brille; and in defiance of the remonstrances of the magistrates, and in violation of the rights of the town, he placed his devoted garrison in that important place. To justify this measure, reports were spread that Barneveldt intended to deliver it up to the Spaniards; and the ignorant, insensate, and ungrateful people swallowed the calumny.

This and such minor efforts were, however, all subservient to the one grand object of utterly destroying, by a public proscription, the whole of the patriot party, now identified with Arminianism. A national synod was loudly clamored for by the Gomarists; and in spite of all opposition on constitutional grounds, it was finally proclaimed. Uitenbogaard, the enlightened pastor and friend of Maurice, who on all occasions labored for the general good, now moderated, as much as possible, the violence of either party; but he could not persuade Barneveldt to render himself, by compliance, a tacit accomplice with a measure that he conceived fraught with violence to the public privileges. He had an inflexible enemy in Carleton, the English ambassador. His interference carried the question; and it was at his suggestion that Dordrecht, or Dort, was chosen for the assembling of the synod. Du Maurier, the French ambassador, acted on all occasions as a mediator; but to obtain influence at such a time it was necessary to become a partisan. Several towns—Leyden, Gouda, Rotterdam, and some others—made a last effort for their liberties, and formed a fruitless confederation.

Barneveldt **solicited** the acceptance of his resignation of **all his offices.** The states-general implored him **not to** abandon the country at such a critical moment: he consequently **maintained his post. Libels the** most vindictive and atrocious were **published and** circulated against him; and at last, forced from his silence by **these** multiplied calumnies, he put forward his "Apology," addressed to the States of Holland.

This dignified vindication only **produced new** outrages; **Maurice, now become** Prince of Orange by the death of his elder brother without children, **employed** his whole authority **to carry his object, and crush Barneveldt.** At the head of his troops he seized on towns, displaced magistrates, **trampled under foot all the** ancient privileges of the citizens, and openly announced **his intention to** overthrow the **federative constitution.** His bold conduct completely terrified **the states-general.** They thanked him; they consented **to disband the militia; formally** invited **foreign** powers to **favor and protect the synod** about to be held at **Dort.** The **return of Carleton from** England, where he had **gone to** receive the more positive promises of support from King James, was **only** wanting, to decide Maurice to take the final step; **and** no sooner did the ambassador arrive at The Hague **than** Barneveldt and his most able friends, Grotius, Hoogerbeets, and Ledenberg, were arrested in the name of the states-general.

The country was taken by surprise; no resistance was **offered.** The concluding scenes of the tragedy were hurried on; violence was succeeded by violence, against public feeling and public justice. Maurice became completely absolute in everything but in name. The supplications of ambassadors, the protests of individuals, the arguments of statesmen, were alike unavailing to stop the torrent of despotism and injustice. The synod of Dort was opened on the 13th of November, 1618. Theology was mystified; religion disgraced; Christianity outraged. And after one hundred and fifty-two sittings, during six months' display of ferocity and fraud, the solemn mockery was closed on the 9th of May, 1619, by the declaration of its president, that "its miraculous labors had made hell tremble."

Proscriptions, banishments, and death were the natural consequences of this synod. The divisions which it had professed to extinguish were rendered a thousand times more violent than before. Its decrees did incalculable ill to the cause they were meant to promote. The Anglican Church was the first to reject the canons of Dort with horror and contempt. The Protestants of France and Germany, and even Geneva, the nurse and guardian of Calvinism, were shocked and disgusted, and unanimously softened down the rigor of their respective creeds. But the moral effects of this memorable conclave were too remote to prevent the sacrifice which almost immediately followed the celebration of its rites. A trial by twenty-four prejudiced enemies, by courtesy called judges, which in its progress and its result throws judicial dignity into scorn, ended in the condemnation of Barneveldt and his fellow patriots, for treason against the liberties they had vainly labored to save. Barneveldt died on the scaffold by the hands of the executioner on the 13th of May, 1619, in the seventy-second year of his age. Grotius and Hoogerbeets were sentenced to perpetual imprisonment. Ledenberg committed suicide in his cell, sooner than brave the tortures which he anticipated at the hands of his enemies.

Many more pages than we are able to afford sentences might be devoted to the details of these iniquitous proceedings, and an account of their awful consummation. The pious heroism of Barneveldt was never excelled by any martyr to the most holy cause. He appealed to Maurice against the unjust sentence which condemned him to death; but he scorned to beg his life. He met his fate with such temperate courage as was to be expected from the dignified energy of his life. His last words were worthy a philosopher whose thoughts, even in his latest moments, were superior to mere personal hope or fear, and turned to the deep mysteries of his being. "O God!" cried De Barneveldt, "what then is man?" as he bent his head to the sword that severed it from his body, and sent the inquiring spirit to learn the great mystery for which it longed.

CHAPTER XVII

TO THE DEATH OF PRINCE MAURICE

A.D. 1619—1625

THE princess-dowager of Orange, and Du Maurier, the French ambassador, had vainly implored mercy for the innocent victim at the hands of the inexorable stadtholder. Maurice refused to see his mother-in-law: he left the ambassador's appeal unanswered. This is enough for the rigid justice of history that cannot be blinded by partiality, but hands over to shame, at the close of their career, even those whom she nursed in the very cradle of heroism. But an accusation has become current, more fatal to the fame of Prince Maurice, because it strikes at the root of his claims to feeling, which could not be impugned by a mere perseverance in severity that might have sprung from mistaken views. It is asserted, but only as general belief, that he witnessed the execution of Barneveldt. The little window of an octagonal tower, overlooking the square of the Binnenhof at The Hague, where the tragedy was acted, is still shown as the spot from which the prince gazed on the scene. Almost concealed from view among the clustering buildings of the place, it is well adapted to give weight to the tradition; but it may not, perhaps, even now be too late to raise a generous incredulity as to an assertion of which no eye-witness attestation is recorded, and which might have been the invention of malignity. There are many statements of history which it is immaterial to substantiate or disprove. Splendid fictions of public virtue have often produced their good if once received as fact; but, when private character is at stake, every conscientious writer or reader will cherish his "historic doubts," when he reflects on the facility with which calumny is sent abroad, the avidity with which it is received, and the careless ease with which men credit what it costs little to invent and propagate, but requires an age of trouble and an almost impossible conjunction of opportunities effectually to refute.

Grotius and Hoogerbeets were confined in the castle of Louvestein. Moersbergen, a leading patriot of Utrecht, De Haan, pensionary of Haarlem, and Uitenbogaard, the chosen confidant of Maurice, but the friend of Barneveldt, were next accused and sentenced to imprisonment or banishment. And thus Arminianism, deprived of its chiefs, was for the time completely stifled. The Remonstrants, thrown into utter despair, looked to emigration as their last resource. Gustavus Adolphus, king of Sweden, and Frederick, duke of Holstein, offered them shelter and protection in their respective states. Several availed themselves of these offers; but the states-general, alarmed at the progress of self-expatriation, moderated their rigor, and thus checked the desolating evil. Several of the imprisoned Arminians had the good fortune to elude the vigilance of their jailers; but the escape of Grotius is the most remarkable of all, both from his own celebrity as one of the first writers of his age in the most varied walks of literature, and from its peculiar circumstances, which only found a parallel in European history after a lapse of two centuries. We allude to the escape of Lavalette from the prison of the Conciergerie in Paris in 1815, which so painfully excited the interest of all Europe for the intended victim's wife, whose reason was the forfeit of her exertion.

Grotius was freely allowed during his close imprisonment all the relaxations of study. His friends supplied him with quantities of books, which were usually brought into the fortress in a trunk two feet two inches long, which the governor regularly and carefully examined during the first year. But custom brought relaxation in the strictness of the prison rules; and the wife of the illustrious prisoner, his faithful and constant visitor, proposed the plan of his escape, to which he gave a ready and, all hazards considered, a courageous assent. Shut up in this trunk for two hours, and with all the risk of suffocation, and of injury from the rude handling of the soldiers who carried it out of the fort, Grotius was brought clear off by the very agents of his persecutors, and safely delivered to the care of his devoted and discreet female servant, who knew the secret and kept it well. She attended the important consignment in the barge to the town of Gorcum; and after various risks of discovery, providentially escaped, Grotius at length found himself safe beyond the limits of his native land. His wife, whose torturing suspense may be imagined the while, concealed the stratagem as long as it was possible to impose on the jailer with the pardonable and praiseworthy fiction of her husband's illness and confinement to his bed. The government, outrageous at the result of the affair, at first proposed to hold this interesting prisoner in place of the prey they had lost, and to proceed criminally against her. But after a fortnight's confinement she was restored to liberty, and the country saved from the disgrace of so ungenerous and cowardly a proceeding. Grotius repaired to Paris, where he was received in the most flattering manner, and distinguished by a pension of one thousand crowns allowed by the king. He soon published his vindication—one of the most eloquent and unanswerable productions of its kind, in which those times of unjust accusations and illegal punishments were so fertile.

The expiration of the twelve years' truce was now at hand; and the United Provinces, after that long period of intestine trouble and disgrace, had once more to recommence a more congenial struggle against foreign enemies; for a renewal of the war with Spain might be fairly considered a return to the regimen best suited to the constitution of the people. The republic saw, however, with considerable anxiety, the approach of this new contest. It was fully sensible of its own weakness. Exile had reduced its population; patriotism had subsided; foreign friends were dead; the troops were unused to warfare; the hatred against Spanish cruelty had lost its excitement; the finances were in confusion; Prince Maurice had no longer the activity of youth; and the still more vigorous impulse of fighting for his country's liberty was changed to the dishonoring task of upholding his own tyranny.

The archdukes, encouraged by these considerations, had hopes of bringing back the United Provinces to their domination. They accordingly sent an embassy to Holland with proposals to that effect. It was received with indignation; and the ambassador, Peckius, was obliged to be escorted back to the frontiers by soldiers, to protect him from the insults of the people. Military operations were, however, for a while refrained from on either side, in consequence of the deaths of Philip III. of Spain and the archduke Albert. Philip IV. succeeded his father at the age of sixteen; and the archduchess Isabella found herself alone at the head of the government in the Belgian provinces. Olivarez became as sovereign a minister in Spain, as his predecessor the duke of Lerma had been; but the archduchess, though now with only the title of stadtholderess of the Netherlands, held the reins of power with a firm and steady hand.

In the celebrated thirty years' war which had commenced between the Protestants and Catholics of Germany, the former had met with considerable assistance from the United Provinces. Barneveldt, who foresaw the embarrassments which the country would have to contend with on the expiration of that truce, had strongly opposed its meddling in the quarrel; but his ruin and death left no restraint on the policy which prompted the republic to aid the Protestant cause. Fifty thousand florins a month to the revolted Protestants, and a like sum to the princes of the union, were for some time advanced. Frederick, the elector palatine, son-in-law of the king of England, and nephew of the prince, was chosen by the Bohemians for their king; but in spite of the enthusiastic wishes of the English nation, James persisted in refusing to interfere in Frederick's favor. France, governed by De Luynes, a favorite whose influence was deeply pledged, and, it is said, dearly sold to Spain, abandoned the system of Henry IV., and upheld the House of Austria. Thus the new monarch, only aided by the United Provinces, and that feebly, was soon driven from his temporary dignity; his hereditary dominions in the palatinate were overrun by the Spanish army under Spinola; and Frederick, utterly defeated at the battle of Prague, was obliged to take refuge in Holland. James's abandonment of his son-in-law has been universally blamed by almost every historian. He certainly allowed a few generous individuals to raise a regiment in England of two thousand four hundred chosen soldiers, who, under the command of the gallant Sir Horace Vere, could only vainly regret the impossibility of opposition to ten times their number of veteran troops.

This contest was carried on at first with almost all the advantages on the side of the House of Austria. Two men of extraordinary character, which presented a savage parody of military talent, and a courage chiefly remarkable for the ferocity into which it degenerated, struggled for a while against the imperial arms. These were the count of Mansfield and Christian of Brunswick. At the head of two desperate bands, which, by dint of hard fighting, acquired something of the consistency of regular armies, they maintained a long resistance; but the duke of Bavaria, commanding the troops of the emperor, and Count Tilly at the head of those of Spain, completed in the year 1622 the defeat of their daring and semi-barbarous opponents.

Spinola was resolved to commence the war against the republic by some important exploit. He therefore laid siege to Berg-op-Zoom, a place of great consequence, commanding the navigation of the Meuse and the coasts of all the islands of Zealand. But Maurice, roused from the lethargy of despotism which seemed to have wholly changed his character, repaired to the scene of threatened danger; and succeeded, after a series of desperate efforts on both sides, to raise the siege, forcing Spinola to abandon his attempt with a loss of upward of twelve thousand men. Frederick Henry in the meantime had made an incursion into Brabant with a body of light troops; and ravaging the country up to the very gates of Mechlin, Louvain, and Brussels, levied contributions to the amount of six hundred thousand florins. The states completed this series of good fortune by obtaining the possession of West Friesland, by means of Count Mansfield, whom they had despatched thither at the head of his formidable army, and who had, in spite of the opposition of Count Tilly, successfully performed his mission.

We must now turn from these brief records of military affairs, the more pleasing theme for the historian of the Netherlands in comparison with domestic events, which claim attention but to create sensations of regret and censure. Prince Maurice had enjoyed without restraint the fruits of his ambitious daring. His power was uncontrolled and unopposed, but it was publicly odious; and private resentments were only withheld by fear, and, perhaps, in some measure by the moderation and patience which distinguished the disciples of Arminianism. In the midst, however, of the apparent calm, a deep conspiracy was formed against the life of the prince. The motives, the conduct, and the termination of this plot, excite feelings of many opposite kinds. We cannot, as in former instances, wholly execrate the design and approve the punishment. Commiseration is mingled with blame, when we mark the sons of Barneveldt, urged on by the excess of filial affection to avenge their venerable father's fate; and despite our abhorrence for the object in view, we sympathize with the conspirators rather than the intended victim. William von Stoutenbourg and Renier de Groeneveld were the names of these two sons of the late pensionary. The latter was the younger; but, of more impetuous character than his brother, he was the principal in the plot. Instead of any efforts to soften down the hatred of this unfortunate family, these brothers had been removed from their employments, their property was confiscated, and despair soon urged them to desperation. In such a time of general discontent it was easy to find accomplices. Seven or eight determined men readily joined in the plot; of these, two were Catholics, the rest Arminians; the chief of whom was Henry Slatius, a preacher of considerable eloquence, talent, and energy. It was first proposed to attack the prince at **Rotterdam**; but the place was soon after changed for Ryswyk, a village near The Hague, and afterward celebrated by the treaty of peace signed there and which bears its name. Ten other associates were soon engaged by the exertions of **Slatius**: these were Arminian artisans and sailors, to whom the actual execution of the murder was to be confided; and they were persuaded that it was planned with the connivance of Prince Frederick Henry, who was considered by the Arminians as the secret partisan of their sect. The 6th of February was fixed on for the accomplishment of the deed. The better to conceal the design, the conspirators agreed to go unarmed to the place, where they were to find a box containing pistols and poniards in a spot agreed upon. The death of the Prince of Orange was not the only object intended. During the confusion subsequent to the hoped-for success of that first blow, the chief conspirators intended to excite simultaneous revolts at Leyden, Gouda, and Rotterdam, in which towns the Arminians were most numerous. A general revolution throughout Holland was firmly reckoned on as the infallible result; and success was enthusiastically looked for to their country's freedom and their individual fame.

But the plot, however cautiously laid and resolutely persevered in, was doomed to the fate of many another; and the horror of a second murder (but with far different provocation from the first) averted from the illustrious family to whom was still destined the glory of consolidating the country it had formed. Two brothers named Blansaart, and one Parthy, having procured a considerable sum of money from the leading conspirators, repaired to The Hague, as they asserted, for the purpose of betraying the plot; but they were forestalled in this purpose: four of the sailors had gone out to Ryswyk the preceding evening, and laid the whole of the project, together with the wages of their intended crime, before the prince; who, it would appear, then occupied the ancient chateau, which no longer exists at Ryswyk. The box of arms was found in the place pointed out by the informers, and measures were instantly taken to arrest the various accomplices. Several were seized. Groeneveld had escaped along the coast disguised as a fisherman, and had nearly effected his passage to England, when he was recognized and arrested in the island of Vlieland. Slatius and others were also intercepted in their attempts at escape.—Stoutenbourg, the most culpable of all, was the most fortunate; probably from the energy of character which marks the difference between a bold adventurer and a timid speculator. He is believed to have passed from The Hague in the same manner as Grotius quitted his prison; and, by the aid of a faithful servant, he accomplished his escape through various perils, and finally reached Brussels, where the archduchess Isabella took him under her special protection. He for several years made efforts to be allowed to return to Holland; but finding them hopeless, even after the death of Maurice, he embraced the Catholic religion, and obtained the command of a troop of Spanish cavalry, at the head of which he made incursions into his native country, carrying before him a black flag with the effigy of a death's head, to announce the mournful vengeance which he came to execute.

Fifteen persons were executed for the conspiracy. If ever mercy was becoming to a man, it would have been pre-eminently so to Maurice on this occasion; but he was inflexible as adamant. The mother, the wife, and the son of Groeneveld, threw themselves at his feet, imploring pardon. Prayers, tears and sobs were alike ineffectual. It is even said that Maurice asked the wretched mother "why she begged mercy for her son, having refused to do as much for her husband?" To which cruel question she is reported to have made the sublime answer—"Because my son is guilty, and my husband was not."

These bloody executions caused a deep sentiment of gloom. The conspiracy excited more pity for the victims than horror for the intended crime. Maurice, from being the idol of his countrymen, was now become an object of their fear and dislike. When he moved from town to town, the people no longer hailed him with acclamations; and even the common tokens of outward respect were at times withheld. The Spaniards, taking advantage of the internal weakness consequent on this state of public feeling in the States, made repeated incursions into the provinces, which were now united but in title, not in spirit. Spinola was once more in the field, and had invested the important town of Breda, which was the patrimonial inheritance of the princes of Orange. Maurice was oppressed with anxiety and regret; and, for the sake of his better feelings, it may be hoped, with remorse. He could effect nothing against his rival; and he saw his own laurels withering from his careworn brow. The only hope left of obtaining the so much wanted supplies of money was in the completion of a new treaty with France and England. Cardinal Richelieu, desirous of setting bounds to the ambition and the successes of the House of Austria, readily came into the views of the States; and an obligation for a loan of one million two hundred thousand livres during the year 1624, and one million more for each of the two succeeding years, was granted by the king of France, on condition that the republic made no new truce with Spain without his mediation.

An alliance nearly similar was at the same time concluded with England. Perpetual quarrels on commercial questions loosened the ties which bound the States to their ancient allies. The failure of his son's intended marriage with the infanta of Spain had opened the eyes of King James to the way in which he was despised by those who seemed so much to respect him. He was highly indignant;

and he undertook to revenge himself by aiding the republic. He agreed to furnish six thousand men, and supply the funds for their pay, with a provision for repayment by the States at the conclusion of a peace with Spain.

Prince Maurice had no opportunity of reaping the expected advantages from these treaties. Baffled in all his efforts for relieving Breda, and being unsuccessful in a new attempt upon Antwerp, he returned to The Hague, where a lingering illness, that had for some time exhausted him, terminated in his death on the 23d of April, 1625, in his fifty-ninth year. Most writers attribute this event to agitation at being unable to relieve Breda from the attack of Spinola. It is in any case absurd to suppose that the loss of a single town could have produced so fatal an effect on one whose life had been an almost continual game of the chances of war. But cause enough for Maurice's death may be found in the wearing effects of thirty years of active military service, and the more wasting ravages of half as many of domestic despotism.

CHAPTER XVIII

TO THE TREATY OF MUNSTER

A.D. 1625–1648

FREDERICK HENRY succeeded to almost all his brother's titles and employments, and found his new dignities clogged with an accumulation of difficulties sufficient to appall the most determined spirit. Everything seemed to justify alarm and despondency. If the affairs of the republic in India wore an aspect of prosperity, those in Europe presented a picture of past disaster and approaching peril. Disunion and discontent, an almost insupportable weight of taxation, and the disputes of which it was the fruitful source, formed the subjects of internal ill. Abroad was to be seen navigation harassed and trammelled by the pirates of Dunkirk; and the almost defenceless frontiers of the republic exposed to the irruptions of the enemy. The king of Denmark, who endeavored to make head against the imperialist and Spanish forces, was beaten by Tilly, and made to tremble for the safety of his own States. England did nothing toward the common cause of Protestantism, in consequence of the weakness of the monarch; and civil dissensions for a while disabled France from resuming the system of Henry IV. for humbling the House of Austria.

Frederick Henry was at this period in his forty-second year. His military reputation was well established; he soon proved his political talents. He commenced his career by a total change in the tone of government on the subject of sectarian differences. He exercised several acts of clemency in favor of the imprisoned and exiled Arminians, at the same time that he upheld the dominant religion. By these measures he conciliated all parties; and by degrees the fierce spirit of intolerance became subdued. The foreign relations of the United Provinces now presented the anomalous policy of a fleet furnished by the French king, manned by rigid Calvinists, and commanded by a grandson of Admiral Coligny, for the purpose of combating the remainder of the French Huguenots, whom they considered as brothers in religion, though political foes; and during the joint expedition which was undertaken by the allied French and Dutch troops against Rochelle, the stronghold of Protestantism, the preachers of Holland put up prayers for the protection of those whom their army was marching to destroy. The states-general, ashamed of this unpopular union, recalled their fleet, after some severe fighting with that of the Huguenots. Cardinal Richelieu and the king of France were for a time furious in their displeasure; but interests of state overpowered individual resentments, and no rupture took place.

Charles I. had now succeeded his father on the English throne. He renewed the treaty with the republic, which furnished him with twenty ships to assist his own formidable fleet in his war against Spain. Frederick Henry had, soon after his succession to the chief command, commenced an active course of martial operations, and was successful in almost all his enterprises. He took Groll and several other towns; and it was hoped that his successes would have been pushed forward upon a wider field of action against the imperial arms; but the States prudently resolved to act on the defensive by land, choosing the sea for the theatre of their more active operations. All the hopes of a powerful confederation against the emperor and the king of Spain seemed frustrated by the war which now broke out between France and England. The states-general contrived by great prudence to maintain a strict neutrality in this quarrel. They even succeeded in mediating a peace between the rival powers, which was concluded the following year; and in the meantime they obtained a more astonishing and important series of triumphs against the Spanish fleets than had yet been witnessed in naval conflicts.

The West India Company had confided the command of their fleet to Peter Hein, a most intrepid and intelligent sailor, who proved his own merits, and the sagacity of his employers on many occasions, two of them of an extraordinary nature. In 1627, he defeated a fleet of twenty-six vessels, with a much inferior force. In the following year, he had the still more brilliant good fortune, near Havana, in the island of Cuba, in an engagement with the great Spanish armament, called the Money Fleet, to indicate the immense wealth which it contained. The booty was safely carried to Amsterdam, and the whole of the treasure, in money, precious stones, indigo, etc., was estimated at the value of twelve million florins. This was indeed a victory worth gaining, won almost without bloodshed, and raising the republic far above the manifold difficulties by which it had been embarrassed. Hein perished in the following year, in a combat with some of the pirates of Dunkirk— those terrible freebooters whose name was a watchword of terror during the whole continuance of the war.

The year 1629 brought three formidable armies at once to the frontiers of the republic, and caused a general dismay all through the United Provinces; but the immense treasures taken from the Spaniards enabled them to make preparations suitable to the danger; and Frederick Henry, supported by his cousin William of Nassau, his natural brother Justin, and other brave and experienced officers, defeated every effort of the enemy. He took many towns in rapid succession; and finally forced the Spaniards to abandon all notion of invading the territories of the republic. Deprived of the powerful talents of Spinola, who was called to command the Spanish troops in Italy, the armies of the archduchess, under the count of Berg, were not able to cope with the genius of the Prince of Orange. The consequence was the renewal of negotiations for a second truce. But these were received on the part of the republic with a burst of opposition. All parties seemed decided on that point; and every interest, however opposed on minor questions, combined to give a positive negative on this.

The **gratitude of** the country for the services of Frederick Henry induced the provinces of which he **was** stadtholder to grant the reversion in this title to his son, a child of three years old; and this dignity had every chance of becoming as absolute, as it was now pronounced almost hereditary, by the means of an army of one hundred and twenty thousand men devoted to their chief. However, few military occurrences took place, the sea being still chosen as the element best suited to the present enterprises of the republic. In the widely-distant settlements of Brazil and Batavia, the Dutch were equally successful; and the East and West India companies acquired eminent power and increasing solidity.

The year 1631 was signalized by an expedition into Flanders, consisting of eighteen thousand men, intended against Dunkirk, but hastily abandoned, in spite of every probability of success, by the commissioners of the states-general, who accompanied the army, and thwarted all the ardor and vigor of the Prince of Orange. But another great naval victory in the narrow seas of Zealand recompensed the disappointments of this inglorious affair.

The splendid victories of Augustus Adolphus against the imperial arms in Germany changed the whole face of European affairs. Protestantism began once more to raise its head; and the important conquests by Frederick Henry of almost all the strong places on the Meuse, including Maestricht, the strongest of all, gave the United Provinces their ample share in the glories of the war. The death of the archduchess Isabella, which took place at Brussels in the year 1633, added considerably to the difficulties of Spain in the Belgian provinces. The defection of the count of Berg, the chief general of their armies, who was actuated by resentment on the appointment of the marquis of St. Croix over his head, threw everything into confusion, in exposing a widespread confederacy among the nobility of these provinces to erect themselves into an independent republic, strengthened by a perpetual alliance with the United Provinces against the power of Spain. But the plot failed, chiefly, it is said, by the imprudence of the king of England, who let the secret slip, from some motives vaguely hinted at, but never sufficiently explained. After the death of Isabella, the prince of Brabançon was arrested. The prince of Epinoi and the duke of Burnonville made their escape; and the duke of Arschot, who was arrested in Spain, was soon liberated, in consideration of some discoveries into the nature of the plot. An armistice, published in 1634, threw this whole affair into complete oblivion.

The king of Spain appointed his brother Ferdinand, a cardinal and archbishop of Toledo, to the dignity of governor-general of the Netherlands. He repaired to Germany at the head of seventeen thousand men, and bore his share in the victory of Nordlingen; after which he hastened to the Netherlands, and made his entry into Brussels in 1634. Richelieu had hitherto only combated the house of Austria in these countries by negotiation and intrigue; but he now entered warmly into the proposals made by Holland for a treaty offensive and defensive between Louis XIII. and the republic. By a treaty soon after concluded (February 8, 1635) the king of France engaged to invade the Belgian provinces with an army of thirty thousand men, in concert with a Dutch force of equal number. It was agreed that if Belgium would consent to break from the Spanish yoke it was to be erected into a free state; if, on the contrary, it would not co-operate for its own freedom, France and Holland were to dismember, and to divide it equally.

The plan of these combined measures was soon acted on. The French army took the field under the command of the marshals De Chatillon and De Breeze; and defeated the Spaniards in a bloody battle, near Avein, in the province of Luxemburg, on the 20th of May, 1635, with the loss of four thousand men. The victors soon made a junction with the Prince of Orange; and the towns of Tirlemont, St. Trond, and some others, were quickly reduced. The former of these places was taken by assault, and pillaged with circumstances of cruelty that recall the horrors of the early transactions of the war. The Prince of Orange was forced to punish severely the authors of these offences. The consequences of this event were highly injurious to the allies. A spirit of fierce resistance was excited throughout the invaded provinces. Louvain set the first example. The citizens and students took arms for its defence; and the combined forces of France and Holland were repulsed, and forced by want of supplies to abandon the siege, and rapidly retreat. The prince-cardinal, as Ferdinand was called, took advantage of this reverse to press the retiring French; recovered several towns; and gained all the advantages as well as glory of the campaign. The remains of the French army, reduced by continual combats, and still more by sickness, finally embarked at Rotterdam, to return to France in the ensuing spring, a sad contrast to its brilliant appearance at the commencement of the campaign.

The military events for several ensuing years present nothing of sufficient interest to induce us to record them in detail. A perpetual succession of sieges and skirmishes afford a monotonous picture of isolated courage and skill; but we see none of those great conflicts which bring out the genius of opposing generals, and show war in its grand results, as the decisive means of enslaving or emancipating mankind. The prince-cardinal, one of the many who on this bloody theatre displayed consummate military talents, incessantly employed himself in incursions into the bordering provinces of France, ravaged Picardy, and filled Paris with fear and trembling. He, however, reaped no new laurels when he came into contact with Frederick Henry, who, on almost every occasion, particularly that of the siege of Breda, in 1637, carried his object in spite of all opposition. The triumphs of war were balanced; but Spain and the Belgian provinces, so long upheld by the talent of the governor-general, were gradually become exhausted. The revolution in Portugal, and the succession of the duke of Braganza, under the title of John IV., to the throne of his ancestors, struck a fatal blow to the power of Spain. A strict alliance was concluded between the new monarch of France and Holland; and hostilities against the common enemy were on all sides vigorously continued.

The successes of the republic at sea and in their distant enterprises were continual, and in some instances brilliant. Brazil was gradually falling into the power of the West India Company. The East India possessions were secure. The great victory of Van Tromp, known by the name of the battle of the Downs, from being fought off the coast of England, on the 21st of October, 1639, raised the naval reputation of Holland as high as it could well be carried. Fifty ships taken, burned, and sunk, were the proofs of their admiral's triumph; and the Spanish navy never recovered the loss. The victory was celebrated throughout Europe, and Van Tromp was the hero of the day. The king of England was, however, highly indignant at the hardihood with which the Dutch admiral broke through the etiquette of territorial respect, and destroyed his country's bitter foes under the very sanction of English neutrality. But the subjects of Charles I. did not partake their monarch's feelings. They had no sympathy with arbitrary and tyrannic government; and their joy at the misfortune of their old enemies the Spaniards gave a fair warning of the spirit which afterward proved so fatal to the infatuated king, who on this occasion would have protected and aided them.

In an unsuccessful enterprise in Flanders, Count Henry Casimir of Nassau was mortally wounded, adding another to the list of those of that illustrious family whose lives were lost in the service of their country. His brother, Count William Frederick, succeeded him in his office of stadtholder of Friesland; but the same dignity in the provinces of Groningen and Drent devolved on the Prince of Orange. The latter had conceived the desire of a royal alliance for his son William. Charles I. readily assented to the proposal of the states-general that this young prince should receive the hand of his daughter Mary. Embassies were exchanged; the conditions of the contract agreed on; but it was not till two years later that Van Tromp, with an escort of twenty ships, conducted the princess, then twelve years old, to the country of her future husband. The republic did not view with an eye quite favorable this advancing aggrandizement of the House of Orange. Frederick Henry had shortly before been dignified by the king of France, at the suggestion of Richelieu, with the title of "highness," instead of the inferior one of "excellency"; and the states-general, jealous of this distinction granted to their chief magistrate, adopted for themselves the sounding appellation of "high and mighty lords." The Prince of Orange, whatever might have been his private views of ambition, had however the prudence to silence all suspicion, by the mild and moderate use which he made of the power, which he might perhaps have wished to increase, but never attempted to abuse.

On the 9th of November, 1641, the prince-cardinal Ferdinand died at Brussels in his thirty-third year; another instance of those who were cut off, in the very vigor of manhood, from worldly dignities and the exercise of the painful and inauspicious duties of governor-general of the Netherlands. Don Francisco de Mello, a nobleman of highly reputed talents, was the next who obtained this onerous situation. He commenced his governorship by a succession of military operations, by which, like most of his predecessors, he is alone distinguished. Acts of civil administration are scarcely noticed by the historians of these men. Not one of them, with the exception of the archduke Albert, seems to have valued the internal interests of the government; and he alone, perhaps, because they were declared and secured as his own. De Mello, after taking some towns, and defeating the marshal De Guiche in the battle of Hannecourt, tarnished all his fame by the great faults which he committed in the famous battle of Rocroy. The duke of Enghien, then twenty-one years of age, and subsequently so celebrated as the great Condé, completely defeated De Mello, and nearly annihilated the Spanish and Walloon infantry. The military operations of the Dutch army were this year only remarkable by the gallant conduct of Prince William, son of the Prince of Orange, who, not yet seventeen years of age, defeated, near Hulst, under the eyes of his father, a Spanish detachment in a very warm skirmish.

Considerable changes were now insensibly operating in the policy of Europe. Cardinal Richelieu had finished his dazzling but tempestuous career of government, in which the hand of death arrested him on the 4th of December, 1642. Louis XIII. soon followed to the grave him who was rather his master than his minister. Anne of Austria was declared regent during the minority of her son, Louis XIV., then only five years of age; and Cardinal Mazarin succeeded to the station from which death alone had power to remove his predecessor.

The civil wars in England now broke out, and their terrible results seemed to promise to the republic the undisturbed sovereignty of the seas. The Prince of Orange received with great distinction the mother-in-law of his son, when she came to Holland under pretext of conducting her daughter; but her principal purpose was to obtain, by the sale of the crown jewels and the assistance of Frederick Henry, funds for the supply of her unfortunate husband's cause.

The prince and several private individuals contributed largely in money; and several experienced officers passed over to serve in the royalist army of England. The provincial states of Holland, however, sympathizing wholly with the parliament, remonstrated with the stadtholder; and the Dutch colonists encouraged the hostile efforts of their brethren, the Puritans of Scotland, by all the absurd exhortations of fanatic zeal. Boswell, the English resident in the name of the king, and Strickland, the ambassador from the parliament, kept up a constant succession of complaints and remonstrances on occasion of every incident which seemed to balance the conduct of the republic in the great question of English politics. Considerable differences existed: the province of Holland, and some others, leaned toward the parliament; the Prince of Orange favored the king; and the states-general endeavored to maintain a neutrality.

The struggle was still furiously maintained in Germany. Generals of the first order of military talent were continually appearing, and successively eclipsing each other by their brilliant actions. Gustavus Adolphus was killed in the midst of his glorious career, at the battle of Lutzen; the duke of Weimar succeeded to his command, and proved himself worthy of the place; Tilly and the celebrated Wallenstein were no longer on the scene. The emperor Ferdinand II. was dead, and his son Ferdinand III. saw his victorious enemies threaten, at last, the existence of the empire. Everything tended to make peace necessary to some of the contending powers, as it was at length desirable for all. Sweden and Denmark were engaged in a bloody and wasteful conflict. The United Provinces sent an embassy, in the month of June, 1644, to each of those powers; and by a vigorous demonstration of their resolution to assist Sweden, if Denmark proved refractory, a peace was signed the following year, which terminated the disputes of the rival nations.

Negotiations were now opened at Munster between the several belligerents. The republic was, however, the last to send its plenipotentiaries there; having signed a new treaty with France, by which they mutually stipulated to make no peace independent of each other. It behooved the republic, however, to contribute as much as possible toward the general object; for, among other strong motives to that line of conduct, the finances of Holland were in a state perfectly deplorable.

Every year brought the necessity of a new loan; and the public debt of the provinces now amounted to one hundred and fifty million florins, bearing interest at six and a quarter per cent. Considerable alarm was excited at the progress of the French army in the Belgian provinces; and escape from the tyranny of Spain seemed only to lead to the danger of submission to a nation too powerful and too close at hand not to be dangerous, either as a foe or an ally. These fears were increased by the knowledge that Cardinal Mazarin projected a marriage between Louis XIV. and the infanta of Spain, with the Belgian provinces, or Spanish Netherlands as they were now called, for her marriage portion. This project was confided to the Prince of Orange, under the seal of secrecy, and he was offered the marquisate of Antwerp as the price of his influence toward effecting the plan. The prince revealed the whole to the states-general. Great fermentation was excited; the stadtholder himself was blamed, and suspected of complicity with the designs of the cardinal. Frederick Henry was deeply hurt at this want of confidence, and the injurious publications which openly assailed his honor in a point where he felt himself entitled to praise instead of suspicion.

The French labored to remove the impression which this affair excited in the republic; but the states-general felt themselves justified by the intriguing policy of Mazarin in entering into a secret negotiation with the king of Spain, who offered very favorable conditions. The negotiations were considerably advanced by the marked disposition evinced by the Prince of Orange to hasten the establishment of peace. Yet, at this very period, and while anxiously wishing this great object, he could not resist the desire for another campaign; one more exploit, to signalize the epoch at which he finally placed his sword in the scabbard.

Frederick Henry was essentially a soldier, with all the

spirit of his race; and this evidence of the ruling passion, while he touched the verge of the grave, is one of the most striking points of his character. He accordingly took the field; but, with a constitution broken by a lingering disease, he was little fitted to accomplish any feat worthy of his splendid reputation. He failed in an attempt on Venlo, and another on Antwerp, and retired to The Hague, where for some months he rapidly declined. On the 14th of March, 1647, he expired, in his sixty-third year; leaving behind him a character of unblemished integrity, prudence, toleration, and valor. He was not of that impetuous stamp which leads men to heroic deeds, and brings danger to the states whose liberty is compromised by their ambition. He was a striking contrast to his brother Maurice, and more resembled his father in many of those calmer qualities of the mind, which make men more beloved without lessening their claims to admiration. Frederick Henry had the honor of completing the glorious task which William began and Maurice followed up. He saw the oppression they had combated now humbled and overthrown; and he forms the third in a sequence of family renown, the most surprising and the least checkered afforded by the annals of Europe.

William II. succeeded his father in his dignities; and his ardent spirit longed to rival him in war. He turned his endeavors to thwart all the efforts for peace. But the interests of the nation and the dying wishes of Frederick Henry were of too powerful influence with the states, to be overcome by the martial yearnings of an inexperienced youth. The negotiations were pressed forward; and, despite the complaints, the murmurs, and the intrigues of France, the treaty of Munster was finally signed by the respective ambassadors of the United Provinces and Spain, on the 30th of January, 1648. This celebrated treaty contains seventy-nine articles. Three points were of main and vital importance to the republic: the first acknowledges an ample and entire recognition of the sovereignty of the states-general, and a renunciation forever of all claims on the part of Spain; the second confirms the rights of trade and navigation in the East and West Indies, with the possession of the various countries and stations then actually occupied by the contracting powers; the third guarantees a like possession of all the provinces and towns of the Netherlands, **as they** then stood in their respective occupation—a clause **highly favorable to the republic, which** had conquered several **considerable places in Brabant and** Flanders. The ratifications of the treaty were exchanged **at Munster** with great solemnity on the 15th of May following **the signature**; the peace was published in that town and in Osnaburg on the **19th**, and in all the different states of the king of **Spain** and **the** United Provinces as soon **as the** joyous intelligence **could** reach such various and widely separated destinations. Thus after eighty years of unparalleled warfare, only interrupted **by** the truce of 1609, during which hostilities had not ceased in the Indies, the new republic rose from the horrors of civil war and foreign tyranny to its uncontested rank as a free and independent state among the most powerful nations of Europe. No country had ever done more for glory; and the result of its efforts was the irrevocable guarantee of civil and religious liberty, the great aim and end of civilization.

The king of France alone had reason to complain of this treaty: his resentment was strongly pronounced. But the United Provinces flung back **the** reproaches of his ambassador on Cardinal Mazarin; and the anger of the monarch was smothered by the policy of the minister.

The internal tranquillity of the republic was secured from all future alarm by the conclusion of the general peace of Westphalia, definitively signed on the 24th of October, 1648. This treaty was long considered not only as the fundamental law of the empire, but as the basis of the political system of Europe. As numbers of conflicting interests were reconciled, Germanic liberty secured, and a just equilibrium established between the Catholics and Protestants, France and Sweden obtained great advantages; and the various princes of the empire saw their possessions regulated and secured, at the same time that the powers of the emperor were strictly defined.

This great epoch in European history naturally marks the conclusion of another in that of the Netherlands; and this period of general repose allows a brief consideration of the progress of arts, sciences, and manners, during the half century just now completed.

The archdukes Albert and Isabella, during the whole course of their sovereignty, labored to remedy the abuses which had crowded the administration of justice. The Perpetual Edict, in 1611, regulated the form of judicial proceedings; and several provinces received new charters, by which the privileges of the people were placed on a footing in harmony with their wants. Anarchy, in short, gave place to regular government; and the archdukes, in swearing to maintain the celebrated pact known by the name of the Joyeuse Entrée, did all in their power to satisfy their subjects, while securing their own authority. The piety of the archdukes gave an example to all classes. This, although degenerating in the vulgar to superstition and bigotry, formed a severe check, which allowed their rulers to restrain popular excesses, and enabled them in the internal quiet of their despotism to soften the people by the encouragement of the sciences and arts. Medicine, astronomy, and mathematics, made prodigious progress during this epoch. Several eminent men flourished in the Netherlands. But the glory of others, in countries presenting a wider theatre for their renown, in many instances eclipsed them; and the inventors of new methods and systems in anatomy, optics and music were almost forgotten in the splendid improvements of their followers.

In literature, Hugo de Groot, or Grotius (his Latinized name, by which he is better known), was the most brilliant star of his country or his age, as Erasmus was of that which preceded. He was at once eminent as jurist, poet, theologian, and historian. His erudition was immense; and he brought it to bear in his political capacity, as ambassador from Sweden to the court of France, when the violence of party and the injustice of power condemned him to perpetual imprisonment in his native land. The religious disputations in Holland had given a great impulse to talent. They were not mere theological arguments; but with the wild and furious abstractions of bigotry were often blended various illustrations from history, art, and science, and a tone of keen and delicate satire, which at once refined and made them readable. It is remarkable that almost the whole of the Latin writings of this period abound in good taste, while those written in the vulgar tongue are chiefly coarse and trivial. Vondel and Hooft, the great poets of the time, wrote with genius and energy, but were deficient in judgment founded on good taste. The latter of these writers was also distinguished for his prose works; in honor of which Louis XIII. dignified him with letters patent of nobility, and decorated him with the order of St. Michael.

But while Holland was more particularly distinguished by the progress of the mechanical arts, to which Prince Maurice afforded unbounded patronage, the Belgian provinces gave birth to that galaxy of genius in the art of painting, which no equal period of any other country has ever rivalled. A volume like this would scarcely suffice to do justice to the merits of the eminent artists who now flourished in Belgium; at once founding, perfecting, and immortalizing the Flemish school of painting. Rubens, Vandyck, Teniers, Crayer, Jordaens, Sneyders, and a host of other great names, crowd on us with claims for notice that almost make the mention of any an injustice to the rest. But Europe is familiar with their fame; and the widespread taste for their delicious art makes them independent of other record than the combination of their own exquisite touch, undying tints, and unequalled knowledge of nature. Engraving, carried at the same time to great perfection, has multiplied some of the merits of the celebrated painters, while stamping the reputation of its own professors. Sculpture, also, had its votaries of considerable note. Among these, Des Jardins and Quesnoy held the foremost station. Architecture also produced some remarkable names.

The arts were, in short, never held in higher honor than at this brilliant epoch. Otto Venire, the master of Rubens, held most important employments. Rubens himself, appointed secretary to the privy council of the archdukes, was subsequently sent to England, where he negotiated the peace between that country and Spain. The unfortunate King Charles so highly esteemed his merit that he knighted him in full parliament, and presented him with the diamond ring he wore on his own finger, and a chain enriched with brilliants. David Teniers, the great pupil of this distinguished master, met his due share of honor. He has left several portraits of himself; one of which hands him down to posterity in the costume, and with the decorations of the belt and key, which he wore in his capacity of chamberlain to the archduke Leopold, governor-general of the Spanish Netherlands.

The intestine disturbances of Holland during the twelve years' truce, and the enterprises against Friesland and the duchy of Cleves, had prevented that wise economy which was expected from the republic. The annual ordinary cost of the military establishment at that period amounted to thirteen million florins. To meet the enormous expenses of the state, taxes were raised on every material. They produced about thirty million florins a year, independent of five million each for the East and West India companies. The population in 1620, in Holland, was about six hundred thousand, and the other provinces contained about the same number.

It is singular to observe the fertile erections of monopoly in a state founded on principles of commercial freedom. The East and West India companies, the Greenland company, and others, were successively formed. By the effect of their enterprise, industry and wealth, conquests were made and colonies founded with surprising rapidity. The town of Amsterdam, now New York, was founded in 1624; and the East saw Batavia rise up from the ruins of Jacatra, which was sacked and razed by the Dutch adventurers.

The Dutch and English East India companies, repressing their mutual jealousy, formed a species of partnership in 1619 for the reciprocal enjoyment of the rights of commerce. But four years later than this date an event took place so fatal to national confidence that its impressions are scarcely yet effaced—this was the torturing and execution of several Englishmen in the island of Amboyna, on pretence of an unproved plot, of which every probability leads to the belief that they were wholly innocent. This circumstance was the strongest stimulant to the hatred so evident in the bloody wars which not long afterward took place between the two nations; and the lapse of two centuries has not entirely effaced its effects. Much has been at various periods written for and against the establishment of monopolizing companies, by which individual wealth and skill are excluded from their chances of reward. With reference to those of Holland at this period of its history, it is sufficient to remark that the great results of their formation could never have been brought about by isolated enterprises; and the justice or wisdom of their continuance are questions wholly dependent on the fluctuations in trade, and the effects produced on that of any given country by the progress and the rivalry of others.

With respect to the state of manners in the republic, it is clear that the jealousies and emulation of commerce were not likely to lessen the vice of avarice with which the natives have been reproached. The following is a strong expression of one, who cannot, however, be considered an unprejudiced observer, on occasion of some disputed points between the Dutch and English maritime tribunals—"The decisions of our courts cause much ill-will among these people, whose hearts' blood is their purse."[1] While drunk-

---

[1] Carleton.

euness was a vice considered scarcely scandalous, the intrigues of gallantry were concealed with the most scrupulous mystery—giving evidence of at least good taste, if not of pure morality. Court etiquette began to be of infinite importance. The wife of Count Ernest Casimir of Nassau was so intent on the preservation of her right of precedence that on occasion of Lady Carleton, the British ambassadress, presuming to dispute the *pas*, she forgot true dignity so far as to strike her. We may imagine the vehement resentment of such a man as Carleton for such an outrage. The lower orders of the people had the rude and brutal manners common to half-civilized nations which fight their way to freedom. The unfortunate king of Bohemia, when a refugee in Holland, was one day hunting; and, in the heat of the chase, he followed his dogs, which had pursued a hare, into a newly sown corn-field: he was quickly interrupted by a couple of peasants armed with pitchforks. He supposed his rank and person to be unknown to them; but he was soon undeceived, and saluted with unceremonious reproaches. "King of Bohemia! King of Bohemia!" shouted one of the boors, "why do you trample on my wheat which I have so lately had the trouble of sowing?" The king made many apologies, and retired, throwing the whole blame on his dogs. But in the life of Marshal Turenne we find a more marked trait of manners than this, which might be paralleled in England at this day. This great general served his apprenticeship in the art of war under his uncles, the princes Maurice and Frederick Henry. He appeared one day on the public walk at The Hague, dressed in his usual plain and modest style. Some young French lords, covered with **gold**, embroidery, and **ribbons**, met and accosted him: a **mob** gathered round; **and while** treating Turenne, although **unknown** to them, with all possible respect, they forced the others to retire, assailed with mockery and the coarsest abuse.

But one characteristic, more noble and worthy than any of those thus briefly cited, was the full enjoyment of the liberty of the press in the United Provinces. The thirst of gain, the fury of faction, the federal independence of the minor towns, the absolute power of Prince Maurice, all the combinations which might carry weight against this grand principle, were totally ineffectual to prevail over it. And the republic was, on this point, proudly pre-eminent among surrounding nations.

CHAPTER XIX

FROM THE PEACE OF MUNSTER TO THE PEACE OF NIMEGUEN

A. D. 1648—1678

THE completion of the peace of Munster opens a new scene in the history of the republic. Its political system experienced considerable changes. Its ancient enemies became its most ardent friends, and its old allies loosened the bonds of long-continued amity. The other states of Europe, displeased at its imperious conduct, or jealous of its success, began to wish its humiliation; but it was little thought that the consummation was to be effected at the hands of England.

While Holland prepared to profit by the peace so brilliantly gained, England, torn by civil war, was hurried on in crime and misery to the final act which has left an indelible stain on her annals. Cromwell and the parliament had completely subjugated the kingdom. The unfortunate king, delivered up by the Scotch, was brought to a mock trial, and condemned to an ignominious death. Great as were his faults, they are almost lost sight of in the atrocity of his opponents; so surely does disproportioned punishment for political offences produce a reaction in the minds that would approve a commensurate penalty. The United Provinces had preserved a strict neutrality while the contest was undecided. The Prince of Orange warmly strove to obtain a declaration in favor of his father-in-law, Charles I. The Prince of Wales and the Duke of York, his sons, who had taken refuge at The Hague, earnestly joined in the entreaty; but all that could be obtained from the states-general was their consent to an embassy to interpose with the ferocious bigots who doomed the hapless monarch to the block. Pauw and Joachimi, the one sixty-four years of age, the other eighty-eight, the most able men of the republic, undertook the task of mediation. They were scarcely listened to by the parliament, and the bloody sacrifice took place.

The details of this event, and its immediate consequences, belong to English history; and we must hurry over the brief, turbid, and inglorious stadtholderate of William II., to arrive at the more interesting contest between the republic which had honorably conquered its freedom, and that of the rival commonwealth, which had gained its power by hypocrisy, violence, and guilt.

William II. was now in his twenty-fourth year. He had early evinced that heroic disposition which was common to his race. He panted for military glory. All his pleasures were those usual to ardent and high-spirited men, although his delicate constitution seemed to forbid the indulgence of hunting, tennis, and the other violent exercises in which he delighted. He was highly accomplished; spoke five different languages with elegance and fluency, and had made considerable progress in mathematics and other abstract sciences. His ambition knew no bounds. Had he reigned over a monarchy as absolute king, he would most probably have gone down to posterity a conqueror and a hero. But, unfitted to direct a republic as its first citizen, he has left but the name of a rash and unconstitutional magistrate. From the moment of his accession to power, he was made sensible of the jealousy and suspicion with which his office and his character were observed by the provincial states of Holland. Many instances of this disposition were accumulated to his great disgust; and he was not long in evincing his determination to brave all the odium and reproach of despotic designs, and to risk everything for the establishment of absolute power. The province of Holland, arrogating to itself the greatest share in the reforms of the army, and the financial arrangements called for by the transition from war to peace, was soon in fierce opposition with the states-general, which supported the prince in his early views. Cornelius **Bikker**, one of the burgomasters of **Amsterdam**, was the leading person in the states of Holland; and a circumstance soon occurred which put him and the stadtholder in collision, and quickly decided the great question at issue.

The admiral Cornellizon de Witt arrived from Brazil with the remains of his fleet, and without the consent of the council of regency there established by the states-general. He was instantly arrested by order of the Prince of Orange, in his capacity of high-admiral. The admiralty of Amsterdam was at the same time ordered by the states-general to imprison six of the captains of this fleet. The states of Holland maintained that this was a violation of their provincial rights, and an illegal assumption of power on the part of the states-general; and the magistrates of Amsterdam forced the prison doors, and set the captains at liberty. William, backed by the authority of the states-general, now put himself at the head of a deputation from that body, and made a rapid **tour of visitation to the** different chief towns of the republic, to sound the depths of public opinion on the matters in dispute. The deputation met with varied success; but the result proved to the irritated prince that no measures of compromise **were to be expected,** and that force alone was to arbitrate the question. The army was to a man devoted to him. The states-general gave him their entire, and somewhat servile, support. He, therefore, on his own **authority,** arrested the six deputies of Holland, in the same **way** that his uncle Maurice **had** seized on Barneveldt, Grotius, and the others; **and they** were immediately conveyed **to the castle of** Louvestein.

In adopting this bold **and** unauthorized measure, he decided on an immediate attempt to gain possession of the city of **Amsterdam, the** central point of opposition to his violent **designs.** William Frederick, count of Nassau, stadtholder of Friesland, at the head of a numerous detachment of troops, marched **secretly and by night to surprise the town;** but the **darkness and a violent** thunderstorm having caused the greater number **to lose** their way, the count found himself **at dawn at the city** gates with a very insufficient **force; and had the further mortification to see the walls well manned, the** cannon **pointed, the drawbridges** raised, **and everything in a** state of **defence. The** courier **from Hamburg, who had** passed through **the scattered bands of soldiers during the** night, had given **the alarm. The first notion was that a** roving band **of Swedish or** Lorraine **troops, attracted by the opulence of Amsterdam,** had resolved **on an attempt to seize and pillage it.** The magistrates **could scarcely credit the evidence of day, which showed them the count of Nassau and his force on their** hostile mission. **A short conference with the deputies from the citizens convinced him that a speedy retreat was the only measure of safety for himself and his force, as the** sluices **of the dikes were in part opened, and a threat of** submerging **the** intended **assailants only required a moment more to be enforced.**

Nothing could exceed the disappointment **and irritation of the Prince of Orange** consequent on **this transaction. He at first threatened,** then negotiated, **and** finally patched up the matter in a manner the least mortifying **to his wounded pride.** Bikker nobly offered himself for a peace-offering, and voluntarily resigned his **employments** in the city he had saved; and **De Witt and his** officers were released. William **was in some measure consoled** for his disgrace by the condolence **of the army,** the thanks of the province **of** Zealand, and **a new treaty with** France, strengthened **by** promises of future support from Cardinal Mazarin; but, before he could profit by these encouraging symptoms, domestic and foreign, a premature death cut short all his projects of ambition. Over-violent exercise in a shooting party in Guelders brought on a fever, which soon terminated in an attack of smallpox. On the first appearance of his illness, he was removed to The Hague; and he died there on the 6th of November, 1650, aged twenty-four years and six months.

The death of this prince left the state without a stadtholder, and the army without a chief. The whole of Europe shared more or less in the joy or the regret it caused. The republican party, both in Holland and in England, rejoiced in a circumstance which threw back the sovereign power into the hands of the nation; the partisans of the House of Orange deeply lamented the event. But the birth of a son, of which the widowed princess of Orange was delivered within a week of her husband's death, revived the hopes of those who mourned his loss, and offered her the only consolation which could assuage her grief. This child was, however, the innocent cause of a breach between his mother and grandmother, the dowager-princess, who had never been cordially attached to each other. Each claimed the guardianship of the young prince; and the dispute was at length decided by the states, who adjudged the important office to the elector of Brandenburg and the two princesses jointly. The states of Holland soon exercised their influence on the other provinces. Many of the prerogatives of the stadtholder were now assumed by the people; and, with the exception of Zealand, which made an ineffectual attempt to name the infant prince to the dignity of his ancestors under the title of William III., a perfect unanimity seemed to have reconciled all opposing interests. The various towns secured the privileges of appointing their own magistrates, and the direction of the army and navy devolved to the states-general.

The time was now arrived when the wisdom, the courage, and the resources of the republic were to be put once more to the test, in a contest hitherto without example, and never since equalled in its nature. The naval wars between Holland and England had their real source in the inveterate jealousies and unbounded ambition of both countries, reciprocally convinced that a joint supremacy at sea was incompatible with their interests and their honor, and each resolved to risk everything for their mutual pretensions—to perish rather than yield. The United Provinces were assuredly not the aggressors in this quarrel. They had made sure of their capability to meet it, by the settlement of all questions of internal government, and the solid peace which secured them against any attack on the part of their old and inveterate enemy; but they did not seek a rupture. They at first endeavored to ward off the threatened danger by every effort of conciliation; and they met, with temperate management, even the advances made by Cromwell, at the instigation of St. John, the chief justice, for a proposed, yet impracticable coalition between the two republics, which was to make them one and indivisible. An embassy to The Hague, with St. John and Strickland at its head, was received with all public honors; but the partisans of the families of Orange and Stuart, and the populace generally, openly insulted the ambassadors. About the same time Dorislas, a Dutchman naturalized in England, and sent on a mission from the parliament, was murdered at The Hague by some Scotch officers, friends of the banished king; the massacre of Amboyna, thirty years before, was made a cause of revived complaint; and altogether a sum of injuries was easily made up to turn the proposed fantastic coalition into a fierce and bloody war.

The parliament of England soon found a pretext in an outrageous measure, under pretence of providing for the interests of commerce. They passed the celebrated act of navigation, which prohibited all nations from importing into England in their ships any commodity which was not the growth and manufacture of their own country. This law, though worded generally, was aimed directly at the Dutch, who were the general factors and carriers of Europe. Ships were seized, reprisals made, the mockery of negotiation carried on, fleets equipped, and at length the war broke out.

In the month of May, 1652, the Dutch admiral, Tromp, commanding forty-two ships of war, met with the English fleet under Blake in the Straits of Dover; the latter, though much inferior in number, gave a signal to the Dutch admiral to strike, the usual salutation of honor accorded to the English during the monarchy. Totally different versions have been given by the two admirals of what followed. Blake insisted that Tromp, instead of complying, fired a broadside at his vessel; Tromp stated that a second and a third bullet were sent promptly from the British ship while he was preparing to obey the admiral's claim. The discharge of the first broadside is also a matter of contradiction, and of course of doubt. But it is of small consequence; for whether hostilities had been hurried on or delayed, they were ultimately inevitable. A bloody battle began: it lasted five hours. The inferiority in number on the side of the English was balanced by the larger size of their ships. One Dutch vessel was sunk; another taken; and night parted the combatants.

The states-general heard the news with consternation: they despatched the grand pensionary Pauw on a special embassy to London. The imperious parliament would hear of neither reason nor remonstrance. Right or wrong, they were resolved on war. Blake was soon at sea again with a numerous fleet; Tromp followed with a hundred ships; but a violent tempest separated these furious enemies, and retarded for a while the rencounter they mutually longed for. On the 16th of August a battle took place between Sir George Ayscue and the renowned De Ruyter, near Plymouth, each with about forty ships; but with no decisive consequences. On the 28th of October, Blake, aided by Bourn and Pen, met a Dutch squadron of nearly equal force off the coast of Kent, under De Ruyter and De Witt. The fight which followed was also severe, but not decisive, though the Dutch had the worst of the day. In the Mediterranean, the Dutch admiral Van Galen defeated the English captain Baddely, but bought the victory with his life. And, on the 29th of November, another bloody conflict took place between Blake and Tromp, seconded by De Ruyter, near the Goodwin Sands. In this determined action **Blake** was wounded and defeated; **five** English ships **taken**, burned, or sunk; and night saved the **fleet** from destruction. After this victory Tromp placed a broom **at his masthead, as if to intimate that he would sweep the Channel free of all** English ships.

Great **preparations were made in** England **to** recover this **disgrace;** eighty sail put **to sea** under Blake, **Dean, and Monk, so** celebrated subsequently **as** the restorer of **the monarchy.** Tromp and De Ruyter, with seventy-six **vessels, were descried on the** 18th of February, escorting three hundred **merchantmen up** Channel. **Three days** of **desperate fighting ended in the defeat of the** Dutch, who lost ten ships **of war and twenty-four merchant vessels.** Several of the **English ships were** disabled, **one sunk; and** the carnage on **both sides was nearly equal. Tromp** acquired prodigious honor **by this battle; having succeeded,** though defeated, in **saving, as has been seen, almost the** whole of his **immense convoy. On the 12th of June and** the day following **two** other actions **were fought: in the** first of which the English admiral **Dean was killed; in the** second, Monk, Pen, and **Lawson** amply revenged **his death** by forcing the Dutch **to regain their** harbors with **great loss.**

The 21st **of July** was the last of these **bloody and obstinate** conflicts for superiority. **Tromp issued out once more,** determined **to conquer or die. He met** the enemy **off Scheveling, commanded by** Monk. Both fleets rushed to the **combat. The** heroic Dutchman, animating his sailors **with his** sword drawn, was shot through the heart with **a musket-ball. This event, and this** alone, won the battle, which was the most decisive **of** the whole war. **The** enemy captured or sunk nearly thirty ships. The body of Tromp was carried with great solemnity to the church of Delft, where **a** magnificent mausoleum was erected over the remains of this eminently brave and distinguished man.

This memorable defeat, and the death of this great naval

hero, added to the injury done to their trade, induced the states-general to seek terms from their too powerful enemy. The want of peace was felt throughout the whole country. Cromwell was not averse to grant it; but he insisted on conditions every way disadvantageous and humiliating. He had revived his chimerical scheme of a total conjunction of government, privileges, and interests between the two republics. This was firmly rejected by John de Witt, now grand pensionary of Holland, and by the States under his influence. But the Dutch consented to a defensive league; to punish the survivors of those concerned in the massacre of Amboyna; to pay nine thousand pounds of indemnity for vessels seized in the Sound, five thousand pounds for the affair of Amboyna, and eighty-five thousand pounds to the English East India Company, to cede to them the island of Polerone in the East; to yield the honor of the national flag to the English; and, finally, that neither the young Prince of Orange nor any of his family should ever be invested with the dignity of stadtholder. These two latter conditions were certainly degrading to Holland; and the conditions of the treaty prove that an absurd point of honor was the only real cause for the short but bloody and ruinous war which plunged the Provinces into overwhelming difficulties.

For several years after the conclusion of this inglorious peace, universal discontent and dissension spread throughout the republic. The supporters of the House of Orange, and every impartial friend of the national honor, were indignant at the act of exclusion. Murmurs and revolts broke out in several towns; and all was once more tumult, agitation, and doubt. No event of considerable importance marks particularly this epoch of domestic trouble. A new war was at last pronounced inevitable, and was the means of appeasing the distractions of the people, and reconciling by degrees contending parties. Denmark, the ancient ally of the republic, was threatened with destruction by Charles Gustavus, king of Sweden, who held Copenhagen in blockade. The interests of Holland were in imminent peril should the Swedes gain the passage of the Sound. This double motive influenced De Witt; and he persuaded the states-general to send Admiral Opdam with a considerable fleet to the Baltic. This intrepid successor of the immortal Tromp soon came to blows with a rival worthy to meet him. Wrangel, the Swedish admiral, with a superior force, defended the passage of the Sound; and the two castles of Cronenberg and Elsenberg supported his fleet with their tremendous fire. But Opdam resolutely advanced; though suffering extreme anguish from an attack of gout, he had himself carried on deck, where he gave his orders with the most admirable coolness and precision, in the midst of danger and carnage. The rival monarchs witnessed the battle; the king of Sweden from the castle of Cronenberg, and the king of Denmark from the summit of the highest tower in his besieged capital. A brilliant victory crowned the efforts of the Dutch admiral, dearly bought by the death of his second in command, the brave De Witt, and Peter Florizon, another admiral of note. Relief was poured into Copenhagen. Opdam was replaced in the command, too arduous for his infirmities, by the still more celebrated De Ruyter, who was greatly distinguished by his valor in several successive affairs: and after some months more of useless obstinacy, the king of Sweden, seeing his army perish in the island of Funen, by a combined attack of those of Holland and Denmark, consented to a peace highly favorable to the latter power.

These transactions placed the United Provinces on a still higher pinnacle of glory than they had ever reached. Intestine disputes were suddenly calmed. The Algerines and other pirates were swept from the seas by a succession of small but vigorous expeditions. The mediation of the States re-established peace in several of the petty states of Germany. England and France were both held in check, if not preserved in friendship, by the dread of their recovered power. Trade and finance were reorganized. Everything seemed to promise a long-continued peace and growing greatness, much of which was owing to the talents and persevering energy of De Witt; and, to complete the good work of European tranquillity, the French and Spanish monarchs concluded in this year the treaty known by the name of the "peace of the Pyrenees."

Cromwell had now closed his career, and Charles II. was restored to the throne from which he had so long been excluded. The complimentary entertainments rendered to the restored king in Holland were on the proudest scale of expense. He left the country which had given him refuge in misfortune, and done him honor in his prosperity, with profuse expressions of regard and gratitude. Scarcely was he established in his recovered kingdom, when a still greater testimony of deference to his wishes was paid, by the states-general formally annulling the act of exclusion against the House of Orange. A variety of motives, however, acting on the easy and plastic mind of the monarch, soon effaced whatever of gratitude he had at first conceived. He readily entered into the views of the English nation, which was irritated by the great commercial superiority of Holland, and a jealousy excited by its close connection with France at this period.

It was not till the 22d of February, 1665, that war was formally declared against the Dutch; but many previous acts of hostility had taken place in expeditions against their settlements on the coast of Africa and in America, which were retaliated by De Ruyter with vigor and success. The Dutch used every possible means of avoiding the last extremities. De Witt employed all the powers of his great capacity to avert the evil of war; but nothing could finally prevent it, and the sea was once more to witness the conflict between those who claimed its sovereignty. A great battle was fought on the 31st of June. The duke of York, afterward James II., commanded the British fleet, and had under him the earl of Sandwich and Prince Rupert. The Dutch were led on by Opdam; and the victory was decided in favor of the English by the blowing **up of** that admiral's ship, with **himself** and his whole crew. The loss **of** the Dutch was altogether nineteen ships. De Witt the pensionary then took in **person** the command of **the** fleet, which was soon equipped; **and he** gave a high proof **of the adaptation** of genius **to a pursuit** previously unknown, by **the** rapid knowledge **and the practical** improvements he introduced into **some of the most intricate** branches of **naval** tactics.

Immense efforts **were now made by** England, but with **a very** questionable **policy, to induce Louis** XIV. **to** join in **the war.** Charles **offered to allow of** his acquiring the whole **of the Spanish** Netherlands, **provided** he would leave him without interruption **to** destroy **the Dutch navy (and,** consequently, **their commerce), in the by no means certain** expectation that **its advantages would all fall to the share** of England. But **the king of France resolved to** support the republic. The king **of** Denmark, **too, formed an** alliance with them, after **a** series **of the** most strange **tergiversations.** Spain, reduced to **feebleness, and** menaced with invasion by France, showed **no alacrity to meet** Charles's overtures for **an** offensive treaty. **Van Galen,** bishop of Munster, a **restless** prelate, **was the** only **ally he** could acquire. This bishop, **at the head** of a **tumultuous** force of twenty thousand men, penetrated **into Friesland;** but six thousand French **were** despatched by Louis **to the** assistance of the **republic, and** this impotent invasion **was** easily repelled.

The republic, encouraged by all these favorable circumstances, resolved to put forward its utmost energies. Internal discords were **once more** appeased; the harbors were crowded with merchant ships; the young **Prince of** Orange had put himself under the tuition of the **states of** Holland and of De Witt, who faithfully executed **his** trust; and De Ruyter was ready to lead on the **fleet.** The English, in spite of the dreadful calamity of **the** great fire of London, the plague which desolated the city, and a declaration of war on the part of France, prepared boldly for the shock.

The **Dutch fleet,** commanded by De Ruyter and Tromp, the gallant **successor** of his father's fame, was soon at sea. **The** English, under Prince Rupert and Monk, now duke of Albemarle, did not lie **idle in port. A battle of** four days' continuance, **one of the** most **determined and** terrible up to this period on record, was the consequence. **The** Dutch claim, and it appears with justice, to have had the advantage. But a more decisive conflict took place on the **25th of July,**[1] **when a** victory **was gained** by the English, **the enemy having three** of their **admirals** killed. "My God!" exclaimed De Ruyter, during this desperate fight, and seeing the certainty of defeat; "what a wretch I am! Among so many thousand bullets, is there not **one to put** an end to my miserable life?"

The king of France hastened forward in this crisis to the assistance of the republic; and De Witt, by a deep stroke of policy, amused the English with negotiation while a powerful fleet was fitted out. It suddenly appeared in the Thames, **under the command of** De Ruyter, and all England was thrown into consternation. The Dutch took Sheerness, and burned many ships of war; almost insulting **the** capital itself in their predatory incursion. **Had the** French power **joined that of the Provinces at this time,** and invaded England, **the most fatal results** to that kingdom might have **taken place. But the** alarm soon subsided with the disappearance **of the hostile fleet;** and the signing the peace of **Breda, on the 10th of July,** 1667, extricated Charles from his present difficulties. The island of Polerone was restored **to the Dutch, and the point** of maritime superiority was, **on this** occasion, undoubtedly theirs.

While Holland was preparing to indulge in the luxury of **n**ational repose, the death of Philip IV. of Spain, and the startling ambition of Louis XIV., brought war once more to their very doors, and soon even forced it across the **threshold**

---

[1] In all these naval battles we have followed Hume and the English historians as to dates, which, in almost every instance, are strangely at variance with those given by the Dutch writers.

of the republic. The king of France, setting at naught his solemn renunciation at the peace of the Pyrenees of all claims to any part of the Spanish territories in right of his wife, who was daughter of the late king, found excellent reasons (for his own satisfaction) to invade a material portion of that declining monarchy. Well prepared by the financial and military foresight of Colbert for his great design, he suddenly poured a powerful army, under Turenne, into Brabant and Flanders; quickly overran and took possession of these provinces; and, in the space of three weeks, added Franche-Comte to his conquests. Europe was in universal alarm at these unexpected measures; and no state felt more terror than the republic of the United Provinces. The interest of all countries seemed now to require a coalition against the power which had abandoned the House of Austria only to settle on France. The first measure to this effect was the signing of the triple league between Holland, Sweden, and England, at The Hague, on the 13th of January, 1668. But this proved to be one of the most futile confederations on record. Charles, with almost unheard-of perfidy throughout the transaction, fell in with the designs of his pernicious, and on this occasion purchased, cabinet, called the Cabal; and he entered into a secret treaty with France, in the very teeth of his other engagements. Sweden was dissuaded from the league by the arguments of the French ministers; and Holland in a short time found itself involved in a double war with its late allies.

A base and piratical attack on the Dutch Smyrna fleet by a large force under Sir Robert Holmes, on the 13th of March, 1672, was the first overt act of treachery on the part of the English government. The attempt completely failed, through the prudence and valor of the Dutch admirals; and Charles reaped only the double shame of perfidy and defeat. He instantly issued a declaration of war against the republic, on reasoning too palpably false to require refutation, and too frivolous to merit record to the exclusion of more important matter from our narrow limits.

Louis at least covered with the semblance of dignity his unjust co-operation in this violence. He soon advanced with his army, and the contingents of Munster and Cologne, his allies, amounting altogether to nearly one hundred and seventy thousand men, commanded by Conde, Turenne, Luxemburg, and others of the greatest generals of France. Never was any country less prepared than were the United Provinces to resist this formidable aggression. Their army was as naught; their long cessation of military operations by land having totally demoralized that once invincible branch of their forces. No general existed who knew anything of the practice of war. Their very stores of ammunition had been delivered over, in the way of traffic, to the enemy who now prepared to overwhelm them. De Witt was severely, and not quite unjustly, blamed for having suffered the country to be thus taken by surprise, utterly defenceless, and apparently without resource. Envy of his uncommon merit aggravated the just complaints against his error. But, above all things, the popular affection to the young prince threatened, in some great convulsion, the overthrow of the pensionary, who was considered eminently hostile to the illustrious House of Orange.

William III., prince of Orange, now twenty-two years of age, was amply endowed with those hereditary qualities of valor and wisdom which only required experience to give him rank with the greatest of his ancestors. The Louvenstein party, as the adherents of the House of Orange were called, now easily prevailed in their long-conceived design of placing him at the head of affairs, with the titles of captain-general and high admiral. De Witt, anxious from personal considerations, as well as patriotism, to employ every means of active exertion, attempted the organization of an army, and hastened the equipment of a formidable fleet of nearly a hundred ships of the line and half as many fire-ships. De Ruyter, now without exception the greatest commander of the age, set sail with this force in search of the combined fleets of England and France, commanded by the duke of

A HOLLAND BEAUTY *Holland.*

TO THE PEACE OF NIMEGUEN

York and Marshal D'Etrees. **He** encountered them, on the 6th of May, 1672, at Solebay. **A** most bloody engagement **was** the result of this meeting. Sandwich, on the side of the English, and **Van Ghent**, a **Dutch admiral**, were slain. The glory of **the day was divided; the** victory doubtful; but the **sea was not the element on which** the **fate of** Holland **was to be decided.**

The French armies poured **like a** torrent into **the territories of the** republic. Rivers were passed, towns taken, **and provinces overrun** with a rapidity much **less** honorable **to France than** disgraceful **to** Holland. **No** victory was **gained—no** resistance **offered; and it is disgusting to** look **back on the** fulsome **panegyrics with which courtiers and** poets lauded Louis **for those facile and inglorious triumphs.** The Prince of **Orange had received the command of a nominal army of seventy thousand men; but with this undisciplined and discouraged mass he could attempt nothing. He** prudently retired into **the province of Holland, vainly hoping that the** numerous **fortresses on the** frontiers would have offered some resistance to the **enemy. Guelders,** Overyssel **and** Utrecht were already **in Louis's hands.** Groningen **and** Friesland **were** threatened. **Holland and** Zealand **opposed obstruction to** such rapid **conquest from** their natural **position; and Amsterdam set a noble example to the remaining towns—forming a regular and** energetic plan of defence, and **endeavoring to infuse its** spirit into the rest. The sluices, **those desperate sources at** once of safety and desolation, **were opened;** the whole country submerged; **and the** other provinces following this example, extensive districts of fertility **and** wealth were given to the sea, for the exclusion of **which so** many centuries **had** scarcely sufficed.

The states-general now assembled, **and** it was decided to supplicate for peace at the hands **of** the combined monarchs. The haughty insolence of Louvois, coinciding with the temper of Louis himself, made the latter propose the following conditions as the price of peace: To take off all duties on commodities exported into Holland; to grant the free exercise of the Romish religion in the United Provinces; to share the churches with the Catholics, and to pay their priests; to yield up all the frontier towns, with several in the heart of the republic; to pay him twenty million livres; to send him every year a solemn embassy, accompanied by a present of a golden medal, as an acknowledgment that they owed him their liberty; and, finally, that they should give entire satisfaction to the king of England.

Charles, on his part, after the most insulting treatment of the ambassadors sent to London, required, among other terms, that the Dutch should give up the honor of the flag without reserve, whole fleets being expected, even on the coasts of Holland, to lower their topsails to the smallest ship under British colors; that the Dutch should pay one million pounds sterling toward the charges of the war, and ten thousand pounds a year for permission to fish in the British seas; that they should share the Indian trade with the English; and that Walcheren and several other islands should be put into the king's hands as security for the performance of the articles.

The insatiable monarchs overshot the mark. Existence was not worth preserving on these intolerable terms. Holland was driven to desperation; and even the people of England were inspired with indignation at this monstrous injustice. In the republic a violent explosion of popular excess took place. The people now saw no safety but in the courage and talents of the Prince of Orange. He was tumultuously proclaimed stadtholder. De Witt and his brother Cornelis, the conscientious but too obstinate opponents of this measure of salvation, fell victims to the popular frenzy. The latter, condemned to banishment on an atrocious charge of intended assassination against the Prince of Orange, was visited in his prison at The Hague by the grand pensionary. The rabble, incited to fury by the calumnies spread against these two virtuous citizens, broke into the prison, forced the unfortunate brothers into the street, and there literally tore them to pieces with circumstances of the most brutal ferocity. This horrid scene took place on the 27th of August, 1672.

The massacre of the **De** Witts completely destroyed the party of which they were the head. **All** men now united under the **only leader left** to the **country.** William **showed** himself **well worthy of the trust, and of** his heroic blood. He **turned his whole force** against the enemy. He sought nothing **for** himself but the glory **of** saving his country; and taking his ancestors **for** models, in the best points of their respective **characters,** he combined **prudence** with energy, and **firmness** with moderation. **His** spirit inspired all ranks of **men.** The conditions **of peace** demanded **by the partner kings were rejected** with **scorn. The whole nation** was moved **by one** concentrated **principle of heroism**; and it was even resolved to **put** the ancient notion of the first William into **practice, and abandon the country to** the waves, sooner than **submit to the political** annihilation with which **it was threatened. The capability of the vessels** in their **harbors was calculated; and they were** found sufficient to transport **two hundred thousand** families to the Indian settlements. **We must hasten from** this sublime picture **of national** desperation. **The glorious hero who** stands **in** its foreground was inaccessible to every overture of corruption. **Buckingham,** the English ambassador, **offered him, on the part of England and** France, the **independent** sovereignty of Holland, if **he** would abandon **the** other provinces to their grasp; and, urging his consent, asked him **if he did not see** that the republic was **ruined?** "There is **one means,"** replied the Prince of Orange, "which will save me from the sight of my country's ruin—I will die in the last ditch."

Action soon proved the reality of the prince's profession. He took the field; having first punished with death some of **the** cowardly commanders of the frontier towns. He besieged and took Naarden, an important place; and, by a masterly movement, formed a junction with Montecuculi, whom the emperor Leopold had at length sent to his assistance with twenty thousand men. Groningen repulsed the bishop of Munster, the ally of France, with a loss of twelve thousand men. The king of Spain (such are the strange fluctuations of political friendship and enmity) sent the count of Monterey, governor of the Belgian provinces, with ten thousand men to support the Dutch army. The elector of Brandenburg also lent them aid. The whole face of affairs was changed; and Louis was obliged to abandon all his conquests with more rapidity than he had made them. Two desperate battles at sea, on the 28th of May and the 4th of June, in which De Ruyter and Prince Rupert again distinguished themselves, only proved the valor of the combatants, leaving victory still doubtful. England was with one common feeling ashamed of the odious war in which the king and his unworthy ministers had engaged the nation. Charles was forced to make peace on the conditions proposed by the Dutch. The honor of the flag was yielded to the English; a regulation of trade was agreed to; all possessions were restored to the same condition as before the war; and the states-general agreed to pay the king eight hundred thousand patacoons, or nearly three hundred thousand pounds.

With these encouraging results from the Prince of Orange's influence and example, Holland persevered in the contest with France. He, in the first place, made head, during a winter campaign in Holland, against Marshal Luxemburg, who had succeeded Turenne in the Low Countries, the latter being obliged to march against the imperialists in Westphalia. He next advanced to oppose the great Conde, who occupied Brabant with an army of forty-five thousand men. After much manœuvring, in which the Prince of Orange displayed consummate talent, he on only one occasion exposed a part of his army to a disadvantageous contest. Conde seized on the error; and of his own accord gave the battle to which his young opponent could not succeed in forcing him. The battle of Senef is remarkable not merely for the fury with which it was fought, or for its leaving victory undecided, but as being the last combat of one commander and the first of the other. "The Prince of Orange," said the veteran Conde (who had that day exposed his person more than on any previous occasion), "has acted in everything like an old captain, except venturing his life too like a young soldier."

The campaign of 1675 offered no remarkable event; the Prince of Orange with great prudence avoiding the risk of a battle. But the following year was rendered fatally remarkable by the death of the great De Ruyter,[1] who was killed in an action against the French fleet in the Mediterranean; and about the same time the not less celebrated Turenne met his death from a cannon-ball in the midst of his triumphs in Germany. This year was doubly occupied in a negotiation for peace and an active prosecution of the war. Louis, at the head of his army, took several towns in Belgium: William was unsuccessful in an attempt on Maestricht. About the beginning of winter, the plenipotentiaries of the several belligerents assembled at Nimeguen, where the congress for peace was held. The Hollanders, loaded with debts and taxes, and seeing the weakness and slowness of their allies, the Spaniards and Germans, prognosticated nothing but misfortunes. Their commerce languished; while that of England, now neutral amid all these quarrels, flourished extremely. The Prince of Orange, however, ambitious of glory, urged another campaign; and it commenced accordingly. In the middle of February, Louis carried Valenciennes by storm, and laid siege to St. Omer and Cambray. William, though full of activity, courage, and skill, was, nevertheless, almost always unsuccessful in the field, and never more so than in this campaign. Several towns fell almost in his sight; and he was completely defeated in the great battle of Mount Cassel by the duke of

---

[1] The council of Spain gave De Ruyter the title and letters patent of duke. The latter arrived in Holland after his death; and his children, with true republican spirit, refused to adopt the title.

Orleans and Marshal Luxemburg. But the period for another peace was now approaching. Louis offered fair terms for the acceptance of the United Provinces at the congress of Nimeguen, April, 1678, as he now considered his chief enemies Spain and the empire, who had at first only entered into the war as auxiliaries. He was, no doubt, principally impelled in his measures by the marriage of the Prince of Orange with the lady Mary, eldest daughter of the duke of York, and heir presumptive to the English crown, which took place on the 23d of October, to the great joy of both the Dutch and English nations. Charles was at this moment the arbiter of the peace of Europe; and though several fluctuations took place in his policy in the course of a few months, as the urgent wishes of the parliament and the large presents of Louis differently actuated him, still the wiser and more just course prevailed, and he finally decided the balance by vigorously declaring his resolution for peace; and the treaty was consequently signed at Nimeguen, on the 10th of August, 1678. The Prince of Orange, from private motives of spleen, or a most unjustifiable desire for fighting, took the extraordinary measure of attacking the French troops under Luxemburg, near Mons, on the very day after the signing of this treaty. He must have known it, even though it were not officially notified to him; and he certainly had to answer for all the blood so wantonly spilled in the sharp though undecisive action which ensued. Spain, abandoned to her fate, was obliged to make the best terms she could; and on the 17th of September she also concluded a treaty with France, on conditions entirely favorable to the latter power.

CHAPTER XX

FROM THE PEACE OF NIMEGUEN TO THE PEACE OF UTRECHT

A.D. 1678—1713

A FEW years passed over after this period, without the occurrence of any transaction sufficiently important to require a mention here. Each of the powers so lately at war followed the various bent of their respective ambition. Charles of England was sufficiently occupied by disputes with parliament, and the discovery, fabrication, and punishment of plots, real or pretended. Louis XIV., by a stretch of audacious pride hitherto unknown, arrogated to himself the supreme power of regulating the rest of Europe, as if all the other princes were his vassals. He established courts, or chambers of reunion as they were called, in Metz and Brisac, which cited princes, issued decrees, and authorized spoliation, in the most unjust and arbitrary manner. Louis chose to award to himself Luxemburg, Chiny, and a considerable portion of Brabant and Flanders. He marched a considerable army into Belgium, which the Spanish governors were unable to oppose. The Prince of Orange, who labored incessantly to excite a confederacy among the other powers of Europe against the unwarrantable aggressions of France, was unable to arouse his countrymen to actual war; and was forced, instead of gaining the glory he longed for, to consent to a truce for twenty years, which the states-general, now wholly pacific and not a little cowardly, were too happy to obtain from France. The emperor and the king of Spain gladly entered into a like treaty. The fact was that the peace of Nimeguen had disjointed the great confederacy which William had so successfully brought about; and the various powers were laid utterly prostrate at the feet of the imperious Louis, who for a while held the destinies of Europe in his hands.

Charles II. died most unexpectedly in the year 1685; and his obstinately bigoted and unconstitutional successor, James II., seemed, during a reign of not four years' continuance, to rush wilfully headlong to ruin. During this period, the Prince of Orange had maintained a most circumspect and unexceptionable line of conduct; steering clear of all interference with English affairs; giving offence to none of the political factions; and observing in every instance the duty and regard which he owed to his father-in-law. During Monmouth's invasion he had despatched to James's assistance six regiments of British troops which were in the Dutch service, and he offered to take the command of the king's forces against the rebels. It was from the application of James himself that William took any part in English affairs; for he was more widely and much more congenially employed in the establishment of a fresh league against France. Louis had aroused a new feeling throughout Protestant Europe by the revocation of the Edict of Nantes. The refugees whom he had driven from their native country inspired in those in which they settled hatred of his persecution as well as alarm of his power. Holland now entered into all the views of the Prince of Orange. By his immense influence he succeeded in forming the great confederacy called the League of Augsburg, to which the emperor, Spain, and almost every European power but England became parties.

James gave the prince reason to believe that he too would join in this great project, if William would in return concur in his views of domestic tyranny; but William wisely refused. James, much disappointed, and irritated by the moderation which showed his own violence in such striking contrast, expressed his displeasure against the prince, and against the Dutch generally, by various vexatious acts. William resolved to maintain a high attitude;

and many applications were made to him by the most considerable persons in England for relief against James's violent measures, and which there was but one method of making effectual. That method was force. But as long as the Princess of Orange was certain of succeeding to the crown on her father's death, William hesitated to join in an attempt that might possibly have failed and lost her her inheritance. But the birth of a son, which, in giving James a male heir, destroyed all hope of redress for the kingdom, decided the wavering, and rendered the determined desperate. The prince chose the time for his enterprise with the sagacity, arranged its plan with the prudence, and put it into execution with the vigor, which were habitual qualities of his mind.

Louis XIV., menaced by the League of Augsburg, had resolved to strike the first blow against the allies. He invaded Germany; so that the Dutch preparations seemed in the first instance intended as measures of defence against the progress of the French. But Louis's envoy at The Hague could not be long deceived. He gave notice to his master, who in his turn warned James. But that infatuated monarch not only doubted the intelligence, but refused the French king's offers of assistance and co-operation. On the 21st of October, the Prince of Orange, with an army of fourteen thousand men, and a fleet of five hundred vessels of all kinds, set sail from Helvoetsluys; and after some delays from bad weather, he safely landed his army in Torbay, on the 5th of November, 1688. The desertion of James's best friends; his own consternation, flight, seizure, and second escape; and the solemn act by which he was deposed; were the rapid occurrences of a few weeks: and thus the grandest revolution that England had ever seen was happily consummated. Without entering here on legislative reasonings or party sophisms, it is enough to record the act itself; and to say, in reference to our more immediate subject, that without the assistance of Holland and her glorious chief, England might have still remained enslaved, or have had to purchase liberty by oceans of blood. By the bill of settlement, the crown was conveyed jointly to the Prince and Princess of Orange, the sole administration of government to remain in the prince; and the new sovereigns were proclaimed on the 23d of February, 1689. The convention, which had arranged this important point, annexed to the settlement a declaration of rights, by which the powers of royal prerogative and the extent of popular privilege were defined and guaranteed.

William, now become king of England, still preserved his title of stadtholder of Holland; and presented the singular instance of a monarchy and a republic being at the same time governed by the same individual. But whether as a king or a citizen, William was actuated by one grand and powerful principle, to which every act of private administration was made subservient, although it certainly called for no sacrifice that was not required for the political existence of the two nations of which he was the head. Inveterate opposition to the power of Louis XIV. was this all-absorbing motive. A sentiment so mighty left William but little time for inferior points of government, and everything but that seems to have irritated and disgusted him. He was soon again on the Continent, the chief theatre of his efforts. He put himself in front of the confederacy which resulted from the congress of Utrecht in 1690. He took the command of the allied army; and till the hour of his death, he never ceased his indefatigable course of hostility, whether in the camp or the cabinet, at the head of the allied armies, or as the guiding spirit of the councils which gave them force and motion.

Several campaigns were expended, and bloody combats fought, almost all to the disadvantage of William, whose genius for war was never seconded by that good fortune which so often decides the fate of battles in defiance of all the calculations of talent. But no reverse had power to shake the constancy and courage of William. He always appeared as formidable after defeat as he was before action. His conquerors gained little but the honor of the day. Fleurus, Steinkerk, Herwinde, were successively the scenes of his evil fortune, and the sources of his fame. His retreats were master-strokes of vigilant activity and profound combinations. **Many eminent sieges** took place during this war. Among other towns, Mons and **Namur were** taken by the French, and **Huy by the** allies; and the army of Marshal Villeroi **bombarded Brussels** during three days, in August, 1695, **with such fury** that the town-house, fourteen churches, **and four thousand houses,** were reduced to ashes. The year following **this event saw** another undecisive campaign. During the continuance of **this war,** the naval transactions present no grand results. **Du Bart,** a celebrated **adventurer** of Dunkirk, occupies **the leading place in those affairs,** in which he carried on a **desultory but active warfare against the** Dutch and English **fleets, and** generally **with great** success.

All the nations which **had taken part in so many wars** were now becoming exhausted **by the contest,** but none so much so as France. The great **despot who** had so long wielded the energies of that country with **such** wonderful splendor and success found that his unbounded love of dominion was gradually sapping all the real good of his people, in chimerical schemes of universal **conquest.** England, though with much resolution voting **new** supplies, and **in** every way upholding William in his plans for the continuance of war, was rejoiced **when Louis** accepted the mediation of Charles XI., **king of** Sweden, and agreed to concessions which made peace feasible. The emperor and Charles II. of Spain, were less satisfied with those concessions; but everything was finally arranged to meet the general views of the parties, and negotiations were opened at Ryswyk. The death of the king of Sweden, and the minority of his son and successor, the celebrated Charles XII., retarded them on points of form for some time. At length, on the **20th** of September, 1697, the articles of the treaty were subscribed by the Dutch, English, Spanish, and French ambassadors. The treaty consisted of seventeen articles. The French king declared he would not disturb or disquiet the king of Great Britain, whose title he now for the first time acknowledged. Between France and Holland were declared a general armistice, perpetual amity, a mutual restitution of towns, a reciprocal renunciation of all pretensions upon each other, and a treaty of commerce which was immediately put into execution. Thus, after this long, expensive, and sanguinary war, things were established just on the footing they had been by the peace of Nimeguen; and a great, though unavailable lesson, read to the world on the futility and wickedness of those quarrels in which the personal ambition of kings leads to the misery of the people. Had the allies been true to each other throughout, Louis would certainly have been reduced much lower than he now was. His pride was humbled, and his encroachments stopped. But the sufferings of the various countries engaged in the war were too generally reciprocal to make its result of any material benefit to either. The emperor held out for a while, encouraged by the great victory gained by his general, Prince Eugene of Savoy, over the Turks at Zenta in Hungary; but he finally acceded to the terms offered by France; the peace, therefore, became general, but, unfortunately for Europe, of very short duration.

France, as if looking forward to the speedy renewal of hostilities, still kept her armies undisbanded. Let the foresight of her politicians have been what it might, this negative proof of it was justified by events. The king of Spain, a weak prince, without any direct heir for his possessions, considered himself authorized to dispose of their succession by will. The leading powers of Europe thought otherwise, and took this right upon themselves. Charles died on the 1st of November, 1700, and thus put the important question to the test. By a solemn testament he declared Philip, duke of Anjou, second son of the dauphin, and grandson of Louis XIV., his successor to the whole of the Spanish monarchy. Louis immediately renounced his adherence to the treaties of partition, executed at The Hague and in London, in 1698 and 1700, and to which he had been a contracting party; and prepared to maintain the act by which the last of the descendants of Charles V. bequeathed the possessions of Spain and the Indies to the family which had so long been the inveterate enemy and rival of his own.

The emperor Leopold, on his part, prepared to defend his claims; and thus commenced the new war between him and France, which took its name from the succession which formed the object of dispute. Hostilities were commenced in Italy, where Prince Eugene, the conqueror of the Turks, commanded for Leopold, and every day made for himself a still more brilliant reputation. Louis sent his grandson to Spain to take possession of the inheritance, for which so hard a fight was yet to be maintained, with the striking expression at parting—"My child, there are no longer any Pyrenees!" an expression most happily unprophetic for the future independence of Europe; for the moral force of the barrier has long existed after the expiration of the family compact which was meant to deprive it of its force.

Louis prepared to act vigorously. Among other measures, he caused part of the Dutch army that was quartered in Luxemburg and Brabant to be suddenly made prisoners of war, because they would not own Philip V. as king of Spain. The states-general were dreadfully alarmed, immediately made the required acknowledgment, and in consequence had their soldiers released. They quickly reinforced their garrisons, purchased supplies, solicited foreign aid, and prepared for the worst that might happen. They wrote to King William, professing the most inviolable attachment to England; and he met their application by warm assurances of support and an immediate reinforcement of three regiments.

William followed up these measures by the formation of the celebrated treaty called the Grand Alliance, by which England, the States, and the emperor covenanted for the support of the pretensions of the latter to the Spanish monarchy. William was preparing, in spite of his declining health, to take his usual lead in the military operations now decided on, and almost all Europe was again looking forward to his guidance, when he died on the 8th of March, 1701, leaving his great plans to receive their execution from still more able adepts in the art of war.

William's character has been traced by many hands. In his capacity of king of England, it is not our province to judge him in this place. As stadtholder of Holland, he merits unqualified praise. Like his great ancestor William I., whom he more resembled than any other of his race, he saved the country in a time of such imminent peril that its abandonment seemed the only resource left to the inhabitants, who preferred self-exile to slavery. All his acts were certainly merged in the one overwhelming object of a great ambition—that noble quality, which, if coupled with the love of country, is the very essence of true heroism. William was the last of that illustrious line which for a century and a half had filled Europe with admiration. He never had a child; and being himself an only one, his title as Prince of Orange passed into another branch of the family. He left his cousin, Prince Frison of Nassau, the stadtholder of Friesland, his sole and universal heir, and appointed the states-general his executors.

William's death filled Holland with mourning and alarm. The meeting of the states-general after this sad intelligence was of a most affecting description; but William, like all master-minds, had left the mantle of his inspiration on his friends and followers. Heinsius, the grand pensionary, followed up the views of the lamented stadtholder with considerable energy, and was answered by the unanimous exertions of the country. Strong assurances of support from Queen Anne, William's successor, still further encouraged the republic, which now vigorously prepared for war. But it did not lose this occasion of recurring to the form of government of 1650. No new stadtholder was now appointed; the supreme authority being vested in the general assembly of the states, and the active direction of affairs confided to the grand pensionary. This departure from the form of government which had been on various occasions proved to be essential to the safety, although at all times hazardous to the independence, of the States, was not attended with any evil consequences. The factions and the anarchy which had before been the consequence of the course now adopted were prevented by the potent influence of national fear lest the enemy might triumph, and crush the hopes, the jealousies, and the enmities of all parties in one general ruin. Thus the common danger awoke a common interest, and the splendid successes of her allies kept Holland steady in the career of patriotic energy which had its rise in the dread of her redoubtable foe.

The joy in France at William's death was proportionate to the grief it created in Holland; and the arrogant confidence of Louis seemed to know no bounds. "I will punish these audacious merchants," said he, with an air of disdain, when he read the manifesto of Holland; not foreseeing that those he affected to despise so much would, ere long, command in a great measure the destinies of his crown. Queen Anne entered upon the war with masculine intrepidity, and maintained it with heroic energy. Efforts were made by the English ministry and the states-general to mediate between the kings of Sweden and Poland. But Charles XII., enamored of glory, and bent on the one great object of his designs against Russia, would listen to nothing that might lead him from his immediate career of victory. Many other of the northern princes were withheld, by various motives, from entering into the contest with France, and its whole brunt devolved on the original members of the Grand Alliance. The generals who carried it on were Marlborough and Prince Eugene. The former, at its commencement an earl, and subsequently raised to the dignity of duke, was declared generalissimo of the Dutch and English forces. He was a man of most powerful genius, both as warrior and politician. A pupil of the great Turenne, his exploits left those of his master in the shade. No commander ever possessed in a greater degree the faculty of forming vast designs, and of carrying them into effect with consummate skill; no one displayed more coolness and courage in action, saw with a keener eye the errors of the enemy, or knew better how to profit by success. He never laid siege to a town that he did not take, and never fought a battle that he did not gain.

Prince Eugene joined to the highest order of personal bravery a profound judgment for the grand movements of war, and a capacity for the most minute of the minor details on which their successful issue so often depends. United in the same cause, these two great generals pursued their course without the least misunderstanding. At the close of each of those successive campaigns, in which they reaped such a full harvest of renown, they retired together to The Hague, to arrange, in the profoundest secrecy, the plans for the next year's operations, with one other person, who formed the great point of union between them, and completed a triumvirate without a parallel in the history of political affairs. This third was Heinsius, one of those great men produced by the republic whose names are tantamount to the most detailed eulogium for talent and patriotism. Every enterprise projected by the confederates was deliberately examined, rejected, or approved by these three associates, whose strict union of purpose, disowning all petty rivalry, formed the centre of counsels and the source of circumstances finally so fatal to France.

Louis XIV., now sixty years of age, could no longer himself command his armies, or probably did not wish to risk the reputation he was conscious of having gained by the advice and services of Turenne, Conde, and Luxemburg. Louvois, too, was dead; and Colbert no longer managed his finances. A council of rash and ignorant ministers hung like a dead weight on the talent of the generals who succeeded the great men above mentioned. Favor and not merit too often decided promotion, and lavished command. Vendome, Villars, Boufflers, and Berwick were set aside, to make way for Villeroi, Tallard, and Marsin, men every way inferior.

The war began in 1702 in Italy, and Marlborough opened his first campaign in Brabant also in that year. For several succeeding years the confederates pursued a career of brilliant success, the details of which do not properly belong to this work. A mere chronology of celebrated battles would be of little interest, and the pages of English history abound in records of those deeds. Blenheim, Ramillies, Oudenarde, and Malplaquet, are names that speak for themselves, and tell their own tale of glory. The utter humiliation of France was the result of events, in which the undying fame of England for inflexible perseverance and unbounded generosity was joined in the strictest union with that of Holland; and the impetuous valor of the worthy successor to the title of Prince of Orange was, on many occasions, particularly at Malplaquet, supported by the devotion and gallantry of the Dutch contingent in the allied armies. The naval affairs of Holland offered nothing very remarkable. The states had always a fleet ready to support the English in their enterprises; but no eminent admiral arose to rival the renown of Rooke, Byng, Benbow, and others of their allies. The first of those admirals took Gibraltar, which has ever since remained in the possession of England. The great earl of Peterborough carried on the war with splendid success in Portugal and Spain, supported occasionally by the English fleet under Sir Cloudesley Shovel, and that of Holland under Admirals Allemonde and Wapenaer.

During the progress of the war, the haughty and long-time imperial Louis was reduced to a state of humiliation that excited a compassion so profound as to prevent its own open expression—the most galling of all sentiments to a proud mind. In the year 1709 he solicited peace on terms of most abject submission. The states-general, under the influence of the duke of Marlborough and Prince Eugene, rejected all his supplications, retorting unsparingly the insolent harshness with which he had formerly received similar proposals from them. France, roused to renewed exertions by the insulting treatment experienced by her humiliated but still haughty despot, made prodigious but vain efforts to repair her ruinous losses. In the following year Louis renewed his attempts to obtain some tolerable conditions; offering to renounce his grandson, and to comply with all the former demands of the confederates. Even these overtures were rejected; Holland and England appearing satisfied with nothing short of—what was after all impracticable—the total destruction of the great power which Louis had so long proved to be incompatible with their welfare.

The war still went on; and the taking of Bouchain on the 30th of August, 1711, closed the almost unrivalled military career of Marlborough, by the success of one of his boldest and best conducted exploits. Party intrigue had accomplished what, in court parlance, is called the disgrace, but which, in the language of common sense, means only the dismissal of this great man. The new ministry, who hated the Dutch, now entered seriously into negotiations with France. The queen acceded to these views, and sent special envoys to communicate with the court of Versailles. The states-general found it impossible to continue hostilities if England withdrew from the coalition; conferences were consequently opened at Utrecht in the month of January, 1712. England took the important station of arbiter in the great question there debated. The only essential conditions which she demanded individually were the renunciation of all claims to the crown of France by Philip V., and the demolition of the harbor of Dunkirk. The first of these was the more readily acceded to, as the great battles of Almanza and Villaviciosa, gained by Philip's generals, the dukes of Berwick and Vendome, had steadily fixed him on the throne of Spain—a point still more firmly secured by the death of the emperor Joseph I., son of Leopold, and the elevation of his brother

Charles, Philip's competitor for the crown of Spain, to the imperial dignity, by the title of Charles VI.

The peace was not definitively signed until the 11th of April, 1713; and France obtained far better conditions than those which were refused her a few years previously. The Belgian provinces were given to the new emperor, and must henceforth be called the Austrian instead of the Spanish Netherlands. The gold and the blood of Holland had been profusely expended during this contest; it might seem for no positive results; but the exhaustion produced to every one of the other belligerents was a source of peace and prosperity to the republic. Its commerce was re-established; its financial resources recovered their level; and altogether we must fix on the epoch now before us as that of its utmost point of influence and greatness. France, on the contrary, was now reduced from its palmy state of almost European sovereignty to one of the deepest misery; and its monarch, in his old age, found little left of his former power but those records of poetry, painting, sculpture, and architecture which tell posterity of his magnificence, and the splendor of which throw his faults and his misfortunes into the shade.

The great object now to be accomplished by the United Provinces was the regulation of a distinct and guaranteed line of frontier between the republic and France. This object had become by degrees, ever since the peace of Munster, a fundamental maxim of their politics. The interposition of the Belgian provinces between the republic and France was of serious inconvenience to the former in this point of view. It was made the subject of a special article in "the grand alliance." In the year 1707 it was particularly discussed between England and the States, to the great discontent of the emperor, who was far from wishing its definitive settlement. But it was now become an indispensable item in the total of important measures whose accomplishment was called for by the peace of Utrecht. Conferences were opened on this sole question at Antwerp in the year 1714;

and, after protracted and difficult discussions, the treaty of the Barrier was concluded on the 15th of November, 1715.

This treaty was looked on with an evil eye in the Austrian Netherlands. The clamor was great and general; jealousy of the commercial prosperity of Holland being the real motive. Long negotiations took place on the subject of the treaty; and in December, 1718, the republic consented to modify some of the articles. The Pragmatic Sanction, published at Vienna in 1713 by Charles VI., regulated the succession to all the imperial hereditary possessions; and, among the rest, the provinces of the Netherlands. But this arrangement, though guaranteed by the chief powers of Europe, was, in the sequel, little respected, and but indifferently executed.

CHAPTER XXI

FROM THE PEACE OF UTRECHT TO THE INCORPORATION OF BELGIUM WITH THE FRENCH REPUBLIC

A.D. 1713—1795

DURING a period of thirty years following the treaty of Utrecht, the republic enjoyed the unaccustomed blessing of profound peace. While the discontents of the Austrian Netherlands on the subject of the treaty of the Barrier were in debate, the quadruple alliance was formed between Holland, England, France and the emperor, for reciprocal aid against all enemies, foreign and domestic. It was in virtue of this treaty that the pretender to the English throne received orders to remove from France; and the states-general about the same time arrested the Swedish ambassador, Baron Gortz, whose intrigues excited some suspicion. The death of Louis XIV. had once more changed the political system of Europe; and the commencement of the eighteenth century was fertile in negotiations and alliances in which we have at present but little direct interest. The rights of the republic were in all instances respected; and Holland did not cease to be considered as a power of the first distinction and consequence. The establishment of an East India Company at Ostend, by the emperor Charles VI., in 1722, was the principal cause of disquiet to the United Provinces, and the most likely to lead to a rupture. But, by the treaty of Hanover in 1726, the rights of Holland resulting from the treaty of Munster were guaranteed; and in consequence the emperor abolished the company of his creation, by the treaty of Seville in 1729, and that of Vienna in 1731.

The peace which now reigned in Europe allowed the United Provinces to direct their whole efforts toward the reform of those internal abuses resulting from feudality and fanaticism. Confiscations were reversed, and property secured throughout the republic. It received into its protection the persecuted sectarians of France, Germany, and Hungary; and the tolerant wisdom which it exercised in these measures gives the best assurance of its justice and prudence in one of a contrary nature, forming a solitary exception to them. This was the expulsion of the Jesuits, whose dangerous and destructive doctrines had been long a warrant for this salutary example to the Protestant states of Europe.

In the year 1732 the United Provinces were threatened with imminent peril, which accident alone prevented from becoming fatal to their very existence. It was perceived that the dikes, which had for ages preserved the coasts, were in many places crumbling to ruin, in spite of the enormous expenditure of money and labor devoted to their preservation. By chance it was discovered that the beams, piles and other timber works employed in the construction of the dikes were eaten through in all parts by a species of sea-worm hitherto unknown. The terror of the people was, as may be supposed, extreme. Every possible resource was applied which could remedy the evil; a hard frost providentially set in and destroyed the formidable reptiles; and the country was thus saved from a danger tenfold greater than that involved in a dozen wars.

The peace of Europe was once more disturbed in 1733. Poland, Germany, France, and Spain, were all embarked in the new war. Holland and England stood aloof; and another family alliance of great consequence drew still closer than ever the bonds of union between them. The young Prince of Orange, who in 1728 had been elected stadtholder of Groningen and Guelders, in addition to that of Friesland which had been enjoyed by his father, had in the year 1734 married the princess Anne, daughter of George II. of England; and by thus adding to the consideration of the House of Nassau, had opened a field for the recovery of all its old distinctions.

The death of the emperor Charles VI., in October, 1740, left his daughter, the archduchess Maria Theresa, heiress of his throne and possessions. Young, beautiful, and endowed with qualities of the highest order, she was surrounded with enemies whose envy and ambition would have despoiled her of her splendid rights. Frederick of Prussia, surnamed the Great, in honor of his abilities rather than his sense of justice, the electors of Bavaria and Saxony, and the kings of Spain and Sardinia, all pressed forward to the spoliation of an inheritance which seemed a fair play for all comers. But Maria Theresa, first joining her husband, Duke Francis of Lorraine, in her sovereignty, but without prejudice to it, under the title of co-regent, took an attitude truly heroic. When everything seemed to threaten the dismemberment of her states, she threw herself upon the generous fidelity of her Hungarian subjects with a dignified resolution that has few examples. There was imperial grandeur even in her appeal to their compassion. The results were electrical; and the whole tide of fortune was rapidly turned.

England and Holland were the first to come to the aid of the young and interesting empress. George II., at the head of his army, gained the victory of Dettingen, in support of her quarrel, in 1743; the states-general having contributed twenty thousand men and a large subsidy to her aid. Louis XV. resolved to throw his whole influence into the scale against these generous efforts in the princess's favor; and he invaded the Austrian Netherlands in the following year. Marshal Saxe commanded under him, and at first carried everything before him. Holland, having furnished twenty thousand troops and six ships of war to George II. on the invasion of the young pretender, was little in a state to oppose any formidable resistance to the enemy that threatened her own frontiers. The republic, wholly attached for so long a period to pursuits of peace and commerce, had no longer good generals nor effective armies; nor could it even put a fleet of any importance to sea. Yet with all these disadvantages it would not yield to the threats nor the demands of France; resolved to risk a new war rather than succumb to an enemy it had once so completely humbled and given the law to.

Conferences were opened at Breda, but interrupted almost as soon as commenced. Hostilities were renewed. The memorable battle of Fontenoy was offered and gloriously fought by the allies; accepted and splendidly won by the French. Never did the English and Dutch troops act more nobly in concert than on this remarkable occasion. The valor of the French was not less conspicuous; and the success of the day was in a great measure decided by the Irish battalions, sent, by the lamentable politics of those and much later days, to swell the ranks and gain the battles of England's enemies. Marshal Saxe followed up his advantage the following year, taking Brussels and many other towns. Almost the whole of the Austrian Netherlands being now in the power of Louis XV., and the United Provinces again exposed to invasion and threatened with danger, they had once more recourse to the old expedient of the elevation of the House of Orange, which in times of imminent peril seemed to present a never-failing palladium. Zealand was the first to give the impulsion; the other provinces soon followed the example; and William IV. was proclaimed stadtholder and captain-general, amid the almost unanimous rejoicings of all. These dignities were soon after declared hereditary both in the male and female line of succession of the House of Orange Nassau.

The year 1748 saw the termination of the brilliant campaigns of Louis XV. during this bloody war of eight years' continuance. The treaty of Aix-la-Chapelle, definitively signed on the 18th of October, put an end to hostilities; Maria Theresa was established in her rights and power; and Europe saw a fair balance of the nations, which gave promise of security and peace. But the United Provinces, when scarcely recovering from struggles which had so checked their prosperity, were employed in new and universal grief and anxiety by the death of their young stadtholder, which happened at The Hague, October 13, 1751. He had long been kept out of the government, though by no means deficient in the talents suited to his station. His son, William V., aged but three years and a half, succeeded him, under the guardianship of his mother, Anne of England, daughter of George II., a princess represented to be of a proud and ambitious temper, who immediately assumed a high tone of authority in the state.

The war of seven years, which agitated the north of Europe, and deluged its plains with blood, was almost the only one in which the republic was able to preserve a strict neutrality throughout. But this happy state of tranquillity was not, as on former occasions, attended by that prodigious increase of commerce, and that accumulation of wealth, which had so often astonished the world. Differing with England on the policy which led the latter to weaken and humiliate France, jealousies sprung up between the two countries, and Dutch commerce became the object of the most vexatious and injurious efforts on the part of England. Remonstrance was vain; resistance impossible; and the decline of the republic hurried rapidly on. The Hanseatic towns, the American colonies, the northern states of Europe, and France itself, all entered into the rivalry with Holland, in which, however, England carried off the most important prizes. Several private and petty encounters took place between the vessels of England and Holland, in consequence of the pretensions of the former to the right of search; and had the republic possessed the ability of former periods, and the talents of a Tromp or a De Ruyter, a new war would no doubt have been the result. But it was forced to submit; and a degrading but irritating tranquillity was the consequence for several years; the national feelings receiving a salve for home-decline by some extension of colonial settlements in the East, in which the island of Ceylon was included.

In the midst of this inglorious state of things, and the domestic abundance which was the only compensation for the gradual loss of national influence, the installation of William V., in 1766; his marriage with the princess of Prussia, niece of Frederick the Great, in 1768; and the birth of two sons, the eldest on the 24th of August, 1772; successively took place. Magnificent fetes celebrated these events; the satisfied citizens little imagining, amid their indolent rejoicings, the dismal futurity of revolution and distress which was silently but rapidly preparing for their country.

Maria Theresa, reduced to widowhood by the death of her husband, whom she had elevated to the imperial dignity by the title of Francis I., continued for a while to rule singly her vast possessions; and had profited so little by the sufferings of her own early reign that she joined in the iniquitous dismemberment of Poland, which has left an indelible stain on her memory, and on that of Frederick of Prussia and Catherine of Russia. In her own dominions she was adored; and her name is to this day cherished in Belgium among the dearest recollections of the people.

The impulsion given to the political mind of Europe by the revolution in North America was soon felt in the Netherlands. The wish for reform was not merely confirmed to the people. A memorable instance was offered by Joseph II., son and successor of Maria Theresa, that sovereigns were not only susceptible of rational notions of change, but that the infection of radical extravagance could penetrate even to the imperial crown. Disgusted by the despotism exercised by the clergy of Belgium, Joseph commenced his reign by measures that at once roused a desperate spirit of hostility in the priesthood, and soon spread among the bigoted mass of the people, who were wholly subservient to their will. Miscalculating his own power, and undervaluing that of the priests, the emperor issued decrees and edicts with a sweeping violence that shocked every prejudice and roused every passion perilous to the country. Toleration to the Protestants, emancipation of the clergy from the papal yoke, reformation in the system of theological instruction, were among the wholesale measures of the emperor's enthusiasm, so imprudently attempted and so virulently opposed.

But ere the deep-sown seeds of bigotry ripened to revolt, or produced the fruit of active resistance in Belgium, Holland had to endure the mortification of another war with England. The republic resolved on a futile imitation of the northern powers, who had adopted the difficult and anomalous system of an armed neutrality, for the prevention of English domination on the seas. The right of search, so proudly established by this power, was not likely to be wrenched from it by manifestoes or remonstrances; and Holland was not capable of a more effectual warfare. In the year 1781, St. Eustache, Surinam, Essequibo, and Demerara, were taken by British valor; and in the following year several of the Dutch colonies in the East, well fortified but ill defended, also fell into the hands of England. Almost the whole of those colonies, the remnants of prodigious power acquired by such incalculable instances of enterprise and courage, were one by one assailed and taken. But this did not suffice for the satisfaction of English objects in the prosecution of the war. It was also resolved to deprive Holland of the Baltic trade. A squadron of seven vessels, commanded by Sir Hyde Parker, was encountered on the Dogher Bank by a squadron of Dutch ships of the same force under Admiral Zoutman. An action of four hours was maintained with all the ancient courage which made so many of the memorable sea-fights between Tromp, De Ruyter, Blake, and Monk drawn battles. A storm separated the combatants, and saved the honor of each; for both had suffered alike, and victory had belonged to neither. The peace of 1784 terminated this short, but, to Holland, fatal war; the two latter years of which had been, in the petty warfare of privateering, most disastrous to the commerce of the republic. Negapatam, on the coast of Coromandel, and the free navigation of the Indian seas, were ceded to England, who occupied the other various colonies taken during the war.

Opinion was now rapidly opening out to that spirit of intense inquiry which arose in France, and threatened to sweep before it not only all that was corrupt, but everything that tended to corruption. It is in the very essence of all kinds of power to have that tendency, and, if not checked by salutary means, to reach that end. But the reformers of the last century, new in the desperate practice of revolutions, seeing its necessity, but ignorant of its nature, neither did nor could place bounds to the careering whirlwind that they raised. The well-meaning but intemperate changes essayed by Joseph II. in Belgium had a considerable share in the development of free principles, although they at first seemed only to excite the resistance of bigotry and strengthen the growth of superstition. Holland was always alive to those feelings of resistance to established authority which characterize republican opinions; and the general discontent at the result of the war with England gave a good excuse to the pretended patriotism which only wanted change, while it professed reform. The stadtholder saw clearly the storm which was gathering, and which menaced his power. Anxious for the present, and uncertain for the future, he listened to the suggestions of England, and resolved to secure and extend by foreign force the rights of which he risked the loss from domestic faction.

In the divisions which were now loudly proclaimed among the states in favor of or opposed to the House of Orange, the people, despising all new theories which they did not comprehend, took open part with the family so closely connected with every practical feeling of good which their country had yet known. The states of Holland soon proceeded to measures of violence. Resolved to limit the power of the stadtholder, they deprived him of the command of the garrison of The Hague, and of all the other troops of the province; and, shortly afterward, declared him removed from all his employments. The violent disputes and vehement discussions consequent upon this measure throughout the republic announced an inevitable commotion. The advance of a Prussian army toward the frontiers inflamed the passions of one party and strengthened the confidence of the other. An incident which now happened brought about the crisis even sooner than was expected. The Princess of Orange left her palace at Loo to repair to The Hague; and travelling with great simplicity and slightly attended, she was arrested and detained by a military post on the frontiers of the province of Holland. The neighboring magistrates of the town of Woesden refused her permission to continue her journey, and forced her to return to Loo under such surveillance as was usual with a prisoner of state. The stadtholder and the English ambassador loudly complained of this outrage. The complaint was answered by the immediate advance of the duke of Brunswick with twenty thousand Prussian soldiers. Some demonstrations of resistance were made by the astonished party whose outrageous conduct had provoked the measure; but in three weeks' time the whole of the republic was in perfect obedience to the authority of the stadtholder, who resumed all his functions of chief magistrate, with the additional influence which was sure to result from a vain and unjustifiable attempt to reduce his former power. We regret to be beyond the reach of Mr. Ellis's interesting but unpublished work, detailing the particulars of this revolution. The former persual of a copy of it only leaves a recollection of its admirable style and the leading facts, but not of the details with sufficient accuracy to justify more than a general reference to the work itself.

By this time the discontent and agitation in Belgium had attained a most formidable height. The attempted reformation in religion and judicial abuses persisted in by the emperor were represented, by a party whose existence was compromised by reform, as nothing less than sacrilege and tyranny, and blindly rejected by a people still totally unfitted for rational enlightenment in points of faith, or practices of civilization. Remonstrances and strong complaints were soon succeeded by tumultuous assemblages and open insurrection. A lawyer of Brussels, named Vander Noot, put himself at the head of the malcontents. The states-general of Brabant declared the new measures of the emperor to be in opposition to the constitution and privileges of the country. The other Belgian provinces soon followed this example. The prince Albert of Saxe-Teschen, and the archduchess Maria Theresa, his wife, were at this period joint governors-general of the Austrian Netherlands. At the burst of rebellion they attempted to temporize; but this only strengthened the revolutionary party, while the emperor wholly disapproved their measures and recalled them to Vienna.

Count Murray was now named governor-general; and it was evident that the future fate of the provinces was to depend on the issue of civil war. Count Trautmansdorff, the imperial minister at Brussels, and General D'Alton, who commanded the Austrian troops, took a high tone, and evinced a peremptory resolution. The soldiery and the citizens soon came into contact on many points; and blood was spilled at Brussels, Mechlin, and Antwerp.

The provincial states were convoked, for the purpose of voting the usual subsidies. Brabant, after some opposition, consented; but the states of Hainault unanimously refused the vote. The emperor saw, or supposed, that the necessity for decisive measures was now inevitable. The refractory states were dissolved, and arrests and imprisonments were multiplied in all quarters. Vander Noot, who had escaped to England, soon returned to the Netherlands, and established a committee at Breda, which conferred on him the imposing title of agent plenipotentiary of the people of Brabant. He hoped, under this authority, to interest the English, Prussian, and Dutch governments in favor of his views; but his proposals were coldly received: Protestant states had little sympathy for a people whose resistance was excited, not by tyrannical efforts against freedom, but by broad measures of civil and religious reformation; the only fault of which was their attempted application to minds wholly incompetent to comprehend their value.

Left to themselves, the Belgians soon gave a display of that energetic valor which is natural to them, and which would be entitled to still greater admiration had it been evinced in a worthier cause. During the fermentation which led to a general rising in the provinces, on the impulse of fanatic zeal, the truly enlightened portion of the people conceived the project of raising, on the ruins of monkish superstition and aristocratical power, an edifice of constitutional freedom. Vonck, also an advocate of Brussels, took the lead in this splendid design; and he and his friends proved themselves to have reached the level of that true enlightenment which distinguished the close of the eighteenth century. But the Vonckists, as they were called, formed but a small minority compared with the besotted mass; and, overwhelmed by fanaticism on the one hand, and despotism on the other, they were unable to act effectually for the public good. Vander Mersch, a soldier of fortune, and a man of considerable talents, who had raised himself from the ranks to the command of a regiment, and had been formed in the school of the seven years' war, was appointed to the command of the patriot forces. Joseph II. was declared to have forfeited his sovereignty in Brabant; and hostilities soon commenced by a regular advance of the insurgent army upon that province. Vander Mersch displayed consummate ability in this crisis, where so much depended upon the prudence of the military chief. He made no rash attempt, to which commanders are sometimes induced by reliance upon the enthusiasm of a newly revolted people. He, however, took the earliest safe opportunity of coming to blows with the enemy; and, having cleverly induced the Austrians to follow him into the very streets of the town of Turnhout, he there entered on a bloody contest, and finally defeated the imperialists with considerable loss. He next manœuvred with great ability, and succeeded in making his way into the province of Flanders, took Ghent by assault, and soon reduced Bruges, Ypres, and Ostend. At the news of these successes, the governors-general quitted Brussels in all haste. The states of Flanders assembled, in junction with those of Brabant. Both provinces were freed from the presence of the Austrian troops. Vander Noot and the committee of Breda made an entrance into Brussels with all the pomp of royalty; and in the early part of the following year (1790) a treaty of union was signed by the seven revolted provinces, now formed into a confederation under the name of the United Belgian States.

All the hopes arising from these brilliant events were soon, however, to be blighted by the scorching heats of faction. Joseph II., whose temperament appears to have been too sensitive to support the shock of disappointment in plans which sprung from the purest motives, saw, in addition to this successful insurrection against his power, his beloved sister, the queen of France, menaced with the horrors of an inevitable revolution. His over-sanguine expectations of successfully rivalling the glory of Frederick and Catherine, and the ill success of his war against the Turks, all tended to break down his enthusiastic spirit, which only wanted the elastic resistance of fortitude to have made him a great character. He for some time sunk into a profound melancholy; and expired on the 20th of January, 1791, accusing his Belgian subjects of having caused his premature death.

Leopold, the successor of his brother, displayed much sagacity and moderation in the measures which he adopted for the recovery of the revolted provinces; but their internal disunion was the best ally of the new emperor. The violent party which now ruled at Brussels had ungratefully forgotten the eminent services of Vander Mersch, and accused him of treachery, merely from his attachment to the noble views and principles of the widely-increasing party of the Vonckists. Induced by the hope of reconciling the opposing parties, he left his army in Namur, and imprudently ventured into the power of General Schoenfeld, who commanded the troops of the states. Vander Mersch was instantly arrested and thrown into prison, where he lingered for months, until set free by the overthrow of the faction he had raised to power; but he did not recover his liberty to witness the realization of his hopes for that of his country. The states-general, in their triumph over all that was truly patriotic, occupied themselves solely in contemptible labors to establish the monkish absurdities which Joseph had suppressed. The overtures of the new emperor were rejected with scorn; and, as might be expected from this combination of bigotry and rashness, the imperial troops under General Bender marched quietly to the conquest of the whole country; town after town opening their gates, while Vander Noot and his partisans betook themselves to rapid and disgraceful flight. On the 10th of December, 1791, the ministers of the emperor concluded a convention with those of England, Russia, and Holland (which powers guaranteed its execution), by which Leopold granted an amnesty for all past offences, and confirmed to all his recovered provinces their ancient constitution and privileges; and, thus returning under the domination of Austria, Belgium saw its best chance for successfully following the noble example of the United Provinces paralyzed by the short-sighted bigotry which deprived the national courage of all moral force.

Leopold enjoyed but a short time the fruits of his well-measured indulgence: he died, almost suddenly, March 1, 1792; and was succeeded by his son Francis II., whose fate it was to see those provinces of Belgium, which had cost his ancestors so many struggles to maintain, wrested forever from the imperial power. Belgium presented at this period an aspect of paramount interest to the world; less owing to its intrinsic importance than to its becoming at once the point of contest between the contending powers, and the theatre of the terrible struggle between republican France and the monarchs she braved and battled with.

The whole combinations of European policy were staked on the question of the French possession of this country.

This war between France and Austria began its earliest operations on the very first days after the accession of Francis II. The victory of Jemappes, gained by Dumouriez, was the first great event of the campaign. The Austrians were on all sides driven out. Dumouriez made his triumphal entry into Brussels on the 13th of November; and immediately after the occupation of this town the whole of Flanders, Brabant, and Hainault, with the other Belgian provinces, were subjected to France. Soon afterward several pretended deputies from the Belgian people hastened to Paris, and implored the convention to grant them a share of that liberty and equality which was to confer such inestimable blessings on France. Various decrees were issued in consequence; and after the mockery of a public choice, hurried on in several of the towns by hired Jacobins and well-paid patriots, the incorporation of the Austrian Netherlands with the French republic was formally pronounced.

The next campaign destroyed this whole fabric of revolution. Dumouriez, beaten at Nerwinde by the prince of Saxe-Coburg, abandoned not only his last year's conquest, but fled from his own army to pass the remainder of his life on a foreign soil, and leave his reputation a doubtful legacy to history. Belgium, once again in the possession of Austria, was placed under the government of the archduke Charles, the emperor's brother, who was destined to a very brief continuance in this precarious authority.

During this and the succeeding year the war was continued with unbroken perseverance and a constant fluctuation in its results. In the various battles which were fought, and the sieges which took place, the English army was, as usual, in the foremost ranks, under the Duke of York, second son of George III. The Prince of Orange, at the head of the Dutch troops, proved his inheritance of the valor which seems inseparable from the name of Nassau. The archduke Charles laid the foundation of his subsequent high reputation. The emperor Francis himself fought valiantly at the head of his troops. But all the coalesced courage of these princes and their armies could not effectually stop the progress of the republican arms. The battle of Fleurus rendered the French completely masters of Belgium; and the representatives of the city of Brussels once more repaired to the national convention of France, to solicit the reincorporation of the two countries. This was not, however, finally pronounced till the 1st of October, 1795, by which time the violence of an arbitrary government had given the people a sample of what they were to expect. The Austrian Netherlands and the province of Liege were divided into nine departments, forming an integral part of the French republic; and this new state of things was consolidated by the preliminaries of peace, signed at Leoben in Styria, between the French general Bonaparte and the archduke Charles, and confirmed by the treaty of Campo-Formio on the 17th of October, 1797.

CHAPTER XXII

FROM THE INVASION OF HOLLAND BY THE FRENCH TO THE RETURN OF THE PRINCE OF ORANGE

A.D. 1794—1813

WHILE the fate of Belgium was decided on the plains of Fleurus, Pichegru prepared to carry the triumphant arms of France into the heart of Holland. He crossed the Meuse at the head of one hundred thousand men, and soon gained possession of most of the chief places of Flanders. An unusually severe winter was setting in; but a circumstance which in common cases retards the operations of war was, in the present instance, the means of hurrying on the conquest on which the French general was bent. The arms of the sea, which had hitherto been the best defences of Holland, now became solid masses of ice; battlefields, on which the soldiers manoeuvred and the artillery thundered, as if the laws of the elements were repealed to hasten the fall of the once proud and long flourishing republic. Nothing could arrest the ambitious ardor of the invaders. The Duke of York and his brave army resisted to the utmost; but, borne down by numbers, he was driven from position to position. Batteries, cannons, and magazines were successfully taken; and Pichegru was soon at the term of his brilliant exploits.

But Holland speedily ceased to be a scene of warfare. The discontented portion of the citizens, now the majority, rejoiced to retaliate the revolution of 1787 by another, received the French as liberators. Reduced to extremity, yet still capable by the aid of his allies of making a long and desperate resistance, the stadtholder took the nobler resolution of saving his fellow-citizens from the horrors of prolonged warfare. He repaired to The Hague; presented himself in the assembly of the states-general; and solemnly deposited in their hands the exercise of the supreme power, which he found he could no longer wield but to entail misery and ruin on his conquered country. After this splendid instance of true patriotism and rare virtue, he quitted Holland and took refuge in England. The states-general dissolved a national assembly installed at The Hague; and, the stadtholderate abolished, the United Provinces now changed their form of government, their long-cherished institutions, and their very name, and were christened the Batavian Republic.

Assurances of the most flattering nature were profusely showered on the new state, by the sister republic which had effected this new revolution. But the first measure of regeneration was the necessity of paying for the recovered independence, which was effected for the sum of one hundred million florins. The new constitution was almost entirely modelled on that of France, and the promised independence soon became a state of deplorable suffering and virtual slavery. Incalculable evils were the portion of Holland in the part which she was forced to take in the war between France and England. Her marine was nearly annihilated, and some of her most valuable possessions in the Indies ravished from her by the British arms. She was at the same time obliged to cede to her ally the whole of Dutch Flanders, Maestricht, Venloo, and their dependencies; and to render free and common to both nations the navigation of the Rhine, the Meuse, and the Scheldt.

The internal situation of the unfortunate republic was deplorable. Under the weight of an enormous and daily increasing debt, all the resources of trade and industry were paralyzed. Universal misery took place of opulence, and not even the consolation of a free constitution remained to the people. They vainly sought that blessing from each new government of the country whose destinies they followed, but whose advantages they did not share. They saw themselves successively governed by the states-general, a national assembly, and the directory. But these ephemeral authorities had not sufficient weight to give the nation domestic happiness, nor consideration among the other powers.

On the 11th of October, 1797, the English admiral, Sir Adam Duncan, with a superior force, encountered the Dutch fleet under De Winter off Camperdown; and in spite of the bravery of the latter he was taken prisoner, with nine ships of the line and a frigate. An expedition on an extensive scale was soon after fitted out in England, to co-operate with a Russian force for the establishment of the House of Orange. The Helder was the destination of this armament, which was commanded by Sir Ralph Abercrombie. The Duke of York soon arrived in the Texel with a considerable reinforcement. A series of severe and well-contested actions near Bergen ended in the defeat of the allies and the abandonment of the enterprise; the only success of which was the capture of the remains of the Dutch fleet, which was safely conveyed to England.

From this period the weight of French oppression became every day more intolerable in Holland. Ministers, generals, and every other species of functionary, with swarms of minor tyrants, while treating the country as a conquered province, deprived it of all share in the brilliant though checkered glories gained by that to which it was subservient. The Dutch were robbed of national independence and personal freedom. While the words "liberty" and "equality" were everywhere emblazoned, the French ambassador assumed an almost Oriental despotism. The language and forms of a free government were used only to sanction a foreign tyranny; and the Batavian republic, reduced to the most hopeless and degraded state, was in fact but a forced appendage chained to the triumphal car of France.

Napoleon Bonaparte, creating by the force of his prodigious talents the circumstances of which inferior minds are but the creatures, now rapidly rose to the topmost height of power. He not only towered above the mass of prejudices which long custom had legalized, but spurned the multitude by whom these prejudices had been overthrown. Yet he was not of the first order of great minds; for he wanted that grand principle of self-control which is the supreme attribute of greatness. Potent, and almost irresistible in every conflict with others, and only to be vanquished by his own acts, he possessed many of the higher qualities of genius. He was rapid, resolute, and daring, filled with contempt for the littleness of mankind, yet molding every atom which composed that littleness to purposes at utter variance with its nature. In defiance of the first essence of republican theory, he built himself an imperial throne on the crushed privileges of a prostrate people; and he lavished titles and dignities on men raised from its very dregs, with a profusion which made nobility a byword of scorn. Kingdoms were created for his brothers and his friends; and the Batavian republic was made a monarchy, to give Louis a dignity, or at least a title, like the rest.

The character of Louis Bonaparte was gentle and amiable, his manners easy and affable. He entered on his new rank with the best intentions toward the country which he was sent to reign over; and though he felt acutely when the people refused him marks of respect and applause, which was frequently the case, his temper was not soured, and he conceived no resentment. He endeavored to merit popularity; and though his power was scanty, his efforts were not wholly unsuccessful. He labored to revive the ruined trade, which he knew to be the staple of Dutch prosperity: but the measures springing from this praiseworthy motive were totally opposed to the policy of Napoleon; and in proportion as Louis made friends and partisans among his subjects, he excited bitter enmity in his imperial brother. Louis was so averse from the continental system, or exclusion of British manufactures, that during his short reign every facility was given to his subjects to elude it, even in defiance of the orders conveyed to him from **Paris** through the medium of the French ambassador at **The Hague**. He imposed no restraints on public opinion, nor would he establish the odious system of espionage cherished by the French police; but he was fickle in his purposes, and prodigal in his expenses. The profuseness of his expenditure was very offensive to the Dutch notions of respectability in matters of private finance, and injurious to the existing state of the public means. The tyranny of Napoleon became soon quite insupportable to him; so much so, that it is believed that had the ill-fated English expedition to **Walcheren** in 1809 succeeded, and the army advanced into the country, he would have declared war against France. After an ineffectual struggle of more than three years, he chose rather to abdicate his throne than retain it under the degrading conditions of proconsulate subserviency. This measure excited considerable regret, and much esteem for the man who preferred the retirement of private life to the meanness of regal slavery. But Louis left a galling **memento** of misplaced magnificence, in an increase of ninety millions of florins (about nine millions sterling) to the already oppressive amount of the national debt of the country.

The annexation of Holland to the French empire was immediately pronounced by Napoleon. Two-thirds of the national debt were abolished, the conscription law was introduced, and the Berlin and Milan decrees against the introduction of British manufactures were rigidly enforced. The nature of the evils inflicted on the Dutch people by this annexation and its consequences demand a somewhat minute examination. Previous to it all that part of the territory of the former United Provinces had been ceded to France. The kingdom of Holland consisted of the departments of the Zuyder Zee, the mouths of the Maese, the Upper **Yssel**, the mouths of the Yssel, Friesland, and the Western and Eastern Ems; and the population of the whole did not exceed one million eight hundred thousand souls.

When Louis abdicated his throne, he left a military and naval force of eighteen thousand men, who were immediately taken into the service of France; and in three years and a half after that event this number was increased to fifty thousand, by the operation of the French naval and military code: thus about a thirty-sixth part of the whole population was employed in arms. The forces included in the maritime conscription were wholly employed in the navy. The national guards were on constant duty in the garrisons or naval establishments. The cohorts were by law only liable to serve in the *interior* of the French empire—that is to say, from Hamburg to Rome; but after the Russian campaign, this limitation was disregarded, and they formed a part of Napoleon's army at the battle of Bautzen.

The conscription laws now began to be executed with the greatest rigor; and though the strictest justice and impartiality were observed in the ballot and other details of this most oppressive measure, yet it has been calculated that, on an average, nearly one-half of the male population of the age of twenty years was annually taken off. The conscripts were told that their service was not to extend beyond the term of five years; but as few instances occurred of a French soldier being discharged without his being declared unfit for service, it was always considered in Holland that the service of a conscript was tantamount to an obligation during life. Besides, the regulations respecting the conscription were annually changed, by which means the code became each year more intricate and confused; and as the explanation of any doubt rested with the functionaries, to whom the execution of the law was confided, there was little chance of their constructions mitigating its severity.

But the conscription, however galling, was general in its operation. Not so the formation of the emperor's guard of honor. The members of this patrician troop were chosen from the most noble and opulent families, particularly those who were deemed inimical to the French connection. The selection depended altogether on the prefect, who was sure to name those most obnoxious to his political or personal dislike, without regard to their rank or occupation, or even the state of their health. No exemption was admitted—not even to those who from mental or bodily infirmity, or other cause, had been declared unfit for general military duty. The victims were forced to the mockery of volunteering their services; obliged to provide themselves with horses, arms, and accoutrements; and when arrived at the depot appointed for their assembling, considered probably but as hostages for the fidelity of their relatives.

The various taxes were laid on and levied in the most oppressive manner; those on land usually amounting to twenty-five, and those on houses to thirty per cent of the clear annual rent. Other direct taxes were levied on persons and movable property, and all were regulated on a scale of almost intolerable severity. The whole sum annually obtained from Holland by these means amounted to about thirty millions of florins (or three million pounds sterling), being at the rate of about one pound thirteen shillings four pence from every soul inhabiting the country.

The operation of what was called the continental system created an excess of misery in Holland, only to be understood by those who witnessed its lamentable results. In other countries, Belgium for instance, where great manufactories existed, the loss of maritime communication was compensated by the exclusion of English goods. In states possessed of large and fertile territories, the population which could no longer be employed in commerce might be occupied in agricultural pursuits. But in Holland, whose manufactures were inconsiderable, and whose territory is insufficient to support its inhabitants, the destruction of trade threw innumerable individuals wholly out of employment, and produced a graduated scale of poverty in all ranks. A considerable part of the population had been employed in various branches of the traffic carried on by means of the many canals which conveyed merchandise from the seaports into the interior, and to the different continental markets. When the communication with England was cut off, principals and subordinates were involved in a common ruin.

In France, the effect of the continental system was somewhat alleviated by the license trade, the exportation of various productions forced on the rest of continental Europe, and the encouragement given to home manufactures. But all this was reversed in Holland: the few licenses granted to the Dutch were clogged with duties so exorbitant as to make them useless; the duties on one ship which entered the Maese, loaded with sugar and coffee, amounting to about fifty thousand pounds sterling. At the same time every means was used to crush the remnant of Dutch commerce and sacrifice the country to France. The Dutch troops were clothed and armed from French manufactories; the frontiers were opened to the introduction of French commodities duty free; and the Dutch manufacturer undersold in his own market.

The population of Amsterdam was reduced from two hundred and twenty thousand souls to one hundred and ninety thousand, of which a fourth part derived their whole subsistence from charitable institutions, while another fourth part received partial succor from the same sources. At Haarlem, where the population had been chiefly employed in bleaching and preparing linen made in Brabant, whole streets were levelled with the ground, and more than five hundred houses destroyed. At The Hague, at Delft, and in other towns, many inhabitants had been induced to pull down their houses, from inability to keep them in repair or pay the taxes. The preservation of the dikes, requiring an annual expense of six hundred thousand pounds sterling, was everywhere neglected. The sea inundated the country, and threatened to resume its ancient dominion. No object of ambition, no source of professional wealth or distinction, remained to which a Hollander could aspire. None could voluntarily enter the army or navy, to fight for the worst enemy of Holland. The clergy were not provided with a decent competency. The ancient laws of the country, so dear to its pride and its prejudices, were replaced by the Code Napoleon; so that old practitioners had to recommence their studies, and young men were disgusted with the drudgery of learning a system which was universally pronounced unfit for a commercial country.

Independent of this mass of positive ill, it must be borne in mind that in Holland trade was not merely a means of gaining wealth, but a passion long and deeply grafted on the national mind: so that the Dutch felt every aggravation of calamity, considering themselves degraded and sacrificed by a power which had robbed them of all which attaches a people to their native land; and, for an accumulated list of evils, only offered them the empty glory of appertaining to the country which gave the law to all the nations of Europe, with the sole exception of England.

Those who have considered the events noted in this history for the last two hundred years, and followed the fluctuations of public opinion depending on prosperity or misfortune, will have anticipated that, in the present calamitous state of the country, all eyes were turned toward the family whose memory was revived by every pang of slavery, and associated with every throb for freedom. The presence of the Prince of Orange, William IV., who had, on the death of his father, succeeded to the title, though he had lost the revenues of his ancient house, and the re-establishment of the connection with England, were now the general desire. Some of the principal partisans of the House of Nassau were for some time in correspondence with his most serene highness. The leaders of the various parties into which the country was divided became by degrees more closely united. Approaches toward a better understanding were reciprocally made; and they ended in a general anxiety for the expulsion of the French, with the establishment of a free constitution, and a cordial desire that the Prince of Orange should be at its head. It may be safely affirmed, that, at the close of the year 1813, these were the unanimous wishes of the Dutch nation.

Napoleon, lost in the labyrinths of his exorbitant ambition, afforded at length a chance of redress to the nations he had enslaved. Elevated so suddenly and so high, he seemed suspended between two influences, and unfit for either. He might, in a moral view, be said to have breathed badly, in a station which was beyond the atmosphere of his natural world, without being out of its attraction; and having reached the pinnacle, he soon lost his balance and fell. Driven from Russia by the junction of human with elemental force, in 1812, he made some grand efforts in the following year to recover from his irremediable reverses. The battles of Bautzen and Lutzen were the expiring efforts of his greatness. That of Leipzig put a fatal negative upon the hopes that sprang from the two former; and the obstinate ambition, which at this epoch made him refuse the most liberal offers of the allies, was justly punished by humiliation and defeat. Almost all the powers of Europe now leagued against him; and France itself being worn out by his wasteful expenditure of men and money, he had no longer a chance in resistance. The empire was attacked at all points. The French troops in Holland were drawn off to reinforce the armies in distant directions; and the whole military force in that country scarcely exceeded ten thousand men. The advance of the combined armies toward the frontiers became generally known: parties of Cossacks had entered the north of Holland in November, and were scouring the country beyond the Yssel. The moment for action on the part of the Dutch confederate patriots had now arrived; and it was not lost or neglected.

A people inured to revolutions for upward of two centuries, filled with proud recollections, and urged on by well-digested hopes, were the most likely to understand the best period and the surest means for success. An attempt that might have appeared to other nations rash was proved to be wise, both by the reasonings of its authors and its own results. The **intolerable** tyranny of France had made the population **not only ripe, but** eager for revolt. This disposition **was acted on by a few** enterprising men, at once **partisans of the House of** Orange and patriots **in** the truest **sense of the word.** It would be unjust to omit the mention **of some of their** names in even this sketch of **the** events **which sprang from their** courage and sagacity. Count **Styrum, Messieurs Repelaer d'**Jonge, Van Hogendorp, **Vander Duyn van Maasdam, and** Changuion, were the **chiefs of the intrepid junta which planned** and executed **the bold measures of enfranchisement, and drew** up the **outlines of the constitution which was afterward** enlarged **and ratified. Their first movements at The Hague were totally unsupported by foreign aid. Their early checks from** the exasperated **French and their** overcautious **countrymen would have deterred most men** embarked in so **perilous a venture; but they never swerved nor** shrank **back. At the head of a force, which** courtesy **and** policy **called an army, of three** hundred national **guards** badly **armed, fifty citizens** carrying fowling-pieces, fifty soldiers **of the old Dutch guard,** four hundred auxiliary citizens **armed with pikes, and a** cavalry force **of** twenty young **men, the confederates boldly** proclaimed the Prince of **Orange, on the 17th** of November, 1813, **in their open village of The Hague, and** in the teeth of a French force **of full ten thousand** men, occupying every fortress in **the** country.

While a few gentlemen thus boldly came forward, at **their own risk, with** no funds but their private fortunes, **and only aided by** an unarmed populace, to declare war **against the French** emperor, they did not even know the **residence of** the exil**ed** prince in whose cause they were now **so** completely compromised. The other towns of Holland **were** in a state of the greatest incertitude: Rotterdam had not moved; and the intentions of Admiral Kickert, who commanded there, were (mistakenly) supposed to be decidedly hostile to the national cause. Amsterdam had, **on** the preceding day, been the scene of a popular commotion, which, however, bore no decided character; the rioters having been fired on by the national guard, no leader coming forward, and the proclamation of the magistrates cautiously abstaining from any allusion to the Prince of Orange. A brave officer, Captain Falck, had made use of many strong but inefficient arguments to prevail on the timid corporation to declare for the prince; the presence of a French garrison of sixty men seeming sufficient to preserve their patriotism from any violent excess.

The subsequent events at The Hague furnish an inspiring lesson for all people who would learn that to be free they must be resolute and daring. The only hope of the confederates was from the British government, and the combined armies then acting in the north of Europe. But many days were to be lingered through before troops could be embarked, and make their way from England in the teeth of the easterly winds then prevailing; while a few Cossacks, hovering on the confines of Holland, gave the only evidence of the proximity of the allied forces.

In this crisis, it was most fortunate that the French prefect at The Hague, M. de Stassart, had stolen away on the earliest alarm; and the French garrison of four hundred chasseurs, aided by one hundred well-armed custom-house officers, under the command of General Bouvier des Eclats, caught the contagious fears of the civil functionary. This force had retired to the old palace—a building in the centre of the town, the depot of all the arms and ammunition then at The Hague, and, from its position, capable of some defence. But the general and his garrison soon felt a complete panic from the bold attitude of Count Styrum, who made the most of his little means, and kept up, during the night, a prodigious clatter by his twenty horsemen; sentinels challenging, amid incessant singing and shouting, cries of "Oranje boven!" "Vivat Oranje!" and clamorous patrols of the excited citizens. At an early hour on the 18th, the French general demanded terms, and obtained permission to retire on Gorcum, his garrison being escorted as far as the village of Ryswyk by the twenty cavaliers who composed the whole mounted force of the patriots.

Unceasing efforts were now made to remedy the want of arms and men. A quantity of pikes were rudely made and distributed to the volunteers who crowded in; and numerous fishing-boats were despatched in different directions to inform the British cruisers of the passing events. An individual named Pronck, an inhabitant of Schævening, a village of the coast, rendered great services in this way, from his influence among the sailors and fishermen in the neighborhood.

The confederates spared no exertion to increase the confidence of the people under many contradictory and disheartening contingencies. An officer who had been despatched for advice and information to Baron Bentinck, at Zwolle, who was in communication with the allies, returned with the discouraging news that General Bulow had orders not to pass the Yssel, the allies having decided not to advance into Holland beyond the line of that river. A meeting of the ancient regents of The Hague was convoked by the proclamation of the confederates, and took place at the house of Mr. Van Hogendorp, the ancient residence of the De Witts. The wary magistrates absolutely refused all co-operation in the daring measures of the confederates, who had now the whole responsibility on their heads, with little to cheer them on in their perilous career but their own resolute hearts and the recollection of those days when their ancestors, with odds as fearfully against them, rose up and shivered to atoms the yoke of their oppressors.

Some days of intense anxiety now elapsed; and various incidents occurred to keep up the general excitement. Reinforcements came gradually in; no hostile measure was resorted to by the French troops; yet the want of success, as rapid as was proportioned to the first movements of the revolution, threw a gloom over all. Amsterdam and Rotterdam still held back; but the nomination of Messrs. Van

Hogendorp and Vander Duyn van Maasdam to be heads of the government, until the arrival of the Prince of Orange, and a formal abjuration of the emperor Napoleon, inspired new vigor into the public mind. Two nominal armies were formed, and two generals appointed to the command; and it is impossible to resist a smile of mingled amusement and admiration on reading the exact statement of the forces, so pompously and so effectively announced as forming the armies of Utrecht and Gorcum.

The first of these, commanded by Major-General D'Jonge, consisted of three hundred infantry, thirty-two volunteer cavalry, with two eight-pounders. The latter, under the orders of Major-General Sweertz van Landas, was composed of two hundred and fifty of The Hague Orange Guard, thirty Prussian deserters from the French garrison, three hundred volunteers, forty cavalry, with two eight-pounders.

The "army of Gorcum" marched on the 22d on Rotterdam: its arrival was joyfully hailed by the people, who contributed three hundred volunteers to swell its ranks. The "army of Utrecht" advanced on Leyden, and raised the spirits of the people by the display of even so small a force. But still the contrary winds kept back all appearance of succor from England, and the enemy was known to meditate a general attack on the patriot lines from Amsterdam to Dordrecht. The bad state of the roads still retarded the approach of the far-distant armies of the allies; alarms, true and false, were spread on all hands—when the appearance of three hundred Cossacks, detached from the Russian armies beyond the Yssel, prevailed over the hesitation of Amsterdam and the other towns, and they at length declared for the Prince of Orange.

But this somewhat tardy determination seemed to be the signal for various petty events, which at an epoch like that were magnified into transactions of the most fatal import. A reinforcement of one thousand five hundred French troops reached Gorcum from Antwerp: a detachment of twenty-five Dutch, with a piece of cannon, were surprised at one of the outposts of Woerden, which had been previously evacuated by the French, and the recapture of the town was accompanied by some excesses. The numbers and the cruelties of the enemy were greatly exaggerated. Consternation began to spread all over the country. The French, who seemed to have recovered from their panic, had resumed on all sides offensive operations. The garrison of Gorcum made a sortie, repulsed the force under General Van Landas, entered the town of Dordrecht, and levied contributions; but the inhabitants soon expelled them, and the army was enabled to resume its position.

Still the wind continued adverse to arrivals from the English coast; the Cossacks, so often announced, had not yet reached The Hague; and the small unsupported parties in the neighborhood of Amsterdam were in daily danger of being cut off.

In this crisis the confederates were placed in a most critical position. On the eve of failure, and with the certainty, in such a result, of being branded as rebels and zealots, whose rashness had drawn down ruin on themselves, their families, and their country, it required no common share of fortitude to bear up against the danger that threatened them. Aware of its extent, they calmly and resolutely opposed it; and each seemed to vie with the others in energy and firmness.

The anxiety of the public had reached the utmost possible height. Every shifting of the wind was watched with nervous agitation. The road from The Hague to the sea was constantly covered with a crowd of every age and sex. Each sail that came in sight was watched and examined with intense interest; and at length, on the 26th of November, a small boat was seen to approach the shore, and the inquiring glances of the observers soon discovered that it contained an Englishman. This individual, who had come over on a mercantile adventure, landed amid the loudest acclamation, and was conducted by the populace in triumph to the governor's. Dressed in an English volunteer uniform, he showed himself in every part of the town, to the great delight of the people, who hailed him as the precursor and type of an army of deliverers.

The French soon retreated before the marvellous exaggerations which the coming of this single Englishman gave rise to. The Dutch displayed great ability in the transmission of false intelligence to the enemy. On the 27th Mr. Fagel arrived from England with a letter from the Prince of Orange, announcing his immediate coming; and finally, the disembarkation of two hundred English marines, on the 29th, was followed the next day by the landing of the prince, whose impatience to throw himself into the open arms of his country made him spurn every notion of risk and every reproach for rashness. He was received with indescribable enthusiasm. The generous flame rushed through the whole country. No bounds were set to the affectionate confidence of the nation, and no prince ever gave a nobler example of gratitude. As the people everywhere proclaimed William I. sovereign prince, it was proposed that he should everywhere assume that title. It was, however, after some consideration, decided that no step of this nature should be taken till his most serene highness had visited the capital. On the 1st of December the prince issued a proclamation to his countrymen, in which he states his hopes of becoming, by the blessing of Providence, the means of restoring them to their former state of independence and prosperity. "This," continued he, "is my only object; and I have the satisfaction of assuring you that it is also the object of the combined powers. This is particularly the wish of the prince regent and the British nation; and it will be proved to you by the succor which that powerful people will immediately afford you, and which will, I hope, restore those ancient bonds of alliance and friendship which were a source of prosperity and happiness to both countries." This address being distributed at Amsterdam, a proclamation, signed by the commissioners of the confederate patriots, was published there the same day. It contained the following passages, remarkable as being the first authentic declaration of the sovereignty subsequently conferred on the Prince of Orange: "The uncertainty which formerly existed as to the executive power will no longer paralyze your efforts. It is not William, the sixth stadtholder, whom the nation recalls, without knowing what to hope or expect from him; but William I. who offers himself as sovereign prince of this free country." The following day, the 2d of December, the prince made his entry into Amsterdam. He did not, like some other sovereigns, enter by a breach through the constitutional liberties of his country, in imitation of the conquerors from the Olympic games, who returned to the city by a breach in its walls: he went forward borne on the enthusiastic greetings of his fellow-countrymen, and meeting their confidence by a full measure of magnanimity. On the 3d of December he published an address, from which we shall quote one paragraph: "You desire, Netherlands! that I should be intrusted with a greater share of power than I should have possessed but for my absence. Your confidence, your affection, offer me the sovereignty; and I am called upon to accept it, since the state of my country and the situation of Europe require it. I accede to your wishes. I overlook the difficulties which may attend such a measure; I accept the offer which you have made me; but I accept it only on one condition—that it shall be accompanied by a wise constitution, which shall guarantee your liberties and secure them against every attack. My ancestors sowed the seeds of your independence: the preservation of that independence shall be the constant object of the efforts of myself and those around me."

CHAPTER XXIII

FROM THE INSTALLATION OF WILLIAM I. AS PRINCE SOVEREIGN OF THE NETHERLANDS TO THE BATTLE OF WATERLOO

A.D. 1814—1815

THE regeneration of Holland was rapid and complete. Within four months, an army of twenty-five thousand men was raised; and in the midst of financial, judicial, and commercial arrangements, the grand object of the constitution was calmly and seriously debated. A committee, consisting of fourteen persons of the first importance in the several provinces, furnished the result of three months' labors in the plan of a political code, which was immediately printed and published for the consideration of the people at large. Twelve hundred names were next chosen from among the most respectable householders in the different towns and provinces, including persons of every religious persuasion, whether Jews or Christians. A special commission was then formed, who selected from this number six hundred names; and every housekeeper was called on to give his vote for or against their election. A large majority of the six hundred notables thus chosen met at Amsterdam on the 28th of March, 1814. The following day they assembled with an immense concourse of people in the great church, which was splendidly fitted up for the occasion; and then and there the prince, in an impressive speech, solemnly offered the constitution for acceptance or rejection. After a few hours' deliberation, a discharge of artillery announced to the anxious population that the constitution had been accepted. The numbers present were four hundred and eighty-three, and the votes as follows: Ayes, four hundred and fifty-eight; Noes, twenty-five.

There were one hundred and seventeen members absent; several of these were kept away by unavoidable obstacles. The majority among them was considered as dissentients; but it was calculated that if the whole body of six hundred had voted, the adoption of the constitution would have been carried by a majority of five-sixths. The dissentients chiefly objected to the power of declaring war and concluding treaties of peace being vested in the sovereign. Some individuals urged that the Protestant interest was endangered by the admission of persons of every persuasion to all public offices; and the Catholics complained that the state did not sufficiently contribute to the support of their religious establishments.

Such objections as these were to be expected, from individual interest or sectarian prejudices. But they prove that the whole plan was fairly considered and solemnly adopted; that so far from being the dictation of a government, it was the freely chosen charter of the nation at large, offered and sworn to by the prince, whose authority was only exerted in restraining and modifying the overardent generosity and confidence of the people.

Only one day more elapsed before the new sovereign was solemnly inaugurated, and took the oath prescribed by the constitution: "I swear that first and above all things I will maintain the constitution of the United Netherlands, and that I will promote, to the utmost of my power, the independence of the state and the liberty and prosperity of its inhabitants." In the eloquent simplicity of this pledge, the Dutch nation found an ample guarantee for their freedom and happiness. With their characteristic wisdom and moderation, they saw that the obligation it imposed embraced everything they could demand; and they joined in the opinion expressed by the sovereign in his inaugural address, that "no greater degree of liberty could be desired by rational subjects, nor any larger share of power by the sovereign, than that allotted to them respectively by the political code."

While Holland thus resumed its place among free nations, and France was restored to the Bourbons by the abdication of Napoleon, the allied armies had taken possession of and occupied the remainder of the Low Countries, or those provinces distinguished by the name of Belgium (but then still forming departments of the French empire), and the provisional government was vested in Baron Vincent, the Austrian general. This choice seemed to indicate an intention of restoring Austria to her ancient domination over the country. Such was certainly the common opinion among those who had no means of penetrating the secrets of European policy at that important epoch. It was, in fact, quite conformable to the principle of *statu quo ante bellum*, adopted toward France. Baron Vincent himself seemed to have been impressed with the false notion; and there did not exist a doubt throughout Belgium of the re-establishment of the old institutions.

But the intentions of the allied powers were of a nature far different. The necessity of a consolidated state capable of offering a barrier to French aggression on the Flemish frontier was evident to the various powers who had so long suffered from its want. By England particularly, such a field was required for the operations of her armies; and it was also to the interest of that nation that Holland, whose welfare and prosperity are so closely connected with her own, should enjoy the blessings of national independence and civil liberty, guaranteed by internal strength as well as friendly alliances.

The treaty of Paris (30th May, 1814), was the first act which gave an open manifestation of this principle. It was stipulated by its sixth article, that "Holland, placed under the sovereignty of the House of Orange, should receive an increase of territory." In this was explained the primitive notion of the creation of the kingdom of the Netherlands, based on the necessity of augmenting the power of a nation which was destined to turn the balance between France and Germany. The following month witnessed the execution of the treaty of London, which prescribed the precise nature of the projected increase.

It was wholly decided, without subjecting the question to the approbation of Belgium, that that country and Holland should form one United State; and the rules of government in the chief branches of its administration were completely fixed. The Prince of Orange and the plenipotentiaries of the great allied powers covenanted by this treaty: first, that the union of the two portions forming the kingdom of the Netherlands should be as perfect as possible, forming one state, governed in conformity with the fundamental law of Holland, which might be modified by common consent; secondly, that religious liberty, and the equal right of citizens of all persuasions to fill all the employments of the state, should be maintained; thirdly, that the Belgian provinces should be fairly represented in the assembly of the states-general, and that the sessions of the states in time of peace should be held alternately in Belgium and in Holland; fourthly and fifthly, that all the commercial privileges of the country should be common to the citizens at large; that the Dutch colonies should be considered as belonging equally to Belgium; and, finally, that the public debt of the two countries, and the expenses of its interest, should be borne in common.

We shall now briefly recapitulate some striking points in the materials which were thus meant to be amalgamated. Holland, wrenched from the Spanish yoke by the genius and courage of the early princes of Orange, had formed for two centuries an independent republic, to which the extension of maritime commerce had given immense wealth. The form of government was remarkable. It was composed of seven provinces, mutually independent of each other. These provinces possessed during the Middle Ages constitutions nearly similar to that of England: a sovereign with limited power; representatives of the nobles and commons, whose concurrence with the prince was necessary for the formation of laws; and, finally, the existence of municipal privileges, which each town preserved and extended by means of its proper force. This state of things had known but one alteration—but that a mighty one—the forfeiture of Philip II. at the latter end of the sixteenth century, and the total abolition of monarchical power.

The remaining forms of the government were hardly altered; so that the state was wholly regulated by its ancient usages; and, like some Gothic edifice, its beauty and solidity were perfectly original, and different from the general rules and modern theories of surrounding nations. The country loved its liberty such as it found it, and not in the fashion of any Utopian plan traced by some new-fangled system of political philosophy. Inherently Protestant and commercial, the Dutch abhorred every yoke but that of their own laws, of which they were proud even in their abuse. They held in particular detestation all French customs, in remembrance of the wretchedness they had suffered from French tyranny; they had unbounded confidence in the House of Orange, from long experience of its hereditary virtues. The main strength of Holland was, in fact, in its recollections; but these, perhaps, generated a germ of discontent, in leading it to expect a revival of all the influence it had lost, and was little likely to recover, in the total change of systems and the variations of trade. There nevertheless remained sufficient capital in the country, and the people were sufficiently enlightened, to give just and extensive hope for the future which now dawned on them. The obstacles offered by the Dutch character to the proposed union were chiefly to be found in the dogmatical opinions, consequent on the isolation of the country from all the principles that actuated other states, and particularly that with which it was now joined: while long-cherished sentiments of opposition to the Catholic religion was little likely to lead to feelings of accommodation and sympathy with its new fellow-citizens.

The inhabitants of Belgium, accustomed to foreign domination, were little shocked by the fact of the allied powers having disposed of their fate without consulting their wishes. But they were not so indifferent to the double discovery of finding themselves the subjects of a Dutch and a Protestant king. Without entering at large into any invidious discussion on the causes of the natural jealousy which they felt toward Holland, it may suffice to state that such did exist, and in no very moderate degree. The countries had hitherto had but little community of interests with each other; and they formed elements so utterly discordant as to afford but slight hope that they would speedily coalesce. The lower classes of the Belgian population were ignorant as well as superstitious (not that these two qualities are to be considered as inseparable); and if they were averse to the Dutch, they were perhaps not more favorably disposed to the French and Austrians. The majority of the nobles may be said to have leaned more, at this period, to the latter than to either of the other two peoples. But the great majority of the industrious and better informed portions of the middle orders felt differently from the other two, because they had found tangible and positive advantages in their subjection to France, which overpowered every sentiment of political degradation.

We thus see there was little sympathy between the members of the national family. The first glance at the geographical position of Holland and Belgium might lead to a belief that their interests were analogous. But we have traced the anomalies in government and religion in the two countries, which led to totally different pursuits and feelings. Holland had sacrificed manufactures to commerce. The introduction, duty free, of grain from the northern parts of Europe, though checking the progress of agriculture, had not prevented it to flourish marvellously, considering this obstacle to culture; and, faithful to their traditional notions, the Dutch saw the elements of well-being only in that liberty of importation which had made their harbors the marts and magazines of Europe. But the Belgian, to use the expressions of an acute and well-informed writer, "restricted in the thrall of a less liberal religion, is bounded in the narrow circle of his actual locality. Concentrated in his home, he does not look beyond the limits of his native land, which he regards exclusively. Incurious, and stationary in a happy existence, he has no interest in what passes beyond his own doors."

Totally unaccustomed to the free principles of trade so cherished by the Dutch, the Belgians had found, under the protection of the French custom-house laws, an internal commerce and agricultural advantages which composed their peculiar prosperity. They found a consumption for the produce of their well-cultivated lands, at high prices, in the neighboring provinces of France. The webs woven by the Belgian peasantry, and generally all the manufactures of the country, met no rivalry from those of England, which were strictly prohibited; and being commonly superior to those of France, the sale was sure and the profit considerable.

Belgium was as naturally desirous of this state of things as Holland was indifferent to it; but it could only have been accomplished by the destruction of free trade, and the exclusive protection of internal manufactures. Under such discrepancies as we have thus traced in religion, character, and local interests, the two countries were made one; and on the new monarch devolved the hard and delicate task of reconciling each party in the ill-assorted match, and inspiring them with sentiments of mutual moderation.

Under the title of governor-general of the Netherlands for his intended elevation to the throne and the definitive junction of Holland and Belgium were still publicly unknown), the Prince of Orange repaired to his new state. He arrived at Brussels in the month of August, 1814, and his first effort was to gain the hearts and the confidence of the people, though he saw the nobles and the higher orders of the inferior classes (with the exception of the merchants) intriguing all around him for the re-establishment of the Austrian power. Petitions on this subject were printed and distributed; and the models of those anti-national documents may still be referred to in a work published at the time.[1]

As soon as the moment came for promulgating the decision of the sovereign powers as to the actual extent of the new kingdom—that is to say, in the month of February, 1815—the whole plan was made public; and a commission, consisting of twenty-seven members, Dutch and Belgian, was formed, to consider the modifications necessary in the fundamental law of Holland, in pursuance of the stipulation of the treaty of London. After due deliberation these modifications were formed, and the great political pact was completed for the final acceptance of the king and people.

As a document so important merits particular consideration, in reference to the formation of the new monarchy, we shall briefly condense the reasonings of the most impartial and well-informed classes in the country on the constitution now about to be framed. Every one agreed that some radical change in the whole form of government was necessary, and that its main improvement should be the strengthening of the executive power. That possessed by the former stadtholders of Holland was often found to be too much for the chief of a republic, too little for the head of a monarchy. The assembly of the states-general, as of old constructed, was defective in many points; in none so glaringly as in that condition which required unanimity in questions of peace or war, and in the provision, from which they had no power to swerve, that all the taxes should be uniform. Both these stipulations were, of sheer necessity, continually disregarded; so that the government could be carried on at all only by repeated violations of the constitution. In order to excuse measures dictated by this necessity, each stadtholder was perpetually obliged to form partisans, and he thus became the hereditary head of a faction. His legiti-

---

[1] History of the Low Countries, by St. Genoist.

mate power was trifling: but his influence was capable of fearful increase; for the principle which allowed him to infringe the constitution, even on occasions of public good, might be easily warped into a pretext for encroachments that had no bounds but his own will.

Besides, the preponderance of the deputies from the commercial towns in the states-general caused the others to become mere ciphers in times of peace; only capable of clogging the march of affairs, and of being, on occasions of civil dissensions, the mere tools of whatever party possessed the greatest tact in turning them to their purpose. Hence a wide field was open to corruption. Uncertainty embarrassed every operation of the government. The Hague became an arena for the conflicting intrigues of every court in Europe. Holland was dragged into almost every war; and thus, gradually weakened from its rank among independent nations, it at length fell an easy prey to the French invaders.

To prevent the recurrence of such evils as those, and to establish a kingdom on the solid basis of a monarchy, unequivocal in its essence yet restrained in its prerogative, the constitution we are now examining was established. According to the report of the commissioners who framed it, "It is founded on the manners and habits of the nation, on its public economy and its old institutions, with a disregard for the ephemeral constitutions of the age. It is not a mere abstraction, more or less ingenious, but a law adapted to the state of the country in the nineteenth century. It did not reconstruct what was worn out by time; but it revived all that was worth preserving. In such a system of laws and institutions well adapted to each other, the members of the commission belonging to the Belgian provinces recognized the basis of their ancient charters, and the principles of their former liberty. They found no difficulty in adapting this law, so as to make it common to the two nations, united by ties which had been broken only for their own misfortune and that of Europe, and which it was once more the interest of Europe to render indissoluble."

The news of the elevation of William I. to the throne was received in the Dutch provinces with great joy, in as far as it concerned him personally; but a joy considerably tempered by doubt and jealousy, as regarded their junction with a country sufficiently large to counterbalance Holland, oppose interests to interests, and people to people. National pride and oversanguine expectations prevented a calm judgment on the existing state of Europe, and on the impossibility of Holland, in its ancient limits, maintaining the influence which it was hoped it would acquire.

In Belgium the formation of the new monarchy excited the most lively sensation. The clergy and the nobility were considerably agitated and not slightly alarmed; the latter fearing the resentment of the king for their avowed predilection in favor of Austria, and perceiving the destruction of every hope of aristocratical domination. The more elevated of the middle classes also saw an end to their exclusive occupation of magisterial and municipal employments. The manufacturers, great and small, saw the ruin of monopoly staring them in the face. The whole people took fright at the weight of the Dutch debt, which was considerably greater than that of Belgium. No one seemed to look beyond the present moment. The advantage of colonial possessions seemed remote and questionable to those who possessed no maritime commerce; and the pride of national independence was foreign to the feelings of those who had never yet tasted its blessings.

It was in this state of public feeling that intelligence was received in March, 1815, of the reappearance in France of the emperor Napoleon. At the head of three hundred men he had taken the resolution, without parallel even among the grandest of his own powerful conceptions, of invading a country containing thirty millions of people, girded by the protecting armies of coalesced Europe, and imbued, beyond all doubt, with an almost general objection to the former despot who now put his foot on its shores, with imperial pretensions only founded on the memory of his bygone glory.

His march to Paris was a miracle; and the vigor of his subsequent measures redeems the ambitious imbecility with which he had hurried on the catastrophe of his previous fall.

The flight of Louis XVIII. from Paris was the sure signal to the kingdom of the Netherlands, in which he took refuge, that it was about to become the scene of another contest for the life or death of despotism. Had the invasion of Belgium, which now took place, been led on by one of the Bourbon family, it is probable that the priesthood, the people, and even the nobility, would have given it not merely a negative support. But the name of Napoleon was a bugbear for every class; and the efforts of the king and government, which met with most enthusiastic support in the northern provinces, were seconded with zeal and courage by the rest of the kingdom.

The national force was soon in the field, under the command of the Prince of Orange, the king's eldest son, and heir-apparent to the throne for which he now prepared to fight. His brother, Prince Frederick, commanded a division under him. The English army, under the duke of Wellington, occupied Brussels and the various cantonments in its neighborhood; and the Prussians, commanded by Prince Blucher, were in readiness to co-operate with their allies on the first movement of the invaders.

Napoleon, hurrying from Paris to strike some rapid and decisive blow, passed the Sambre on the 15th of June, at the head of the French army, one hundred and fifty thousand strong, driving the Prussians before him beyond Charleroi and back on the plain of Fleurus with some loss. On the 16th was fought the bloody battle of Ligny, in which the Prussians sustained a decided defeat; but they retreated in good order on the little river Lys, followed by Marshal Grouchy with thirty thousand men detached by Napoleon in their pursuit. On the same day the British advanced position at Quatre Bras, and the *corps d'armée* commanded by the Prince of Orange, were fiercely attacked by Marshal Ney; a battalion of Belgian infantry and a brigade of horse artillery having been engaged in a skirmish the preceding evening at Frasnes with the French advanced troops.

The affair of Quatre Bras was sustained with admirable firmness by the allied English and Netherland forces, against an enemy infinitely superior in number, and commanded by one of the best generals in France. The Prince of Orange, with only nine thousand men, maintained his position till three o'clock in the afternoon, despite the continual attacks of Marshal Ney, who commanded the left of the French army, consisting of forty-three thousand men. But the interest of this combat, and the details of the loss in killed and wounded, are so merged in the succeeding battle, which took place on the 18th, that they form in most minds a combination of exploits which the interval of a day can scarcely be considered to have separated.

The 17th was occupied by a retrograde movement of the allied army, directed by the duke of Wellington, for the purpose of taking its stand on the position he had previously fixed on for the pitched battle, the decisive nature of which his determined foresight had anticipated. Several affairs between the French and English cavalry took place during this movement; and it is pretty well established that the enemy, flushed with the victory over Blucher of the preceding day, were deceived by this short retreat of Wellington, and formed a very mistaken notion of its real object, or of the desperate reception destined for the morrow's attack.

The battle of Waterloo has been over and over described and profoundly felt, until its records may be said to exist in the very hearts and memories of the nations. The fiery valor of the assault, and the unshakable firmness of the resistance, are perhaps without parallel in the annals of war. The immense stake depending on the result, the grandeur of Napoleon's isolated efforts against the flower of the European forces, and the awful responsibility resting on the head of their great leader, give to this conflict a romantic sublimity, unshared by all the manœuvring of science in a hundred commonplace combats of other wars. It forms an epoch in the history of battles. **It is to** the full as memorable, as an individual event, **as** it is for **the** consequences which followed it. It was fought by no rules, and gained by no tactics. It was a fair stand-up fight on **level** ground, where downright manly courage was alone to decide the issue. **This** derogates in nothing from the splendid talents **and deep knowledge of** the rival commanders. Their reputation for all **the intricate** qualities of generalship rests on the broad **base of previous** victories. This day was to be **won by strength of nerve and** steadiness of **heart**; and a moral grandeur is **thrown over its** result by **the** reflection that human skill **had little to do where so much was left to Providence.**

We abstain from entering on details of the battle. It is enough to state that **throughout the day the troops of the** Netherlands sustained **the** character for **courage which so** many centuries had established. Various **opinions have** gone forth as to the conduct of **the** Belgian **troops on this** memorable occasion. **Isolated instances were possibly found,** among a mass of several **thousands, of that nervous weakness** which **neither** the noblest **incitements nor the finest** examples can conquer. Old associations **and feelings not** effaced might **have slackened the efforts of a few, directed** against former comrades or personal friends whom the stern necessity **of** politics had placed in opposing **ranks.** Raw troops might here **and** there have **shrunk** from attacks the most desperate on **record; but** that the great principle of public duty, on grounds purely national, pervaded the army, is to be found in the official reports of its loss; two thousand and fifty-eight men **killed** and one thousand nine hundred and thirty-six wounded prove indelibly that the troops of the Netherlands had their full share in the honor of the day. The victory was cemented by the blood of the Prince of Orange, who stood the brunt of the fight with his gallant soldiers. His conduct was conformable to the character of **his** whole race, and to his own reputation during a long series of service with the British army in the Spanish peninsula. He stood bravely at the head of his troops during the murderous conflict; or, like Wellington, in whose school he was formed and whose example was beside him, rode from rank to rank and column to column, inspiring his men by the proofs of his untiring courage.

Several anecdotes are related of the prince's conduct throughout the day. One is remarkable as affording an example of those pithy epigrams of the battlefield with which history abounds, accompanied by an act that speaks a fine knowledge of the soldier's heart. On occasion of one peculiarly desperate charge, the prince, hurried on by his ardor, was actually in the midst of the French, and was in the greatest danger; when a Belgian battalion rushed forward, and, after a fierce struggle, repulsed the enemy and disengaged the prince. In the impulse of his admiration and gratitude, he tore from his breast one of those decorations gained by his own conduct on some preceding occasion, and flung it among the battalion, calling out, "Take it, take it, my lads! you have all earned it!" This decoration was immediately grappled for, and tied to the regimental standard, amid loud shouts of "Long live the prince!" and vows to defend the trophy, in the very utterance of which many a brave fellow received the stroke of death.

A short time afterward, and just half an hour before that terrible charge of the whole line, which decided the victory, the prince was struck by a musket-ball in the left shoulder. He was carried from the field, and conveyed that evening to Brussels, in the same cart with one of his wounded aides-de-camp, supported by another, and displaying throughout as much indifference to pain as he had previously shown contempt of danger.

The battle of Waterloo consolidated the kingdom of the Netherlands. The wound of the Prince of Orange was perhaps one of the most fortunate that was ever received by an individual, or sympathized in by a nation. To a warlike people, wavering in their allegiance, this evidence of the prince's valor acted like a talisman against disaffection. The organization of the kingdom was immediately proceeded on. The commission, charged with the revision of the fundamental law, and the modification required by the increase of territory, presented its report on the 31st of July. The inauguration of the king took place at Brussels on the 21st of September, in presence of the states-general: and the **ceremony received** additional **interest from** the appearance of the sovereign supported by his two sons who had so valiantly fought for **the** rights **he now swore to** maintain; the heir **to the crown yet bearing his wounded arm in a scarf,** and showing in **his countenance the** marks **of recent** suffering.

The constitution was finally **accepted by the nation, and** the principles of the government **were stipulated and fixed in** one grand view—that of the **union, and,** consequently, the force of the **new state.**

It has been asked **by a profound and sagacious inquirer,** or at least the question **is put forth on** undoubted authority in his name, "Why did England **create for** herself a difficulty, and what will be by and by a natural **enemy, in uniting** Holland **and Belgium, in place of managing those two immense resources** to her commerce by keeping them separate? **For Holland,** without manufactures, was the natural mart for those of England, **while Belgium** under an English prince had been the **route for constantly inundating** France and Germany."

So asked Napoleon, **and** England may answer and justify her conduct so impugned, on principles consistent with the general wishes and **the** common good of Europe. **The discussion** of the question is foreign to our **purpose,** which is **to** trace the circumstances, not to argue on the policy, that led to the formation of the Netherlands **as** they now exist. But it appears that the different integral parts of the nation were amalgamated from deep-formed designs for their mutual benefit. Belgium was not given to Holland, as the already-cited article of the treaty of Paris might at first sight seem to imply; nor was Holland allotted to Belgium. But they were grafted together, with all the force of legislative wisdom; not that one might be dominant and the other oppressed, but that both should bend to form an arch of common strength, able to resist the weight of such invasions as had perpetually perilled, and often crushed, their separate independence.

SUPPLEMENTARY CHAPTER

A.D. 1815—1899

IN the preceding chapters we have seen the history of Holland carried down to the treaty which joined together what are now known as the separate countries of Holland and Belgium. And it is at this point that the interest of the subject for the historian practically ceases. The historian differs from the annalist in this—that he selects for treatment those passages in the career of nations which possess a dramatic form and unity, and therefore convey lessons for moral guidance, or for constituting a basis for reasonable prognostications of the future. But there are in the events of the world many tracts of country (as we might term them) which have no special character or apparent significance, and which therefore, though they may extend over many years in time, are dismissed with bare mention in the pages of the historian; just as, in travelling by rail, the tourist will keep his face at the window only when the scenery warrants it; at other times composing himself to other occupations.

The scenery of Dutch history has episodes as stirring and instructive as those of any civilized people since history began; but it reached its dramatic and moral apogee when the independence of the United Netherlands was acknowledged by Spain. The Netherlands then reached their loftiest pinnacle of power and prosperity; their colonial possessions were vast and rich; their reputation as guardians of liberty and the rights of man was foremost in the world. But further than this they could not go; and the moment when a people ceases to advance may generally be regarded as the moment when, relatively speaking at least, it begins to go backward. The Dutch could in no sense become the masters of Europe; not only was their domain too small, but it was geographically at a disadvantage with the powerful and populous nations neighboring it, and it was compelled ever to fight for its existence against the attacks of nature itself. The stormy waves of the North Sea were ever moaning and threatening at the gates, and ever and anon a breach would be made, and the labor of generations annulled. Holland could never enter upon a career of conquest, like France or Russia; neither could she assume the great part which Britain has played; for although the character of the Dutchmen is in many respects as strong and sound as that of the English, and in some ways its superior, yet the Dutch had not been dowered with a sea-defended isle for their habitation, which might enable them to carry out enterprises abroad without the distraction and weakness involved in maintaining adequate guards at home. They were mighty in self-defence and in resistance against tyranny; and they were unsurpassed in those virtues and qualities which go to make a nation rich and orderly; but aggression could not be for them. They took advantage of their season of power to confirm themselves in the ownership of lands in the extreme East and in the West, which should be a continual source of revenue; but they could do no more; and they wasted not a little treasure and strength in preserving what they had gained, or a part of it, from the grasp of others. But this was the sum of their possibility; they could not presume to dictate terms to the world; and the consequence was that they gradually ceased to be a considered factor in the European problem. In some respects, their territorial insignificance, while it prevented them from aggressive action, preserved them from aggression; their domain was not worth conquering, and again its conquest could not be accomplished by any nation without making others uneasy and jealous. They became, like Switzerland, and unlike Poland and Hungary, a neutral region, which it was for the interest of Europe at large to let alone. None cared to meddle with them; and, on the other hand, they had native virtue and force enough to resist being absorbed into other peoples; the character of the Dutch is as distinct to-day as ever it had been. Their language, their literature, their art, and their personal traits, are unimpaired. They are, in their own degree, remarkably prosperous and comfortable; and they have the good sense to be content with their condition. They are liberal and progressive, and yet conservative; they are even with modern ideas as regards education and civilization, and yet the tourist within their boundaries continually finds himself reminded of their past. The costumes and the customs of the mass of the people have undergone singularly little change; they mind their own affairs, and are wisely indifferent to the affairs of others. Both as importers and as exporters they are useful to the world, and if the prophecies of those who foretell a general clash of the European powers should be fulfilled, it is likely that the Dutch will be onlookers merely, or perhaps profit by the misfortunes of their neighbors to increase their own well-being.

As we have seen in the foregoing pages, Belgium did not unite with the Hollanders in their revolt of the sixteenth century; but appertained to Burgundy, and was afterward made a domain of France. But after Napoleon had been overthrown at Waterloo, the nations who had been so long harried and terrorized by him were not satisfied with banishing the ex-conqueror to his island exile, but wished to prevent any possibility of another Napoleon arising to renew the wars which had devastated and impoverished them. Consequently they agreed to make a kingdom which might act as a buffer between France and the rest of Europe; and to this end they decreed that Belgium and Holland should be one. But in doing this, the statesmen or politicians concerned failed to take into account certain factors and facts which must inevitably, in the course of time, undermine their arrangements. Nations cannot be arbitrarily manufactured to suit the convenience of others.

There is a chemistry in nationalities which has laws of its own, and will not be ignored. Between the Hollanders and the Belgians there existed not merely a negative lack of homogeneity, but a positive incompatibility. The Hollanders had for generations been fighters and men of enterprise; the Belgians had been the appanage of more powerful neighbors. The Hollanders were Protestants; the Belgians were adherents of the Papacy. The former were seafarers; the latter, farmers. The sympathies or affiliations of the Dutch were with the English and the Germans; those of the Belgians were with the French. Moreover, the Dutch were inclined to act oppressively toward the Belgians, and this disposition was made the more irksome by the fact that King William was a dull, stupid, narrow and very obstinate sovereign, who thought that to have a request made of him was reason sufficient for resisting it.

But over and above all these causes for disintegration of the new kingdom lay facts of the broadest significance and application. The arbiters of 1815 did not sufficiently apprehend the meaning of the French Revolution. The wars of Napoleon had made them forget it; his power had seemed so much more formidable and positive that the deeper forces which had brought about the events of the last decade of the eighteenth century were ignored. But they still continued profoundly active, and were destined ere long to announce themselves anew. They were in truth the generative forces of the nineteenth century.

They have not yet spent themselves; but as we look back upon the events of the past eighty or ninety years, we perceive what vast differences there are between what we were in Napoleon's day and what we are now. A long period of intrigue and misrule, of wars and revolutions, has been followed by material, mental and social changes affecting every class of the people, and especially that class which had hitherto been almost entirely unconsidered. The wars of this century have been of another character than those of the past; they have not involved basic principles of human association, but have been the result of attempts to gain comparatively trifling political advantages, or else were the almost inevitable consequence of adjustments of national relations. Several small new kingdoms have appeared; but their presence has not essentially altered the political aspect of Europe. It is the conquests of mind that have been, in this century, far more important than the struggles of arms. Steam, as applied to locomotion on sea and land, and to manufactures, has brought about modifications in social and industrial conditions that cannot be exaggerated. Steamboats and railroads have not only given a different face to commerce and industry, but they have united the world in bonds of mutual knowledge and sympathy, which cannot fail to profoundly affect the political relations of mankind. Isolation is ignorance; as soon as men begin to discover, by actual intercourse, the similarities and dissimilarities of their several conditions, these will begin to show improvements. To be assured that people in one part of the world are better off than those in another, will tend inevitably to bring about ameliorations for the latter. The domain of evil will be continually restricted, and that of good enlarged. In the dissemination of intelligence and the spread of sympathy, the telegraph, and other applications of electricity, have enormously aided the work of steam. Every individual of civilized mankind may now be cognizant, at any moment, of what is taking place at any point of the earth's surface to which the appliances of civilization have penetrated. This unprecedented spread of common acquaintanceship of the world has been supplemented by discoveries of science in many other directions. We know more of the moon to-day than Europe did of this planet a few centuries ago. The industrial arts are now prosecuted by machinery with a productiveness which enables one man to do the work formerly performed by hundreds, and which more than keeps up the supply with the demand. Conquests of natural forces are constantly making, and each one of them adds to the comfort and enlightenment of man. Men, practically, **live** a dozen lives such as those of the past in their single **span of** seventy years; and we are even finding means of prolonging the Scriptural limit of mortal existence physically **as** well **as** mentally.

But is all this due to that **great moral** and social earthquake to which we **give the name of the** French Revolution? Yes; for that upheaval, like the **plow of** some titanic **husbandman, brought to the surface elements of** good and use **which had been lying fallow for unnum**bered ages. It brought into view the **People, as against mere** rulers and aristocrats, **who had hitherto lived upon what the** People **produced, without working themselves, and without** caring **for anything except to conserve** things **as they were. Human progress will never be advanced by** oligarchies, no **matter how gentle and well-disposed. We see their** results **to-day in Spain and in Turkey, which are still** mediæval, **or worse, in their condition and methods. It is the** brains **of the common people that have wrought** the mighty change; **their personal interests demand that they** go forward, and **their fresh and unencumbered minds** show them the way. **The great scientists, the inventors, the** philanthropists, the **reformers, are all of the common** people; the statesmen who **have really governed the** world in this century have sprung **from the common stock. The** French Revolution destroyed **the dominance of old ideas,** and with **them** the **forms in which they were em**bodied. Political, **personal and** religious **freedom are now** matters **of** course; **but a** hundred **years ago they were** almost unheard of, save in the dreams **of optimists and fanatics.** The rights of labor have been **vindicated; and** the right of every human being to the benefit **of what he** produces has been claimed and established. **Along with** this improvement has come, of course, a **train of evils** and abuses, due to our ignorance of how best to manage and apply our new privileges and advantages; but such evils **are** transient, and the conditions which created them will suffice, ere long, to remove them. The conflict between labor and capital is not permanent; it will yield to better knowledge of the true demands of political economy. The indifference or corruption of law makers and dispensers will disappear when men realize that personal selfishness is self-destructive, and that only care for the commonweal can bring about prosperity for the individual. The democracy is still in its swaddling clothes, and its outward aspect is in many ways ugly and unwelcome, and we sigh for the elegance and composure of old days; but these discomforts are a necessary accompaniment of growth, and will vanish when the growing pains are past. The Press is the mirror of the aspirations, the virtues and the faults of the new mankind; its power is stupendous and constantly increasing; many are beginning to dread it as a possible agent of ill; but in truth its real power can only be for good, since the mass of mankind, however wedded to selfishness as individuals, are united in desiring honesty and good in the general trend of things; and it is to the generality, and not to the particular, that the Press, to be successful, must appeal. It is the great critic and the great recorder; and in the face of such criticism and record abuses cannot long maintain themselves. Men will be free, first of external tyrannies, and then of that more subtle but not less dangerous tyranny which they impose upon themselves. As might have been expected, extremists have arisen who sought to find a short road to perfection, and they have met with disappointment. The dreams of the socialists have not been realized; men will not work for one another unless they are at the same time working for themselves. The communist and the nihilist are yet further from the true ideal; there will always remain in human society certain persons who rule, and others who obey. There must always, in all affairs, be a head to direct as well as hands to execute. Men are born unequal in intelligence and ability; and it will never be possible to reduce leaders to the level of followers. The form of society must take its model from the human form, in which one part is subordinate to another, yet all work together in harmony. Only time—and probably no very long time—is required to bring a recognition of these facts. Meanwhile, the very violence of the revolts against even the suspicion of oppression are but symptoms of the vigorous vitality which, in former centuries, seemed to have no existence at all. On the other hand, industrial co-operation seems to promise successful development; it involves immense economies, and consequent profit to producers. The middleman has his uses, and especially is he a convenience; but it is easy to pay too dear for conveniences; and there seems no reason why the producer should not, as time goes on, become constantly better equipped for dealing direct with the consumer, to the manifest advantage of both.

All these and many other triumphs of civilization, which we see now in objective form, were present in potency at the beginning of this century, though, as we have said, they were not duly taken into account by the framers of the agreement which sought to make Holland and Belgium one flesh. Had the sun not yet risen upon the human horizon, the attempt might have had a quasi success; but the light was penetrating the darkened places, and men were no longer willing to accept subjection as their inevitable doom. It might be conducive to the comfort of the rest of Europe that Batavian and Belgian should dwell together under one political roof; but it did not suit the parties themselves; and therefore they soon began to make their incompatibility known. But nothing was heard beyond the grumblings of half-awakened discontent until, in 1830, the new revolution in Paris sent a sympathetic thrill through all the dissatisfied of Europe. A generation had now passed since the first great upheaval, and men had had time to digest the lesson which it conveyed, and to draw various more or less reasonable inferences as to future possibilities. It had been determined that, broadly speaking, what the people heartily wanted, the people might have; and the disturbances in Paris indicated that the people were prepared to resent any attempt on the part of their rulers to bring back the old abuses. When the Pentarchy, in 1815, had made its division of the spoils of Napoleon, the Bourbons were reseated on the throne which Louis XIV. had made famous; but Louis XVIII. was but a degenerate representative of the glories that had been. He adopted a reactionary policy against the Napoleonic (or imperialist), the republican and the Protestant elements in France; and outrages and oppressions occurred. As a consequence, secret societies were formed to counteract the ultra-royalist policy. When Louis died, it was hoped that his successor, Charles X., might introduce improvements; but on the contrary he only made matters worse. The consequence was the gradual growth of a liberal party, seeking a monarchy based on the support of the great middle class of the population. In 1827 Charles disbanded the National Guard; and in the following year the liberals elected a majority in the Chamber. Charles foolishly attempted to meet this step by making the prince de Polignac his minister, who stood for all that the people had in abhorrence. The prince issued ordinances declaring the late elections illegal, narrowing down the rights of suffrage to the large landowners, and forbidding all liberty to the press. Hereupon the populace of Paris erected barricades and took up arms; and in the "Three Days" from the 27th to the 29th of July, 1830, they defeated the forces of the king, and after capturing the Hotel de Ville and the Louvre, sent him into exile, and made the venerable and faithful Lafayette commander of the National Guard. But the revolutionists showed forbearance; and instead of beheading Charles, as they might have done, they let him go, and punished the ministers by imprisonment only. This put an end to the older line of the Bourbons in France, and the representative of the younger branch, Louis Philippe ("Philippe Egalite"), was set on the throne, in the hope that he would be willing to carry out the people's will.

All this was interesting to the Belgians, and they profited by the example. They regarded William as another Charles, and deemed themselves justified in revolting against his rule.

They declared that they were no longer subject to his control, and issue was joined on that point. But the Powers were not ready to permit the dissolution of their anxiously constructed edifice; and they met together with a view to arranging some secure modus vivendi. The issue of their deliberations took the form of proposing that the duchy of Luxemburg, at the southeast corner of Belgium, should be ceded to Holland on the north. This suggestion was favorably received by the Hollanders, but was not so agreeable to the Belgians; and an assembly at Brussels devised and adopted a liberal constitution, and invited Leopold of Saxe-Coburg to occupy their throne. Leopold was at this time about forty years of age; he was the youngest son of Francis, duke of Saxe-Coburg; he had married, in 1816, the daughter of George IV. of England, the princess Charlotte, and had, a few months before the Belgians' proposal, been offered and had refused the crown of Greece. But the Belgian throne was more to his liking; and after taking measures to sound the Powers on the subject, and to assure himself of their good will, he accepted the proffer, and was crowned under the title of Leopold I. His reign lasted thirty-four years, and was comparatively uneventful and prosperous.

But the Dutch refused to tolerate this change of sovereignty without a struggle; William raised an army and suddenly threw it into Belgium; and the chances are that he would have made short work of Belgian resistance had the two been permitted to fight out their quarrel undisturbed. This, however, could not happen; since the independence of Belgium had been recognized by England, Austria, Russia, and Prussia; and the triumphal march of the Dutch was arrested by a French army which happened to be in the place where they could be most effective in the circumstances. The Dutch had occupied Antwerp, a town on the borderland of Belgium and Holland. It had been in the possession of the French in 1794, but had been taken from them at the Restoration in 1814. The French now laid siege to it, being under the command of Gérard, while the Dutch were led by Chassé. The citadel was taken in 1832, and the resistance of the Dutch to the decree of Europe was practically at an end, though William the Obstinate refused for several years to accept the fact. The duchy of Luxemburg had sided with the Belgians all along, as might have been anticipated from its position and natural affiliations; and though no immediate action was taken relative to its ownership till 1839, it remained during the interval in Belgian hands. Matters remained in this ambiguous condition for some time; but though the Dutch might grumble, they could not fight. At length the treaty of 1839 was signed in London, on the 19th of April, according to the terms of which part of the duchy of Luxemburg was retained by the Belgians, and part was ruled by the king of Holland as grand duke. In other respects, the status quo ante was preserved, and the partition of Holland and Belgium was confirmed, as it has ever since remained. The history of Belgium thenceforward has been almost wholly devoid of incidents; the little nation may quote the apothegm as applying to themselves, "Short are the annals of a happy people!" Their insignificance and their geographical position secure them against all disturbance. They live in their tiny quarters with economy and industry; the most densely populous community in Europe, and one of the most prosperous. Around their borders rises the sullen murmur of threatening armies and hostile dynasties; but Belgium is free from menace, and their sunshine of peace is without a cloud. It is of course conceivable that in the great struggle which seems impending, the Belgian nation may suddenly vanish from the map, and become but a memory in the minds of a future generation; but their end, if it come, is likely to be in the nature of a euthanasia, and so far as they are physically concerned, they will survive their political annihilation. The only ripples which have varied the smooth surface of their career since the treaty, have been disputes between the liberal and clerical parties on questions of education, and disturbances and occasional riots instigated by socialists over industrial questions. Leopold, dying at the age of seventy-six, was succeeded by his son as Leopold II., and his reign continued during the remainder of the century.

The treaty of 1839, in addition to its provisions already mentioned, gave Limburg, on the Prussian border, to the Dutch, and opened the Scheldt under heavy tolls. In October of the year following the treaty, William I. abdicated the throne of Holland in favor of his son. He had not enjoyed his reign, and he retired in an ill humor, which was not without some excuse. His career had been a worthy one; he had been a soldier in the field from his twenty-first year till the battle of Wagram in 1809, when he was near forty; after that he dwelt in retirement in Berlin until he was called to the throne of the Netherlands. At that time he had exchanged his German possessions for the grand duchy of Luxemburg; and was therefore naturally reluctant to be deprived of the latter. The old soldier survived his abdication only a few years, dying in 1843 at Berlin.

William II. was a soldier like his father. He had gained distinction under Wellington in the Spanish campaign, and in the struggle against Napoleon during the Hundred Days he commanded the Dutch contingent. He married Anne, sister of Alexander I. of Russia, in 1816, and at the outbreak of the revolution of 1830 he was sent to Belgium to bring about an arrangement. On the 16th of October of that year he took the step, which was repudiated by his rigid old father, of acknowledging Belgian independence; but he subsequently commanded the Dutch army against the Belgians, and was forced to yield to the French in August, 1832. After his accession, he behaved with firmness and liberality, and died in 1849 leaving a good reputation behind him.

Meanwhile, the new revolution of 1848 was approaching. Insensibly, the states of Europe had ranged themselves under two principles. There were on one side the states governed by constitutions, including Great Britain, France, Holland,

Belgium, Switzerland, Sweden and Norway, Denmark, and, for the time being, Spain and Portugal. On the other side were Russia, Prussia, Austria, the Italian States, and some of those of Germany, who held that the right of rule and the making **of laws belonged absolutely to certain** dynasties, which were, indeed, morally bound to consult the interests of their populations, yet were not responsible to their subjects **for the** manner in which they might choose to do it. In **the last mentioned states there** existed **a** chronic strife between the people and their rulers. **It was an irrepressible** conflict, and its crisis **was reached in 1848.**

It was in France that things first came to a head. Louis Philippe and his minister, Guizot, tried to render the **government** gradually independent **of the nation, in imitation** of the absolutist empires; and the uneasiness caused by this policy was emphasized by the scarcity that prevailed during the years 1846 and 1847. The Liberals **began** to demand electoral reform; **but the king, on opening** the Chambers, intimated that **he was convinced that no reform** was needed. Angry debates ensued, and finally the opposition arranged for a great banquet in the Champs Elysee on February 22, 1848, in support of the reform movement. This gathering, however, was forbidden by Guizot. The **order was** regarded as arbitrary, **and the Republicans seized the** opportunity. Barricades appeared in **Paris,** the king was **forced** to abdicate, and took refuge with his family in England. France was thereupon declared to be **a Republic,** and the **government** was intrusted to **Lamartine** and others. There was now great danger of excesses similar to those of the first great revolution; but the elements of violence were kept under by the opposition of the middle and higher classes. The communistic clubs were **overawed by** the National Guards, and on April 16th the Communistic party was defeated. General Cavaignac, who had been made dictator during the struggle, laid down his office after the battle which began on the 23d of June between the rabble of idle mechanics, eighty thousand in number, and the national forces had been decided in favor of the latter, who slew no less than sixteen thousand of the enemy. Cavaignac was now appointed chief of the Executive Commission with the title of President of the Council. A reaction favoring a monarchy was indicated; but meanwhile a new constitution provided for a quadriennial presidency, with a single legislature of seven hundred and fifty members. Louis Napoleon, the nephew of the great emperor, was chosen by a majority vote for the office in December of 1848. Four years later he was declared emperor under the title of Napoleon III.

The revolutionary movement spread to other countries of Europe, with varying results. In Hungary, Kossuth in the Diet demanded of the emperor-king a national government. Prince Metternich, prime minister, attempted to resist the demand with military force, but an insurrection in Vienna drove him into exile, and the Hungarians gained a temporary advantage, and were granted a constitution. The Slavs met at Prague, at the instigation of Polocky, and held a congress; but it was broken up by the impatience of the inhabitants, and a success of the imperialists was followed by the rising of the southern Slavs in favor of the emperor. A battle took place in Hungary on September 11, 1848, but the imperialists under Jellachich were routed and driven toward the Austrian frontier. The war became wider in its scope; the insurrectionists at first met with success; but in spite of their desperate valor the Hungarian forces were finally overthrown by the aid of a Russian army; and their leader, Goergy, was compelled to surrender to the Russians on August 13, 1849. It was thought that the Czar might annex Hungary; but he handed it back to Francis Joseph, who, by way of vengeance, permitted the most hideous cruelties.

In Germany, the issue had no definite feature. The people demanded freedom of the Press and a German parliament, and the various princes seemed acquiescent; but when it was proposed that Prussia should become Germany, there was opposition on all sides; a Diet of the Confederation was held, but Frederick William IV., king of Prussia, refused to accept the title of hereditary emperor which was offered him. Austria and Prussia came into opposition; two rival congresses were sitting at the same time in 1850, and war between the two states was only averted by the interference of Russia. Czar Nicholas, then virtually dictator of Europe, ordered Prussia's troops back, and the Convention of Olmutz, in November, seemed to put a final end to Prussia's hopes of German hegemony.

All the local despotisms of Italy collapsed before the breath of revolution; but the country then found itself face to face with Austria. Charles Albert of Sardinia had the courage to head the revolt; but was defeated, and abdicated in favor of his son Victor Emmanuel. Venice was taken after a severe siege by the Austrians; and King Bomba managed to repossess himself of Naples, after a terrible massacre. Sicily was subdued. In the Papal States, Pio Nono was deposed; but after a time a reaction set in, the provisional government under Mazzini was overthrown, and the French occupied Rome and recalled the Pope.

The question as to the Danish or German ownership of the duchies of Schleswig-Holstein had already been agitated, and they became acute at this time; but the spirit of the new revolution had no direct bearing upon the matter. By the end of the first half of the nineteenth century, Europe was outwardly quiet once more.

And what part had Holland taken in these proceedings? A very small one. The phlegmatic Dutchmen found themselves fairly well off, and were nowise tempted to embark in troubles for sentiment's sake. The constitution given them in 1814 was revised, with the consent of the king, and the changes, which involved various political reforms, went into effect on April 17, 1848. William II. died just eleven months afterward, and was succeeded by his son William III., at that time a man of two-and-thirty. He favored the reforms granted by his father, and showed himself to be in harmony with such sober ideas of progress as belonged to the nation over which he ruled. His aim in all things was peace, and the development of the resources of the country; he understood his people, and they placed confidence in him, and Holland steadily grew in wealth and comfort. In 1853, after the establishment by the papacy of Catholic bishoprics had been allowed, there was a period of some excitement; for Roman Catholicism had found a stern and unconquerable foe in the Dutch, when it had come with the bloody tyranny of Spain. But those evil days were past, and the Dutch, who had pledged themselves to welcome religious freedom in their dominions, were disposed to let bygones be bygones, and to permit such of their countrymen as preferred the Catholic ceremonial to have their way. It was evident that no danger existed of Holland's becoming subject to the papacy; and, indeed, the immediate political sequel of the establishment of the bishoprics was the election of a moderate, liberal, Protestant cabinet, which thoroughly represented the country, and which represented its tone thereafter, with such modifications as new circumstances might suggest. The Dutch were philosophic, and were victims to no vague and costly ambitions. They felt that they had given sufficient proofs of their quality in the past; the glory which they had won as champions of liberty could never fade; and now they merited the repose which we have learned to associate with our conception of the Dutch character. Their nature seems to partake of the scenic traits of their country; its picturesque, solid serenity, its unemotional levels, its flavor of the antique: and yet beneath that composure we feel the strength and steadfastness which can say to the ocean, Thus far and no further, and can build their immaculate towns, and erect their peaceful windmills, and navigate their placid canals, and smoke their fragrant pipes on land which, by natural right, should be the bottom of the sea. Holland is a perennial type of human courage and industry, common sense and moderation. As we contemplate them to-day, it requires an effort of the imagination to picture them as the descendants of a race of heroes who defied and overcame the strongest and most cruel Power on earth in their day, and then taught the rest of Europe how to unite success in commerce with justice and honor. But the heroism is still there, and, should need arise, we need not doubt **that it** would once more be manifested.

Because Holland is so quiet, some rash critics fancy that she may be termed effete. But this is far from the truth. The absence of military burdens, rendered needless by the intelligent selfishness, if not the conscience, of the rest of Europe, implies no decadence of masculine spirit in the Dutch. In no department of enterprise, commercial ability, or intellectual energy are they inferior to any of their contemporaries, or to their own great progenitors. "Holland," says Professor Thorold Rogers, "is the origin of scientific medicine and rational therapeutics. From Holland came the first optical instruments, the best mathematicians, the most intelligent philosophers, as well as the boldest and most original thinkers. Amsterdam and Rotterdam held the printing presses of Europe in the early days of the republic; the Elzevirs were the first publishers of cheap editions, and thereby aided in disseminating the new learning. From Holland came the new agriculture, which has done so much for social life, horticulture and floriculture. The Dutch taught modern Europe navigation. They were the first to explore the unknown seas, and many an island and cape which their captains discovered has been renamed after some one who got his knowledge by their research, and appropriated the fruit of his predecessor's labors. They have been as much plundered in the world of letters as they have been in commerce and politics. Holland taught the Western nations finance—perhaps no great boon. But they also taught commercial honor, the last and hardest lesson which nations learn. They inculcated free trade, a lesson nearly as hard to learn, if not harder, since the conspiracy against private right is watchful, incessant, and, as some would make us believe, respectable. They raised a constant and for a long time ineffectual protest against the barbarous custom of privateering, and the dangerous doctrine of contraband of war, a doctrine which, if carried out logically, would allow belligerents to interdict the trade of the world. The Dutch are the real founders of what people call international law, or the rights of nations. They made mistakes, but they made fewer than their neighbors made. The benefits which they conferred were incomparably greater than the errors they committed. There is nothing more striking than the fact that, after a brief and discreditable episode, the states were an asylum for the persecuted. The Jews, who were contemned because they were thrifty, plundered because they were rich, and harassed because they clung tenaciously to their ancient faith and customs, found an asylum in Holland; and some of them perhaps, after they originated and adopted, with the pliability of their race, a Teutonic alias, have not been sufficiently grateful to the country which sheltered them. The Jansenists, expelled from France, found a refuge in Utrecht, and more than a refuge, a recognition, when recognition was a dangerous offence.

"There is no nation in Europe," continues the professor, "which owes more to Holland than Great Britain does. The English were for a long time, in the industrial history of modern civilization, the stupidest and most backward nation in Europe. There was, to be sure, a great age in England during the reign of Elizabeth and that of the first Stuart king. But it was brief indeed. In every other department of art, of agriculture, of trade, we learned our lesson from the Hollanders. I doubt whether any other small European race, after passing through the trials which it endured after the peace of Aix-la-Chapelle to the conclusion of the continental war, ever had so entire a recovery. The chain of its history, to be sure, was broken, and can never, in the nature of things, be welded together. But there is still left to Holland the **boast** and the reality of her motto, 'Luctor et emergo.'"

The events of Holland's history since the Catholic concessions can be briefly told. In 1863 **slavery** was abolished in the Dutch West Indies, the owners being **compensated**; and forty-two thousand slaves were set **free**, chiefly in Dutch Guiana. In **the same year** the navigation **of the** Scheldt was freed, by purchase **from** Holland by the **European** powers, **of the** right to **levy** tolls. **In 1867,** Louis **Napoleon** raised the question **of** Luxemburg by negotiating to buy the grand duchy **from** Holland; **but Prussia** objected to the **scheme, and** the matter **was finally settled by a Conference** in London; **the Prussian garrison evacuating the** fortifications, which **were then** dismantled, **and Luxemburg was declared neutral territory. Capital punishment was** abolished in **1869; and on the 15th of July of the** same year the Amsterdam **National Exposition was opened** by Prince Henry. In 1870, **at the outbreak of war between** Germany and France, **the neutrality of Holland as to both** belligerents was **secured by the other Powers. In 1871** the Hollanders ceded **Dutch Guinea to England, and in** 1876 the canal between **Amsterdam and the North Sea,** which had been begun in 1865, was **completed, and** the **passage** through it was accomplished **by a monitor. Another Exposition** was opened in 1883, and in the **same year the constitution** underwent **a further** revision. **On the 24th of June,** 1884, the Prince **of Orange,** heir-apparent **to the throne,** died, and the succession thus devolved upon the **princess** Wilhelmina, then a child of four years. William **III.** himself died in 1890, and Queen Emma thereupon assumed the regency, which **she** was to **hold** until Wilhelmina came of age **in** 1898; an agreeable consummation which we have just witnessed.

A word may here be said concerning **the** physical and political constitution of the present kingdom of Holland. The country is divided into eleven provinces—North and South Holland, Zealand, North Brabant, Utrecht, Limburg, Gelderland, Overyssel, Drenthe, Groningen, and Friesland. There are three large rivers—the Rhine, the Meuse, and the Scheldt. The inhabitants are Low Germans (Dutch), Frankish, Saxon, Frisian, and Jews, the latter numbering some sixty thousand, though their influence is, owing to their wealth and activity, larger than these figures would normally represent. The leading religion of the country is Lutheran; but there are also many Catholics and persons of other faiths, all of whom are permitted the free enjoyment of their creeds. Holland was at one time second to no country in the extent of its colonies; and it still owns Java, the Moluccas, part of Borneo, New Guinea, Sumatra and Celebes, in the East; and in the West, Dutch Guiana and Curacoa. In Roman times the Low Countries were inhabited by various peoples, chiefly of Germanic origin; and in the Middle Ages were divided into several duchies and counties—such as Brabant, Flanders, Gelderland, Holland, Zealand, etc. The present government is a hereditary monarchy, consisting of a king or queen and states-general; the upper chamber of fifty members, the lower of one hundred. It is essentially a country of large towns, of five thousand inhabitants and upward. The Frisians are in North Holland, separated by the river Meuse from the Franks; the Saxons extend to the Utrecht Veldt. The Semitic race is represented by the Portuguese Jews; and there is an admixture of other nationalities. In no part of the country do the Dutch present a marked physical type, but, on the other hand, they are sharply differenced, in various localities, by their laws, their customs, and particularly by their dialects; indeed the Frisians have a distinct language of their own.

The constitution of 1815, though more than once revised, remains practically much the same as at first. The son of the monarch, the heir-apparent, is called the Prince of Orange. The administration of the Provinces is in the hands of the provincial states; these meet but a few times in the year. The Communes have their communal councils, under the control of the burgomasters. There is a high court of justice, and numerous minor courts.

The population is divided between about two million two hundred thousand Protestants, and half as many Roman Catholics, together with others. There are four thousand schools, with six hundred thousand pupils, and about fourteen thousand teachers. Not more than ten per cent of the people are illiterate, and the women are as carefully educated as the men. There are four great universities: Leyden, founded in 1575; Utrecht, founded in 1636; Groningen, in 1614; and Amsterdam, which has existed since 1877. These seats of learning give instruction to from three hundred to seven hundred students each. The total expenses of the universities average about six hundred thousand dollars. There are also in Holland excellent institutions of art, science, and industry.

Agriculture is generally pursued, but without the extreme science and economy shown in Belgium. The cultivation and produce vary, in part, according as the soil is sand or clay; but the same kind of soil, in different parts of the country, produces different results. Cattle are largely raised and are of first-rate quality; Friesland produces the best, but there are also excellent stocks in North Holland and South Holland. In Drenthe, owing to the extensive pasturage, great numbers of sheep are raised. But perhaps the most important industry of Holland is the fisheries, both those of the deep sea, and those carried on in the great Zuyder Zee, which occupies a vast area within the boundaries of the country. These fisheries, however, are not in all years successful, owing to the ungovernable vagaries of ocean currents, and other causes.

Holland has taken a prominent part in European thought since about 1830. The Dutch language, instead of yielding to the domination of the German, has been cultivated and enriched. The writers who have achieved distinction could hardly even be named in the space here available, and any approach to a critical estimate of them would require vol-

umes. One of the earlier but best-known names is that of
Jacobus Van Lennep, who is regarded as the leader of the
Dutch Romantic school. He was born in Amsterdam on
the 24th of March, 1802, and died at Oosterbeek, near Arnheim, August 25, 1868. His father, David, was a professor and a poet; Jacobus studied jurisprudence at Leyden,
and afterward practiced law at Amsterdam. For a while
he took some part in politics as a member of the second
chamber; but his heart was bent on the pursuit of literature, and he gradually abandoned all else for that. His
first volume of poems was published when he was but four-and-twenty; and he was the author of several dramas. But
his strongest predilections were for romantic novel-writing;
and his works in this direction show signs of the influence of
Walter Scott, who dominated the romantic field in the first
half of this century, and was known in Holland as well as
throughout the rest of Europe. "The Foster Son" was
published in 1829; the "Rose of Dekama" in 1836; "The
Adventures of Claus Sevenstars" in 1865. His complete
works, in prose and poetry, fill six-and-thirty volumes. A
younger contemporary of Van Lennep was Nikolas Beets,
born at Haarlem in 1814; he also was both poet and prose
writer, and his "Camara Obscura," published in 1839, is
accounted a masterpiece of character and humor, though
it was composed when the author was barely twenty-four
years of age. Van den Brink was a leading critic of the
Romanticists; Hasebroek, author of a volume of essays
called "Truth and Dream," has been likened to the English Charles Lamb. Vosmaer is another eminent figure in
Dutch literature; he wrote a "Life of Rembrandt" which
is a masterpiece of biography. Kuenen, who died but ten
years ago, was a biblical critic of European celebrity. But
the list of contemporary Dutch writers is long and brilliant,
and the time to speak critically of them must be postponed.

Nothing impresses the visitor to Holland more than the
vast dikes or dams which restrain the sea from overwhelming the country. They have to be constantly watched and

renewed, and to those unused to the idea of dwelling in the presence of such constant peril, **the** phlegm of the Hollanders is remarkable. M. Havard, who has made a careful study of the country and its people, and who writes of them in a lively style, has left **excellent** descriptions **of** these unique works. "We know," he says, "**what the** Zealand soil is—how **uncertain,** changing, **and** mutable; nevertheless, **a** construction is placed upon it, one **hundred and twenty** yards long, **sixteen** yards wide **at** the entrance, **and more** than **seven and a** half yards deep below high **water. Add to** this, **that the enormous** basin (one thousand **nine hundred** square **yards) is** enclosed within granite walls of extraordinary thickness, **formed** of solid blocks of stone of tremendous weight. **To** what depth must the daring workmen who undertook the Cyclopean task have gone in search **of a stable** standpoint, on which **to** lay the foundation of such **a** mass! **In** what subterranean layer could they have had such confidence, in this country where the earth **sinks in,** all of a sudden, where islands disappear without **leaving a** trace—that they ventured to build upon it so **mighty an edifice! And** observe that not only one **dam** is **thus built**; in the two islands of Zuid Beveland **and** Walcheren a dozen have been constructed. There **are** two at Wormeldingen. In the presence of these achievements, of **problems** faced with such courage and solved **with such success, one is** almost bewildered."

Elsewhere, in **speaking of Kampveer,** one of the towns **which** suffered **an** inundation, he says, "Poor **little** port! once **so** famous, lively, populous, and noisy, **and** now so solitary and still! Traces of its former military and mercantile character are yet to be seen. On the left stands a majestic building with thick walls and few apertures, terminating on the sea in a crenellated round tower; and these elegant houses, with their arched and trefoiled windows, and their decorated gables, on the right, once formed the ancient Scotschhuis. Every detail of the building recalls

the great trade in wool done by the city at that period.
Far off, at the entrance of the port, stands a tower, the
last remnant of the ramparts, formerly **a** fortification; it
is now a tavern. In vain do we **look for** the companion
tower; it has disappeared with the **earth on** which its foundations stood deep and strong for ages. If, from the summit of the surviving tower, you search for that mysterious
town upon the opposite bank, you will look for it in **vain**
where it formerly stood and mirrored its houses and steeples
in the limpid waters. Kampen also has been swallowed up
forever, leaving no trace that it ever existed in this world.
The land that stretches out before us is all affected by that
subtle, cancerous disease, the *val*, **whose ravages are so terrible.** Two centuries ago this great bay **was** so filled up
with sand that it was expected the two islands would in a
short time be reunited and thenceforth **form** but one. Then,
on a sudden, the gulf yawned anew. That huge **rent,** the
Veer Gat, opened once again, more deeply **than before;**
whole towns were buried, and their inhabitants drowned.
Then the water retired, the earth rose, shaking off its humid
winding sheet, and the old task was resumed; **man began
once more to** dispute the soil with **the** invading **waves.** A
portion of the land, which seemed to have been forever lost,
was regained; but at **the cost** of what determined strife,
after how many battles, with what dire alternations!
Within **a century,** three entire polders on the north coast
of **Noordbeveland have** again vanished, and **in the** place
where they were there flows a stream forty yards deep.
In 1873, **the polder of** Borselen, thirty-one acres in extent,
sank into the waters. Each year the terrible *val* devours
some space or other, carrying away the land in strips. The
Sophia polder is now attacked by the *val*. Every possible
means is being employed **for** its defence; no sacrifice is
spared. The game is almost up; already one dike has
been swallowed, and a portion of the conquered ground
has had to be abandoned. The dams are being strengthened in the rear, while every effort is being made **to fix**

the soil so as to prevent the slipping away of the reclaimed land. To effect this, not only are the dams reinforced and complicated by an inextricable network of stones and interlaced tree-branches, but *Zinkstukken* are sunk far off in the sea, which by squeezing down the shifting bottom avert those sudden displacements which bring about such disasters. The Zinkstukken—enormous constructions in wicker work—are square rafts, made of reeds and boughs twisted together, sometimes two or three hundred feet long on a side. They are made on the edge of the coast and pushed into the sea; and no sooner is one afloat than it is surrounded by a crowd of barges and boats, big and little, laden with stones and clods of earth. The boats are then attached to the Zinkstuk, and this combined flotilla is so disposed along shore that the current carries it to the place where the Zinkstuk is to be sunk. When the current begins to make itself felt, the raft is loaded by the simple process of heaping the contents of the barges upon the middle of it. The men form in line from the four corners to the centre, and the loads of stone and earth are passed on to the centre of the raft, on which they are flung; then the middle of the Zinkstuk begins to sink gently, and to disappear under the water. As it goes down, the operators withdraw; the stones and clods are then flung upon it from boats. At this stage of the proceedings the Zinkstuk is so heavy that all the vessels, dragged by its weight, lean over, and their masts bend above it. But now the decisive moment approaches, and the foreman, standing on the poop of the largest boat, in the middle of the flotilla, on the side furthest from the shore, awaits the instant when the Zinkstuk shall come into precisely the foreordained position. At that instant he utters a shout and makes a signal; the ropes are cut, the raft plunges downward, and disappears forever, while the boats recover their proper position."

M. Havard merits the space we have given him; for he describes a work the like of which has never been seen elsewhere in the world, any more than have the conditions which necessitated it. But the picturesqueness of the actual scene can hardly be conveyed in words. Under an azure sky we behold outstretched a sparkling sea, its waters shading from green to blue and from yellow to violet, harmoniously blending. In the distance, as though marking the horizon, stretches a long, green strip of land, with the spires of the churches standing out in strong relief against the sky. At our feet is the Zinkstuk, surrounded by its flotilla. The great red sails furled upon the masts, the green poops, the rudders sheathed with burnished copper, the red streaks along the sides of the boats, the colored shirts, brown vests, and blue girdles of the men, touched by the warm rays of the sun, compose a striking picture. On all sides the men are in motion, and five hundred brawny arms are flinging the contents of the boats upon the great raft; a truly Titanic stoning! Projectiles rain from all sides without pause, until the moment comes when the decisive command is to be given. Then silence, absolute and impressive, falls upon the multitude. Suddenly the signal is given; a creaking noise is heard; the fifty boats right themselves at the same instant, and turn toward the point where the great raft which had separated them has just disappeared. They bump against one another, they get entangled, they group themselves in numberless different ways. The swarming men, stooping and raising up, the uplifted arms, the flying stones, the spurting water covering the boats with foam; and in the midst of the confusion the polder-jungens flinging the clods of earth with giant strength and swiftness upon the raft. At certain points the tumult declines; flags are hoisted from the tops of masts, the large sails are shaken out, and aided by the breeze some vessels get loose, sail out, and desert the field of battle. These are they whose task is done, and which are empty. They retire one by one upon the great expanse of water, which, save in one spot, was a little while ago deserted, and is now overspread with the vessels making their various ways toward that green line on the horizon.

This is a conflict not of days, nor of years, nor of generations, but of all time; and what the end will be none can foretell. It is the concrete symbol of the everlasting fight of man with nature, which means civilization. The day may come when, where once Holland was, will be outspread the serene waters of the sea, hiding beneath them the records of the stupendous struggle of so many centuries. Or, perhaps, some mysterious shifting of the ocean bottom may not only lift Holland out of peril, but uncover mighty tracts of land which, in the prehistoric past, belonged to Europe. Meanwhile it is easy to understand that the people who can wage this ceaseless war for their homes and lives, are the sons of those heroes who curbed the might of Spain, and taught the world the lessons of freedom and independence.

THE END

www.ingramcontent.com/pod-product-compliance
Lightning Source LLC
Chambersburg PA
CBHW022120290426
44112CB00008B/746